RIGHT-WING AUTHORITARIANISM

All of us submit to established authority to some extent, but are many of us astonishingly accepting of governmental injustice and tyranny? All of us are sometimes aggressive, but do some of us seethe with a self-righteous hostility waiting to be licenced? All of us follow social conventions, but do some of us sanctify our notion of conventionality as though it were the only defense against catastrophe? And do these things occur together in many people?

Is there a broadly based right-wing authoritarianism in many western democracies that supports unjust and unwise wars, that despises protest and dissent, that believes the unbelievable because high officials have said so, that longs for authorities to "crack down on the deviants," that does not care how many times the government breaks the law, that when marshalled can determine elections and pass repressive laws, and that, by its sheer numbers, continually invites dictatorship? It is the thesis of this book that the answer to all these questions is yes.

Professor Altemeyer begins by closely examining the scientific literature on right-wing authoritarianism. He argues that, because of vague conceptualizations and poorly developed measures, many earlier approaches were doomed to failure.

In the second part of the volume, the author describes his previously unpublished twelve-year research program on right-wing authoritarianism. The construct is defined as the covariation of three attitudinal clusters—authoritarian submission, authoritarian aggression, and conventionalism—and it is operationally determined by the score on an attitude measure, the Right-Wing Authoritarianism Scale. The author describes a large pitting experiment which established the psychometric and predictive advantages of the RWA Scale over its predecessors. A number of studies of the covariates and dynamics of authoritarianism then investigated the way in which the construct interacts with other variables in determining behavior.

In the final section, the author presents a social learning theory of the origins of right-wing authoritarianism which he compares with the psychoanalytic theory advanced thirty years ago in *The Authoritarian Personality*.

This timely volume surveys the history of social psychological research on right-wing authoritarianism and describes a more fruitful direction for future work. It concludes with a disturbing comment on the pervasiveness of authoritarian behavior in our society.

Bob Altemeyer is a graduate of Yale University and Carnegie-Mellon University. He is a member of the Psychology Department of the University of Manitoba.

Right-Wing Authoritarianism

BOB ALTEMEYER

THE UNIVERSITY OF MANITOBA PRESS

HM
271
.A47

Canadian Cataloguing in Publication Data

Altemeyer, Robert A. (Robert Anthony), 1940-
  Right-wing authoritarianism

  Bibliography: p.
  Includes index.
  ISBN 0-88755-124-6

  1. Authority.   2. Attitude (Psychology).
  3. Dogmatism.   I. Title
  HM271.A47   303.3'8   C81-091194-9

To Jean
Robert, Jennifer, and Michael

Contents

Acknowledgments

I have been ably assisted in my research on authoritarianism during the past twelve years by students at the University of Manitoba. Foremost among these have been my three PhD graduates, and good friends, Bruce Hunsberger, Tim Fullerton and Wendy Josephson. Professor Hunsberger, now at Wilfrid Laurier University, has been my closest research ally over the years. Dr. Fullerton made many valuable suggestions for revisions of an earlier draft of this book. At one time or another Cathy Casserly, Rene Villa, Bob Worcester, Ted Palys and Alex Jopling also conducted experiments for me, usually for small remuneration. Many of these people, hoping that I would publish this book in time to help them land jobs, have been asking for the past six or eight years, "When is your book coming out?" It is too late to help any of them, if it ever would have, but at last the book "is out."

A number of my Manitoba colleagues have provided support and encouragement over the years. Dan Perlman has often suggested that various psychological organizations invite me to speak on my unpublished research. They never did, but it was nice of Dan to make the suggestions. John Adair, Marion Aftanas, Ross Hartsough, Terry Hogan, Michel Janisse, John McIntyre, Alf Shephard, Barry Spinner, Fred Stambrook, John Whiteley, and Neil Malamuth have each asked me, at least twice in the past eight years, "When is your book coming out?" Many of these gentlemen have had the singular misfortune to have been head of my department, or dean of my faculty. They have shown great tolerance for a colleague who kept gobbling up research funds and computer time year after year, but published nothing. True, no one ever suggested I should be promoted; but I have not been fired yet either.

Richard Christie of Columbia University wrote a very generous review of this book in 1977 for the Social Science Federation of Canada, which helped lead the Federation to support its publication. I am most grateful for that recommendation, without which I am sure you would be reading something else right now. Professor Christie used to phone about once a year, starting in 1978, to find out when the book was coming out, but lately he has given up.

I am almost as indebted to an unknown assessor who in 1978 wrote a trenchant, damning, and detailed critique of the first draft of this book for another organization. (S)He may not be any more impressed by the finished product, but I think the final manuscript is much improved because of these criticisms.

The University of Manitoba Press has been a joy to work with. Carol Dahlstrom has wrestled with me on the reader's behalf over my writing style, Norman Schmidt did the design work and drew the cover, and Patricia Lagacé supervised the overall editorial process. Unfortunately, production delays held up the printing of the book, and I fear I have made a nuisance of myself by constantly barging into the Press' office and demanding, "When is my book coming out? When is my book coming out?"

My wife Jean helped with none of the research, did none of the typing, and did not read a single word of the proofs. She may not even know I have written a book. She is not a very good wife for a writer, but she *is* the most interesting person I know. This book is rightly dedicated to her, and to those three marvelous enrichments to our lives, our children.

If there could be a secondary dedication, it would be to the many people who have served as subjects in my experiments. They got very little for doing so, not even an accurate explanation of what the studies were about. I hope their service will lead to a safer, freer society, and they would be satisfied with that.

The research reported in this book was supported by Grant Numbers 69-0825 and S73-0811 from the Canada Council, and Grant Numbers 03-195-64, 431-1665-04, 432-1665-02, 432-1665-03, 432-1665-41, 432-1665-44, and 432-1665-64 from the University of Manitoba.

This book has been published with the help of a grant from the Social Science Federation of Canada, using funds provided by the Social Sciences and Humanities Research Council of Canada.

Winnipeg, Canada
April 23, 1981

Right-Wing Authoritarianism

Introduction

THREE RECENT EPISODES

In the fall of 1970, a terrorist group in Quebec kidnapped a provincial official and a British diplomat and offered to exchange them for a number of "political prisoners." When 10 days of intense police activity failed to locate the kidnappers, the federal government invoked the War Measures Act. This act, similar to laws most democracies have on the books for use in the gravest national emergencies, had never been used in Canada in peacetime, but could be promulgated in a case of "apprehended insurrection." It gave authorities the power to search and seize property without warrant, to arrest and hold persons without charging them with any crime, to censor the media, and to outlaw any organization considered dangerous to the national welfare.

I live in Winnipeg, over a thousand miles from Quebec. Soldiers did not appear in the streets, nor were people arrested overnight as they were by the hundreds in Montreal. There were small demonstrations in my city and elsewhere in Canada against the use of the War Measures Act; the protestors argued that the known facts about the situation in Quebec did not justify so Draconian a step. But all the evidence indicates that the vast majority of Canadians supported the government: the prime minister's mail was 96% favorable; a poll of 1,650 Canadians from Halifax to Vancouver found that 87% supported the use of the War Measures Act; and the House of Commons endorsed promulgation of the act by a margin of 190 to 16 (*Toronto Globe and Mail*, Oct. 19, 1970, p.9; Oct. 22, p. 9; Nov. 16, p. 9).

For many citizens and politicians, the terrorists' acts by themselves justified the government's reactions, especially when one of the hostages was murdered the day after the act was promulgated. Others, including the Leader of the Opposition in Parliament, assumed that the government knew of plans for an insurrection in Quebec, and that this secret intelligence justified the use of the War Measures Act. Indeed, several members of the government spoke in such terms. A senior minister in the federal cabinet declared that the terrorists were a "widespread, well-armed and thoroughly trained guerrilla movement." Another minister stated in the House of Commons that the organization had up to 3,000 members and had "infiltrated every strategic place in the province of Quebec."

It turned out, however, that the kidnappings were carried out by perhaps a dozen people. They were not even dreaming of causing a general insurrection. Nor has anyone in Quebec ever been accused of promoting an insurrection during the October crisis.[1] By now, we are so used to hostage takings, hijackings, and murders that we no longer fear they will trigger revolution. But in 1970, the actions of this small group of terrorists caused an advanced Western democracy to suspend its most precious freedoms, and very little protest was heard across the nation. Instead, people seemed spring-loaded to support the government. I well remember the dominant sentiment of the day: "Don't speak out now, at this of all times. The country is in real danger." I felt it myself.

Shortly before the October crisis in Canada, the vice-president of the United States was travelling the breadth of his country creating a political force known as the "Silent Majority." We now know that his efforts were the more public aspect of a broad campaign by the Nixon administration to intimidate the press and discredit political opposition. The response to the alliterating Spiro Agnew was not altogether positive, and the campaign ultimately failed to cow the press. But the vice-president's speeches— which were basically an attack on the Bill of Rights cloaked as an appeal for balance in news reporting—apparently struck a responsive chord in millions of Americans who received Agnew as a hero of the little man and a moral leader.

A few years later, as Richard Nixon and Spiro Agnew were seeking another term in office, a group of men connected with their re-election committee were caught photographing documents and placing wiretaps in the campaign headquarters of their political opponents. High administration officials said the Watergate break-in was an isolated act organized by a few overzealous campaign workers, and President Nixon promised a complete investigation. A Harris Poll in October, 1972, found that 62% of the voters believed him, and dismissed the controversy over Watergate as "mostly politics." The Nixon team was re-elected by a similar margin a few weeks later.

Soon however the cover-up of the break-in began to come apart, and Americans had good reason to doubt the president's word. After Nixon "cleaned house" with the removal of Haldeman, Erlichman, Kleindienst and Dean in April, 1973, 50% of a Gallup sample believed that the president was still concealing facts about the break-in. Few Americans, though, felt that the president should be impeached if he were implicated in the scandal.

The Ervin Committee Hearings produced a further dent in Richard Nixon's credibility. A Gallup Poll taken after the president's August 15 speech "refuting" the testimony of John Dean indicated that the number doubting him had grown to 60%. After President Nixon fired Archibald Cox and the Attorney General and announced the dissolution of the Office of the Special Prosecutor, the figure grew larger yet, and pollsters began asking the public if they thought the president should resign. A Gallup Poll taken in late October, 1973, found that 48% favored resignation, while 39% were against it. But when the "firestorm" had died down a few weeks later, a Harris Poll found a 47–43% plurality against resignation. The issue was still virtually deadlocked, 43–41%, in January, 1974.

It soon became clear that Nixon was not going to resign easily, and the pollsters began asking if the president should be forced from office. In April, 1974, following the discovery of the 18.5 minute "gap" and Nixon's refusal to release any more materials to the investigators, a Harris Poll found the issue too close to call. After the White House released 1,200 pages of edited transcripts, a 49–41% plurality favored removal. In late July, just before the House Judiciary Committee began its televised deliberations on articles of impeachment, the margin had widened to 47–34%. But, as White House spokesmen pointed out, the "majority of Americans" still did not support impeachment. At the end of the House hearings, however, that milestone too was passed: the Harris Poll found that 56% of its sample favored removal, while 31% did not.

A few days later Richard Nixon resigned, not directly because of public opinion, but because his attorney had forced the disclosure of evidence so damaging that it seemed certain he would be convicted of high crimes by the Senate. Nevertheless, a Gallup Poll found, shortly thereafter, that 22% of the electorate still felt that Richard Nixon's misdeeds did not warrant the resignation. The figure is close to the 24% of an August, 1974, Gallup Poll who still approved, in the dying moments of his presidency, of the way Nixon was doing his job. These percentages translate into approximately 30 million American adults.

The American public thus was slow to react to the Watergate

disclosures, and to the very end, Richard Nixon could count on a very large number of hard-core supporters who demanded "smoking gun" evidence of his guilt. Beyond that, there were tens of millions to whom the discovery of the "smoking howitzer" apparently meant little. There were, and still are, many people in the United States who will believe the unbelievable about a president simply because they want to. There is apparently no conceivable evidence which will shake their confidence.[2]

A conclusion

These three episodes were certainly major events in the recent history of Canada and the United States. They all suggest that many citizens in a democracy will support highhanded, repressive, and antidemocratic policies by government officials to a degree probably unenvisioned by democratic philosophers. Such sentiments are a force to be reckoned with; they are an assurance of support to the official contemplating repression; they can, when marshaled, elect certain candidates and defeat others. If one of the assumptions of democratic theory is that the citizen cherishes his freedoms and will resist tyranny from above as well as from abroad, the system may be based on an untenable assumption.

SITUATIONAL VERSUS PERSONAL DETERMINANTS OF BEHAVIOR

It is probable that in a crisis, nearly everyone will support the government when it suspends constitutional rights, as Canadians did in 1970. One can cite many events in Western history in which antidemocratic acts during emergencies received widespread support. The Nazis' use of the Reichstag fire in 1933 to consolidate their power in Germany is perhaps the most notorious example. At the same time, there are other instances when antidemocratic activities evoked a decidedly mixed response among the populace. Some Americans agreed with Spiro Agnew's attacks on the press, but others were appalled. Some Americans wanted to suppress the protest against the war in Viet Nam, but others believed the dissenters were well within their rights. Some believed the students killed at Kent State "got what they had coming to them"; others called the killings a massacre. Sixty-one percent of a representative sample of American adults said that Lt. Calley should have shot women and children at My Lai if he had been ordered to; the rest of the sample was less sure (Kelman and Lawrence, 1972). Some Americans believed President Nixon's account of Watergate to the very end; others had their doubts from the beginning;

but the majority of Americans seemed to change eventually from believers to skeptics. Many Canadians in the late 1970s considered it acceptable for the Royal Canadian Mounted Police (RCMP) to open mail illegally to "control subversives," but not to commit burglary or arson for the same reason. Thus, while there was almost universal support for some antidemocratic acts committed by officials, there were other circumstances in which the support varied considerably.

The main question this book attempts to answer is: *are there individual differences in the support of antidemocratic governmental actions which are general enough across situations that we ignore them at our scientific and social peril?* That is, given that everyone submits to established authority to some extent, and certain situations will make most of us highly submissive, is it meaningful to talk about "authoritarian people"? Are there some people who are so generally submissive to established authority that it is scientifically useful to speak of "authoritarians"? And, if there are, are there so many people so generally submissive to established authority that they constitute a real threat to freedom in countries such as Canada and the United States? It is the thesis of this book that the answer to these questions is yes.

THE ISSUE OF "TRAITS"

Many psychologists would doubt this thesis from the outset, however. I am proposing that we organize certain behaviors in terms of a trait of authoritarianism, meaning by "trait" a hypothetical construct created for its explanatory convenience and power (Mischel, 1968, p. 5). I am not the first to make this suggestion; most people analyze behavior in terms of traits such as honesty, dependency, and friendliness. However, the scientific utility of "traits" has been strongly challenged lately. Mischel (1968) found three grounds for argument:

1 While studies of intellectual and cognitive variables have shown some intersituational consistencies in behavior, studies of personality variables have shown almost none. That is, individuals who behave one way (e.g., respectful toward authority) in one situation may behave very differently in another.

2 Studies of trait attribution have not demonstrated that people judged to behave kindly or aggressively, for instance, across situations actually do so, but only that they are perceived to do so. The consistency in the perceptions may be due to the social stereotypes and the conceptual

dimensions of the judges, the vagueness of the labels used, and so forth.
3 Paper-and-pencil assessments of traits have shown very weak relationships (typically less than .30) with criterion behaviors measured
in other ways. Higher relationships found with paper-and-pencil measures
of criteria may be attributed to shared method variance due to a common
"apparatus factor" such as the effect of response sets (Campbell and
Fiske, 1959), or to mutual relationships with intelligence.

One cannot help but agree with these points, but they still do not lead
to Mischel's conclusion.[3] My hesitation springs from methodological
problems found in the research literature, particularly problems with the
reliability of the measures used. The very first case Mischel cites to
illustrate his first point, for example, happens to involve attitudes toward
authority figures (Mischel, 1968, pp. 21–23). In 1953, Burwen and Campbell
(1957) administered a series of seven measures to 155 Air Force personnel;
this series was designed to elicit attitudes toward (a) each subject's
father, (b) symbolic authority, (c) his aircraft commander, (d) his peers,
and (e) symbolic peers. The "instruments" used to gauge these attitudes
were (a) an interview, (b) Thematic Apperception Test (TAT) type stimuli
(scored both "nonclinically" and "clinically"), (c) checklist ratings of
oneself, one's father, etcetera, (d) evaluations of strangers based on their
photographs, (e) an autobiographical inventory, (f) an attitude scale
measuring sentiments toward the Air Force, superiors and peers, and (g)
a sociometric questionnaire. Not all of these measures were used to
collect data on all of the five dependent variables. "Attitudes toward the
father," for example, were gauged in the interview, the checklist ratings,
and the autobiographical inventory.

It was found that there was very little relationship between theoretically linked variables (e.g., "father" and "symbolic authority") once
a strong "apparatus factor" was taken into account. In particular, attitudes toward one sort of authority figure were about as poorly correlated
with attitudes toward peers as they were with attitudes toward another
sort of authority figure.

But what was the reliability of the measures used? Mischel's only
comment (1968, p. 22) on this quite relevant matter was that "the interjudge reliability of *all* ratings on *each* instrument was adequately high"
(emphasis mine). In fact Burwen and Campbell reported interjudge reliabilities on only three of the seven instruments they used: .83 (between two
judges) on "nonclinical" TAT ratings; .95 (between one pair of judges) and
.86 (between another pair of judges) on a photo judging measure; and .86

(between two judges) on evaluations of subjective material from an autobiographical inventory. Mischel's assurances notwithstanding, there was no reported interjudge reliability check on interview scorings, nor on the "clinical" TAT scores, and the agreement among the three (or four) judges used on the photo-based ratings was only partially reported.

More distressing than this, however, were the internal consistency estimates of reliability which Burwen and Campbell reported for their measures, but which Mischel did not mention at all. They were as follows: TAT (symbolic authority) "nonclinical"—.55, "clinical"—none reported; Checklist Ratings, of father—.24, of "boss"—.34; Photo Judging (symbolic authority)—.46; Autobiographical Inventory, of father—.56, of "boss"—.56; Attitude Survey (symbolic authority) —.59; Sociometric Questionnaire, of boss—.75. There was no internal estimate of the interview scorings, as they consisted of a single rating on a five-point scale. The reliabilities of the peer measures were a little higher than those for the authority figure measures, ranging from .29 to .90 and averaging .64.

Obviously the measures of attitudes toward one's father, toward symbolic authority, and toward "bosses" were not measuring anything with consistency. Nearly all of the information gathered with them was "noise." Accordingly, expecting evaluations of the father (the variance of which was 94% "nonsignal" on the checklist measure, 69% "nonsignal" on the autobiographical inventory, and of totally unknown quality in the interview data) to correlate substantially—for this is what Mischel asks of the data—with attitudes toward symbolic authority and one's boss (which were also mostly noise) is a little silly. If reinforcement contingencies were measured so inconsistently, the Empirical Law of Effect would be in the gravest danger.[4]

Later, Mischel (1968, p. 38) acknowledged some of the problems inherent in interpreting correlation coefficients, but suggested that "the low reliability of tests, subtests and items may reflect true differences in the person across situations." This is indeed possible, but the way to test it (against the alternate explanation that a test has low reliability because it involves a [small] number of ambiguous, nondiscriminating or largely irrelevant components) is to see if a reliable index can be developed. Nearly all of Burwen and Campbell's measures appear to have been expressly developed for their study, and there is no mention of any effort having been made to pretest the measures and to improve their reliability.

In summary, Burwell and Campbell's study shows only that very unreliable measures of a trait will not correlate well with other very unreliable measures of that trait. This does not seem good reason for arguing, as Mischel does after examining this study, that the trait of authoritarianism has little scientific utility. Nothing would have scientific utility in these circumstances; the question is still open.

Mischel's second point, concerning the ambiguity of the findings on trait attribution, does not pertain to our discussion. But his third, concerning the low validity coefficients of paper-and-pencil measures of traits, is quite relevant and we shall examine it in great detail in a later chapter.

THE PLAN OF THIS BOOK

If I have established the thesis and an antithesis for this book, let me preview what follows. It is necessary, first of all, to review earlier attempts to establish the trait of authoritarianism. There have been many efforts, and some of them have large research literatures. The critique is consequently long, even exhausting, and still far short of exhaustive.

In the end, I shall conclude that all previous efforts have failed to produce a viable scientific construct of authoritarianism, and the reader may well ask whether this trip is necessary. I believe it is, and not just because there are hosts of behavioral scientists who still swear by one or another of these attempts. These research efforts failed for very understandable reasons. The same mistakes were made over and over again; they have hardly been unique to research on authoritarianism; and they continue to be made today. It can and must be illustrated how futile it is, in the long run, to do research in such ways. It is a major goal of chapter 1 to make this point.

As we review the tortured literature on authoritarianism, we shall quickly encounter the nearly impenetrable tangle caused by the "response set issue." The two literatures are historically intertwined, and uncertainty about the extent to which response sets shape answers to authoritarianism scales has clouded interpretation of authoritarianism research for several decades. In chapter 2, I present the results of an investigation which I believe clarifies the matter and has important implications for other research areas as well.

The rest of the book describes the construct of right-wing authoritarianism which I have to propose, and the research which bears upon it. I propose that this and the earlier models should be evaluated in terms of the following questions:

1 Is the definition of the model sufficiently clear? Is the construct

described in enough detail that what is and what is not meant by authoritarianism is well understood?

2 Is the construct measured faithfully and powerfully? Since all the major definitions of authoritarianism have been operationalized through attitude scales, does the content of these scales reflect the conceptualization of the construct? And are these scales psychometrically powerful enough to be effective research instruments?

3 Does research produce expected relationships between the construct and criterion behaviors of authoritarianism? Are these relationships large enough to be important, beyond being statistically significant?

Finally, a word of inducement. Some of my readers are probably white-haired veterans of the scientific wars which raged over authoritarianism in the 1950s and 1960s. They are likely sick to death of the subject, and their first reaction to this book may well be "Oh no! Not another one!" But it appears that, even after all the setbacks, research on authoritarianism will not finally die, for one so often senses that there is a vast, continuing authoritarian sentiment dwelling in the land and this sentiment threatens the dearest freedoms we have. We cannot afford to ignore authoritarianism, even if it has proven difficult to study, and we had better come to understand and learn to control it.

A critique of previous social psychological research on right-wing authoritarianism

1

While modern psychological speculation about authoritarianism may be traced to Fromm (1941) and Maslow (1943), the first major experimental investigation of the subject arose from a multi-disciplinary team at the University of California at Berkeley in the late 1940s. Not only were they the first, but their book *The Authoritarian Personality (TAP)* (Adorno, Frenkel-Brunswik, Levinson and Sanford, 1950) remains the major work in the field 30 years later. Its conclusions have long since been assimilated into our cultural wisdom and, to an appreciable extent, integrated into our scientific thinking as well. Most of this chapter is devoted to a critique of this work and the enormous literature it has spawned.

A considerable number of other scientific expeditions have struck out after authoritarianism since 1950, and some editorial discretion is required in deciding what to review. I have reduced the number to five: the works of Eysenck (1953); Rokeach (1960); Wilson and Patterson (1968); Lee and Warr (1969); and Kohn (1972). (Or, alphabetically speaking, the "R," "T," "D," "C," "Revised F" and "A-R" Scales.) Eysenck's work was discontinued following a storm of criticism in 1956, but the approach and the criticism are of historical interest and deserve to be remembered. Rokeach's study of dogmatism is only mentioned in passing as the construct, while termed "general authoritarianism," is theoretically orthogonal to the authoritarianism under discussion here. Wilson's work has attracted considerable interest among contemporary researchers and should be covered in any review. The more recent efforts of Lee and Warr, and Kohn, have very small literatures but are included to illustrate the latest developments in the field.[1]

THE BERKELEY MODEL OF
THE AUTHORITARIAN PERSONALITY

The theory of the authoritarian personality
The original goal of the Berkeley research team was to study social prejudice, and in 1944 the team set out to construct a "scale that would measure prejudice without appearing to have this aim and without mentioning the name of any minority group (*TAP,* p. 222). The researchers turned to their clinical experience with prejudiced persons to find material for such a scale, and as they reviewed this group's comments on the self, family, sex, and so forth, it seemed that their indirect measure of prejudice could also be considered an estimate of "antidemocratic tendencies" at the personality level. The pursuit of this second goal produced the major theoretical development of their research program, and its apparent success was their most striking finding. The scale which resulted was labelled the Fascism Scale (F Scale), because the investigators theorized that prejudice was often caused by a fascist personality syndrome.

How did this hypothesis arise? Besides being guided by the results of their early studies of prejudice, the Berkeley investigators were influenced by Freudian conceptions of how personalities are organized and operate. Highly prejudiced people, it seemed to them, had externalized superegos and poorly controlled ids whose aggressive and sexual drives were largely fended off through such ego defence mechanisms as repression, projectivity, and displacement. This general model was given a detailed, nine-trait expression from the start, and the model was changed very little during the three subsequent studies in which the F Scale was distilled from tests involving altogether 77 items. The final nine traits were: (a) Conventionalism: rigid adherence to conventional, middle-class values. (b) Authoritarian submission: submissive, uncritical attitude toward idealized moral authorities of the ingroup. (c) Authoritarian aggression: tendency to be on the lookout for and to condemn, reject, and punish people who violate conventional norms. (d) Anti-intraception: opposition to the subjective, the imaginative, the tenderminded. (e) Superstition and stereotypy: the belief in mystical determinants of the individual's fate; the disposition to think in rigid categories. (f) Power and "toughness": preoccupation with the dominance-submission, strong-weak, leader-follower dimension; identification with power figures; overemphasis upon the conventionalized attributes of the ego; exaggerated assertion of strength and toughness. (g) Destructiveness and cynicism: generalized hostility, vilification of the human. (h) Projectivity: the disposition to believe that wild and dangerous things go on in the world; the projection outwards of unconscious emotion impulses. (i) Sex: exaggerated concern with sexual "goings-on" (*TAP,* p. 228).

Several things should be noted about these nine traits before we examine the research which bears on their existence. First, there actually are more than nine distinguishable variables in the above list. Superstition (the belief in mystical determinants of the individual's fate) is hardly the same thing as stereotypy (the disposition to think in rigid categories). In fact, stereotypy was conceived to be a component of the fascist personality only after the initial development of the F Scale (*TAP,* p. 236) and apparently was attached to the nine-level model where it seemed to fit best, rather than enlarge the list of traits. A consequence was that items written to tap superstition (e.g., "Some day it will probably be shown that astrology can explain a lot of things") have little to do with stereotypy. Similarly, one can question the isomorphism of "power" and "toughness," and of "destructiveness" and "cynicism."

The looseness of the theoretical model of the fascist or, as it soon came to be called, the authoritarian personality, is also evident in the details of the definitions given each trait. Calling conventionalism "the rigid adherence to conventional, middle-class values," for example, does not give a very specific idea of what the trait is supposed to be. The point here is that it was theoretically unlikely, from the start, that responses to the F Scale would ever support the nine-trait model advanced in *The Authoritarian Personality* very precisely. The model was too vague.

It was also methodologically all but impossible, because from the start, many of the items on the F Scale were intended to tap several traits at once. On the final (Form 45/40) version (*TAP* pp. 255–257), half of the items supposedly measured two traits simultaneously, and another was designed to tap three.[2] Moreover, this is a minimal statement of the actual trait overlap in the items. Consider the item: "There is hardly anything lower than a person who does not feel a great love, gratitude and respect for his parents." Which of the nine traits would the reader say this item measures? Conventionalism? Authoritarian submission? Authoritarian aggression? I think it taps at least these three, but it is listed as one of the items on the F Scale thought to measure just one trait, authoritarian aggression.

Numerous other instances of unacknowledged trait overlap could be cited, and there probably are not any "pure" items on the test. The problem is endemic to any attitude scale which ventures beyond asking the same question over and over again. But the result is that if the items are misread, the data will not support the details of the hypothesized model.

The fact that most of the items on the F Scale tapped more than one trait may have made it difficult to find the hypothesized dimensions in a set of responses, but the trait overlap was consonant with the central tenet of the model, which was that the traits covaried to an appreciable extent in the population. Thus the Berkeley model of the authoritarian personality could have been confirmed at the level of item covariation, even if the pattern of covariation did not support the model any further than that. The extent to which research has supported the model, either grossly or in detail, is dealt with in the next section.

The construct validity of the California F Scale

The question of a test's validity is a complex one (Cronbach, 1970, chap. 5). Over the years, researchers have discussed "face validity," "content validity," "predictive validity," "concurrent validity," "convergent" and "discriminant" and still other aspects of validity. Our concern is with "construct validity," that is, the extent to which tests such as the F Scale can be said to measure the psychological construct (and just the construct) for which they are named. This evaluation will take place in two stages. First the internal, psychometric properties of a test will be considered. Attention will be focused on the extent of interitem correlation, and on the factor structure which can be interpreted to underlie the items. Then the test's empirical relationships with other measures will be considered. Attention will be focused on relationships with variables which can be theoretically linked with the concept of authoritarianism which the test's inventors have proposed.

Psychometric properties of the California F Scale

Interitem correlations

To what extent was the Berkeley nine-trait model of the authoritarian personality confirmed by the original investigators' own results? The interitem correlations of the final version of the F Scale was, in those precomputer days, ascertained directly in just one sample: 512 women in a large group of Berkeley introductory psychology students. The mean interitem (and presumably Pearsonian) correlation was .13, which is both typical of later findings and none too good. It hardly supports the central tenet of covariation, especially since all the items on the F Scale were written in the protrait (i.e., authoritarian) direction. Agreement with an item thus always indicated authoritarianism, and disagreement, non-authoritarianism. If some subjects tend to agree with items regardless of content, this "response set" will create higher correlations among answers to the F Scale than the items themselves warrant. The same effect occurs if subjects tend to disagree with items, regardless of content.

At first, the Berkeley investigators acknowledged the low interitem correlations on the F Scale, noting they were "considerably lower" than those of acceptable intelligence tests. But over time that assessment of matters changed: by 1974, Sanford wrote that the F Scale had "fairly high internal consistency" which justified the conclusion "that the F Scale measures one thing."*

The items which were supposed to be measuring the nine different traits of the authoritarian personality were obviously not highly inter-correlated. In fact, the items in any one hypothesized cluster correlated no better with one another than they did with numerous items from other clusters. As we have seen, this is not surprising, since the heterogeneity of some of the traits and the ambiguity of which items measured which trait would have obscured any relationships there could have been. The Berkeley investigators concluded that they were justified in using the traits only as "a priori aids to discussion" and left unanswered the question of exactly what scores on the F Scale represent. That has remained "a good question" to this day. I shall try to answer it in this and the next chapter.

Before turning to factor-analytic investigations of the F Scale, we should note one interesting feature of the original Berkeley study. While the correlations among the items on the test were low overall, some of

---

* Sanford's reference to the *internal consistency* of the F Scale raises an important point. While the term denotes the correlations among items on a test, it is also synonymous with Cronbach's "alpha coefficient" of test reliability, which is determined by both the interitem correlations *and* the length of a test. To illustrate, the 30-item F Scale with mean intercorrelation of .13 would have an alpha reliability of about .82. If the test had been 60 items long and maintained the same level of interitem correlation, the alpha reliability would have been .90. Summed scores on the 60-item test would be more stable to be sure, but the degree of cohesion among the items on the two tests would still be identical.

Researchers occasionally cite the high "internal consistency" of a test (i.e., its alpha coefficient) as proof that the test is unidimensional, but the length of the test must always be taken into account. Summed test scores can be made more reliable (stable) by making the tests longer, but this cannot compensate for low correlations among responses to the items. The interitem correlations are the real and only source of unidimensionality.

TABLE 1

The seven F Scale items (Form 40/45) with the best
discriminatory power in the original Berkeley Study

---

1 Sex crimes, such as rape and attacks on children, deserve more than mere imprisonment; such criminals ought to be publicly whipped, or worse.

2 What the youth needs most is strict discipline, rugged determination, and the will
to work and fight for family and country.

3 There is hardly anything lower than a person who does not feel a great love, gratitude, and respect for his parents.

4 Every person should have complete faith in some supernatural power whose decisions he obeys without question.

5 Young people sometimes get rebellious ideas, but as they grow up they ought to
get over them and settle down.

6 Obedience and respect for authority are the most important virtues children should
learn.

7 Homosexuals are hardly better than criminals and ought to be severely punished.

---

the items naturally correlated with the rest of the test better than the
others did. Table 9 in chapter 7 of *The Authoritarian Personality* lists
the Likert "discriminatory powers" of the F Scale items for all the 14
groups who served in the final, definitive studies. The most discriminating items on the test are reproduced in Table 1, in order of their
discriminatory powers.

It seems to me that nearly all of the items in Table 1 tap *aggressive*
impulses, either explicitly or implicitly. Furthermore the aggression is
couched in *conventional* terms, or is directed against unconventional
targets. Most of the items seem to tap sentiments of *submission* as well.

I shall be more precise about these terms in a later chapter, but I
offer these interpretations now because they may help explain some things
later on. While many researchers have used shortened F Scales composed
of the most discriminating items in the original study, it has not, to my
knowledge, been noted before that the most discriminating items have
some things more or less in common.

"Factor analytic" studies of the F Scale
The major approach to determining the factorial nature of the F Scale
has been, naturally enough, through factor analysis. A simple point
about the nature of this approach should be recognized before we review
this literature, however. Factor analyses do not yield *the* results of a
scientific investigation so much as they provide an interpretation of the

results. It is true that the procedures involved in a factor analysis are usually quite laborious, for humans anyway, and this can create the impression that the outcome is necessarily independent of the investigator's inclinations and prejudices, that it is a *deus ex machina*. But this is not so; there are many ways a researcher can shape the results of a factor analysis.

Two such ways have a special bearing on the literature we are about to review: (a) the manner in which the factor matrix is rotated, and (b) the interpretation which is made of the rotated dimensions which emerge. (The reader has just had some experience with the latter point, if he disagreed with the interpretation I made of the items in Table 1.) With regard to rotation, the psychological interpretation given to factors on a scale depends heavily on how the factors are positioned, both absolutely, and relative to one another. In trying to determine whether responses to the F Scale can be organized around the nine-trait model of the Berkeley investigators, for example, one should use oblique rotations, since the traits were conceived to be interrelated, not independent. But most researchers have imposed orthogonality among the factors rotated through F Scale matrices. It is legitimate to use orthogonal rotations to interpret the data; these studies did not test the model of right-wing authoritarianism developed by Adorno et al., however.

Christie and Garcia (1951) were the first to report the results of a "factor analytic" study of the F Scale.[3] Their main objective was to see if the findings of the original Berkeley studies, which had used mainly Californians, would be obtained elsewhere. Accordingly, they compared the F Scale scores of 386 introductory psychology students at Berkeley with those of 114 similar students enrolled in a private university (probably the University of Tulsa) in "Southwest City." It was found that students in this university had much higher scores than did those at Berkeley. Subsamples of 57 students each were then composed, matched for sex, age, size of family, and several income, religious and political preference factors. The difference in F Scale scores between these two subsamples still remained; in fact, in one of the few detailed item analyses found in the literature, Christie and Garcia reported that 18 of the 30 items on the scale received significantly higher scores in the Southwest City sample. (All of the seven items listed in Table 1 were among these, but in this study they showed only a moderate tendency to be the most discriminating.)

The investigators then calculated tetrachoric coefficients among the 30 items in each sample, and performed "cluster analyses" (Tryon, 1939) within each sample's matrix. They found seven clusters in the Berkeley matrix and eight within the other.

Realizing that "interpreting the meaning of a given cluster necessarily involves a certain degree of subjectivity," they each interpreted each set of clusters, compared their results, and discussed them with other investigators who had worked with the F Scale. In addition, two classes of undergraduates interpreted the clusters. Christie and Garcia report that "the interpretation made by psychologically naive subjects agreed with one another as well as with those made by experienced investigators." The resulting cluster names sometimes were identical for both samples, but mostly the clusters differed and the various items on the scale showed practically no tendency to end up in the same cluster in both samples. Thus the psychological organization of responses to the F Scale seemed to vary considerably between two samples which supposedly differed mainly in geographic region. The investigators concluded that these differences were due more to social factors in the two regions than to personality factors attributable to childhood experiences.

While one would hesitate to quarrel with this conclusion, the data cited to support it could be more convincing. The interitem correlations ranged enormously in this study (−.46 to +.89 for the Southwest City sample; −.50 to +.77 for the Berkeley students). By comparison, the values reported for the sample of 517 Berkeley coeds in *The Authoritarian Personality* were −.05 to .44. The wide fluctuation in values found by Christie and Garcia was probably due to the rather small sample size ($N = 57$ in each case) used in their investigations — a limitation which makes the results of a cluster analysis decidedly unreliable. In addition, the use of tetrachoric rather than Pearson product-moment correlations creates certain problems. Another research team undertaking a similar task, (O'Neil and Levinson, 1954) reported that tetrachoric coefficients varied considerably, depending on which point on the response scale was used as the cutting point for each item.

Finally, there is the typical uncertainty regarding cluster interpretations, despite the pains the investigators took to objectify this phase of their work. For example, the first-named cluster in the Berkeley sample contained the following items, in the order of their "loadings":

Most of our social problems would be solved if we could somehow get rid of the immoral, crooked and feebleminded people.

There is hardly anything lower than a person who does not feel a great love, gratitude and respect for his parents.

No weakness or difficulty can hold us back if we have enough will power.

Young people sometimes get rebellious ideas, but as they grow up they ought to get over them and settle down.

The reader is invited to discern the common thread running through these items. The cluster was named "Conformity" by Christie, Garcia and their judges. Conformity can be found, I submit, most directly in the item with the lowest loading, not at all in the third statement, and only with some straining in the first two. This objection is by no means the only one which can be raised with the cluster interpretations given in the original report.[4]

Pursuing alternate interpretations is probably not worthwhile, however, since it is doubtful the original pattern of correlations would have been repeated very precisely had another set of subjects from these populations been tested. It is not surprising that the two sets of clusters obtained in such small samples differed, but the meaning of the difference is unclear. The study by Christie and Garcia thus tells us little about the factor structure of the F Scale, except of course that the scale is decidedly multidimensional. This is a foregone conclusion anyway, given the low level of item intercorrelation in the original study.

Oddly enough, the next factor analysis of the F Scale to appear was performed on some of the original Berkeley data and it reached the opposite conclusion. Eysenck (1954, p. 152) reported that one of his collaborators, Dr. Melvin, carried out a factor analysis of data provided by the Berkeley investigators. Melvin reportedly "found that a very strong general factor ran through all of the items, thus confirming the main hypothesis of the Californian group."

Nevertheless, it is difficult to believe that anything but a weak factor could run through all of the items, given the intercorrelations reported in *The Authoritarian Personality*. No details of Melvin's analysis were reported by Eysenck, such as the factor extraction method, the rotations performed, and the amount of variance controlled by this general factor. It might be noted that factor extraction techniques frequently produce a first, general, factor in the *unrotated* matrix on which all of the variables tend to have appreciable loadings. The factor is in fact mathematically placed to account for as much of the test's variance as possible. But such a factor is usually psychologically meaningless as it has merged some of the influence of all of the factors whose identification is the goal of the exercise. The importance of the first unrotated factor will almost always drop dramatically once the factor structure is rotated into a meaningful configuration.

Comrey (1973) has noted that some investigators have mistakenly interpreted "general" factors in unrotated matrices as evidence for unidimensionality, and we encounter several cases in this chapter in which this definitely occurred. This may be what happened in Melvin's/ Eysenck's analysis as well. In any event, Melvin is the only investigator I have found who concluded from a factor analysis of the F Scale that the test was unidimensional.

Aumack (1955) administered a 55-item scale (containing the 30 original F Scale items) to 85 convicted murderers imprisoned in San Quentin. The items were found to be clustered in 14 groups; these groupings reportedly did not conform to the Berkeley model nor to the clusters Christie and Garcia (1951) obtained. Both the F and non-F Scale items loaded on the 14 clusters, so the apparent lack of unidimensionality cannot be attributed to the 25 "outside" items. The nature of the population sampled of course limits the generality of the findings.

Camilleri (1959) approached the problem in a novel way, purposely rotating a centroid-extracted factor matrix so as to approximate the Berkeley model as closely as possible. As the initial analysis of the responses of 100 UCLA anthropology students provided seven factors, the seven (of nine) traits supposedly most represented on the F Scale were used to formulate the target. Camilleri then calculated the number of items which had "positive" correlations (i.e., > .20) with the factors they were supposed to load on. He found that 35 of the 41 possible correlations were positive, which is rather impressive at first glance. On the other hand, there were 63 other, unscheduled, positive correlations (on supposedly inappropriate factors). In addition, about half (14/27) of the items had their highest loadings on a wrong factor. Finally, it was noted that the seven factors did not correlate among themselves as hypothesized by the Berkeley model (e.g., conventionalism, authoritarian submission, and authoritarian aggression should especially covary because theoretically they represent the "externalized superego.") Camilleri concluded that the F Scale is not a unidimensional instrument: "In its present form the F Scale is not a good measure of the authoritarian personality as that structure is viewed in theory" (p. 322).

Krug (1961) administered the F Scale to 704 incoming freshmen at Carnegie-Mellon University and analyzed the results both by (1) Thurstone's multiple group method with graphic rotation to simple structure, and (2) a centroid extraction with Quartimax rotation. Both rotations were orthogonal. The different procedures reportedly produced similar results, except that the Quartimax rotation merged two hand-graphed factors into a first, general factor. The factor names given by Krug were: (a) "General, with an embedded group factor of Conventionalism"; (b) "Cynicism"; (c) "Aggression"; (d) "Superstition and Stereotypy"; (e) "Projectivity"; (f) "Good versus Bad Persons." Most of these titles coincide with or approximate trait names used by the Berkeley researchers, as Kerlinger and Rokeach (1966) noted. Krug concluded that "the emergence of a general factor...supports the contention that most F Scale items share some common variance," but also that "the relatively clean orthogonal simple structure" indicates that "several independent dimensions are necessary if we are to understand the item responses" (p. 290).

Krug's results come closer to verifying the model of authoritarianism presented in *The Authoritarian Personality* than any other study in the literature. Even so, the model is not verified very completely, especially when one takes a closer look at the data. The emergence of a general factor can be disputed. Quartimax rotations tend to exaggerate the importance of the first factor rotated (Harman, 1967, p. 304), and even with this exaggertion, only five of the 29 items tested had loadings greater than .40 on this first factor (including, incidentally, four of the items listed in Table 1).

As for the similarity of Krug's factors to the traits supposedly assessed by the scale, the reader is invited once again to find a common factor running through the following items:

Nowadays more and more people are prying into matters that should remain personal and private.

The wild sex life of the old Greeks and Romans was tame compared to some of the goings-on in this country, even in places where people might least expect it.

The true American way of life is disappearing so fast that force may be necessary to preserve it.

If people would talk less and work more, everybody would be better off.

What this country needs most, more than laws and political programs, is a few courageous, tireless, devoted leaders in whom the people can put their trust.

Familiarity breeds contempt.

Most of these items, it seems to me, are concerned with things that are wrong in society and what is needed to correct them. I would call the factor "social concern" if I had to give it a name; but I find little in these items which merits the name "Cynicism," which is what Krug called it. Actually only two of the six items (the third and the last) were originally written to tap "Destructiveness and Cynicism." The first two items, which are the only ones with loadings greater than .40, were intended to measure "Projectivity" but do not fall on Krug's "Projectivity factor"...a factor that has no item loadings greater than .40. Similar comments could be made about the other coincidences between Krug's factor names and the trait names in the Berkeley model.

Finally, Kerlinger and Rokeach (1966) studied the factorial nature of the F Scale and Dogmatism Scale (D Scale) (Rokeach, 1960) using over 1,200 students from Michigan, New York, and Louisiana as subjects. Their main purpose was to see if the scales would separate factorially; the extent to which they did and did not, while a matter of some contention, is less relevant here than an analysis of the responses to just the F Scale.

The scale was here factored by the principal axes method and rotated obliquely through an analytical technique, Promax, which pursues simple structure. Unfortunately the results of this analysis were not reported in detail, but supplementary information deposited with the American Documentation Institute (Document No. 8944) shows that five factors were extracted and rotated. The factors were not named and the relationships among them unfortunately were not reported. Inspection of the correlations among the items which "loaded" on the various factors indicates that Factors I and II would be somewhat related, while the remaining three factors were relatively independent. Nearly all of the items with significant loadings on Factors I and II are those listed in Table 1 of this chapter, which suggests that the factors together may have something to do with aggression, conventionalism, and submission. The remaining factors are not readily interpretable. The highest loading items on Factor III, for example, were: "So many different kinds of people," "Astrology," and, "Secret plots hatched."

In summary, the factor analytic studies confirm what one would expect from the initial Berkeley studies regarding the validity of the F Scale.[5] There is no convincing evidence that the test measures any single construct which can be called "fascist potential," "authoritarianism" or the like. This in itself is the most powerful criticism one could level against the validity of the test, and as we have seen, it was evident from the start.

Given multiple dimensionality, then, it is possible that the dimensions conform to the theoretical model which the F Scale was designed to represent, even if they do not covary appreciably. A number of investigations have suggested that at least some of the dimensions are represented. But examination of these results indicates that the representation is very limited, and requires a certain amount of imagination, overlooking of contrary findings, and perhaps preknowledge of what "ought" to be there.

What constructs are represented on the scale then? By and large, it would seem that the test measures very little which is identifiable and comprehensible. I have noted that those items which had the highest discriminatory power in the Berkeley studies also tended to covary in the factor analytic studies, and in several investigations were found to compose the first factor(s) extracted from the scale. The interpretation of what these items have in common is, as always, a subjective matter. I interpret them to tap, more than anything else, sentiments of aggression, conventionality and submission. Of course these are just a few of the items on the scale, and it is doubtful that even these sentiments (if that is what is represented) are measured very powerfully.

One would think this simple fact — that the psychometric properties of the F Scale indicate that it cannot measure the construct it was intended to measure — would preclude any further discussion of the scale's validity. I think it should, but unfortunately it does not. A considerable number of behavioral scientists have apparently believed over the years that, despite its obvious psychometric failures, the scale still "works," that is, that scores on the test are significantly related with other variables.[6] Insofar as these other variables represent plausible criteria of authoritarianism, they can be used to establish the construct validity of a test, especially when the "divergent" validity of the test is also established (Campbell and Fiske, 1959). But the odds are surely against such successful empirical validation when the test is as psychometrically weak as the F Scale is.

It is a consistent theme in this book that research with conceptually or psychometrically weak tools is largely a waste of time. More specifically, it is contended that relationships found with attitude scales having very low interitem correlations and incoherent factor structures are extremely ambiguous and can demonstrate very little about the nature of the test. The contention should be undramatic because it seems so obvious.

But researchers are often attracted to a new test the way moths are drawn to a light. It is so easy to do research with attitude scales that the temptation to use even the poorest tests seems to overwhelm some.

Instruments that are "suggestive, and not too difficult to use," have what Brown (1965, p. 445) has called the "hula hoop effect" among behavioral scientists. "The journals become full of reports of one-shot studies correlating the new kind of score with all the old kinds of score." Hundreds of F Scale relationships have appeared in the literature, through some of which our expedition unavoidably must now proceed.

The F Scale's relationships with other measures
The research literature on the F Scale is huge. After Christie and Cook (1958) had organized the literature through 1956 into as much topical sense as they could, they still had 95 papers on topics which did not fit into their schema. And the literature now is at least twice the size it was then. The F Scale has probably been correlated with every "personality" test ever printed, and been used in conjunction with every social psychological paradigm mentioned more than once in the journals.

For the purpose of this book, we need not review all this material. (See Kirscht and Dillehay, 1967, for a broader if less intense critique.) Instead, we shall concentrate on the issues which bear most directly on the F Scale's construct validity, or which have produced the greatest interest in the journals. We shall consider how high F scores are associated (a) with prejudice; (b) with certain kinds of childhood backgrounds; (c) with rigidity and intolerance of ambiguity; (d) with high conformity; (e) with group behavior; (f) with socioeconomic class; (g) with aggressive behavior; and (h) with political conservatism.

Relationships with prejudice
The F Scale was originally developed to measure ethnocentrism indirectly. Given this intention and the fact that the major result of the Berkeley investigations was a personality-based explanation of social prejudice, it is appropriate that a critique of the F Scale's empirical validity begin with prejudice.

Ethnocentrism was conceived by the Berkeley researchers as an ideological system which made sharp distinctions between "ingroups" (those with which the individual identifies himself) and "outgroups" (with which there is no identification and which are regarded as antithetical to the ingroup) (*TAP*, p. 104). This conceptualization, in itself, is quite general and rather resistant to scientific disproof. Furthermore, one could apply the label with equal justification to various Protestants, Catholics, Jews, and atheists, and to Fascists, Conservatives, Liberals, and Communists alike. As defined in *The Authoritarian Personality*, ethnocentrism is a very common social orientation.

As the Berkeley researchers operationalized the term, however, ethnocentrism meant something more specific: prejudice among Americans against (a) Jews, (b) blacks, (c) other American minorities (including organized groups such as small political parties and religious sects, ethnic minorities and "moral minorities," and (d) ("pseudo") patriotism. The Ethnocentrism Scale (E Scale) which was developed concurrently with the F Scale, contained items from each of these four categories. The final form of this scale (*TAP*, p. 142) contained twenty unidirectionally worded items, most of them dealing explicitly with Jews and blacks. Pseudopatriotism, despite its theoretical importance as the ingroup half of ethnocentrism, was only represented by a few items, and research on "ethnocentrism" has in fact concentrated on prejudice.

The average correlation among items on the final E Scale was .42, several times as large as that of the F Scale (*TAP*, p. 140). Furthermore the correlations between summed scores on the E and F Scales ranged from .56 to .87 and averaged about .75. These very substantial values, based upon five- or ten-item versions of the E Scale and uncorrected for attenuation, indicated that a very strong connection existed between ethnocentrism and authoritarianism, a connection which seemingly explained on a deep psychological level some of the most irrational and horrible events in recent history. It should be noted that it was the close fit between scores on the two scales, not the fact of mere correlation, that seemingly confirmed the theoretical model of the authoritarian personality.

Hyman and Sheatsley (1954) soon pointed out, however, that the high correlations could have resulted more from the Berkeley investigators' methodological procedures than from the validity of their theoretical model. For one thing, the authors of *The Authoritarian Personality* kept track of how well each item on the developing F Scale correlated with the developing Anti-Semitism and Ethnocentrism Scales (see Tables 3 and 6 in chapter 7 of *TAP*). Items which were poorly correlated with prejudice had a poorer chance of surviving "the cut." For instance, the "anti-intraception" item, "Books and movies ought not to deal so much with the sordid and seamy side of life; they ought to concentrate on themes that are entertaining or uplifting," was one of the most discriminating items on the first version of the F Scale, but it also had one of the lowest relationships with scores on the Anti-Semitism Scale. Despite the statement (*TAP*, p. 250) that the most discriminating items on the initial form were carried over to the next model "in the same or slightly revised form," the "books and movies" item simply disappeared, forever. It is not hard to construct a scale which will correlate highly with another if you eliminate items that are insufficiently related with the target.

It must be said that most of the items which made their way to the final form of the F Scale had some relationship with prejudice all along the way. The cases of unwarranted selectivity which Hyman and Sheatsley cited often are quite defendable in terms of the Likert-scale criteria the Berkeley team used to construct the F Scale. A far more serious problem with the procedures followed was that the Berkeley researchers intended the F Scale to be an indirect measure of prejudice, and their contact with prejudiced persons could have strongly influenced which items were even tested. The F Scale was built "from the basement up" to be correlated with prejudice.

A second aspect of the Berkeley investigators' methodology, one which has received far more attention in the literature, also compromised the high relationship between the F and E Scales. This was the possibility that response sets contributed to the relationships between these unidirectionally worded scales, a matter we shall deal with in detail in the next chapter. For the moment, it can simply be said that the response set possibility has been too real to be ignored, and has raised continuing doubts about the extent to which social prejudice is related to scores on the F Scale.

A final caveat on this matter, on historical grounds, is in order. Doubtless the terrible events in Nazi Germany, where institutionalized anti-Semitism and authoritarian submission undeniably coexisted, provided much of the motivation for the Berkeley investigation and may even have been what the researchers were most trying to understand. But the conclusion they reached about prejudice and authoritarianism receives little historical support beyond the case of Germany.[7] The prototype Fascist government in Italy was devoid of anti-Semitism, both in theory and practice for over 15 years, until Hitler pressured Mussolini to institute persecutions; however, they were not carried out with any particular enthusiasm by Italian Fascists. Similarly, fascist governments in Austria and Spain did not persecute racial minorities, while one can name democratic and "leftist" governments which have. The argument is not on behalf of fascism, of course, but against the notion that anti-Semitism was "the spearhead of fascism" (Adorno, 1950). Racial and ethnic prejudice long predated facism, and has hardly been a distinguishing feature of fascism.

Most of the investigations of F Scale scores and prejudice since 1950 have used questionnaire and survey techniques. Campbell and McCandless (1951) compared responses to the E and F Scale with those on a "Xenophobia Scale" developed by Campbell. Xenophobia, a generalized hatred and fear of strangers, was considered an indication of general prejudice toward minority groups. The researchers asked subjects to respond to 25 statements about a minority group (e.g., "Negro people should not be allowed to stay in this country"), and it was completed five times for the following groups: blacks, Japanese, Jews, Mexicans and the English. By and large, the scale was balanced for direction-of-wording effects, so simple response sets would not produce a positive correlation between Xenophobia and F Scale scores. One hundred and fifty-nine students at San Francisco State College, who were participating in a two-day testing program "designed to survey students needs," served in the study. The school was described as "engaged in conspicuous efforts to achieve democratic ideals in racial and religious group relations" at the time (1947).

Scores on the F and E Scales correlated .73; but the meaning of this relationship is difficult to interpret for reasons just described.[8] Responses to the F Scale also correlated with prejudice against the five minority groups, but at a lower level (.42–.57). The difference between these correlations and that with the E Scale may have been due to the lack of response set effects on the Xenophobia scales. The nonetheless significant correlations between Xenophobia and the F Scale were considered by the investigators "substantial enough to remove any doubt about the generalizability of previous findings to other tests of social prejudice" (p. 189).

Some doubts linger on about the interpretation of these findings, however. As we have seen, there is reason to expect scores on the F Scale to correlate with at least some measures of prejudice, since the items on the test tended to be selected for their anticipated and then demonstrated relationship with prejudice. Furthermore, the similarity of F Scale correlations with prejudice against the English (.42) and others (especially the Japanese in 1947, which was only slightly higher at .49) seems a little peculiar. Campbell and McCandless also expressed surprise at the figure for prejudice against the English in light of the "low communality" of this prejudice with attitudes toward other minority groups. Unfortunately no indices of central tendencies were presented in the report, to help one judge just how much prejudice there was in the sample.

Martin and Westie (1959), in a widely cited study, investigated personality and attitudinal differences between racially tolerant and anti-Negro persons living in Indianapolis. The nine most efficient items from the F Scale were included in their battery of measurements. Subjects were randomly selected whites living in all-white neighborhoods who were given a short prejudice measure "at the doorstep." If the subject seemed tolerant of blacks, or highly prejudiced against them, the interviewer left a long survey to be completed and mailed back. Two hundred (of 212) such requests were accepted, and eventually 139 usable surveys were returned.

The measure of prejudice in the long survey was a 192-item bipolar scale whose final score would not reflect the influence of response sets such as acquiescence. The scores on this measure could range from −432 to +432 (see Westie, 1953). It was decided to call people with scores between −70 and +70 "tolerant" and those with scores greater than +174 "prejudiced." Thirty-nine of the 139 usable surveys did not fall in these ranges, leaving a sample of 100 subjects. The mean F Scale score of the 41 tolerant people (−4.39 on a −18 to +18 continuum) was significantly lower than that of the 59 prejudiced people (+5.07, $p < .001$).

Unfortunately the interpretation of this finding is compromised by several aspects of the researchers' analysis. The placement of the cutting points for identifying "tolerant" and "prejudiced" subjects can obviously have a strong effect upon the results of a study, so it is important that the placement be as nonarbitrary as possible. Martin and Westie wished to compare people who were "neutral" toward blacks with persons who were quite prejudiced against them. They could have compared subjects who fell in equal-sized ranges in (a) the center, and (b) the extreme right of the response scale. Another way would have been to compare equal-sized samples of subjects, such as the most prejudiced quartile of the sample with the most neutral quartile. However, Martin and Westie compared those who fell in the middle 16% of the response scale with those who fell in the upper 30% of the range; the latter sample was nearly half again as large as the former. The cutting mark of +175 for prejudiced subjects was used, it was reported, on the basis of unspecified "previous application of the scale in Indianapolis." No explanation of the −70 to +70 boundaries for the neutral category was given.

A second problem with Martin and Westie's analysis is related to their very welcome use of a nonstudent sample. The meaning of a relationship between F Scale scores and prejudice in a sample of the general population is less than clear when the effect of level of education is not taken into account.[9] Educational attainment was not controlled in Martin and Westie's comparisons, although it was known that "tolerant" subjects were significantly better educated than the prejudiced subjects.

Triandis and Triandis (1960) administered a 14-item version of the F Scale to 86 introductory psychology students at the University of Illinois along with a social distance scale. The latter presented brief descriptions of a number of stimulus persons (e.g., a "Swedish physician, white, of the same religion as you"; a "Negro, Portugese coalminer of a different religion) and asked each subject to say, on a 15-point scale, how close they were willing to be to such a person. The stimulus persons varied in race, nationality, occupational status, and religion. A general social distance score based on the total sum of squares of each subject's ratings was computed, and was found to be about twice as great among the upper half of the F Scale distribution as among the lower half ($p < .01$). However this index does not indicate the nature of the differentiations which the high F subjects were more likely to make.

Hites and Kellogg (1964) administered the entire F Scale to 141 students at a private liberal arts college in the southern United States; they included two questions concerning separate schools and church services for blacks and whites. Both of these prejudice questions and all of the F Scale items were worded in the same direction, however. The investigators collapsed the responses to the prejudice items, which had been given on a five-point scale, into three categories. No justification was given for this. The correlation between the F Scale and a summed score on the two prejudice items was .55, but the usual caveat about the effects of response sets applies.

Finally Triandis, as part of a cross-cultural study (Triandis, Davis and Takezawa, 1965) administered 10 items from the original F Scale (mixed with 10 reversals) to 183 University of Illinois students along with a social distance scale which again varied the race, religion, occupation and nationality of the stimulus persons. This time, correlations were computed and scores on the F Scale were found to correlate from .11 to .28 with a variety of measures of social distance. As one can judge from the range of the results, the differences in relationship attributable to racial factors, religious factors, and so forth were relatively minor.

Two widely-cited studies by Pettigrew have challenged the Berkeley investigators' contention that prejudice is mainly caused by personality disorders. In the first (Pettigrew, 1958) a 13-item version of the F Scale and an 18-item "anti-African" scale were administered to over 500 English-speaking students at the University of Natal in South Africa. These students were found to be highly prejudiced against native Africans, but their F Scale scores were only modestly higher than those of much less prejudiced students in the United States. Pettigrew made the very sensible ble point that the high degree of prejudice among South African students probably resulted from their cultural learnings, and not from personality problems ("externalization" in the functional system of Smith, Bruner and White, 1956). Nevertheless, scores on the two scales correlated .46, which indicates the F Scale was still somewhat predictive of prejudice among these members of a highly prejudiced population. A third test in the battery, intended to measure social conformity, also correlated .46 with anti-African prejudice, which strengthened Pettigrew's point. However, the relationships among all of the tests may well have been heightened by response sets, as all three measures were worded in the same direction.

Subsequent research in South Africa has tended to confirm Pettigrew's conclusion insofar as the relationships found between F Scale scores and prejudice have tended to be small. Coleman and Lambley (1970) found weak correlations between scores on a 15-item forced-choice version of the F Scale, (a) two versions of an anti-African prejudice scale ($r = .23, .33$), and (b) a nonwhite social distance scale ($r = .27$). The subjects were 60 University of Capetown students. Using very similar, if not identical, scales, Orpen (1971) found even lower correlations ($r = .19, .20$) among 88 other students from the same university. Lambley and Gilbert (1970) found r's of .32 – .47 with the same tests (supplemented by a partially-balanced version of the F Scale) among 106 different Capetown students; and Lambley (1973) reported correlations of .38 – .41 between the counterbalanced F Scale and prejudice and social distance measures among 190 more students from the University of Capetown. It might be noted that these correlations, obtained with at least partially-balanced F Scales were almost always lower than the figure Pettigrew obtained with totally unbalanced measures.

Pettigrew's contention that prejudice is shaped by local social norms as well as by personality factors received further support from an American study he reported in 1959. Ten F Scale, eight anti-Semitism and 12 anti-Negro items were administered to randomly-selected white adults in four small towns in New England, and also in four small towns in North Carolina and Georgia. All of the F Scale and Anti-Semitism (A-S) Scale items and four of the anti-Negro items were taken from the Berkeley surveys, though not always from the final scales, and thus again all of the items were worded in the same direction. The total sample size was 366.

Pettigrew found that his southern respondents were significantly more prejudiced against Negroes on all 12 of the anti-Negro items. Differences in anti-Semitism for the entire sample were not reported, but from various subsample analyses it seems that any such differences would have been relatively small. However, there was virtually no difference in the level of authoritarianism in the northern and southern samples.

On the correlational level, summed scores on the F Scale items again correlated with anti-Negro sentiments in both the north and south, but were not large (.27 and .34 respectively) when education and age were held constant.[10]

The 16 studies described above[11] bear most directly upon the hypothesis that scores on the F Scale are strongly related to prejudice. An examination of the results, summarized in Table 2, indicates how far the evidence falls short of confirming the original hypothesis of the Berkeley researchers. No study yet has produced a strong relationship between F Scale scores and prejudice that is not plausibly interpretable in a number of alternate ways. Foremost among these is the possibility that response sets inflate the relationship between F Scale scores and unidirectionally-worded measures of prejudice. As Table 2 indicates, F Scale correlations with other unbalanced scales typically ranged from the .50s to the .70s, while those between balanced scales usually fell in the .20s to the .40s. This is a very substantial difference in results, and suggests in itself that response sets control an appreciable amount of the variance of scores on the original F Scale. I shall consider this more fully in chapter 2.

The implications of the .20 – .40 correlations, if they are the truer indicators of the real relationship with prejudice, are obvious. The major conclusion in *The Authoritarian Personality*—that authoritarianism is highly related to prejudice—is still unconfirmed, long after it has been assimilated into our culture.[12]

The childhood origins of "authoritarianism"
There is a considerable literature on the hypothesis that high scores on the F Scale are the result of certain childhood experiences. Few studies have tested this premise very directly, but because many indirect tests have become prominent in the literature, our frame of reference here is necessarily wide. As we consider this literature, we shall move farther and farther away from the kind of evidence which can support the hypothesis most clearly. Many of the studies can at best provide results which are not inconsistent with the Berkeley model. But even such indirect support is in short supply.

TABLE 2

Summary of studies relating scores on the F Scale to prejudice

Study	Version of the F Scale	Measure of prejudice	Sample	Finding
Adorno et al., 1950	Original F Scale	5- or 10-item E Scale	Variety of groups	Correlations ranging from .56 to .87 between F and E Scale scores, averaging about .75.‡
Campbell & McCandless (1951)	30-item scale (3 modified)	E Scale & Xeno-phobia Scale	American students	F and E Scales correlated .73‡ F and Xenophobia correlated .42-.57 for different targets.
Christie & Garcia (1951)	30-item F Scale	E Scale	American students	F and E Scales correlated .56-.63.‡
Kates & Diab (1955)	Original F Scale	E Scale	American students	F and E Scales correlated .66.‡
Kaufman (1957)	15 unspecified F Scale items	Anti-Semitism Scale	American students	F and A-S Scales correlated .53‡
Gaier & Bass (1959)	Original F Scale	E Scale	American students	F and E Scales correlated .49, .60 and .62 at different schools.‡
Martin & Westie, (1959)	9 items from F Scale	Anti-Negro social distance	Indianapolis adults	Moderate difference in mean F Scale scores between unmatched extremes (tolerant and prejudiced) of the sample.
Triandis & Triandis (1960)	14 items from F Scale	Social distance for a variety of targets	American students	Modest tendency for high F subjects to discriminate more among different stimulus persons.
Hites & Kellog, (1964)	30-item F Scale	Two questions about separating Negroes & Whites	American students	F Scale correlated .55 with prejudice against Negroes.‡
Triandis et al., (1965)	10 items from F Scale	Social distance for a variety of targets	American students	F Scale correlated .11 to .28 with various measures of social distance.

Pettigrew (1958)	13 items from F Scale	Anti-African scale	South African students	F Scale correlated .46 with prejudice against native Africans.‡
Coleman & Lambley (1970)	15-item forced choice F Scale	Anti-African & social distance scales	South African students	F Scale correlated .23, .33 and .27 with prejudice against native Africans.
Orpen (1971)	15-item forced choice F Scale	Anti-African & social distance scales	South African students	F Scale correlated .19 and .20 with prejudice against native Africans.
Lambley & Gilbert (1970)	Forced choice & partially balanced F Scales	Anti-African & social distance scales	South African students	F Scale scores correlated .32 to .47 with prejudice against native Africans.
Lambley (1973)	Partially counter-balanced F Scale	Anti-African & social distance scales	South African students	F Scale scores correlated .38 to .41 with prejudice against native Africans.
Pettigrew (1959)	10 items from the F Scale	12 Anti-Negro items	Adults in New England and Southern towns	F Scale scores correlated .27 to .34 when age and education were controlled.‡

‡ Indicates the relationship may have been inflated by the effects of response sets acting upon unbalanced measures.

The original Berkeley study. While Fromm (1941) had theorized earlier that authoritarianism was primarily rooted in early childhood experiences, the first scientific evidence on the matter was collected by the Berkeley research team. Indeed, it was the "early childhood" studies of the Berkeley investigation which seemingly demonstrated that authoritarianism and prejudice originated in the same set of family dynamics and were actually two sides of the same coin.

The evidence on this point came from an interview study supervised by Frenkel-Brunswik. Twenty men and 25 women who had high scores on the E Scale were interviewed some time after they had completed the Berkeley questionnaires, as were 20 men and 15 women who had scored low. The records of these interviews were then analyzed, according to a scoring manual prepared ahead of time, by judges who were blind as to the subjects' E scores. Remarks which would give away the subjects' prejudices or political opinions were reportedly deleted from the protocol.

It was found that prejudiced subjects were scored as showing significant tendencies to overidealize their parents. They were also judged as being highly submissive to their parents, and they seemed to have been dependent in an exploitive way on them for "things." The highly prejudiced males portrayed their fathers as being distant and bad tempered, and they recalled being disciplined "traumatically" for violating specific rules (rather than being taught general principles.) Males also reported their families as being dominated by the father and being highly concerned with social status. Tables 1–3 in chapter 10 of *The Authoritarian Personality* reveal that these eight findings are the only statistically significant relationships found in the study.

It was then concluded (*TAP*, pp. 384–387) that the highly *prejudiced* person comes from a distinctive home environment in which the discipline was relatively harsh, threatening and arbitrary, the parents were forbidding and distant, status-conscious and highly intolerant of unconventional impulses. As a result, the children quickly repressed hostility towards the parents and became highly submissive and overglorifying instead. The repressed aggression in turn reappeared in the form of prejudice against outgroups. While these conclusions were advanced tentatively (the problems inherent in comparing only extremes of a distribution were explicitly acknowledged) the conclusions have since been so widely cited and been transfered to the *authoritarian* personality (by the Berkeley researchers and others) that this picture of the authoritarian's childhood has become almost a stereotype in our culture.

Unbelievable as it may seem, the picture is not really supported by the data of the original study. Even without resorting to the plethora of methodological shortcomings which Hyman and Sheatsley (1954) found in the Berkeley interview studies, it can be demonstrated that the investigation had little to do with authoritarianism. Only 12 of the 20 highly prejudiced men, for example, had scored in the upper quartile of scores on the F Scale, and only 10 of the 15 nonprejudiced women were in the bottom quartile of F Scale scores (*TAP*, pp. 296–297). So right at the outset, whatever differences there were between the high E and the low E subjects hardly translated into differences between high and low F's.

The study was methodologically flawed from beginning to end. The groups compared were roughly matched for age and religion and, very roughly for political outlook, but not for education. Moreover, 40% of the high scoring men were prisoners in San Quentin Penetentiary (compared to 20% of the low scoring men). It would have been far better to exclude such subjects altogether from a study seeking generalizations about the general populace; the error was compounded by having twice as many convicts in one comparison group as in the other. The error turns out to be critical: Table 1 in chapter 9 of *The Authoritarian Personality* reveals that these San Quentin prisoners were almost certainly the backbone of the significant differences found in the interviews; each one performed overall as expected, whereas nonprisoner subjects often did not. In view of the fact that most of the significant relationships (e.g., distant, stern fathers), applied only to males, the part these very atypical men were allowed to play in shaping generalizations about a whole culture is astounding.

The interviews themselves were only loosely structured around a predetermined schedule. Not only were the interviewers given access to the interviewee's scores on the E Scale, but they were instructed to study all of the subject's questionnaire responses in detail ahead of time to suggest "hypotheses which can be verified in the interview" (*TAP*, p. 304). The interviewer recorded the subject's responses in "a 'shorthand' of his own" (*TAP*, p. 33) and then reprocessed his notes onto a dictaphone. There were thus three opportunities for the interviewer to shape what the subject "said" according to his very real and deliberately created preconceptions of what the subject ought to say. The way in which the interviews were scored can also be criticized from several points of view (see Hyman and Sheatsley, 1954).

Actually there is convincing evidence that the biases of the interviewers and scorers did not operate, on a broad front at least, to confirm the expectations of the principal investigator. Only eight of 45 hypothesized differences were statistically significant. Sometimes the "misses" were inconsequential to the conclusions which have been drawn from the study, but often they were highly relevant. For example, the highly prejudiced subjects were not significantly more "victimized" by their parents, nor did they seem to have a higher sense of obligation and duty to their parents, nor did they display a more ingroup conception of the family (*TAP*, p. 341). One reason that these "misses" have largely gone unnoticed may be the way in which the results were written up in the text of the discussion. Nearly all of the hypotheses were treated as though they had been confirmed, with extensive quotes from selected interviews, post hoc differentiations and considerable theoretical ramifications used to fill the gaps usually left by the data.

The reader familiar with the matter knows that most of these criticisms are over 25 years old, and now they might be considered little more than flaying a dead horse. Unfortunately the flaying is necessary, for the horse is not dead, but still trotting around—in various introductory psychology and developmental psychology textbooks, for example. Methodological criticisms seem to travel a shorter circuit and die a much quicker death than do "scientific breakthroughs." In conclusion then, no matter how often it is stated that the Berkeley investigators discovered the childhood origins of authoritarianism, the facts of the matter are anything but convincing.

Studies of how "authoritarian" children are treated by their parents. The most convincing evidence on the issue of the childhood determinants of F Scale scores would come from a longitudinal study of how children reared in different ways turn out to have reliably different scores on the test. Because such a study would be very expensive, time consuming, and potentially a methodological quagmire, the study of childhood origins of authoritarianism has always proceeded in less direct fashion.

One tack, taken three times in the studies I have tracked down, has been to study the parents of "authoritarian" children, either directly or through their children's reporting of them, to see if they are different from the parents of nonauthoritarian children. In such investigations the measure of childhood authoritarianism is of first importance. The most frequently cited study of this sort, by Harris, Gough and Martin (1950) is of doubtful relevance to our purpose insofar as it was concerned with prejudice, not authoritarianism, in children. Fourth- to sixth-grade children in two Minneapolis schools were tested for prejudice against blacks with an 18-item attitude scale (Gough, Harris, Martin and Edwards, 1950), and a childrearing questionnaire was mailed to their mothers as well ($N = 240$). The childrearing attitudes of the mothers of 38 prejudiced children were then compared with those of 38 mothers whose children were among the least prejudiced.

It was found that the mothers of prejudiced children were significantly more likely to agree that "obedience is the most important thing a child can learn," "it is wicked for children to disobey their parents," and "a child ought to be whipped for any sassy remark." These relationships would fit into the schema of the distant, stern, punative parent "found" in the interviews (of men) in the concurrent Berkeley study. The phi-coefficients among these relationships however were only .23–.30, despite the fact that extremes of the distributions were being compared.

Other significant relationships were less directly related to the Berkeley model (e.g., mothers of prejudiced children showed a slight tendency to prefer quiet children) or else were seemingly contradictory. ("My child gets his own way.") More to the point, however, is the fact that only seven of 71 attitude statements thought to bear on the child-rearing techniques of the parents were significantly related to prejudice in the children, sensibly or otherwise. In addition, the mothers were asked which of five or six techniques they would use to handle 10 different problem areas (e.g., child refuses to go to bed). The choice of treatments were related to the high-low distinction only once, and that relationship was seemingly contradictory to expectations (with the bedtime problem, mothers of prejudiced children were significantly more likely not to insist on a regular bedtime). There was no significant difference in the way the mothers said they would handle masturbation, temper tantrums, and the other seven situations.

The data in Harris, Gough and Martin's study thus indicate that child rearing techniques are in general unrelated to prejudice in children. The low incidence of the (very weak) relationships which were found have been overlooked by later writers, who cite the study as an independent confirmation of the Berkeley findings.

Lyle and Levitt (1955) reported two investigations of the relationship between authoritarianism in children and their parents' reported punitiveness. The measure of the former was the "Children's Anti-Democratic Scale" (Gough, Harris, Martin and Edwards, 1950), which consists of 24 statements bearing some resemblance to items on the F Scale. The parents' punitiveness in turn was assessed through an incomplete-sentence test which contained 12 statements expected to elicit a description of the parents' usual disciplinary technique (e.g., "When I disobey my parents they..."). Responses which indicated physical or verbal abuse, deprivation (of food, play, etc.) or coercion were scored as punitive. Interjudge reliability of these assessments between two judges was .97; the split-half reliability of the 12-item measure was a less satisfactory .80.

In the first study of 57 fifth-graders (probably in Iowa), the children's authoritarianism correlated .28 with the measure of inferred parental punitiveness. A replication with 148 other fifth-graders produced a similar correlation of .32. It was concluded that the evidence "is in accord with, and reflects favorably upon, the theory of the origin of ethnocentrism-authoritarianism proposed by Frenkel-Brunswik and her associates."

This pleasantly replicated study indicates that about 10% of the variance of the children's "anti-democratic" attitudes can be accounted for in terms of their parents' reported punitiveness. If one is willing to convert covariation to causation, punativeness can be considered a factor which produces authoritarianism. But even if we take the measures at face value, there is little indication that parental punitiveness is a very important determinant of anti-democratic attitudes.

Unfortunately there is practically no evidence that the Children's Anti-Democratic Scale is a valid measure of authoritarianism in children. Furthermore, it is not clear that Lyle and Levitt's list of punitive acts (e.g., scolding the child or sending him to his room) entirely squares with the "traumatizing" discipline Frenkel-Brunswik concluded was involved in forming the prejudiced-authoritarian personality. And of course we do not know how the parents actually disciplined their children, only the children's reports on the matter. It is difficult to be certain, therefore, that even 10% of the variance of "childhood authoritarianism" has been associated with parental "heavy-handedness."

Finally Richert (1963) administered the F Scale and a 95-item questionnaire seeking retrospective information on "everyday parent-child interaction" to 86 introductory psychology students (probably at the University of Texas). Only three of the items showed a significant correlation with F Scale scores, with the highest coefficient being .34. The other 92 items, contrary to expectations, were unrelated to F Scale scores. Interestingly enough, these results led Richert to the conclusion that questionnaire methods cannot readily point out parental behaviors significant in the development of authoritarianism.

None of these three "most direct" studies then, convinces one that authoritarianism has early childhood origins.

Studies of how high F adults currently describe their parents. Next we consider five investigations which relate authoritarianism in adults to their current attitudes toward their parents. It should be noted at the outset that the most these studies can show is that behaviors hypothesized to be connected with the childhood origins of authoritarianism are related to authoritarianism among adults. Whether the authoritarianism actually began in childhood, and in the way hypothesized, is beyond the scope of these data. We thus move one more step away from the experimental design necessary to test the hypothesis directly.

Jourard (1954) administered a "parent-cathexis scale" and a "moral indignation scale" to 115 subjects (most of them undergraduates) whose mean age was 23 years. The parent-cathexis scale listed 61 traits (e.g., your father's sense of humor, your father's temper) and asked the subject how much he liked each one. The scale was completed for each parent. The moral indignation scale in turn asked the subject to indicate the degree of his annoyance with 50 persons or events which seemed to describe "breaches of common decency" (e.g., "a communist making a speech to you about his beliefs," "a person who avoids the army draft because of 'nervous illness'"). Both scales had split-half reliabilities $\geq .90$.

It was found that moral indignation correlated .39 with a liking of the father's traits and .37 with a liking of the mother's. These results can be construed, as Jourard suggests, as support for the repression-displacement model used by Frenkel-Brunswik in *The Authoritarian Personality*. They do not relate directly to authoritarianism however, except that "conventionalism" is one of the hypothesized traits of the authoritarian personality. Since the examples Jourard provided of items from the moral indignation scale seem particularly likely to be offensive to conservatives, it is not clear how general the relationship might be.

Stagner (1954) administered a 10-item "attitude toward authority" scale to 575 male students taking a course from him, as well as scales designed to measure, among other things, current attitudes towards one's mother and father. He then compared students who scored on the "pro-authority" side of the distribution ($N = 88$) with the 145 most "anti-authority subjects. He found no difference between the two extremes in the extent to which they reportedly liked either parent.

In this instance our methodological concerns cut the other way, The comparison of such unmatched extremes as the top 15% and bottom 25% of a distribution can be questioned. The evidence cited for the internal consistency of the attitude-toward-authority-scale is very weak, that is that the groups who scored in the extremes on the total scores on the scale were also significantly different in their responses on all of its 10 items. The scales used to measure "liking father" and "liking mother" are difficult to assess as they do not appear to have been published (Stagner and Drought, 1935). Thus while Stagner's data do not confirm the hypothesis that highly authoritarian subjects will overglorify their parents, the failure to confirm may have been due to the measures used and the procedures followed.

Melikian (1956), as part of a cross cultural study, administered an authoritarianism scale consisting of 19 items from the F Scale to 97 undergraduates at Cornell and Colgate Universities. The subjects also filled out, six times, a 21-item scale designed to measure the extent to which their parents were perceived as "accepting or rejecting." Both the subject's own father and mother, the typical father and mother, and the ideal father and mother were described on this scale. The corrected split-half reliability of the 19-item F Scale was .76, and the reliabilities of the various parent scales were usually even lower.

While the subject's F Scale scores correlated low but significantly with their ideas of how accepting the ideal parent should be ($-.23$ for the ideal father, $-.19$ for the ideal mother), there was no relationship between their F Scale scores and how accepting or rejecting their actual parents were described to have been. This seemingly disconfirms the hypothesis that authoritarianism is caused by parental rejection. On the other hand there were significant but again low correlations ($-.28$, $-.23$) between F Scale scores and the discrepancy between one's own and the ideal parent, which supports the hypothesis that authoritarians tend to overglorify their parents. Only 7% of the variance of the scores is accounted for by the relationship, however.

Phares (1960) administered a balanced 30-item F Scale (containing 15 original items) to 64 undergraduates, and then asked them to list (anonymously) both positive and negative characteristics of each of their parents. The percentage of negative traits listed by the most and least authoritarian 20 subjects were then compared. High F subjects tended to give significantly fewer negative traits of their mothers (19% vs. 30%). The figures for descriptions of the father were in the same direction (25% vs. 30%) but were reportedly only significant by a one-tailed test.[13]

Finally Koutrelakos (1968) administered the original F Scale and selected scales from the Edwards Personality Preference Schedule (EPPS) to 100 members of Protestant social clubs in Southern New Hampshire. The EPPS scales (need Intraception, Aggression, Dominance and Change) were answered three times, for oneself, one's father, and one's

perception of the ideal person. Also, an "authoritarian father" questionnaire was administered which contained 69 items designed to measure
how dominating, punishing, distant and conventional the subject's father
was perceived to be.

F Scale scores were non-significantly correlated with the similarity
between the needs of one's self and one's father, and also with the similarity of one's own needs and those of the ideal person. There was a significant correlation (.31) between F Scale scores and the similarity between
one's father and the ideal person, just as there was in Melikian's (1956)
study. This time the relationship accounted for about 10% of the variance.

F Scale scores were also significantly correlated (by a point-biseral
correlation corrected for coarse grouping) with reports that the father
had been punitive (.22), conventional (.33) and distant (.29), but not with
being dominating (.17). One notes, however, that 53 of the 69 items used
to assess these recollections were worded and keyed in the same direction
as the items on the F Scale; the correlations above, none too big to begin
with, may have been inflated by response sets.

As was noted at the beginning of this section, studies of adults'
current perceptions of their parents are of limited value in testing a hypothesis about the childhood origins of authoritarianism.[14] As it turns out,
the results of these studies can provide little support, even indirectly,
for the model advanced in *The Authoritarian Personality*. The best one
can say is that four of the five studies found a weak tendency for high
F subjects to "overglorify" their parents. (It is at least possible, incidentally, that these parents really were a little better than most, and that
the small relationships found have a perfectly factual, nonpsychodynamic
explanation.) As for the rest of the model, there is no support at all
and sometimes even disconfirmation.

Studies of how high F adults treat their children. We now consider
a series of studies which are yet another step removed from the issue of
the childhood origins of authoritarianism. A number of investigators
have sought to determine if high F subjects have punitive and restrictive
child rearing attitudes. Such relationships of course imply nothing about
how the subjects themselves became high F. It is only necessary to review
these studies in fact because their results are sometimes cited as supporting the Berkeley model of the origin of authoritarianism.

Block (1955) administered the F Scale and a 20-item "Child-Rearing
Attitude Scale" to 100 male military officers. Scores on the F Scale correlated .50 with a questionnaire measuring "restrictive" approaches to child-

rearing (.41 when intelligence was partialed out). While the author notes the qualifications necessary because of the particular sample used, he also goes on to "hazard the interpretation" that his restrictive parents underwent the same traumatic childhood experiences as Frenkel-Brunswik's (1954) highly prejudiced adolescents supposedly did, and in turn were avenging themselves on the next generation.

The study contains no information about the childhood of the subjects, nor about the authoritarianism of their children. Even the connection between F Scale scores and restrictive child rearing attitudes is less convincing than it might be, as the scale measuring the latter is only partially balanced (8–12) against response sets. Some of its items seem relevant to the kinds of tough child rearing attitudes "uncovered" by Frenkel-Brunswik, but others seem very indirectly connected at best (e.g., "For his own sake a child should be pressed to excel in school"; "Jealousy among brothers and sisters is a very common thing.") No information was presented on the internal consistency and unidimensionality of the child rearing scale.

Kates and Diab (1955) conducted a study similar to Block's, with the notable exception that probably very few of their subjects (172 introductory psychology students at the University of Oklahoma) actually were parents. In this instance the child rearing scale used was the University of Southern California Parent Attitude Survey (Shoben, 1949) which yielded scores on the extent to which the "parents" would be dominant, possessive and ignoring of their children. F Scale scores were only significantly related to possessiveness ($r = .21$), although when the scores were analyzed separately for both sexes, all of the traits were significantly related to F Scale scores for one sex or the other. The pattern of relationship was rather different from what one might expect, however. F Scale scores were unrelated to dominance among the males ($r = .12$), but were significantly related to dominance among the females ($r = .34$). The latter correlation was the highest produced in the study. Again data on the reliability and validity of the Parent Attitude Survey among these subjects were not given.

Gallagher (1957) administered the F Scale and a 19-item "harshness scale" (in childrearing) to 59 students enrolled in a child psychology course at Michigan State. Unlike previous investigations, no significant correlation was found between scores on the two scales. This finding may have resulted from the kind of subjects used in the study, who were probably unrepresentative of the population at large in terms of their interests and sophistication regarding childrearing. No data were presented on the reliability and validity of the Harshness Scale.

Hart (1957), in the most frequently cited paper among this group, studied the relationship between authoritarianism and childrearing in the context of a model provided by one of the authors of *The Authoritarian Personality*, Levinson and Huffman (1955). Contending that "certain childrearing practices are both antecedents and consequences of authoritarianism," (p. 232) the model stipulates that the authoritarian parent disciplines children primarily through bodily harm, social isolation and/or shaming, but not through loss of love. These in turn are seen by Hart as being essentially the "nonlove orientations" distinguished by Whiting and Child (1953), namely actual or threatened physical punishment and punishment by ridicule. Other punishments are considered "love oriented" (viz., denial of love, threats of denial of reward, and threats of ostracism); actual denial of rewards and actual ostracism were considered "ambiguous" by Whiting and Child because they could promote either avoidance or approach tendencies. From this, Hart drew the hypothesis that authoritarian parents would tend to use nonlove punishment techniques while nonauthoritarian parents would tend to use the love-oriented disciplines. No prediction was made for the use of the "ambiguous" techniques.

Mothers ($N = 126$) of young children accordingly were asked, in the context of an interview, to indicate how they would handle 38 different child behavior situations. The subjects' responses were independently rated as non-love-oriented, love-oriented, or ambiguous by three graduate students in psychology, with agreement by two of the judges determining the score in cases of disagreement. At the end of the interview a 24-item F Scale was administered; this scale contained 10 items from the final form of the scale, and several which dealt specifically with childrearing.

Scores on this F Scale were found to correlate .63 with the number of instances in which the mother's responses were scored as non-love-oriented. This is one of the strongest relationships ever found with "the F Scale" and it is the statistic typically cited as *the* result of Hart's study.

Other aspects of the study bear consideration, however. For one thing, the correlation between authoritarianism and the use of love-oriented techniques (which of course bears on the other half of the hypothesis) was never reported. Instead the sample was trichotomized by F Scale scores and the mean love-oriented scores of these groups were presented. The means follow the order expected but no analysis of variance (ANOVA) of these scores was reported. One wonders what would have resulted if a simple and direct test of the study's main hypothesis, involving the difference score for each subject between frequencies of love-oriented and non-love-oriented punishments, had been correlated with scores on the F Scale.

Hart does use this technique in a later analysis involving responses to two open-ended questions at the end of the interview. The responses were scored by two additional judges, but for just the subjects in the upper and lower quartiles of the F Scale distribution. Interjudge reliability, which was not reported for the main analysis, was reported here as .73. A t test for differences between these extremes and their net inclinations to produce "approach tendencies" in their children yielded a statistically significant value of 3.08, but the implication of this figure for the overall correlation between the two measures is vague.

Other observations further limit the generalizations one can draw from this study. Predictions that authoritarian mothers would be especially likely to use non-love techniques in aggression and sex training were not confirmed. Also, the sample used was narrow, consisting of middle class women who recommended one another to the investigator. The format followed in conducting the interviews is only briefly described. It is not known if the raters who scored the main body of the interview were blind as to the investigator's main hypothesis, although it is noted that the two other raters used later were kept blind.

The theoretical framework on which the study was based could have been sounder. The model of authoritarian childrearing habits provided by Levinson and Huffman is even less strongly supported by experimental data than that of Frenkel-Brunswik. In turn the "considerable congruence" of this model to Whiting and Child's findings does not survive close examination. Levinson and Huffman make no distinction between threatening certain punishments and actually carrying out the acts, which is an important distinction in Whiting and Child's system. In fact the acts which Levinson and Huffman list as typical of the authoritarian parent would often be called "ambiguous" by Whiting and Child. "Punishing by shaming" is not necessarily the same as "punishing by ridicule." And punishing by social isolation, which is supposedly one of the main tactics of the authoritarian according to Levinson and Huffman) seems rather similar to threatening ostracism, one of the love-oriented techniques according to Whiting and Child. Thus there is little congruency between the authoritarian's alleged preferences in punishment and the non-love techniques identified by Whiting and Child. If Hart's data were as well-gathered, thoroughly analyzed, and as generalizable as one could wish, and the results as powerful as the often-cited correlation of .63 would seem to imply, they would still not support the conclusions reached.

In 1958, Zuckerman, Barrett-Ribback, Monashkin and Norton reported a factor analysis of the Parental Attitude Research Inventory (Schaefer and Bell, 1958) which identified two orthogonal factors in the 115-item inventory: "Authoritarian Control" and "Hostility-Rejection." As part of a test of the validity of these factors, Zuckerman and Oltean administered the inventory and the F Scale to 32 female patients in a psychiatric hospital and to 88 student nurses. (None of the nurses was a mother, so not a single person in these "validating" samples was a normal mother.) Scores on the "authoritarian control" factor correlated .61 with F Scale scores among the nurses and .51 among the psychiatric patients. All of the items on the tests were worded in the same direction however, so response sets could account for much of the supposed relationships. The rest of Zuckerman and Oltean's results, moreover, do not convince one that the factors they were seeking to validate are in fact validly interpreted. If they are, then the F Scale should correlate significantly with the Hostility-Rejection factor, which it did not.

Studies of the similarity in levels of F Scale scores between parents and their offspring. We now turn to several studies which have investigated the relationship between F Scale scores in parents and their college-age offspring. If authoritarianism is caused by parental behavior which is related to the parents' own level of enduring authoritarianism, we might expect rather substantial relationships between these scores. Such correlations would not necessarily imply that the children's authoritarianism was caused by the parents' harshness or remoteness. It could be due simply to the imitative learning of the parents' attitudes for example. But the data have not yet led to such interpretative struggles, for only contradictory results involving small relationships have been reported so far.

Williams and Williams (1963) administered the F Scale to 614 introductory psychology students at the University of Miami, and then mailed copies of the scale to the students' parents, asking them to complete the test as well. The response rate from the parents was 44%. The correlations between the F Scale scores of sons and fathers was .12 and between sons and mothers it was .28. The correlation between the F Scale scores of daughters and fathers was .24, and between daughters and mothers it was .19. Only the cross-sex correlations were significant, which the authors suggest may have been due to "a residual manifestation of Oedipal relationships" among other things.

In a similar study involving 108 introductory psychology students at the University of Texas and their parents, Byrne (1965) obtained nearly the opposite set of results. Scores on a 32-item partially balanced version of the F Scale correlated .38 between sons and fathers, while those between sons and mothers correlated .30. The relationship between daughters and fathers was .13 while that between daughters and mothers was .32. All of the coefficients were significant except that between daughters' and fathers' scores.

It is not easy to decide which set of relationships are the valid ones (assuming that the difference is not due to the particular populations involved). While Byrne had a very good response rate from the parents (76%), his overall sample is less than half of that of Williams and Williams. Besides, the F Scale used (which contained 25 items from the Form 40/45 Scale, two other items from the earlier versions of the scale, and five antiauthoritarian items from reversals created by Christie, Havel and Seidenberg, 1958) is difficult to assess. Byrne did however, perform some interesting subanalyses of his data. He found that low F Scale scores were significantly more likely to occur among offspring if at least one of the parents was low F (in a trichotomization of the distributions). He also found that high F offspring were most likely when neither parent was low F and the parent of the same sex was high F. The presence or absence of a low F parent then appeared to be a more important covariant of the students' F Scale score than any other aspect of these data, although understandably the generalization would have numerous exceptions.

Comparison of the Williams and Williams and Byrne studies produces only one consistent finding: that the F Scale scores of sons are weakly correlated with those of their mothers. The finding does little to support the Berkeley investigators' contention that it was the father who played the dramatic role in causing authoritarianism in the son.

Summary of the literature on the childhood origins of authoritarianism. It has been widely concluded that authoritarianism usually has its roots in early childhood experiences. But an examination of the literature on the subject, summarized in Table 3, indicates that the conclusion very definitely lacks experimental support. Instead, one finds that the indirect tests of the proposition reviewed above have seldom produced relationships higher than .35 between F Scale scores and some childrearing variable if the latter was balanced against response sets. This is what we found in our review of the prejudice literature, and in this case the low correlations may be largely due to the items on the F Scale which directly tap childrearing attitudes. In conclusion, we can easily agree with a recent statement of one of the original Berkeley researchers that "rightist authoritarianism...owe(s) less to early childhood experiences than the authors of *The Authoritarian Personality* supposed" (Sanford, 1974, p. 166).

Rigidity and intolerance of ambiguity

The authors of *The Authoritarian Personality* reported, on the basis of the 80 interviews described earlier, that their highly ethnocentric subjects were rigid and intolerant of ambiguity (*TAP*, pp. 461–464). While the terms were nearly identical operationally (since most interviewees received the same score on the two variables) subsequent researchers have distinguished between them roughly as follows: "rigidity" refers to a tendency to maintain a perceptual or problem-solving set when such maintenance is inappropriate; "intolerance of ambiguity" refers to a tendency to form such a set when the cues do not warrant it. For example, a person can be intolerant of ambiguity but not rigid, or tolerant but rigid once the set is formed. But it has seemed plausible that intolerance and rigidity would covary. Both are hypothesized to characterize the authoritarian, and in fact are among the most frequent characterizations of the authoritarian personality to be found in the literature.

The research on rigidity was shaped to some extent by a Berkeley study which appeared before *The Authoritarian Personality* was published. Rokeach (1948) reported that students who scored high on a 10-item version of the Ethnocentrism Scale were significantly more likely to use rigid solutions to Einstellung Water Jar problems than were low E subjects. Brown (1953) reported that repeated attempts to replicate Rokeach's finding failed until he deliberately manipulated the testing situation to make it more formal and ego-involving (as he judged Rokeach's to have been). F Scale scores then correlated .40 with rigidity in solving the Water Jar tasks. Neuringer (1964) provided somewhat ambiguous support for Brown's model when he found that F Scale scores were insignificantly related to rigidity in another Einstellung-type test (a version of Rokeach's [1948] "Map Test") among normal subjects, but were correlated .37 among chronically anxious subjects.

French (1955), however, found no significant relationship between F Scale scores and the Water Jar Test among 100 Air Force trainees tested in either relaxed ($r = .10$) or ego-involved ($r = -.06$) conditions. F Scale scores were also unrelated to three other measures of rigidity included in

TABLE 3

Summary of studies relating F Scale scores to childhood origins

Study	Version of the F Scale	Dependent measure	Sample	Findings
"I" Studies				
Adorno et al., 1950	E Scale	Results of interviews	High & Low E adults	High and low E subjects scored differently on 8 of 45 scoring categories.
Harris, Gough & Martin, 1950	Anti-Negro Scale	Childrearing questionnaire	Mothers of preju- diced, unpreju- diced children	Mothers of prejudiced children gave different responses on 8 of 81 measures.
Lyle & Levitt, 1955	Children's A-D Scale	Sentence completion regarding parents	Fifth graders	A-D Scale scores correlated .28–.32 with inferred parental punitiveness.
Richert, 1963	Original F Scale	Parent-child relations survey	College students	Three of 95 items correlated with F Scale scores
"II" Studies				
Jourard, 1954	None	"Moral Indignation," "Liking for parents"	College students	"Moral indignation" correlated .37–.39 with liking for the parents.
Stagner, 1954	None	Liking for parents, "Attitudes toward authority"	College students	No difference in the extent to which "pro- authority" and "anti-authority" subjects liked their parents.
Melikian, 1956	19 original F Scale items	Ratings of own, typical & ideal father and mother	College students	Correlations of -.19 to -.28 with various measures, some confirmatory, others not so.
Phares, 1960	30-item balanced	Number of positive & negative parental traits	College students	High F subjects gave fewer negative traits of mothers, and possibly of fathers.

Koutralakos, 1968	Original F Scale	Ratings of self, father & ideal person, & other ratings	Adult males in Protestant social clubs	Correlation of .31 with similarity of father to ideal person; r's of .22-.33 with other aspects of father's behavior, one disconfirmation.

"III" Studies

Block, 1955	Original F Scale	Childrearing Attitude Scale	Air Force Officers	Correlation of .50 between tests (.41 with intelligence controlled; some response set effects possible.)
Kates & Diab, 1955	Original F Scale	Parent Attitude Scale	College students	Correlation of .21 with possessiveness, .34 with dominance of daughters, .29 with ignoring of sons.
Gallagher, 1957	Original F Scale	Harshness in child-rearing scale	College students	No relationship.
Hart, 1957	24-item test (10 originals)	Childrearing techniques	Middle class mothers	Correlation of .63 with use of nonlove-oriented techniques; other r's unknown or disconfirmatory.
Zuckerman et al., 1958	Original F Scale	"Authoritarian Control" factor of PARI	Student nurses & psychiatric patients	Correlations of .51-.61 with (unidirectionally-worded) "authoritarian control" items from test.

"IV" Studies

Williams & Williams, 1963	Original F Scale	—	College students & their parents	Correlations of .12-.28 between students' and parents' scores on the F Scale.
Byrne, 1965	32-item F Scale (24 originals)	—	College students & their parents	Correlations of .13-.38 between students' and parents' scores on the F Scale.

the test battery. Jackson, Messick and Solley (1957) found that "rigid Einstellungers" did score a little higher on the F Scale, but they also scored significantly lower on an F Scale composed of reversals of the original items. (It should be noted that Levitt [Levitt and Zelen, 1953; Levitt, 1956; Levitt and Zuckerman, 1959] has raised some very serious questions about the validity of the Water Jar Test as a measure of rigidity, or anything else.)

Several studies have pursued the matter with other measures of rigidity. Jones (1955) found that F Scale scores were slightly correlated (.22–.25) with an inability to reverse figure and ground in the Necker Cube. The subjects were several hundred naval aviation cadets tested under relaxed, non-ego-involving conditions. Harvey and Caldwell (1959) allowed subjects to form opinions about the distance between two fixed lights and then attempted to change that perception by sometimes flashing a third light instead of one of the original pair. F Scale scores correlated .44 with resistance to change. Harvey and Campbell (1963) found a similar relationship (–.32) when attempts were made to change judgements of weights. Millon (1957), on the other hand, found that F Scale scores were unrelated to changes in judgment of movement in a one-light autokinetic situation when a second light was introduced, whether the subject was serving in "ego-involved" circumstances or not.

The evidence that F Scale scores are related to intolerance of ambiquity is not much clearer. On the positive side, Millon (1957) found that high F subjects tended to reach a criterion of stability somewhat faster than did low F subjects; the extent of ego-involvement made no difference. Also Harvey and Caldwell (1959) and Harvey and Campbell (1963) both found that F Scale scores were correlated (.33 and .28 respectively) with narrowness of initial judgments about distances and weights in their studies. Finally, with what is by far the most dramatic F Scale relationship ever reported, Harvey and Rutherford (1958) found that scores on the scale correlated .90–.95 with the speed with which subjects said they saw the light moving in the autokinetic situation when the experimenter either praised or attacked them periodically for their performance.

On the negative side, however, Davids (1955) found no tendency for high F subjects either to structure or to deny structure in Rorschach inkblots, nor to grasp or fail to grasp meaning in structurally confused sentences. Davids (1956) repeated his experiment under more ego-involving conditions and obtained the same results. French (1955) found no relationship between F Scale scores and responses to a "Changing Figures Test" based on a study by Frenkel-Brunswik. Finally, I twice attempted to replicate the dramatic findings of Harvey and Rutherford (1958) during 1970 and both times failed to find a significant, much less large, relationship between F Scale scores and latency of reporting movement in the autokinetic situation. In the first study, 18 male and 31 female undergraduates served under a female experimenter who praised the subjects for their judgments. The highest correlation between F Scale scores and latency was .20 (*ns*). In the second study, both "praise" and "attack" conditions were run with sexually balanced samples of 27 and 26 undergraduates respectively. The experimenter was a large and powerful male. Again only nonsignificant correlations were obtained, the highest being −.28. The procedures used in both studies followed those given in Harvey and Rutherford (1958) exactly.

In summary, the research described above does not provide clear support for the contention that high F subjects are rigid and intolerant of ambiguity. It is true that many of the tests used to measure the latter constructs have "little more in common than the name" (Millon, 1957; see also Chown, 1959), and it is possible that clearly valid measures of rigidity and intolerance of ambiguity would be related to the F Scale. But the ambiguity presently associated with these concepts itself deserves some intolerance, and until more convincing evidence appears, the verdict must necessarily be that matters are presently inconclusive.

Are F Scale scores predictive of conforming behavior?
It follows most directly from the concept of the authoritarian personality that people who score high on the F Scale should tend to submit to authority figures. Oddly enough, relatively few studies have tested this hypothesis (and as will be seen, nearly all those which have found negative results). Far more research has been aimed at the more indirect premise that high F subjects, because of their weak ego structures, will tend to conform to pressure from peers. As much as anything else, the popularity of the experimental methodologies developed by Sherif (1935) and Asch (1956) may have led to this emphasis on peer conformity.

The first intimation that F Scale scores might be related to peer conformity came in fact from Asch's research. Barron (1953) administered an unspecified number of items from the F Scale to 86 students who had been either very yielding or very independent in Asch's experiments. The yielders scored significantly higher on three of the items; they also scored significantly lower on another.

The best known link between F Scale scores and conformity to peer pressure, however, was provided by Crutchfield (1955). Fifty men participating in an intensive personality assessment program were placed in automated Asch-type conformity situations. Scores on the F Scale correlated .39 with total conformity on the critical items. This finding has been replicated by Nadler (1959), who obtained a correlation of .48 in a similar study involving students, and by Wells, Weinert and Rubel (1956) who used a one-item conformity measure in an Asch-type situation with students. Similarly, Steiner and Johnson (1963) obtained a correlation of .42 in the condition of their study most closely approximating Asch's procedure. Harvey and Rutherford (1958) found a similar relationship in the autokinetic situation, when F Scale scores correlated .32 with changes in judgments induced by a confederate.

Vaughan and White (1966) compared scores on Berkowitz and Wolkon's (1964) Forced Choice F Scale with three different measures of conformity. The correlations among 312 undergraduates (probably from New Zealand) were .15 in a Crutchfield-type situation, .21 in a "bogus norm" attempt to change opinions, and .28 with Bass' (1958) Social Acquiescence Scale. Vaughan (1969) essentially repeated this experiment later, and found significant differences between high and low conforming subjects on both the original and Berkowitz and Wolkon's (1969) scales, with the former being somewhat more predictive.

What would thus seem to be the best established finding in the F Scale literature is sullied, however, by just as many studies which failed to find significant relationships with conformity. Berkowitz and Lundy (1957) attempted to influence students' opinions on several social issues by presenting bogus opinions attributed either to other students or to prominent military officials. F Scale scores were not predictive of conformity with either kind of source. Hoffman (1957) also tried to change attitudes through bogus norms and found no relationship between the F Scale scores of the subjects and the amount of their conformity.

Hardy (1957) put students into discussion groups one at a time with six confederates who "innocently" gave arguments against the subject's position on divorce. F Scale scores were found to be unrelated to attitude change measured either publicly at the end of the discussion or privately later when the subject was alone.

Beloff (1958) ranked students, probably from Northern Ireland, on the extent to which they acquiesced to the opinions of confederates concerning war. They were also ranked on the extent to which their judgments in aesthetic and "politicosocial" matters were conventional (i.e., corresponded to ratings of the sample as a whole). None of these behaviors was significantly related to scores on the F Scale.

Gorfein (1961) found that behavior in an Asch-type line-judging situation was unrelated to scores on the F Scale among University of Alberta students. Similarly in a second study, scores were unrelated to conformity when the experimenter attempted to influence judgments of triangle sizes. Weiner and McGinnes (1961) also placed subjects in an Asch-type situation in which they were to judge whether a briefly-presented face was smiling or frowning. Although the naive subjects had scored either extremely high or extremely low on the F Scale, there was no difference in the amount of their conformity to two confederates' opinions. Steiner and Vannoy (1966) also failed to find a significant correlation ($r = .02$) with conformity under Asch-type circumstances which, in fact, approximated those of Steiner and Johnson (1963) when one was found.

Lasky (1962) took the intersting tack of giving nursing students false norms about their scores on the F Scale itself. Students who had scored low on the scale were told in some detail that such scores were usually much higher. High scoring students were told the opposite. Both groups then took the F Scale again, and as one would expect, both sets of scores regressed toward the mean. When one controls for the tendency for scores on the scale to drop somewhat upon retesting (which is seen in all of the control groups in Lasky's study), both high and low F subjects conformed to the influence attempt equally. Also, the influence attempt for half of the subjects was made by the director of the nursing school; the other subjects heard the same message, although much more poorly delivered, from a clerk-typist just out of high school. There was no difference in the effect of these two communicators, and as was true in Berkowitz and Lundy's (1957) study, high F subjects were not more likely to be influenced by the authority figure.

Finally, Johnson and Steiner (1957) attempted to modify male students' impressions of themselves by giving them (adverse) evaluations of their behavior discrepant from their own self ratings. Eight levels of discrepancy were used in the study. Overall F Scale scores were unrelated to the amount of conformity to the feedback ($r = .04$), and in only one of the eight levels of discrepancy was there a significant correlation between scores on the test and conformity.

In conclusion, it is not easy to reconcile these conflicting sets of findings. Berkowitz and Lundy (1957), while finding conformity unrelated to F Scale scores overall, did find that high F subjects with low "interpersonal confidence" (as measured by the Guilford-Zimmerman Sociability Scale) were particularly likely to conform. It is difficult to extend this explanation to other studies, however, as it seems unlikely that the high F subjects in Crutchfield (1955), Nadler (1959), etcetera, were predominantly low in interpersonal confidence, while those in the nonconforming studies were high on this dimension.

One generalization may be offered. The studies which have reported a relationship between conformity and scores on the F Scale involved primarily judgments of geometric relationships, logical problems, and other nonsocial matters. It has been much harder to find the relationship when social issues are involved. This is not because social issues are easier, or harder, to change. Some change occurs in all these studies. But it is usually not related to scores on the F Scale if social attitudes are at issue. Since authoritarianism has been studied primarily because of its potential effect on social events, and not because of its influence on judgments of geometry, the former set of findings are more pertinent. And that is where the connection is least demonstrated.

Are F Scale scores predictive of behavior in groups?
A seemingly obvious derivation of the theory of the authoritarian personality is that persons who score high on the F Scale should act in characteristic ways in group situations and should be especially comfortable in certain kinds of organizaitons (e.g., the military). There has been far more research on the latter point than on the former, but again the results have often been at considerable odds with expectations.

Insofar as nonmilitary groups are concerned, Bass, McGhee, Hawkins, Young and Gebel (1953) found a weak linear correlation of -.16 between scores on the F Scale and emergent leadership in formally leaderless student group discussions. (A curvilinear eta of .30 indicated that subjects with moderate F Scale scores were somewhat more likely to emerge as leaders than those with either high or low scores.)

McCurdy and Eber (1953) made up student problem-solving groups composed of either three high or three low scorers on the F Scale. Half of the teams were then organized into "authoritarian" groups in which one (designated) person had some centralized control over the team's efforts; the other groups were organized along equalitarian principles. One might expect that high F subjects would perform better in groups with a designated, "powerful" leader, and that low F subjects would perform best in equalitarian groups. However there was no reliable difference in problem solving ability among the four kinds of groups across a number of dependent variables.

Haythorn, Couch, Haefner, Langham and Carter (1956) adopted a similar approach in a thorough study of the interactions of four-person groups composed entirely of either high F or low F subjects. The results of their study may be summarized as follows:

1 In most respects the interactions within the groups and the behavior of the persons who emerged as leaders in the groups were not significantly different for the high and low F teams. Some of these nondifferences are very noteworthy: high F groups were not more autocratic in their behavior, and low F groups were not more equalitarian.

2 Among those few categories in which there was a significant difference between the two types of groups, some of the results seem to confirm expectations (e.g., low F leaders were rated as being significantly more equalitarian, sensitive and submissive to others).

3 A few of the significant differences seem to contradict expectations (i.e., low F leaders made more initial acts, high F leaders sought more approval for their actions).

In the main, however, the study showed, like that of McCurdy and Eber (1953), that groups composed of high or low scorers on the F Scale do not act very differently.

Finally, in a well-known study concerned more with the effects of reference and membership groups than with authoritarianism per se, Siegel and Siegel (1957) studied 28 Stanford coeds who at the end of their freshman year (spent in a large dormitory) wanted to move into much smaller housing units on campus called row houses. It had independently been determined that the randomly assigned occupants of these facilities had higher scores on Gough's (1951) version of the F Scale than did residents of other dorms (perhaps because the houses' small size insulated their occupants somewhat from the usual effect of college life, which is to lower scores on the F Scale: Feldman and Newcomb, 1969). Testing at the end of the sophomore year indicated that the scores of the students who had spent the year in row houses had dropped very little, while those who had continued to live in large dorms and who had decided *not* to try for row houses again had dropped considerably. Scores of students who had spent their sophomore year in the larger dorms but who still aspired to live in row houses had dropped an intermediate amount.

Siegel and Seigel's results suggest that a person's attitudes are a joint function of the group he belongs to and the group he identifies with. It would seem to follow then that people who join a distinctly authoritarian organization will become more authoritarian, especially those who decide to make that organization their "home." As plausible as this seems, there is very little support for it in the research which has been done with the F Scale and membership in military organizations.

The first researcher to report a study of the F Scale and adaptation to military life was Christie (1952), who gave a "modified form" of the test to 182 inductees prior to and at the end of their basic training. While one might expect military training to increase authoritarianism there was no significant change in F Scale scores for the group as a whole. Subanalyses with sociometric data indicated that recruits who were accepted by both their peers and trainers were the only ones to show a significant rise in F Scale scores over the training period. Christie interpreted this to mean these men fit well into military life. On the other hand, those who were high on the F Scale, whom one would expect to fit especially well into the army, were not particularly popular.

This latter nonfinding was replicated by Hollander (1954), who administered the F Scale to 268 naval aviation cadets at the end of their training. Hollander hypothesized that high F subjects would be perceived by their peers and by their trainers as more fit to lead a military unit. Earlier, another group of cadets serving in a role-playing study had indicated that high scores on the F Scale would be related to "military leadership potential." In fact, however, F Scale scores were negatively related to peer nomination for a hypothetical leadership position ($r = -.23$), and there was no relationship between F Scale scores and the trainers' ratings ($r = -.06$).

A third study indicates that high F Scale scores are negatively related to popularity (and performance) in the military. Rohde (1955) asked twenty Air Force pilots to rate the members of their crew on several dimensions. "Desirability as a friend" correlated $-.46$ with crewmembers' scores on the F Scale, while "willingness to take into combat" correlated $-.33$. "Confidence in the individual" was not significantly related ($-.11$).

A well-known study by Thibaut and Riecken (1955) provided mixed support for the relationship of authoritarianism to behavior in a military situation. Air Force reservists were administered a 20-item authoritarianism scale which contained nine of the original Berkeley items. They then were introduced to a confederate playing the role of another reservist about to enter active service on an important assignment. Sometimes the confederate was of high rank (e.g., a major), at other times he supposedly held a lower rank (e.g., a sargeant). Subjects were asked to evaluate the confederate before the two began a task and again after the job was completed. The confederate purposely botched up his part of the task initially, but following feedback his performance was quite good.

While one might expect that high F subjects would initially rate the confederate higher when he held high rank, this was not the case. But high F subjects were quite unfavorable toward the lower status confederate after the exercise was completed, while they did not downgrade a high ranking confederate nearly as much for making the same mistakes.

In a finding reminiscent of Hollander's (1954) discovery that high F Scale scores were associated with *hypothetical* leadership potential in the military, French and Ernest (1955) found correlations of .29 −.54 between the F Scale and a Military Ideology Scale given to enlisted men and officer candidates undergoing training in the Air Force. Again, however, scores on the F Scale did not change over the course of training. Furthermore, they did not correlate with intentions to stay in the Air Force after the men's initial duty expired, which may be taken as a measure of the extent to which the Air Force had become a "reference group" for the subjects.[15]

Medalia (1955) gave an F Scale consisting of the 12 best discriminating items in the original Berkeley study to personnel in three Air Force radar squadrons. The men also rated their commanders on scales designed to measure how "human relations minded" the commanders were (i.e., showed "concern for obtaining spontaneous cooperation," "other centeredness," and "interpersonal sensitivity.") While one might expect that high F Scale scorers would tend not to describe their commanders as being human relations minded (assuming they respected them) there was a modest tendency for them to do so. Also, Medalia's implication to the contrary notwithstanding, high F subjects did not indicate they planned to re-enlist more often than did low F subjects.

Campbell and McCormack (1957) administered a 20-item F Scale (containing 16 original items) to 146 Air Force pilots at the beginning of their training, and again a year later. Contrary to expectation, the year's experience in the military was associated with a significant drop in scores on the scale.[16]

The studies described above, which have attempted to relate scores on the F Scale to reasonably predictable behavior in group situations, have done little to validate the scale. Groups composed of high F subjects have not been found to act very differently from those composed of low F subjects, even when an authoritarian structure was imposed upon them. And while there is some evidence that certain items on the F Scale correlate appreciably with military ideology, there is no evidence that military training increases scores on the scale, nor that high F persons do particularly well in the military nor that persons who wish to make a career of military service score particularly high on the F Scale. Perhaps this is because the military system in a democracy is not authoritarian enough for the expected effects to occur. But it is also possible that these results occurred because the F Scale lacks validity.

Are F Scale scores related to socioeconomic class?
While fascism has historically been termed a "middle class" movement, there is no compelling theoretical reason in Adorno et al. (1950) for F Scale scores to be particularly associated with any socioeconomic stratum. Nevertheless a number of writers have suggested that there is such an association, and interestingly enough the association is thought to be with the lower classes. The case has been put forth most strongly by Lipset (1959), who gathered evidence from a wide variety of sources to argue that the lower classes were more authoritarian than the middle class in noneconomic matters. Lipset attributed this difference to a number of factors, including low educational attainment, low participation in political or voluntary organizations, little reading, isolated occupations, and other things.

Unfortunately for our purposes, most of the evidence which bears on this point has nothing to do with the F Scale. Janowitz and Marvick (1953) and McKinnon and Centers (1956) did find negative relationships between socioeconomic status (SES) indicators and versions of F. H. Sanford's Short Authoritarian-Equalitarian Scale administered as part of public opinion polls. Similarly several of the "anomie versus authoritarianism" studies mentioned in footnote 11 to the section on prejudice (Srole, 1956; Roberts and Rokeach, 1956; McDill, 1961) found negative correlations between SES and the five-item "authoritarianism scale" developed by Flowerman, Stewart and Strauss (1950). But the validity of each of these scales is far from established, either among the working class as Miller and Riesman (1961) have noted, or among any other class.

By way of contrast, several studies which did use the original F Scale (Davidson and Kruglov, 1953; Johnson, Johnson and Martin, 1961) reported no relationship with the usual occupational indicators of social class. It should be noted, however, that these studies sampled only university students.

If right-wing authoritarianism is more prevalent in certain social classes, there is no evidence so far that the F Scale can detect it. Matters will not end, incidentally, even if the premise is true and a valid measure of authoritarianism is found to covary with SES. Here as elsewhere the covariation will not be very useful if it is easily explainable on other grounds. Lipsitz (1965), for example, has shown that differences found in various nationwide polls in the "authoritarianism" of blue collar and white collar workers are almost entirely due to differences in educational attainment in these two groups. Similar findings in the future would not negate the relationship with SES, but why should one invoke authoritarianism to account for differences more simply explained in educational terms?

Hostility toward certain targets
We now turn to two areas in which the F Scale seems to have some reliable empirical validity. The first of these is hostility toward certain kinds of people. As was noted at the beginning of our discussion, one of the defining traits of the authoritarian personality was authoritarian aggression, defined as the "tendency to be on the lookout for, and to condemn, reject, and punish people who violate conventional values." The theoretical expectation thus is that F Scale scores will be associated with aggression against persons who are deemed unconventionable. It may also be directly inferred from the Berkeley model that high F people, because of their authoritarian submission, will be less aggressive toward authority figures, at least insofar as overt, conscious aggression is concerned. It is not clear on the other hand whether F Scale scores should be related to aggression against conventional people, or toward people of equal status.

Relationships with paper-and-pencil measures of aggression. Most of the studies in this area have used paper-and-pencil measures of aggression, and not all of them found the expected relationship. Siegel (1956), for example, administered the F Scale and two such measures to samples of (a) college males, and (b) armed forces veterans seeking psychiatric help. One of the measures of aggression was a 50-item questionnaire called the Manifest Hostility Scale (which apparently had a very low level of internal consistency even though 44 of its 50 items were keyed in the same direction). The samples were each trichotomized according to F Scale scores, and significant if modest overall differences were found in the hostility scores within each sample. The relationships of course could be due simply to response sets.

Siegel's second measure of aggressiveness was based upon responses to a Rorschach test. Here there was no significant difference in the latent hostility manifested by high, middle, and low F students, while the veterans showed a significant negative relationship. The data thus failed to support the notion that high F people are on fire with unconscious aggressive impulses, if one accepts the validity of the Rorschach measure. However, the two measures of hostility were not significantly correlated in either sample, and the validity of each is undemonstrated.

Roberts and Jessor (1958) reported results far more confirmatory of the Berkeley model. Twenty-four drawings similar to those used in the Rosenzweig Picture Frustration Study (Rosenzweig, 1945) were shown to students who had scored very high, or very low on the F Scale. In half of the cartoons a high-status person was frustrating a lower-status person; the situation was reversed in the other cartoons. Subjects were asked to assume the role of the frustrated person in each case and give a response for him to the frustrator. These responses were scored for hostility directed against the frustrator, some other object, or oneself.

It was found that when the frustrator was lower in status than the role-playing subject, high F students were significantly more hostile toward the frustrator than were low F subjects, who tended to direct their aggression elsewhere. But when the frustrator was of high status, the pattern was neatly reversed. The differences between the high and low F groups were often substantial, but it is also true that the mean scores of the two groups were more than two standard deviations apart. Also, contrary to theoretical expectations high F subjects showed no tendency to blame themselves when frustrated by a high status figure.

Singer and Feshbach (1959), on the other hand, found evidence that high F subjects do tend to be intrapunitive. As part of a larger study involving 147 college males, they administered the F Scale and a "response to frustration" scale employed previously by Waterhouse and Child (1953). The latter purportedly yielded independent scores on the extent to which subjects tend to aggress against themselves, others, or act constructively when frustrated. An "intrapunitive" item, for example, would be of the sort: "I am apt to be very critical of myself when I fail."

F Scale scores were found to be well correlated with intrapunitiveness ($r = .50$), less so with extrapunitiveness ($r = .23$), and negatively with "constructiveness" ($r = -.20$). The significant correlation with extrapunitiveness seemingly contradicts Roberts and Jessor's conclusion that there should be no relationship if the status of the frustrator is uncontrolled (which it was not in Waterhouse and Child's scale). Similarly it is not clear why intrapunitiveness should be correlated with F Scale scores when the frustration was not at the hands of an authority figure. Both relationships could have been shaped by response sets, however, as the Intrapunitiveness and Extrapunitiveness Scales may have been uni-directionally worded.

A study by Wright and Harvey (1965) provided more direct contra-diction of Roberts and Jessor's findings. As part of a more involved experiment, student subjects were administered both the F Scale and Rosenzweig's Picture Frustration Study. Later three independent judges agreed that in three of the cartoons used the frustrator was clearly of lower status, and in four others, of higher status. Roberts and Jessor's manipulation was thus replicated post hoc. High and low F subjects (divided at the median) did not significantly differ in their responses to the two sets of cartoons. While the authors suggest this may have been due to the smaller number of cartoons used, it is also true that they studied the effect across the entire range of F Scale scores, and not just between extremes.[17]

Taking a somewhat different tack, Sherwood (1966) asked 75 graduate students in an industrial administration program to solve a hypothetical human relations case involving the control of slacking workers. He then scored their solutions for the kinds of punishments involved (if any). With scores on the F Scale trichotomized, high F subjects were found to be significantly more likely to use "coercive or arbitrary" punishments, while middle and low F subjects were more likely to use a nonpunishing, educational approach to the problem.

Recently research in this area has focused on punitiveness toward persons accused or convicted of crimes. Gladstone (1969) provided stu-dent subjects in a counterbalanced design with descriptions of crimes committed by high or low status persons, and asked them to recommend punishments in each case. High F subjects tended to be more punitive overall, and contrary to expectations, there was no significant F Scale x status-of-criminal interaction. Both results thus contradict Roberts and Jessors' findings. The type of crime committed was also varied systemati-cally, and was found to interact with F Scale scores, high F subjects being especially punitive toward crimes against propriety, compared to those against people or property.

Thayer (1970) sought personality differences between students who said they could, or could not, recommend the death penalty if they were jurors. Unexpectedly the two groups did not differ in F Scale scores.

Finally, Mitchell and Byrne (1973) gave undergraduates a description of a fictitious student accused of stealing an examination. Half of the subjects were led to believe that the accused's attitudes on five unrelated topics were extremely similar to their own; the other half were led to believe that the accused's attitudes were quite dissimilar. Scores on a 22-item partially balanced F Scale were available for each subject.

Overall, high F subjects (divided at the mean) were more punitive toward the accused when his attitudes were very dissimilar from their own. Attitude similarity did not affect the punishments recommended by the low F subjects, nor did high and low F subjects differ in the punishments given the "similar" student. If we assume that high F subjects would tend to consider people with attitudes very dissimilar to their own to be unconventional, then the rsults support the Berkeley model. (The finding is somewhat compromised, on the other hand, by the use of an ANOVA to analyze scores obtained with an obviously noninterval punishment scale. Also, somewhat unexpectedly, high F subjects did not rate the accused as being less "moral" than did low F subjects in either the similar or dissimilar condition.)

Relationships with more direct measures of aggression. Most of the more direct studies of aggression have used the familiar technique of inducing subjects to deliver (supposedly) electric shocks to a victim. Two relevant studies predate this technique, however. Meer (1955) compared the dreams reported by very high or very low F student subjects. Aggressive content in these dreams was scored in terms of whether they involved the subject with a member of his "ingroup" (family, friends and acquaintances) or his "outgroup" (i.e. strangers). Unfortunately, no distinction was made as to whether the subject was the aggressor, observer or victim in the dreams. Also the number of aggressive events was not compared, but only the average intensity of the encounters, the average being taken of scores on a rank-order scale.

The data were classified as "intense" or "nonintense" if they were above or below an arbitrary point (2.0) on an eight-level intensity scale, and it was found that high F subjects tended to have more intensely aggressive dreams involving strangers than they did with the "ingroup." Very low F subjects showed no significant differences in the intensity of aggressive events experienced with the different groups. Of course one can doubt that all of a person's acquaintances are members of his "ingroup." Also one would expect from the theory of the authoritarian personality that high F subjects would have a lot of aggressive content in dreams involving their parents. If such dreams followed the pattern "found" for the rest of the ingroup, the results would disconfirm the theory.

In an experiment described earlier in the section on group behavior, Thibaut and Riecken (1953) put Air Force reservists onto a work team with a confederate who then performed his end of the job very poorly for a while. Sometimes the confederate was of relatively high rank; in other cases he was of low rank. When the content of the subjects' feedback to the confederate was analyzed for overt aggressiveness, it was found that high F subjects were significantly more aggressive against low status confederates than they were against high status ones (Table II, p. 110, $t = 2.45$, $p < .05$). There was no tendency, however, for high F subjects to be less aggressive against the high status confederate than the low F subjects.

The literature on F Scale relationships to behavior in "shocking experiments" began with two studies by Epstein. In the first, Epstein (1965) arranged to have very high or very low F student subjects administer electrical shocks to a high or low status student confederate as part of a bogus learning experiment. The status of the confederate was varied by having him wear old, disheveled clothing (vs. being well dressed), saying he came from a poor family (vs. one well off), being about to drop out of school (vs. being headed for graduate school), and so forth.

Overall, high F subjects delivered stronger shocks than did low F subjects, and were especially likely to do so against a low status target. (The fact that high F subjects administered stronger punishment against the "high status" target as well is not as damaging here as in other cases since the high status target was not an authority figure for the subjects, just a well off, ambitious peer.)

Epstein's (1966) second experiment differed in a number of respects from the first. Only males were used, and they delivered shocks to a victim after a second confederate had done so. The victim was black, while the modeling confederate was sometimes white, sometimes black, and also varied in status as the victim in the first study had. Also, instead of treating average shocks delivered as the measure of aggression, as he had before, Epstein (1965) used only the number of "very strong" shocks delivered as the dependent variable.

High F subjects were again more aggressive (on the changed dependent variable at least) than were low F subjects, but the subjects' F Scale scores did not interact with either the race or social status of the model in determining aggressiveness. While off the point of whether high F subjects are more aggressive against low status targets, the failure of these interactions seemingly disconfirms other aspects of the theory of the authoritarian personality.

The best-known research program using the bogus shocking machine paradigm is undoubtedly that of Milgram (1963, 1964, 1965, 1974), which at one point produced findings that bear on the validity of the F Scale. Elms and Milgram (1966) administered a true-false version of the F Scale to subjects who had either been very defiant when situationally it was hard to be so (in the "remote" and "voice feedback" conditions) or very compliant when the situational pressures made it hard to be so (in the "proximity" and "touch proximity" conditions). The very compliant subjects scored significantly higher than did the very defiant ones. The status of the victim was the same in both of these conditions, and unlikely to be considered lower class or unconventional by the subjects.[18]

In a rather different variation on the shock-a-confederate theme, Lipetz and Ossorio (1967) induced male college students to shock their experimenters as part of a bogus study on changing strong habits. Attempts were made to vary the status of the experimenters (i.e., the victims) so that half the subjects believed they were shocking professors, the others just "someone helping out." Half the time, furthermore, the experimenters had just berated the subject's performance in an earlier part of the session; in other cases no such disparaging remarks were made. Needless to say, the power was turned off.

F Scale scores were unrelated to shock intensity (or shock duration), nor were there any significant interactions with the status of the experimenter-victim or the "pull for aggression" (provocation) variables on these measures. The same was true for a less overt dependent variable, the amount of pressure applied to the shock keys, except in one (of four) F Scale x Status condition, where the disparaging remarks may have had a significant effect. It is difficult to place much credence in this one result, however. Lipetz and Ossario thus failed to find any meaningful relationship between scores on the F Scale and their measures of behavioral aggression. That may be due to the F Scale of course; it may also have resulted from the direct and indirect consequences of placing subjects in a situation where they were expected to believe they had the power to deliver very painful shocks to the experimenter (Orne, 1961).

Lipetz and Ossario also administered the Buss-Durkee Hostility-Guilt Inventory (Buss and Durkee, 1957) to their subjects, and found a low correlation (.25) with F Scale scores. Self-ratings of aggressiveness were also related to F Scale scores ($r = .32$).

Finally, Dustin and Davis (1967) induced students to play the role of supervisor over another student performing a boring task. The subjects were instructed to use rewards (congratulatory notes and pennies) and punishments (derogatory notes and small fines) as they saw fit to maximize the worker's performance. It was found that high F subjects were significantly more likely to use punishments to attain that end than were low F subjects. It is not clear whether the findings were pertinent to aggression against peers, or to aggression against persons of lower status.

Summary. Table 4 summarizes the results of the 15 studies just reviewed, studies which bear on the relationship between F Scale scores and aggressiveness. With regard to the main prediction that high F subjects will be more punitive against persons considered unconventional, only a few studies (Epstein, 1965; Gladstone, 1969; and perhaps Mitchell and Byrne, 1973) really presented unconventional targets for aggression, and all of them found positive relationships. Six other studies (listed in Table 4) placed the target in a position of lower status to the potential aggressor, and five of these also found a positive relationship. The evidence thus supports, in the main, the modified hypothesis that high F subjects tend to be more aggressive against unconventional or low status targets than do low F persons.

It should be noted that this support is based almost entirely upon student samples, that there were methodological hesitations about several of these experiments, and that there is little to suggest that the relationship is a very powerful one. The evidence for the F Scale's empirical validity here appears reasonably consistent but it is hardly electrifying.

As for the second hypothesis, that F Scale scores will be negatively correlated with aggression against authority (and high status) figures, the studies are clearly nonsupportive. The intriguing thing about this conclusion is that it is consonant with other findings we have encountered before, which show that people who score high on the F Scale are not particularly likely to cower before authority.

As for aggression against peers, three of the four pertinent studies listed in Table 4 found a significant relationship, and these studies seem relatively sound methodologically. It may be, then, that high F subjects also tend to be aggressive against people of equal status, although at least one of the studies (Epstein, 1965) indicated they will be even more aggressive against low status or unconventional targets.

Finally the evidence on aggression against undifferentiated or unspecified targets is plainly ambiguous. The above analysis suggests that characteristics of the victim mediate the aggressive impulses of high F persons, and studies which have been vague on this point might well have turned up conflicting results because of this vagueness.

TABLE 4

Summary of studies relating F Scale scores to aggression

Study	Version of the F Scale	Measure of Aggression	Sample	Were F Scale scores related to aggression against			
				Unconventional or low status victims?	Authority or high status victims?	Peers?	Unspecified targets?
Siegel (1956)	Original F Scale	Hostility Scale Rorschach	College males neurotic vets				Yes & No
Roberts & Jessor (1958)	Original F Scale	Responses to 24 cartoon scenes	College students	Positively	Negatively		
Singer & Feshbach (1959)	Original F Scale	Questionnaire responses	College students				Yes
Wright & Harvey (1965)	Original F Scale	Responses to 7 cartoon scenes	College students	No relationship	No relationship		No relationship
Sherwood (1966)	Original F Scale	How solve human relations problem	Graduate students	Positively			
Gladstone (1969)	Original F Scale	(Questionnaire) criminal sentences	College students	Positively	Positively		
Thayer (1970)	Original F Scale	(Questionnaire) Death sentence?	College students				No relationship
Mitchell & Byrne (1973)	22-item balanced	Mock student trial	College students	Positively		No relationship	
Meer (1952)	Original F Scale	Aggression in dreams	College students				Unclear
Thibaut & Riecken (1953)	20-item (9 orig.)	Feedback to co-worker	Air Force reservists	Positively	No relationship		

Epstein (1965)	Original F Scale	Electric shock	College students	Positively		Positively
Epstein (1966)	Original F Scale	Electric shock	College students	Positively		
Elms & Milgram (1966)	Original F Scale	Electric shock	Male adults		Positively	
Lipetz & Ossorio (1967)	Original F Scale	Electric shock; paper-and-pencil measures	College students		No relationship	Yes & No
Dustin & Davis (1967)	Original F Scale	Negative verbal feedback, fines	College students	(Positively)		(Positively)

The F Scale and conservative political sentiment
Although the Berkeley researchers named the F Scale a measure of "implicit antidemocractic trends," the test was clearly conceived to tap just
"fascist" (as opposed to communistic) tendencies (Shils, 1954). Assuming
that fascism is a radical right-wing political movement, scores on the
scale should be more associated with conservative political attitudes
than with center and leftist ones if the scale is valid.

The original investigation sought to demonstrate this connection
directly through correlations between the F and the Political-Economic
Conservatism (PEC) Scale. The latter was developed concurrently with
the E and F Scales (*TAP*, chap. 5) and in its final, five-item form correlated about .57 with Form 40/45 of the F Scale. Two of the PEC items
were worded in the anticonservative direction, so it is unlikely that response sets contributed much to this relationship. However the brevity
of the PEC Scale presented a grave problem; it did not have enough
items "to obtain an adequate measure of reliability, and hardly enough
to be called a 'scale'" (*TAP*, p. 168).

While other investigators have found significant (if usually lower)
correlations between the F and PEC Scales (e.g., Barker, 1963; Campbell
and McCandless, 1951) and other paper-and-pencil measures of conservatism (Thompson and Michael, 1972), the more telling studies in this area
have concerned themselves with actual political affiliation, electoral
preference, and orientations toward particular issues such as the war in
Viet-Nam. We shall consider each of these now.

Relationships with political affiliation. Two well-known British
experiments have tested the F Scale's hypothesized relationship with
political affiliations, including one which actually involved some
fascists. This study, conducted by Coulter soon after World War II
and reported briefly in Eysenck (1954), compared the F Scale scores
of working-class London males who were either active Fascists or
Communists.

The reported mean item score of the 43 Fascists involved was (a
very high) 5.30, while that of 43 Communists was significantly lower
at 3.13. A control group of 86 soldiers apparently tested in a hospital
scored even lower than the Communists (2.50). Eysenck concluded,
somewhat extraordinarily, that both Fascists and Communists appear
to score high on the F Scale. In fact, as Christie (1965a) very rightly
pointed out, the Communist score is quite low, and is only "high" compared to the exceedingly low score of the "normals." To my knowl-

(in England or anywhere else) has ever scored so low as these British soldiers, most of whom must have disagreed with practically every statement on the F Scale.

At a later date Eysenck (1972) provided a little more information on the procedures used by Coulter in her study; the elaboration compromises the results further. Different "cover stories" were used to involve the fascists and communists in the research. The latter were told that the 2.5-hour battery of tests given them measured social insight. The Fascists, on the other hand, were expected to believe that the battery, which included the TAT and a number of "rigidity" measures, was a public opinion poll "on questions that are commonly discussed over the radio." Eysenck (1972) provided very little information on the procedures used in testing the "normals" however, despite the questions which had long been raised (Christie, 1956a) about them.

Rokeach (1960) in the meanwhile had reported the results of a study conducted in 1954 among British university students. Those who said they identified with the Communist party scored significantly lower (item mean = 2.86) on the F Scale than did those who were Liberal party supporters (3.39). The latter score in turn was significantly lower than that of Conservative students (3.98). The scores of those who belonged to several smaller political groups of the day ("Bevanites" and "Attleeites") were intermediate and sensibly close to the Communist party and Liberal party supporters respectively.

In America, Barker (1963) reported the results of two experiments which compared F Scale scores of university students who were categorized as politically right- or left-wing. In the first study, a number of tests measuring constructs supposedly relevant to authoritarianism were administered to at least 160 graduate students in psychology or eduction in New York City. A 30-item F Scale (Gough, 1951) containing 26 of the original items was included in the battery. Scores on this scale correlated .57 with a tendency to censor leftist speakers and .55 with Rokeach's (1960) Right Opinionation Scale; as the reader by now might suspect from the size of the correlations, both tests were unidirectionally worded. The relationships obtained with four other "authoritarianism" measures included in the battery were not reported.

In his second study, Barker compared (among other things) the F Scale scores of (1) 29 "leftist" Ohio State undergraduates who had actively opposed a campus speakers ban, (2) 61 comparable students who had not been active in any organized political activity, and (3) 26 active student conservatives. The mean (item) F Scale scores of these groups were reedge, no normal, unselected group spectively 2.14, 2.98 and 3.58, with all groups being significantly different from one another.[19]

F Scale scores and presidential preference. Milton (1952) was among the first to test the F Scale's relationship to electoral behavior. He administered the test to 390 University of Tennessee students immediately after Douglas MacArthur's keynote address to the 1952 Republican convention. Then subjects were asked to indicate which of six candidates they preferred to be the next president: the Republican possibilities were Eisenhower, MacArthur and Robert Taft; the Democrats were Estes Kevauver, Richard Russell and Adalai Stevenson.

It was found that MacArthur supporters had significantly higher F Scale scores than did the combined values for the rest of the sample. Taft enthusiasts also scored higher than most, and just as high as the Mac-Arthur supporters. Among the Democrats, Stevenson's supporters were significantly lower than either Kefauver's or Russell's supporters. Thus while the results are somewhat compromised by the fact that the sample was drawn from Kefauver's home state (Kefauver outpolled Stevenson by more than 4-1 in the sample) they are in line with theoretical expectations if both MacArthur and Taft can be labelled more conservative than Eisenhower, and if Stevenson can be labelled more left-wing than Kefauver and Russell. This is consistent at least with the journalistic labels used at the time.

It would appear from Milton's data, incidentally, that students who preferred a Republican contender had slightly but significantly higher F Scale scores than did Democratic supporters. A parallel difference, which was slight but significant, existed in Milton's data between the preconvention supporters of the eventual nominees, Eisenhower and Stevenson. Stotsky and Lachman (1956) similarly reported that Eisenhower supporters scored significantly higher on the F Scale among 102 Wayne University students.

Wrightsman, Radloff, Horton and Mercherikoff (1961) administered an unspecified short form of the F Scale to over a thousand students in California, Connecticut, Minnesota and Tennessee prior to the 1960 political conventions. The subjects also expressed preference among eight possible presidential nominees: two Republicans (Nixon and Rockefeller) and six Democrats (Faubus, Humphrey, Johnson, Kennedy, Stevenson and Symington). The data provided spotty support for the F Scale's validity in terms of the journalistic images of the candidates at the time. There was no difference in the F Scale scores of Nixon and Rockefeller supporters, which is somewhat surprising. The differences among the Democrats were a little more supportive: Stevenson and Humphrey enthusiasts (as well as Symington supporters) scored relatively low on the F Scale, while Faubus and Johnson supporters had the highest means in the sample. Although an ANOVA of the scores for all eight candidates revealed a significant overall effect, it was not reported which individual candidates were significantly different from one another.

In Wrightsman's (et al., 1961) overall sample, Republicans and Democrats had very similar F Scale scores. The mean scores of the preconvention supporters of Nixon (29.3) and Kennedy (29.8), the eventual nominees, were also very similar.

The 1964 election apparently attracted more F Scale research than any other, perhaps because of interest in Barry Goldwater's campaign. Three studies found that Goldwater supporters scored higher on the F Scale than did Johnson enthusiasts: Goldberg and Stark, 1965 (who studied 34 Connecticut College students who were at least moderately enthusiastic about one of the candidates); Higgins, 1965 (who tested all of 20 students in California); and Kerpelman, 1968, (who administered 24 F Scale items to 258 students attending university day and evening classes in the Chicago area).

Zippel and Norman (1966), however, administered the F Scale to 381 University of New Mexico students in October, 1964. There was no significant difference in the responses of Goldwater and Johnson supporters (who had mean total scores of 97.6 and 99.8 respectively). An analysis of those who had switched parties in 1964 also produced confounding results. "Democrats for Goldwater" had higher F Scale scores than the rest of the Democrats, as one might predict, but "Republicans for Johnson" also had higher scores than did the rest of the Republicans. Zippel and Norman's results may be specific to a certain region of the country; New Mexico in fact is right between the home states of both contenders, and they both may have alienated certain segments of the state's population over regional issues. But it should be noted that the authors' sample was the largest of the four studies conducted during the 1964 election.

A study by Schwenidman, Larsen and Cope (1970) provides further disconfirmation. They administered 10 items from the F Scale to 282 randomly selected students at Brigham Young University in conjunction with a study of presidential preference in the 1968 election. (The ten items chosen, for reasons which are difficult to imagine, were those consticuting the authoritarian aggression and superstition "subscales" of the test.) The mean scores on these ten items ranged from 35.4 for supporters of "peace candidates" (e.g., Eugene McCarthy) to 38.8 for George Wallace supporters, with Humphrey (35.9) and Nixon (37.7) supporters scoring in between. None of these very small differences appear to be statistically significant.

Lück and Gruner (1970) administered the F Scale to 110 University of Georgia undergraduates in July of 1969 and then asked them whom they would prefer for president in the 1972 election. The results were analyzed in terms of the political parties supported, and the students who expressed a preference for the American Independent Party of George Wallace scored significantly higher on the F Scale (mean = 117.4) than did either supporters of a Republican (mean = 103.9) or a Democrat (mean = 97.4). The latter two means were not significantly different.

Finally Hanson and White (1973) reported that 15 Clarkson College students who supported Richard Nixon in the 1972 presidential election had significantly higher scores on the F Scale (mean = 91.5) than did 19 McGovern supporters (mean = 67.2). Results for twenty other students who participated in the study at least initially were not reported. The difference between Nixon and McGovern supporters is consistent with expectations, but the representativeness of this small sample is doubtful.

In summary, studies of candidate preference during American presidential elections offer some marginal support of the hypothesis that F Scale scores are related to right-wing political sentiment. Candidates who were generally described as "conservatives" at the time (i.e., Douglas MacArthur, Robert Taft, Barry Goldwater and George Wallace) drew high F supporters, while "liberal" candidates (i.e., Adalai Stevenson, Hubert Humphrey and George McGovern) tended to draw low F enthusiasts.

It should be noted, however, that this summary glosses over many deficiencies in the data, not the least of which is that all the studies used student samples. In addition, three of the studies reviewed (Wrightsman et al., 1961; Zippel and Norman, 1966; and Schwendiman et al., 1970) failed to find at least some differences in F Scale scores one might reasonably expect to occur; and all three of these studies of presidential preferences used "large" samples. In fact, if one excludes those studies which sampled only twenty or thirty subjects, the support of the validity of the F Scale in this area is much more equivocal, and certainly less convincing than that on general political affiliation reviewed at the beginning of this section.

Relationships with specific issues. Several studies, some more compelling than others, have investigated the relationship between scores on the F Scale and certain "right-wing" political attitudes. Gump (1953), for instance, administered the F Scale and a 10-item questionnaire to 405 University of Colorado students which surveyed reactions to President Truman's firing of General MacArthur. In four of the six classes tested, students who disagreed with the statement, "MacArthur should have been dismissed," had significantly higher F Scale scores than those who agreed. Overall, the difference was significant but modest (item means of 3.71 vs. 3.33). For some reason, results for the other nine items on the "dismissal" questionnaire were not reported.

The relationship is in line with theoretical expectations only if one assumes that MacArthur's appeal to high F subjects was stronger than their hypothesized need to submit to the president's authority. The theory of the authoritarian personality could also have "explained" matters if the results had turned out directly opposite to the way they did.

Handlon and Squier (1955) administered the F Scale to 23 graduate students at Berkeley who had refused to sign the California Regents' "loyalty oath," and to 21 others who did sign the oath. The former, who more often described themselves as political liberals (and who strongly preferred Wallace or Thomas in the 1948 election) scored significantly lower on the test (item means of 1.88 vs. 2.73). This study is particularly impressive because probably no other finding in the entire F Scale literature relates to so personally crucial a piece of behavior as Handlon and Squier's. The consequences to the students who refused to sign the oaths were often quite severe (Stewart, 1950).

Smith and Rosen (1958) compared F Scale scores of students attending summer school in New York City who had scored in either the upper or lower 10% of the distribution on the "Worldmindedness Scale" (Sampson and Smith, 1957). The latter may be considered a measure of the nationalism versus internationalism dimension which received such limited representation on the E Scale. It was found that the most nationalistic subjects had significantly (and very much) higher scores on the 22 F Scale items used than did the extremely internationalistic students. Of course subjects preselected by their extreme differences on an attitude scale might be expected to disagree on a wide range of topics. Unfortunately the correlation between scores on the two scales for all of the sample was not reported.

A study by Mischel and Schopler (1959) provided both confirmation and disconfirmation of the relationship between F Scale scores and nationalism. University of Colorado students were asked, shortly after the launching of Sputnik I, if they thought the USA or the USSR would "get to the moon first." The question was then asked again about a month later after Sputnik II was launched. Finally responses to either a 10-item or 30-item version of the F Scale were gathered from the subjects.

By way of disconfirmation, F Scale scores were unrelated to initial estimates of whether the USA would win the moon race (most subjects initially thought it would), nor to a variety of opinions about Russian people, politics or culture. However, the relatively few subjects who "kept the faith" after Sputnik II did score significantly higher on the F Scale than did those who switched opinions and believed the USSR would win. Mischel and Schopler believed their results demonstrated that high F subjects are rigid and resist change, but this ignores the usual definitional stipulation that such persistence in beliefs must be inappropriate to be labeled "rigidity." It was not known in 1957 who would land on the moon first, and we now know in fact that the high F students tended to be right.

Finally several studies reported small-to-moderate correlations between F Scale scores and attitudes toward the war in Viet-Nam. Izzett (1971) found that students at a New York State university who missed classes on the October 15, 1969, Moratorium Day scored significantly lower on the F Scale than did those who attended classes (point-biserial $r = .29$). F Scale scores also correlated significantly (.25 to .39) with responses to four (of six) questions concerning the war. Granberg and Corrigan (1972) found similar correlations between scores on Berkowitz and Wokkon's (1964) forced-choice version of the F Scale and reports of opposition to the war among University of Missouri students.

While the six studies about the F Scale's relationship with specific issues reviewed above do not validate the F Scale as firmly as one might wish, none of them produced a negative finding. Like the research described earlier, they do therefore suggest that scores on the scale are modestly associated with right-wing political sentiment.[20]

Considering all of the studies on this topic (see Table 5) the F Scale's strongest relationship appears to be with political party affiliation; correlations with electoral preference and specific issues are somewhat weaker. It must be mentioned once more, however, that few of the relationships are strong, and there are many inconsistencies and methodological hesitations regarding the data.

*Summary and conclusions regarding the theory of the
authoritarian personality*

All of the research bearing on the empirical correlations of the F Scale
reviewed above[21] may be summarized as follows:

1 F Scale scores are only strongly correlated with unidirectionally
worded prejudice measures; the relationships are much smaller when the
possible effects of response sets have been controlled. These very modest
relationships in turn may be partly due to the biased way in which items
were developed and selected for the F Scale by the Berkeley researchers.

2 There is no convincing evidence that high F Scale scores result from
certain early childhood experiences and family situations. The psycho-
dynamic model of the childhood origins of the authoritiarian personality
is dramatically lacking in experimental support.

3 There is conflicting evidence as to whether scores on the F Scale are
associated with marked rigidity and intolerance of ambiguity. Some
investigators have found such a relationship, but others have not. It
seems clear that if there is a relationship, it is much more complicated
than that proposed by the Berkeley researchers.

4 There is also highly conflicting evidence as to whether persons who
score high on the F Scale conform more to peer pressure than do nonauthoritarians. There are very few studies which show conformity when
socially relevant stimuli are involved.

5 There is little evidence linking F Scale scores to predictable behavior
in group settings. Scores on the test also do not seem linked to experience
with, or to success in relatively authoritarian organizations.

6 There is no evidence that F Scale scores are particularly high in any
certain socioeconomic class.

7 F Scale scores do seem to be moderately associated with tendencies
to be aggressive against people considered unconventional and lower in
status. High F subjects may also be relatively aggressive against peers.

8 F Scale scores do seem to be modestly associated with right-wing
political sentiment.[22]

Before we took up the evidence on the F Scale's empirical correlations, some doubts were expressed about the eventual outcome because
the scale was so weak psychometrically. It was hard to see how the test
could "work" as a measure of right-wing authoritarianism (or anything
else), although obviously hundreds of researchers have believed it would.
Now the chickens have come home to roost, and we can see that the test

TABLE 5

Summary of studies relating F Scale scores to conservative political sentiment

Study	Version of the F Scale	Dependent Measure	Sample	Findings
I. Political party affiliation				
Coulter, 1954	Original F Scale	Political party membership in England	Working class English males	Fascists scored higher than Communists, who scored higher than "normals."
Rokeach, 1960	Original F Scale	Political party membership in England	College students in England	Conservatives scored higher than Liberals, who scored higher than Communists.
Barker, 1963	30-item scale, (26 originals)	PEC and other tests; membership in campus political groups	College students	Some significant correlations with other tests. "Right-wing" activists scored higher than "left-wing" activists.
II. Electoral preference				
Milton, 1952	Original F Scale	Pres. preference, 1952	College students	Generally confirmatory.
Stotsky & Lachman, 1956	Original F Scale	Pres. preference, 1952	College students	Einsenhower supporters scored higher than Stevenson supporters.
Wrightsman et al., 1961	Unknown	Pres. preference, 1960	College students	Some confirmatory, some not so.
Goldberg & Stark, 1965	Original F Scale	Pres. preference, 1964	College students	Goldwater supporters scored higher than Johnson supporters.
Higgins, 1965	Original F Scale	Pres. preference, 1964	College students	Goldwater supporters scored higher than Johnson supporters.
Kerpelman, 1968	24-item F Scale	Pres. preference, 1964	College students	Goldwater supporters scored higher than Johnson supporters.
Zippel & Norman, 1966	Original F Scale	Pres. preference, 1964	College students	No difference between Goldwater and Johnson supporters. Mixed results for party switchers.

Study	Scale	Measure	Subjects	Results
Schwenidman et al., 1970	10-item F Scale	Pres. preference, 1968	College students	No difference in the scores of supporters of four contenders.
Lück & Gruner, 1970	Original F Scale	Pres. preference, 1972	College students	American Independent Party supporters scored higher than Republicans or Democrats.
Hanson & White, 1973	Original F Scale	Pres. preference, 1972	College students	Nixon supporters scored higher than McGovern supporters.

III. Specific issues

Study	Scale	Measure	Subjects	Results
Adorno et al., 1950	Original F Scale	Scores on the PEC Scale	Many different groups	Overall correlation of .57.
Gump, 1953	Original F Scale	Questionnaire on Gen. MacArthur's firing	College students	MacArthur's supporters scored higher than Truman's.
Handlon & Squire, 1955	Original F Scale	Signing of U. of Calif. "loyalty oath"	Berkeley Graduate students	Those who signed the "loyalty oath" scored higher than those who refused to sign.
Smith & Rosen	22-item F Scale	"Worldmindedness" Scale	College students	High F subjects less "worldminded."
Mischel & Schopler, 1959	10- or 30-item Scale	Reactions to Sputnik	College students	Mixed results.
Izzett, 1972	Original F Scale	Participation in Viet-Nam Moratorium Day	College students	Observers of the moratorium scored lower than nonobservers.
Granberg & Corrigan, 1972	30-item balanced scale	Opinions about the war in Viet-Nam	College students	Supporters of the war scored higher than opponents.

does not work very well at all. That should come as no surprise whatsoever.

What can we make of the test's very limited success at predicting (a) hostility toward certain targets, and (b) conservative political sentiment? These findings might be insightful if we knew more about them, but as matters stand now, there is a perfectly straightforward interpretation of them: they may just be due to those items on the F Scale whose content reflects (respectively) aggressive and conventional sentiments. Thus the studies on aggression listed in Table 4 may carry no more psychological significance than the fact that people who indicate on the F Scale that they are particularly hostile toward sex criminals, disrespectful youth, rebellious youth, and homosexuals are also aggressive on other measures against these and similarly unconventional individuals. That should not knock anyone off his horse. *A major failing of the research we have just reviewed is that nearly all of the investigators who found positive results failed to determine if these results were attributable to the scale as a whole, or mainly to subsets of items with rather obvious connections to the criterion.*

Before leaving the California F Scale, we might pause for a moment to reflect on the enormous wreckage behind us. Considering the number of subjects who have completed the F Scale (surely hundreds of thousands) and the number of dollars which have been spent on F Scale research (probably millions) it is rather stupifying to realise that we end up knowing so little. For we found not only that the theory is unconfirmed (that is the chance one always takes), but also that all of this research was *incapable of testing the theory from the start.* Why ever on earth, then, was most of it done?

EYSENCK'S TWO-FACTOR THEORY OF POLITICAL BEHAVIOR

Origin of the theory

A few years after *The Authoritarian Personality* was published, H. J. Eysenck (1954) presented a summary of research he had conducted in England on *The Psychology of Politics.* In this book he suggested that political behavior could be conceptualized in terms of two independent dimensions. The first was the traditional left-to-right continuum of political-economic attitudes. Eysenck in fact stated that this is the only ideological factor present in the attitude field. The second dimension was how "tenderminded" or "toughminded" a person was, and it was not an attitudinal dimension at all, but rather a projection of "introversion" ("tendermindedness") and "extraversion" ("toughmindedness") (Eysenck, 1953) onto the attitude field. Thus Eysenck, like the Berkeley researchers, presented a theoretical model which connected personality factors with social attitudes.

Unlike the Berkeley model (which was to some extent deducted from Freudian theory), Eysenck's two-dimensional analysis was inductive in that it was based on his interpretation of the results of factor analytic studies of certain social attitudes. In the definitive study (1947), he first selected 40 items from a larger pool, including all of those which reportedly had been "shown to be of some importance or relevance in any previous research." Eysenck gave five to fifteen copies of a questionnaire containing these 40 items to his students at the University of London and instructed them to administer them to friends and acquaintances. Nearly 1,000 middle-class and (apparently) 137 working-class subjects completed the survey in this way. In the basic analysis, the responses of 250 middle class supporters of the Conservative, Liberal and Socialist parties, roughly matched for age, sex and education, were factor analyzed.

Two essentially orthogonal, bipolar factors emerged from Eysenck's analysis. He chose not to rotate these factors so that they would pass through the most obvious clusterings of the items, however. Instead he passed the first factor much closer to two plainly economic-political items (Eysenck, 1971, p. 210). The items which loaded highest on Factor I as a result of this placement were as follows:

Loading	Item
.72	The nationalization of the great industries is likely to lead to inefficiency, bureaucracy, and stagnation.
−.68	Ultimately, private property should be abolished, and complete socialism introduced.
.65	Crimes of violence should be punished by flogging.
.65	The Japanese are by nature a cruel people.
−.62	In the interests of peace, we must give up part of our national sovereignty.
−.60	The death penalty is barbaric, and should be abolished.

Eysenck, 1954, p. 129

As I mentioned earlier, a factor analyst may rotate his factors to whatever position he chooses. Eysenck's choice enabled him to define Factor I as a left-to-right political-economic attitude factor (although for most of the remaining high loading items the connection with such a factor seems extremely oblique. Eysenck called his first factor "Radicalism-

Conservatism" (R); it controlled about 18% of the total variance among the 40 items.

A direct consequence of Eysenck placing Factor I where he did was that there were very few items that loaded on Factor II; as a result the factor was relatively unimportant, controlling only about 8% of the remaining total test variance. The only items with loadings $\geq$ .40 are given below:

Loading	Item
−.65	Only by going back to religion can civilization hope to survive.
.56	Men and women have the right to find out whether they are sexually suited before marriage (e.g., by companionate marriage).
.49	Sunday observance is old fashioned, and should cease to govern our behavior.
.47	Divorce laws should be altered to make divorce easier.
−.42	Birth control, except when medically indicated, should be made illegal.

Eysenck, 1954, p. 129

It seems obvious to me that the thing these items have most in common is a concern with religion and sex-related (or marriage-related) morality. If I had to give the factor a name, I would call it "Morality" or "Religion and Sexual Morality" or the like. I must confess it would be a long time before I thought of calling the dimension "Tendermindedness-Toughmindedness" (T). Moreover, it is difficult to know how justified this latter interpretation is since Eysenck did not present an independent definition of this construct; the closest he came to such a delineation was in suggesting that the "T" dimension seemed similar to William James' (1907) comments about tenderminded and toughminded people.

The reader may find it difficult to believe that the items which loaded highest on Factor II were uncorrelated with the radical-conservative dimension. All of these items did have appreciable loadings on Factor I as well. It was only the hypothetical dimension invented by the factor analysis which was relatively independent of Factor I. There were in fact no relatively pure Factor II items, and Eysenck has consistently maintained that none exist, that tendermindedness can only be measured in the context of some social issue. Whatever the merits of this contention, the basic operational reason Factor II had no pure items was simply because of the way Factor I was positioned.

Other researchers soon observed that had Eysenck rotated the factor structure approximately 45°, both factors would have been interpretable and similar to those found previously by other investigators (Ferguson, 1941; Kirkpatrick, 1949) with other sets of items. Eysenck has consistently chosen to keep his factors where he originally placed them, however, believing that the R factor inherited a definite semantic advantage and that the T factor amounted to a genuine psychological insight.

The evidence for the "insight" is as follows. Eysenck calculated scores on the R and T factors for each of his subjects by summing the responses to 14 particular items in each case. The 14 T items were chosen so that half of them had positive loadings on the R factor, the others negative. An analysis of these scores in terms of the political party allegience of the subjects revealed that the R Scale sensibly differentiated the three major British political parties, but the T Scale did not (This is not surprising, since the items had been selected to make the summed score on T uncorrelated with R). Then, however, Eysenck recruited 146 Communists for his study through their "Party Branches," and seven Fascists in an unspecified manner. The Communists and the Fascists scored significantly lower on the Tendermindedness Scale (i.e., they were "toughminded" leftists and conservatives respectively.) Eysenck then proceeded to equate tendermindedness with introversion, and toughmindedness with extraversion, and to explain how "learning theory" could account for the development of these types. The explanation he offers is exceedingly hard to accept both theoretically and in terms of supporting evidence, but it is off the subject here and will not be pursued.

Criticisms of Eysenck's study

Soon after Eysenck's research was published, a barrage of intense criticism was leveled at it, a barrage which provided some lively reading in the *Psychological Bulletin* during 1956. The antagonists were Eysenck (1956a, b) on the one hand, and Rokeach and Hanley (1956; Hanley and Rokeach, 1956) and Christie (1956a, b) on the other. The exchanges are still remarkable in many respects, and well worth the effort necessary to follow the debate in detail. The reader is encouraged to read these papers himself if he has not done so already, but in essence they can be summarized as follows:

1 Samples drawn: Eysenck (1954, p. 127) specifically stated that his findings could be applied to the British middle class as a whole. Christie demonstrated, however, that the people in the sample were far younger and better educated than the overall English middle class (as one would expect, given the extraordinary way in which they were recruited). He

also observed that Communists were very active politically, while the vast majority of the Conservatives, Liberals and Socialists probably were not. Christie wondered if the more active members of the major parties would have been as different from the Communists as the overall samples were.

2 Items used: It is rather doubtful that the 40 statements Eysenck used for his item pool covered the entire field of social attitudes as completely as he apparently believed they did. The results of any factor analysis depend in the first instance on what is being factored; it is clear that factoring another set of "important and relevant" items could produce a different structure. In particular, no pure T items may have been found by the analysis simply because no pure T items were included among the 40 items factored.

3 Scoring of the T Scale: The T Scale, which consists of five "tenderminded" and nine "toughminded" items, was scored in a most peculiar fashion. Any form of agreement ("+ +" or "+") with a tenderminded item was scored +1; any form of neutrality ("0") or disagreement ("−" or "− −") was scored a zero. If the item was toughminded, any disagreement was called a +1, while neutrality or agreement was scored a zero. Thus as Christie pointed out a person who gave a "neutral" response to all 14 items on the T Scale would receive a score of zero, which is the most toughminded score possible. Someone who disagreed with every item would have a score of nine, and hence be more tenderminded than anyone who agreed with everything. Obviously the scoring system was all cockeyed, and differences found between certain groups implied nothing about how "tenderminded" they were.

4 Calculations of the scores for various groups: Eysenck employed a rather dubious method for calculating the mean T Scale scores of the samples in his study, whereby subgroups' average scores were averaged regardless of their respective sample sizes. For example, the mean of the 250 middle-class Liberals (7.9) was averaged with the 7.4 obtained from 27 working-class Liberals, producing a new "mean" of 7.65. This figure was rounded up to 7.7, which at least is in the direction of the weighted mean (7.9). On the other hand, a combined score for the Communists and the Fascists was apparently arrived at by averaging the 6.8 mean of 50 middle-class and 6.0 of 96 working-class Communists, and then averaging the resulting 6.4 with the 4.7 for the seven Fascists, and rounding the resulting 5.55 down to 5.5. It is unlikely that more than a dozen or two of the 153 subjects in the composite sample had scores lower than this "mean." Christie observed further that the rule Eysenck apparently followed when deciding to round means up or down was to round in what-

ever direction would maximize the difference between the Communists-Fascists and the other groups.

An even more damaging discovery about these group scores, this one made by Rokeach and Hanley, was that calculation of the T Scale scores on an item-by-item basis using information provided by Eysenck (1951, Table III) produced very different totals from those cited by Eysenck. In particular, the Communists' mean among the middle-class subjects rose to 7.4 where it was barely below that of the Conservatives (7.6) and only 0.8 points below the highest mean in the group (8.2 for the Liberals). Recalculation of the working-class samples produced an even more dramatic shift as the Communists (7.3) were found to have scored higher (i.e., were more tenderminded) than both the Conservatives (6.7) and the Socialists (6.6) (the Liberals scored 8.3). Thus the Communists were by no means significantly more toughminded than the rest of the subjects in either sample.

5 Ambiguity of responses to the items: Rokeach and Hanley also pointed out that according to Eysenck's 1951 data, the Communists were the most toughminded of the subjects on only six of the 14 items on the T Scale; on the other eight items, in fact, they were the least toughminded. An examination of these two sets of items yields an obvious explanation of the difference between them. Most (4/6) of the items on which the Communists appeared most toughminded loaded appreciably (about .50) on the Radical end of the R dimension; most (5/8) of the items on which the Communists appeared least toughminded loaded appreciably (about .45) on the Conservative end of the R dimension. It seems eminently plausible then that the Communists were responding to the radical-conservativism content of most of these items, rather than their "toughmindedness." Christie in fact observed that, overall, the items on the T Scale correlated better with the R factor (about .48 on the average) than they did with the T dimension (about .38 on the average) which they were being used to measure.

Christie went on to point out that the 14 T-Scale items were very unequally distributed among the four quadrants defined by the high and low halves of the R and T dimensions. Just one consequence of this was that equally toughminded Fascists and Communists would not receive the same scores on the T Scale.

The above five points summarize the major criticisms which Rokeach and Hanley, and Christie, leveled against Eysenck's study. Each of them is so damaging as to destroy altogether one's confidence in the validity of Eysenck's conclusions about the relationship between "tendermindedness" and political affiliation. Several more general criticisms should also be reported here. First, Eysenck was extremely brief in describing his experimental procedures; he gave only a vague account of how samples were drawn, how subjects were instructed, how scores were calculated, and how statistical operations were carried out. Sometimes the most elementary pieces of information, such as the mean scores of subjects in different groups, were not reported (and when searched out, they are found to be rather damaging to Eysenck's conclusions.) Secondly, there are many inconsistencies in Eysenck's writings. For example, the date of one of his students' dissertations was variously given as 1953, 1954, and 1955. At other times the reader's credulity is strained to the limit to believe that certain miscitations and miscalculations were merely due to sloppiness on Eysenck's part. At one point, for example, he argues against a rotation of his factor structure to one approximating simple structure because it would drop a "reasonably high" correlation with extraversion to a "rather low and unimportant one"; Hanley and Rokeach found that the correlation in fact dropped from .41 to about .36.

Eysenck's reply to the critics and their rejoinders
Eysenck (1956a, b) replied to each set of criticisms, and the critics each wrote rejoinders to the reply. There the matter ended. The gist of the various arguments is given below—but again the reader is directed to the original sources for a full understanding of the issues involved.

1 Samples drawn: Eysenck replied to the criticisms of his sampling techniques by stating that any sampling system has its deficiencies, that he had to use what was available, and that he had supplied enough information about his procedures to allow the reader to form an intelligent opinion about his sampling deficiencies. He then proceeded to defend at some length his use of "analytic" sampling (drawing 250 middle class subjects for each of the major parties) rather than drawing a proportionate or random sample of the middle class, which would have produced very few members of particular parties. As to the confounding of comparisons with the Communists because of their high degree of political activity, Eysenck contended that it was impossible to find members of the major parties as active as the Communists, and that he was being asked to do the impossible.

   Christie replied that in all of this, Eysenck was evading the issue. The issue in the first instance had nothing to do with using analytic samples, what was available, and so forth, but rather was Eysenck's generalizing the results found in a plainly unrepresentative sample to the population as a whole. As for the active Communists, Christie said that he had not asked for the impossible, but rather for a comparison of the scores of relatively active Conservatives, Liberals and Socialists to see if they were as different from the Communists as the entire samples in the major parties had been.

2 Items used: Eysenck contended that he and his students had been trying for years to write "pure T" items, without success, and that if Christie "had himself some practical experience in carrying out work of this kind he might be less inclined to dismiss the concentrated efforts of several people over many years in this superficial fashion" (Eysenck, 1956b, p. 432). Christie in turn responded that there was no record, or even an allusion to this concentrated effort in any of Eysenck's writings, and that Eysenck had never even formally defined the Tendermindedness construct, such a definition seemingly being a first step toward the development of pure T items.

3 Scoring of the T Scale: Eysenck did not respond to the criticisms made of his scoring system. The critics noted this.

4 Calculations of the scores for various groups: Eysenck similarly did not reply to the criticism of his use of "average of the averages" statistics, nor did he explain the rationale he had been using to round various means up or down. He did say, however, that the reason Rokeach and Hanley's T Scale scores for the political groups were different from his own was that they did not have a complete breakdown of the data for their calculations. He said the reason he did not provide a more complete breakdown of the data originally (in the 1951 paper) was that the 1952 (sic!) APA Publication Manual prohibited duplicate presentation of results. But he did not provide the missing breakdown in 1956 either. He also implied that Rokeach and Hanley did not know exactly how he had scored the responses, but given the chance, he still did not say exactly how he had scored the responses.

The critics observed that these criticisms went unanswered, and noted that, given what information was available about Eysenck's scoring system and the responses his subjects made, it was impossible to obtain the means Eysenck reported.

5 Ambiguities of responses to the items: Eysenck devoted a large portion of his responses to "elementary" explanations of the "chief charactertistics of dimensional analysis." He argued that if one item had loadings of $+.6$ on R and $+.5$ on T, and another had loadings of $-.6$ and

+.5 on R and T respectively, and a subject answered yes to both, the individual items might correlate higher with R but their sum would be a better indicator of T. He also argued that the imbalance Christie pointed out in the R-T quandrants would imply that the Communists' score should be increased by one point. This, according to Eysenck, would make them more like the Fascists (who were more toughminded than the Communists) and support his position that the two were equally toughminded.

Hanley and Rokeach remarked that Eysenck was inconsistent in his analysis of whether subjects were responding to the R or the T content of items, using whichever interpretation simply suited his purpose. Christie in turn pointed out that Eysenck's hypothetical example was far simpler than the reality of the items' actual loadings on the two dimensions, and that the items Eysenck had cited in making his analysis actually had loadings far different from how he represented them. Furthermore, the fact that the T Scale items were balanced with respect to their loadings on the R dimension was irrelevant to his criticisms of the asymetrical distribution of items in the R-T quadrants. Finally he observed that adding a score of one to the Communists' T Scale scores would make them even more tenderminded than the Fascists, not less so, since the T Scale is scored in the tenderminded direction.

Additional evidence

In addition to his own investigation, Eysenck argued that dissertations by three of his students all provided support for the conclusions he had reached in *The Psychology of Politics*. Two of these, one by Melvin (1955) and the other by Coulter (1953), became available to the critics; they did not provide very convincing support for Eysenck's position, and in some respects made it even worse. (See the comments on Coulter's study, for example, in the earlier section of this chapter on the F Scale's relationship to political behavior.) The data for the third dissertation, by Nigniewitzky (1956) were collected in France and were unavailable to the critics.

Conclusions

Seldom has a study been shown to be so seriously flawed from beginning to end as Eysenck's was, and never, moreover, have criticisms of a study been answered so ineffectively as Eysenck answered Rokeach and Hanley, and Christie.[23]

The R-T Scales do not appear to have generated much research interest among other investigators during the past 25 years. Eysenck's attention turned almost completely to other matters. Lately by his own report, however (Eysenck, 1972), his interest has returned to the field of social attitudes, and in 1971 he reported a study in which approximately 2,000 members of a BBC viewing sample answered a 28-item questionnaire. The items (and age and sex) were subjected to a principal-components factor analysis, and for various sub-groupings, nine to 10 factors were extracted and obliquely rotated to Promax criteria so as to analytically achieve simple structure. The first two dimensions, which Eysenck called authoritarian and religious dimensions, were considerably more important than the rest (controlling 14% and 12% of the total variance respectively—assuming the figures given in Table 5 of Eysenck [1971] are for an intermediate orthogonal rotation). Other factors were named, in diminishing importance: Ethnocentrism, Humanitarianism, Sexual Mores and Toughmindedness.

The oblique first-order factor matrix was then factored (presumably according to the Promax criterion again), and two relatively independent second-order factors resulted. The analysis, set to blindly pursue simple structure, produced Ferguson's "Humanitarianism-Religion" structure which others had earlier suggested was the clearest interpretation of Eysenck's 1947 data. Eysenck argued that this happened because the two highest-loading R items in the original study were, for unspecified reasons, not included in the present study. (However, rotation to simple structure in the original study would have approximated Ferguson's model anyway, even with the two economic-political items present.) Eysenck argued that it was preferrable even in the present case to rotate the Promax factors approximately 45° to produce the R and T factors, with the usual justification of semantic convenience and connections with extraversion-introversion.

Eysenck refers the reader of his 1971 paper to his earlier writings in this area, but makes no mention of the criticisms directed at these studies in 1956.

Even if one ignores the difference between a first-order factor structure and a second-order one, the 1971 study merely shows that a factor structure found in some items in 1947 was also somewhat detectable in a set of similar items in 1971. The nature of the factors is highly debatable, and even if one places them where Eysenck would, his interpretation of Factor II as "tendermindedness" (which still has not been defined) still seems to require one to close both eyes. Even if one grants Eysenck's interpretation, however, it remains to be demonstrated that the conceptualization is useful to the understanding of political behavior.

ROKEACH'S THEORY OF DOGMATISM

In 1956 and 1960, one of Eysenck's major critics, Milton Rokeach, presented his own conceptualization of how personality dispositions affect political behavior. If Rokeach's intentions had a bearing on the matter, his theory of dogmatism would have no place in a critique of the literature on right-wing authoritarianism, since his goal was to develop a concept (and measure) of "general authoritarianism." This authoritarianism would be no more associated with right-wing political sentiment than it would with that in the "center" or on the "left,"—and indeed would be just as applicable outside the realm of politics as within. Unfortunately, scores on the Dogmatism Scale (D Scale) (which serves as the operational definition of this "general authoritarianism") have frequently been found to be higher among right-wing political groups than among others (Barker, 1963; Direnzo, 1968; Kirtley and Harkness, 1969; Granberg and Corrigan, 1972; Thompson and Michel, 1972) and so we shall consider the conceptualization here, if only briefly.

The focus of Rokeach's theorizations is the structure of belief systems, not their content, and the conceptualization is rather complex. A model of cognitive structure was developed, organized along three basic dimensions, which each consisted of several subcomponents, which in turn often had numerous sub-subcomponents. Statements were written to tap the elements of this rather complicated model, and after five item-analysis studies involving altogether 87 statements, the final (Form E) 40-item D Scale emerged.

Technically, the D Scale is an even bigger nightmare than the F Scale. Virtually every criticism leveled against the F Scale's construction, including those concerning trait-representation, item ambiguity, and unidirectional wording, apply to the D Scale as well. Rokeach (1956, 1960) did not report the mean interitem correlation on the scale, but from the reliability coefficients given (and subsequent research) it appears to be about .10 or less—unidirectional wording and all. Indeed it was necessary to make the scale 40 items long to attain even the relatively poor reliabilities (usually between .75 and .80) it has. Factor analyses of the scale (e.g., Kerlinger and Rokeach, 1966) show that the scale is not at all unidimensional, and that the complex theoretical model of dogmatism used to develop the items is not discernable in any detail among the intercorrelations on the test.

Despite the fact that the D Scale (1) does not measure what it was intended to measure, and (2) is psychometrically so poor an instrument that it is difficult to know what it is measuring, it has been used in hundreds of studies on the rigidity of belief systems. Its literature is by now as large as the F Scale's, and is heading unavoidably toward the same fate.[24]

A small number of D-Scale studies should be mentioned, however, because some investigators have used the test as a measure of right-wing authoritarianism. Theoretical expectations notwithstanding, the D Scale has frequently been found to correlate about .60 with the F Scale, and some researchers have interpreted this to mean both must measure rightist authoritarianism. (The reader, who by now is used to seeing large F Scale correlations only with other unidirectionally worded tests, can probably offer a different interpretation.) These researchers have generally found that the D Scale has even poorer relationships with "rightist" behavior than does the F Scale, however (Barker, 1963; Vacchiano, Scheffman and Crowell, 1966; Vaughan, 1969; Schwendiman, Larsen and Cope, 1970; Granberg and Corrigan, 1972). Zippel and Norman (1966), on the other hand, found that the D Scale differentiated party switchers from nonswitchers in the 1964 election better than did the F Scale; unfortunately the difference contradicts expectations, since switchers scored higher on the D Scale than did nonswitchers.

WILSON'S THEORY OF CONSERVATISM

Perhaps the most novel approach taken in this field in recent years has been that of Glenn D. Wilson and his collaborators in New Zealand, England, and Australia (Wilson and Patterson, 1968; Wilson, 1973). Relatively little attention has been paid to this research program in North America, despite the fact that many articles describing it have appeared in British and American journals. Because of this, and because of the promise which some investigators believe this approach holds, Wilson's theory is reviewed here in some detail.

By "conservatism" Wilson means "resistance to change and the tendency to prefer safe, traditional and conventional forms of institutions and behaviour" (Wilson, 1973, p. 4). The construct is thought by Wilson to be an extremely important one. In fact, somewhat reminiscent of Eysenck's position on a similar construct, conservatism "is conceived as a general factor underlying the entire field of social attitudes" (p. 3). As such, it is thought to reflect a single personality dimension "similar to that which has previously been described in the semiscientific literature[25] in terms of a variety of labels such as 'fascism,' 'authoritarianism,' 'rigidity,' and 'dogmatism'" (p. 4) and also the "antiscientific attitude" (Wilson and Patterson, 1968, p. 264). Wilson suggests that the term "conservatism" is a more accurate name for this dimension, and that it is also less derogatory than authoritarianism or dogmatism.

Wilson's more specific understanding of the term "conservatism" is based, he states, largely on the popularly held stereotype of the extreme conservative. Initially, Wilson stated, this stereotype implied, (a) religious fundamentalism, (b) right-wing political orientation, (c) insistence on strict rules and punishments, (d) intolerance of minority groups, (e) preference for conventional art, clothing and institutions, (f) antihedonistic outlook, and (g) superstitious resistance to science (Wilson and Patterson, 1968). The Conservatism Scale (C Scale) was designed to tap these seven clusters. Later (Wilson, 1973), "militarism" was inserted into the list (after the scale was constructed, and with no mention of the post-hoc nature of the enlargement), and the last category became two ("opposition to scientific progress" and "superstition"), so that the term conservatism then implied the extent to which the nine attitudinal clusters were held. Wilson, Ausman and Mathews (1973), however, provided yet another list (this one with 10-clusters), of the ideal conservative's characteristics: "conventional, conforming, antihedonistic, authoritarian, punitive, enthnocentric, militaristic, dogmatic, superstitious, and antiscientific." Thus, there has been a certain imprecision in the definition of the construct, since elements have been added and subtracted over time without explanation. Also, the clusters are generally expected to covary, but Wilson allows that some of them may prove to be independent. However, he does not present a detailed explanation of which ones will be independent and why. Like the varying definitions, this ambiguity makes it hard to test the model.

In one respect, the operational definition of the construct, the C Scale, is the most distinctive feature of the approach. Wilson contends that attitude items presented in the usual form of propositional statements (as in the F and D Scales) "can never provide an adequate basis for the measurement of attitudes" (Wilson and Patterson, 1968, p. 264) because they draw a two-stage response from the subject: an immediate emotional response, and a more cautious, cognitive response triggered by the details and qualifications of the statement. It is assumed that the first, affective response will be the better predictor of actual behavior. (An underlying assumption seems to be that behavior is controlled more by emotional than cognitive factors.) High scores on traditional authoritarianism scales, it was argued, result more often from "ignorance and confusion rather than true authoritarianism," and so a new approach was needed.

Wilson's new approach was to present subjects with a list of brief labels and catch phrases representing the attitudinal clusters involved in conservatism. Examples are "death penalty," "evolution theory," and "school uniforms." Subjects were instructed to give their first reaction to each item by giving either a positive, negative, or uncertain response.

The initial pool for the C Scale contained 130 labels, which after three successive item analyses reduced to 50 items—half of which were "liberal" expressions for which no is the conservative response. Conservative and liberal items were alternated systematically throughout the scale, and the responses were scored on a 0-1-2 basis so that summed scores on the test could range from 0 to 100. The resulting scale was described in its initial publication as "a remarkably reliable, valid and economical instrument," and Wilson has been so impressed with its subsequent performance that he wrote in 1973, "the onus is now squarely upon proponents of traditional statement-form attitude scales to demonstrate that their approach has some measurable advantage. Otherwise it must be regarded as obsolete" (p. 69).

The construct validity of the Conservatism Scale:
psychometric properties

Wilson and Patterson (1968) initially administered the C Scale to 496 adults from varying occupational backgrounds in Christchurch, New Zealand; and the split-half reliability of the scale for a subsample of 244 was .943. It was concluded that this result was "evidence of very high internal consistency" (p. 267). Subsequent studies mentioned by Wilson (1973, p. 56) have found reliabilities ranging from .63 to .94 with an average value around .88. Most psychologists would probably agree that this represents adequate, if not admirable, reliability for the sum score on an attitude survey, but it is not indicative of high consistency among responses to the items (see note, p. 17). A 50-item test with a Cronbach "alpha" coefficient of .88 would have a mean interitem correlation of about .13. The reliability of the summed score on the C Scale may indeed be higher than that of other authoritarianism scales, but that is simply because it is based on 50 responses by the subject (as compared to say 30), not because the information "hangs together" better or is based on truer indicators of the subject's "real" attitudes so far as one can judge. C Scale scores may be stable, but that does not imply they mean anything. While there are many references to the "remarkable reliability" of the C Scale in Wilson's writings, the less impressive level of interitem correlation has not, to my knowledge, been mentioned yet.

Several factor analytic studies of the C Scale have appeared in the literature, and they have reached some very different conclusions about the factorial structure of the test. Wilson (1970) performed a principal-components analysis of the responses given by 200 London males (50 students, 50 professionals, 50 white-and 50 blue-collar workers) analyzing only the unrotated factor matrix. Fifteen factors with latent roots (eigenvalues) greater than 1.0 were extracted, but the first factor accounted for 18.7% of the variance on the test, and none of the remaining ones more than 6.5%. It was also noted that the highest loading items on this first factor represented divergent areas (which Wilson regarded "as covering all major areas of social controversy") and nearly all of the items on the test had positive loadings on this factor. Bageley, Wilson and Boshier (1970) reported the results of similar analyses carried out in the Netherlands and New Zealand, where the first factor accounted for 15.3 and 14.0% of the variance respectively and showed similar general representation among the items of the test. It was concluded in both papers that the test could "for practical purposes be regarded as unidimensional in content" thus supporting the basic premise of a major, general factor underlying all social attitudes.

The evidence cited, however, by no means warrants this conclusion, insofar as it is based on the unrotated factor matrices. The first factor extracted in a principal components analysis is defined so as to maximize mathematically the amount of variance that can be accounted for. That is, it is placed in such a position that as many of the elements in the correlation matrix as possible have substantial projections on it, whether the elements are related to one another or not. When the factor matrix is rotated so that correlated elements tend to land on the same factors (this being the goal of the analysis), the first factor naturally loses some of the variance it seemingly explained in the unrotated structure. This is the point raised earlier as a potential explanation of Melvin's factor analysis of the F Scale (Eysenck, 1954). As Comrey (1973, p. 104) has noted, "Failure to understand how the first (unrotated) factor can pull variance from uncorrelated variables has led some investigators to infer mistakenly that a general factor exists in the data just because all the variables have positive loadings on the first factor."

To put it another way, if one judges unidimensionality according to the importance (in terms of variance) and generality (in terms of item loadings) of the first factor of an unrotated principal components matrix, then practically every scale in existence can be considered unidimensional, including the F Scale. The evidence put forward that the C Scale is unidimensional is thus unconvincing.

A Varimax rotation was performed on 10 (of the 15) Wilson (1970) factors by Bagley in 1970. These were named "Conservative-Militaristic," "Sexual Morality," "Racialist," "Roman Catholic," "Anti-artistic," and so on. The amount of variance allegedly controlled by these various factors was only generally reported, and in fact is identical to the figures Wilson (1970) cited for the unrotated matrix.[26] Bagley then performed a third-order factor analysis on 10 primary (and presumably oblique) factors, which produced two factors that correlated .60. Wilson (1970) refers to this correlation as further evidence for the unidimensionality of the C Scale.

Boshier (1972), however, reported the results of an identical analysis of the New Zealand data reported in Bagley, Wilson and Boshier (1970) which came to quite a different ending. The subjects were 238 women and 122 men enrolled in an adult education program. (Unlike other studies with the C Scale, the sample in this study was described in some detail.) Fifteen factors were initially extracted, which together accounted for 56.7% of the total variance. The first factor, following rotation, had four items with loadings greater than .40 and was labelled "Religiosity." The second factor ("flouridation," "jazz" and "apartheid") fairly defied interpretation, while the third seemed concerned with "Feminine Repression." The fourth ("modern art," "computer music," "pyjama parties," "student pranks," "beatniks," "conventional clothing") is also difficult to interpret, as are many of the others.

These oblique factors still could be highly correlated, but unlike Bagley, Boshier found no evidence of this. Second-order factoring yielded eight factors, none of which controlled more than 11.2% of the variance. Even third-order factoring could only reduce the structure to four factors, whose average intercorrelation (ignoring signs) was .10 and whose highest value was −.19. The findings were thus strongly inconsistent with the contention that the C Scale is unidimensional.

Nias and Wilson (1972) responded to Boshier's findings in several ways. First they conceded that Boshier's rotated factors did make more intuitive sense than Bagley's (Bagley et al., 1970) unrotated factors, but curiously enough, they used this as an argument for leaving the matrix unrotated since this tactic produced results "of definite 'psychological' interest" (p. 324). This "more interesting finding" was that seemingly unrelated items such as "death penalty" and "chastity" loaded on the general factor. (We have however, already seen the reason for these "unanticipated" loadings, and in fact they are quite easily anticipated in an unrotated matrix, and psychologically meaningless to boot. One can only add that it would be wonderful if patterns of item loadings made more intuitive sense, rather than less, which Nias and Wilson say they prefer.)[27]

Nias and Wilson's second point is that Boshier's higher-order factor analysis did not show a general factor because higher order solutions are rather unreliable. (That they are so unreliable as to produce the marked difference between Bagley's and Boshier's findings is somewhat doubtful —expecially since Bagley et al. [1970] initially argued that both studies found the same thing.) They thus conclude that little weight can be placed on higher-order solutions as tests of a general factor hypothesis. (Nevertheless, Wilson (1973, pp. 84-85) later cites the correlation of .60 between Bagley's third-order factors as just such evidence for the general factor in the C Scale, and makes no mention whatsoever of Boshier's results.)

The only other factor-analytic study of the C Scale I have found in the literature was performed by Robertson and Cochrane (1973) on 329 undergraduates at Edinburgh University. Again a principal-components analysis was employed and 17 factors with eigenvalues greater than 1.0 were extracted. A Varimax rotation was performed, but no oblique ones. The first factor accounted for 12.9% of the test's variance following rotation, and, like Boshier's, seemed to be religious in nature (the highest loading items were "divine law," "Bible truth," "church authority," "sabbath observance," and "chastity.") Factor II had sexual overtones (with some inconsistencies) but only controlled 6.3% of the variance. Factor III seemed clearly racial, but had only three items with loadings greater than .40 and controlled only 4.6% of the remaining total variance. Factor IV, with only two high-loading items and controlling only 3.7% of the variance, seemed related to aggression. Robertson and Cochrane (p. 429-430), concluded "that the C Scale does not measure a general dimension of conservatism."

In summary, then, although the C Scale has been described as "predominantly unidimensional in content" (Wilson, 1973, p. 59) with "very high internal consistency," (Wilson and Patterson, 1968, p. 267), there is simply no sound evidence for these claims. The average correlation among the items on the scale appears to be about .13; the only reason the test has a higher reliability than, say, the F Scale is that it has many more items. As for unidimensionality, no one has yet found fewer than fifteen factors in the scale through factor analysis; the most important of these seems to control only about 13 to 14 percent of the test's total variance. The instrument thus seems to tap, even more so than the F and D Scales, a very large number of poorly correlated factors.

It is a matter of some speculation as to what these factors are. It is even more difficult to judge in the case of the C Scale, I believe, because we have even less information about what caused the subjects' behavior than we do with the traditional attitude scale. What is one to make of the fact that someone said no to "pyjama parties" and yes to "casual living"? If the test stimulus had been, "Pyjama parties are good because they give young girls a chance to socialize without a lot of adult supervision," there still could be many different reasons why a subject might say no. But at least the interpretive search is somewhat narrowed. Subjects probably would not have disagreed with this statement because they thought "pyjama parties" referred to heterosexual pyjama parties, for instance. But what can we eliminate when a subject says no to, simply, "pyjama parties"? In short, items on the C Scale seem to be more ambiguous, not less so, to both the subject and the interpreter than do the usual propositional statements.

This does not mean that it is impossible to interpret factors in the new format. When "divine law," "Bible truth," "church authority" and "sabbath observance" all load at least .64 on a factor, and are higher than any other item (as they did on the first, rotated, factor in both Boshier's and Robinson and Cochrane's studies), then some sort of religious factor is clearly implied. But this is the rare example. All of the items on the scale have multifaceted connotations, and without more information about what the stimuli probably meant to the subjects, it is that much more difficult to make sense of a cluster like Boshier's (1972) Factor II: "flouridation," "jazz," and "apartheid."

The main advantage of Wilson's format seems to be that a great deal of information (i.e., many responses) can be gathered from subjects in a short time. It may be a poor bargain, however, if all we are getting is a great deal of information with relatively little meaning.

The Conservatism Scale's relationships with other measures
Despite its "youth," the C Scale has been used in quite a lot of published research, much of which indicates (at least at first glance) that the scale possesses considerable predictive power. The more impressive findings may be summarized as follows:

1 Groups which one would expect to be significantly more conservative

than others have been found to be so: Politically active Conservative students versus active Socialist students (Wilson and Patterson, 1968); "Gideons" (members of the organization which places Bibles in hotel rooms) versus a group of scientists and medical practitioners (Wilson and Patterson, 1968); Salvation Army cadets versus Young Humanists (Wilson and Lillie, 1973). Wilson (1973, p. 67) also cites as another example of "known group validation" a study by Insel and Wilson (1971), in which Catholic convent school girls scored higher on the C Scale than girls attending a state school.

2 Thomas (1974; 1975) reported that C Scale scores correlated .42 and .62 with various measures of prejudice, and .43 to .84 with child-rearing practices among 56 Australian mothers.

3 Webster and Stewart (1973) found C Scale scores correlated .75 with theological conservatism and −.72 with theological liberalism among a group of New Zealand Baptist ministers. The C Scale also correlated .65 with a measure of ethnocentrism.

4 Orpen and Rodenwoldt (1973) found that C Scale scores correlated .69 with a questionnaire measure of "South African Values," .51 with a self-rating on conservatism, and also distinguished significantly among supporters of South Africa's three political parties. The subjects were 56 English-speaking students in what seems to be the equivalent of their senior year in high school.

5 Wilson, Ausman and Mathews (1973) found that C Scale scores correlated .56 with a preference for simplicity (as opposed to complexity) in paintings among 30 American young adults.

6 Mikesell and Perensky (1971) found that subjects (36 American students) asked to role play liberal and conservative responses to the C Scale produced quite different (and validating) scores on the scale.

7 Kish, Netterberg and Leahy (1973) found correlations of −.33 to −.54 between scores on the C Scale and versions of Zuckerman's "Sensation-seeking Scale" among American college students and social workers.

8 Wilson and Patterson (1969) found correlations ranging from −.24 to .27 among 139 English secondary school students between C Scale scores and preference for various types of humor. Thomas, Shea and Rigby (1971) similarly found an r of −.44 with reactions to a sexual cartoon among 39 Australian college students.

9 C Scale scores have been found to have a positive, monotonic relationship with age (Wilson and Patterson 1968). Boshier (1973) in turn found a large difference between the C Scale scores of some 17-19 year olds in New Zealand and their parents.

10 C Scale scores seem to be related to measures of social desirability (Hartley and Holt, 1971; Schneider, 1973).

Other findings, perhaps less relevant to the validity of the scale than those above, are that C Scale scores: (a) varied with intensity of classical conditioning (Wilson, 1968); (b) correlated negatively with self concept (Boshier, 1969); (c) correlated with attitudes toward patient care among nurses and patients (Caine and Leigh, 1972); (d) were related to fear of death (Wilson, 1973); (e) did not differ when the test was administered under anonymous or named conditions (Nias, Wilson and Woodbridge, 1971); (f) but were related to a preference for anonymity (Patterson and Wilson, 1969; Orpen and Rodenwoldt, 1973).

As encouraging as these relationships appear to be, there are a number of problems with these studies. First among these is a frequent and almost maddening absence of detail about the experimental procedures used. For example, in the "known-group" studies we do not know what rationales were given the subjects for their participation in the studies. What were they (and their leaders) told the test measured? If the subjects were approached at group meetings, and it appears that they were, how well was their membership in these groups played down during the testing, or did it remain salient (Hovland, Janis and Kelley, 1953, pp. 157-160)? We also do not know, in any detail, the extent to which the contrasted groups were matched for demographic variables which could themselves produce significant differences on the C Scale. Instead we are told that the groups were "essentially matched" or "roughly matched" for age, sex and socioeconomic status (Wilson and Patterson, 1968, p. 268; Wilson, 1973, p. 67). Conspicuously absent from this list of variables is an indication of the extent of subjects' formal education, despite all the criticism which has been directed at earlier research on just this point. (One wonders how different the Gideons were from the scientists in educational attainment, and what would have happened to the difference between these two groups had education been controlled.) In fact, none of the studies described above which used nonstudent samples reported controlling for education.

Another detail almost always missing from these studies is how the sample was drawn. The papers by Thomas (1974, 1975) provide no information on who the mothers were (except that they varied considerably in socioeconomic status) nor how they were selected (and self-selected) for the investigation. Similarly the paper by Wilson et al. (1973) gives no description of how the subjects (aged 23–34 and interviewed in their homes) were chosen for and involved in the study. Nor does the original study (Wilson and Patterson, 1968) of the 496 New Zealand adults specify how the "standardizing groups" were drawn, nor how 360 of these subjects were chosen to fulfill the (totally unspecified) "quota sample" which supplied the data that led to the relationship with age.[28] A further illustration of the vagueness of sampling procedures in this literature is found in Wilson (1970). There is no mention of how the 200 London males used in the factor analysis of the C Scale were drawn, only that it was "neither random nor representative" (p. 103). The mind boggles at imagining all the different collections of subjects which could be described as nonrandom and nonrepresentative.

Other pieces of important information are missing from individual studies. Thomas' (1975) findings about the child-rearing practices of conservative mothers were based on interviews conducted with the subjects. The interview schedule was only vaguely described ("a modified version of the Sears et al., 1957 interview schedule") and there is no description of how the child-rearing "practices" were scored (nor how reliably). These reports, once scored, were factor analyzed (in an unspecified way), and seven extracted factors were reduced to three internally consistent scales. The details of this reduction were unreported, however. The first scale was interpreted as measuring "Authoritarianism" and it was this scale that correlated .84 with the C Scale. Only two-thirds of the items on this scale were reported, however, and only a few of them seem more relevant to "authoritarianism" than they do to the names given the other scales. For example, the first-named item on the authoritarianism scale, "restrictions during eating," seems as related to the second scale ("Orderliness Training") as it does to "authoritarianism." "Mother's expectation of immediate obedience" does seem more pertinent to authoritarianism, and it was placed on this scale. But "father's expectation of immediate obedience" ended up on the "Family Adjustment Scale." And so on.

Thomas' (1975) entire paper, like many others in this literature, is extremely brief (it takes up less than one and a half journal pages) and will probably be cited for years to come as having demonstrated an extremely close relationship exists between C Scale scores and child-rearing practices. But who can say how good the evidence is? Very little of it was reported.

Beyond the skimpiness and vagueness of many of these reports (and at least half a dozen other examples could be given), there are a number of nonconfirmations in the literature which are usually glossed over but which should be taken into account. For example, in the Wilson and Patterson (1969) study of humor preferences, C Scale scores were expected (for unconvincing reasons) to be positively related to preference for puns (and they were—$r = .27$) and for "incongruity" jokes (but they were not—$r = .10$). C Scale scores were also, for clearer reasons, expected to be negatively related to appreciation of "sick" and "sexual" jokes (and they were—$r = -.18$ and $-.24$ respectively.)[29] There were also two other kinds of jokes in the battery: "antiradical" (which spoofed radicals and beatniks) and "antiauthority" jokes (which made fun of "respectable" persons and institutions). These would seem to be the most pertinent of the stimuli for testing the concept underlying the C Scale, and the reader might agree that one would expect positive and negative relationships respectively. Actually, C Scale scores correlated negatively with antiradical cartoons ($r = -.22$) and not at all with antiauthority ones ($r = -.10$). The study thus weakly confirmed expectations in three instances, and disconfirmed them in three others, with one of the latter being a significant reversal. It has nonetheless been cited without qualification by Wilson (1970), Insel and Wilson (1971), Boshier (1972) and Wilson (1973) as having validated the C Scale.

Another example of this "accentuating the positive" can be found in Wilson, Ausman and Mathews' (1973) study of art preferences. The paintings which were shown the subjects had been chosen to vary in two ways: (1) abstract-representational (referring to the extent to which the elements in the paintings were familiar and corresponded to visual reality); and (2) simplicity-complexity (referring to the number and concentration of different elements in the paintings). Given that one of the original defining characteristics of the ideal conservative was a preference for conventional art (Wilson and Patterson, 1968) one would expect high C subjects to prefer representational to abstract paintings. There was no such relationship, however ($r = -.14$), but there was a strong one with preference for simplicity ($r = .56$). Much was made of the latter; it supposedly confirmed that "the extreme conservative perceives the world as 'falling apart.'" But the failure to find the more directly expected dislike for abstract art was hardly noted, except that there was almost a sigh of relief that no relationship was found, for such a relationship "might have been regarded as tautological and trivial."[30]

Another negative finding which was put in the best possible light was obtained by Nias (1973), who expected for several reasons that high C English subjects would be opposed to England joining the European Common Market. There was no relationship, however, among a group of "volunteers" from the general population (the method of sample selection was unspecified) and there was a significant, if small, tendency among a group of students for high C subjects to favor entry into the Common Market. To deal with these disconfirmations, Nias broke the 50-item C Scale into five subscales (see Wilson, 1973, p. 89) and found that scores on the "Ethnocentrism Subscale" did correlate with opposition to joining the European Common Market—at least for the nonstudent sample. The validity of the subscales is even more doubtful than that of the C Scale, however. The "Ethnocentrism Subscale" for example contains three pro-trait and nine contrait items, only five of which have any apparent connection with ethnocentrism (compared to "working mothers," "women judges," "learning latin," "beatniks," "teenage drivers," "student pranks," and "jazz.")

Nias also found, incidentally, that while supporters of the Conservative Party tended to score high on the C Scale, there was no difference between members of the Liberal and Labour parties. This lack of differentiation was not commented upon.

Like previous researchers with other scales, investigators who have found significant correlations between summed scores on the C Scale and some other variable have seldom reported the results of an item analysis which could establish that the findings have some nonobvious explanation. To my knowledge only the study by Boshier (1973), which compared the C Scale scores of a group of New Zealand "Peace Corps" volunteers with those of their parents, presents a complete item analysis. Overall, there was a large difference between the mean scores of the parents ($\overline{X} = 45.3$) and the "children" ($\overline{X} = 34.2$). But the parents were significantly more conservative on only 28 of the 50 items. Furthermore Boshier reported that the items which best discriminated parents from their offspring were those which loaded highly on the "intolerance for youth" factor on the test.

A rather sketchy item analysis was reported by Wilson and Lillie (1972) in conjunction with their study of the Salvation Army cadets and the Young Humanists. Only the mean item scores were given, however, and those only graphically. There was no report as to whether the differences in means were statistically significant. It was nonetheless concluded that "the Salvationists were not only more conservative in terms of religion, but were relatively more antihedonistic, punitive, militaristic, politically conservative and conventional" (p. 220).

It is clear from the graphical presentation of the results however, as the authors observe, that the biggest differences between the two groups existed on the religious items (e.g., "Bible truth," "sabbath observance," "divine law"). Other large differences between these two very different groups on the items "self-denial," "nudism" and "stripteases" are not exactly surprising either. The extent to which the groups differed significantly with regard to attitudes less directly related to their organizations' central purposes cannot be determined by the results presented of course. But inspection of the means indicates that even with these groups, surveyed at organizational meetings, with the effects of education uncontrolled, the responses to many of the items on the scale were not significantly different.[31]

Summary and conclusions
It is not easy to state what these various studies do and do not show. Some of the research with the C Scale appears to support the scale's validity. But as we have seen, there are several problems with this literature which make one hesitant to accept many of the findings at face value. Until such time as the ambiguities regarding sampling and experimental procedures are clarified, the potential effect of education is controlled, the inconsistencies in the findings are squarely faced and resolved, and the relationships are shown to have widespread, nontrivial bases in the items on the C Scale, the findings reported so far are not convincing.

If well-documented studies in the future were to replicate the high relationships encountered so far, with relevant criteria, they would suggest that the scale is a measure of general conservatism. But here the item analyses would become crucial, because the hypothesized general conservatism would not be convincingly demonstrated if it turned out that C Scale relationships with religious conservatism were caused by the religion-related items, or those with prejudice were similarly due to the racial items, for instance. The proposition that there is an important general factor of conservatism which underlies social attitudes requires much stronger proof than that.

Our examination of the psychometric properties of the C Scale leads to a rather pessimistic prediction about the eventual outcome. The items on the scale do not intercorrelate very strongly, and thus it seems unlikely that they will, together, correlate significantly with many other measures. The test is very multifactored, and the factors do not seem highly interrelated. The C Scale might eventually prove to be correlatable with a wide range of behaviors; its scope is wide. But whether these correlations would mean very much remains to be demonstrated.

An evaluation of the C Scale must also consider the uniqueness of its item format. While a number of writers have praised the test's simplified structure, questions have been raised here about the difficulties seemingly inherent in interpreting responses to catch-phrases. It can similarly be doubted that the format yields "emotional" responses, and that emotional responses will correlate better with behavior than with responses about which the subject has had time to think. In this context it is curious that, for all the gauntlets which have been thrown down before "proponents of traditional attitude scales," C Scale enthusiasts have so seldom subjected the matter to experimental test. Webster and Stewart (1973) found that the C Scale was appreciably more predictive of religious orthodoxy, ethnocentrism, and other variables among a sample of Baptist ministers than was the D Scale. As we have noted, however, the D Scale is an even weaker instrument than the F Scale. On the other hand, Ray (1972) compared the original and a revised C Scale with a balanced 24-item "General Conservatism Scale" of his own design; he concluded that his own scale was better because responses to the conservative and liberal items on the original C Scale correlated positively (with unreversed keying). The revised C Scale was slightly more predictive of political party preference, however.

In closing, one can note that the concept of conservatism is very commonly used in social psychology and elsewhere; it obviously is relevant to the construct of right-wing authoritarianism. But it is not at all clear that the two constructs should be merged into one, any more than it is clear that dogmatism, fascism and "the antiscientific attitude" should also be collapsed into an all-encompassing conceptualization labelled "conservatism." The most compelling theoretical reason for resisting this amalgamation is that concepts such as right-wing authoritarianism and dogmatism have been sensibly differentiated. For example, Rokeach's conceptualization that dogmatism can be found at all stops along the left-right, liberal-conservative continuum is plausible to me, even if the operationalization of the concept is seriously lacking. Thus the position that all the constructs which Wilson and Patterson name should be treated as one entity probably deserves some resistance. Conservatism should not be equated with right-wing authoritarianism and dogmatism so glibly.

LEE AND WARR'S "BALANCED F SCALE"

Origins
The final two approaches to right-wing authoritarianism which we shall

consider in this review have not received a great deal of attention from other researchers. Both of them (Lee and Warr, 1969; Kohn, 1972) apparently began as nothing more than attempts to balance the "F Scale" against direction-of-wording effects. Lee and Warr chose, however, not to pursue this goal by writing contrait versions of the original F Scale items; such attempts have resulted in very unsatisfactory "reversals," as we shall see in the next chapter. Instead, they collected responses to an unpublished set of 100 items developed by Christie, Lane, N. Sanford, Stern and Webster for a study of "stereotypy." (These items were reportedly culled "from the research literature on the measurement of authoritarianism" (Smith, 1965) and fifty of them were written in the contrait direction.) The 100 items were administered to 54 Peace Corps volunteers undergoing training at Princeton University, and standard Likert scaling procedures were used to determine the most cohesive items in the pool. A 30-item "Balanced F Scale" (or, the Lee and Warr Scale), resulted, which was administered to 421 undergraduate and 135 graduate students at Princeton.[32] The responses of this large cross-validating sample were merged with those of the initial Peace Corps trainees, and the psychometric properties of the scale were reported most completely for the composite sample of 610.

The average interitem correlation among the items on this test was the same as that typically associated with the original F Scale and the C Scale, namely .13. Lee and Warr were not troubled by this low figure, however, arguing instead that since "authoritarianism" is a multifaceted construct, the items should not be too highly intercorrelated. (They did not, however, address themselves to the problems inherent in using multi-faceted constructs to account for behavior.) The split-half reliability of the scale was .84, and its test-retest reliability over a six-week period among 34 Princeton undergraduates was .82.

The multifaceted nature of the test became apparent when factor analyses were performed on the responses of the 610 subjects. A maximum-likelihood analysis (Lawley and Maxwell, 1963) indicated that ten factors were necessary to account for the correlations among the 30 items. These factors were rotated according to Varimax criteria and were named "Parental Authority," "Censorship," "Institutional Toughmindedness," "Authoritarian Submission," "Conventionalism," "Authoritarian Aggression," "Authoritarian Moralism," "Religious Belief," "National Assertiveness" and "Military Ideology." These titles play no subsequent role in the literature on Lee and Warr's scale, so we shall not pick bones over factor interpretations here. They did account for only a pittance of the total variance on the test (e.g., the first three factors account for 4%, 3% and 5% of the variance respectively following rotation) but maximum likelihood factoring does not attempt to maximize the variance explained.

A principal components analysis, which does seek to maximize this, was also performed on the data, and five factors emerged which were Varimax rotated. Lee and Warr argued that these factors were various combinations of the 10 factors listed above, but again there is no point in pursuing the matter. The item loadings on these factors and the amount of variance they controlled were not reported.

The theoretical significance of these findings had to be determined *post hoc* since the conceptualization of authoritarianism which Christie et al. had used to compile the 100 statements for their item pool was unknown. Lee and Warr, however, did not subsequently define authoritarianism either in terms of the 10 or five factors which emerged from the factor analyses, or in any other terms. Their work thus produced a 30-item attitude scale which apparently taps quite a number of different factors implied to be relevant to the rubric "authoritarianism." One is at a loss to know more precisely what scores on the test are meant to measure.

Empirical correlations

Lee and Warr investigated the empirical validity of their test by seeking its correlations with various other tests among samples of 54, 60, 64 and 152 unspecified subjects, using largely unspecified procedures. Their scale correlated .15 to .39 (ignoring signs) with various measures of "rigidity," .17 to .35 with the D Scale, .14 to .29 with measures of intelligence, not at all with the Embedded Figures Test, and .51 with Tomkins' C Scale (1964). Lee and Warr also reported that scores on their scale correlated .40 with accuracy in predicting which undergraduates would join which Princeton dining clubs (the measure of accuracy being only vaguely described). There was also a tendency ($r = .43$) for high scoring subjects to be more "evaluative" when perceiving others. Furthermore, they tended in another study to prefer certain academic majors, and to do better in certain kinds of courses than in others.

Lee and Warr also reported that scores on their scale correlated .43 with prejudice against blacks. By way of "known-group" comparisons, the Peace Corps trainees scored rather low on the scale, a group of fundamentalist students scored high. Young Americans for Freedom tested on two campuses scored significantly higher than a group of "neutral" students; Americans for Democratic Action students scored much lower. As usual, no item analyses were reported for any of these findings.

I have been able to locate only three papers which report using Lee and Warr's scale in subsequent research, and they have largely reported nonfindings. Warr and Coffman (1970) investigated the hypothesis that authoritarians are more likely to use extreme categories in judging various stimuli (Mogar, 1960). But neither the Lee and Warr Scale nor the D Scale produced any significant relationships with extremity of response to a host of stimuli in four different student samples. Cook and Smith (1974) used Lee and Warr's test as a criterion measure in a study of person perception involving a variety of English subjects. Test scores were correlated with peer rankings of "authoritarians" among same-sex subjects who knew one another, and the mean correlations within the various groups ranged from −.23 to +.60. The mean of these means (sample sizes varying from 10 to 14) was about .12, however. Finally, Warr and Rogers (1974) used the test along with an English Ethnocentrism Scale to study the extremity-of-response issue again, using another student sample. The results were presented in terms of the E Scale scores, however.

Evaluation

Lee and Warr's contribution to the study of authoritarianism has essentially been in the application of scaling techniques to an existing item pool. The test which resulted may be characterized as an improvement on the original F Scale insofar as it attains comparable interitem correlations without the possible binding effects of response sets. But the test is still quite multidimensional, and the evidence for its empirical usefulness is unconvincing. Conceptually, Lee and Warr have little to tell us about their construct beyond saying that it is multifaceted, which is, of course, leaving a great deal unsaid. It is yet another test searching for its identity after the fact of its creation.

KOHN'S CONCEPTUALIZATION OF AUTHORITARIANISM AND REBELLIOUSNESS

The last approach to right-wing authoritarianism we shall consider is that of Kohn (1972), who, like Lee and Warr, set out to develop a balanced version of the F Scale. The development proceeded on rather different lines, however. Kohn initially tried to write contrait versions of the original F Scale items, a tack Lee and Warr and others had warned against. Even though his criteria for an acceptable reversal were not as demanding as one might wish he was able to write only nine "successful" reversals.

He therefore repeated the process with items from another "F Scale" (by Pflaum, 1964), and was successful in six more instances. Both the original items and their reversals were then compiled, with a fixed but unspecified number of statements separating each element of a pair, to form a 30-item attitude survey named the Authoritarianism-Rebellion (A-R) Scale.

The reader will note that the test's format is different from any we have encountered before, consisting of 15 pairs of items rather than 30 statements which were more distinctly different. It is quite possible that some subjects would recognize the "flip-flop" nature of the test as they made their way through it. Kohn offered no explanation of why he chose to "balance" the F Scale in this particular way.

Following its development, the A-R Scale was cross-validated with unspecified samples of 58 and 69 subjects (presumably York University students, and possibly upperclassmen enrolled in advanced psychology courses). The only reliability data reported were corrected split-half coefficients of .81 and .78 respectively. If these are a true index of the scale's alpha reliability, then the average interitem correlation on the A-R Scale would have been about .12 in these Canadian samples, which represents no improvement over previous efforts. Kohn did not report on the interitem correlations.

Responses to the 15 original items correlated only −.22 (in both samples) with responses to the set of 15 "reversals," suggesting either the presence of very powerful response sets, or that the contrait items were not very good reversals of the originals. Kohn noted that there was considerable double disagreement with the original-reversal pairs, but said he was not concerned about this because it was not response acquiescence. However, if one is trying to build a test with pairs of matched items (which Kohn was), then double nay-saying is just as problematical as double yea-saying.

Actually, the extensive double-disagreement in Kohn's data is not too surprising. Rorer (1965) had previously pointed out that many "reversals" of F Scale items found in the literature were just as hard to agree with as the originals were. For example, if one is trying to draw agreement from subjects who disagree with the original statement, "Obedience is the mother of success," a statement such as, "Obedience is the mother of enslavement," is bound to be a poor statement for subjects who think that obedience is not automatically associated with either success or enslavement. In fact, the above pair of items is from Kohn's test, and many other examples of such poor reversing could be cited.

Construct validity of the A-R Scale: two independent constructs?
The most distinctive feature of Kohn's investigation emerged from factor analyses of the A-R Scale. No information about the initial factoring was reported in the 1972 paper, but it appears to have been some version of a principal components solution (Kohn, 1974, p. 253). Both Varimax and Oblimin rotations were performed. In the former, five factors allegedly accounted for 26%, 9%, 6%, 7%, and 4%, respectively, of the test's variance. The item loadings for this Varimax solution were not reported, however. Instead, those of the oblique rotation were given. All of the 15 contrait items had loadings in excess of .40 on Factor I, while 10 of the fifteen protrait items loaded at that level on Factor II. Kohn termed Factor I "Rebelliousness" and Factor II "General Right-Wing Authoritarianism." Factor III was labelled "Authoritarian Cynicism;" Factors IV and V were more difficult to interpret.

The interesting feature of this analysis was the discovery that the five Oblimin-rotated factors were still essentially orthogonal, the average intercorrelation among them being −.02. In particular, Factors I and II correlated only .06. Kohn interpreted this to mean that rebellion and authoritarianism are not end points on a single dimension (as they are usually conceived to be) but rather are two independent dimensions. He concluded that among the general North American student population there was no tendency for right-wing authoritarians to be more accepting of things as they are, nor was there any tendency for nonauthoritarian students to be more rebellious.

Kohn did not dwell upon the implications of this conceptualization, even to explain the apparent contradiction in claiming that authoritarian submission and rebelliousness are independent. The evidence which led Kohn to this novel interpretation is subject to an obvious alternate interpretation, however, namely that the correlation between protrait and contrait items on a test are lowered by direction-of-wording effects. Balancing a test with protrait and contrait items does not prevent a response set such as acquiescence from affecting responses to the individual items; it merely prevents these tendencies from affecting the summed score on the test. A tendency to yea-say will (1) raise the correlations among protrait items, (2) similarly raise the correlations among contrait items, and (3) lower the correlations between protrait and contrait items. Nay-saying has the same effects. Thus the fact that protrait and contrait items loaded on different factors could simply be due to such response sets. Kohn himself noted that there was extensive double disagreement among his item pairs.

Empirical correlations of the A-R Scale
Kohn and Mercer (1971) reported that A-R Scale scores were negatively associated with reported use of marijuana and psychedelic drugs among a sample of York University students, but not with amphetamine use. Kohn (1972) reported correlations of .66 with Right Opinionation and −.32 with Left Opinionation among York students who completed an unpublished version of Rokeach's (1960) Opinionation Scale. There was also a tendency for older and less religious students to score lower on the test. On the other hand, there was no significant relationship with sex, family income, size of the hometown or participation in extracurricular activities. The scale was also administered to students affiliated with five political groups, being (from left to right) Trotskyists, New Democrats, Liberals, Conservatives and members of the Edmund Burke Society. Overall, there was a significant difference among the several groups, but the Trotskyists were not significantly differentiated from the New Democrats, nor were the Liberals different from the Conservatives. Following the well-established precedent, Kohn (1974) described these validation studies as having been "highly successful."

The British version of the A-R Scale
Kohn (1974) reported on a British version of the A-R Scale consisting of nine pairs of protrait-contrait items and twelve unmatched statements. (He did not say why he relaxed the "pairing requirement" among these items.) This test had a better split-half reliability (.81 to .93) among samples of undergraduates in England, which would indicate a relatively high interitem correlation of about .20. The protrait and contrait items also correlated better with one another (−.42 to −.56, compared to −.22 in the Canadian student samples). Kohn attributes this improvement in internal consistency to "greater ideological consistency" among English students, rather than to any superiority of the British version of the scale over the Canadian one.

A principal components factor analysis was performed on the responses of all 244 English students, and eight factors with eigenvalues greater than 1.0 were extracted. Following another tradition, Kohn mistakenly cited the substantial loadings on the first unrotated factor as evidence for "the validity of the scale." (If it were valid evidence that a single factor dominated the scale, it would of course contradict the "two-independent-factors" interpretation we just considered—a point Kohn does not comment upon.) Only five of the eight factors were retained and rotated to Varimax and Oblimin criteria; again, rebellious items tended to dominate Factor I in the oblique solution, while authoritarian items loaded on Factor II. The correlation between Factor I and II in the oblique rotation would appear to be substantial, given the correlations of −.42 to −.56 between the protrait and contrait items. Such correlation would also disconfirm Kohn's original finding of no relationship, the finding that led to the theory that authoritarianism and rebelliousness are independent. We do not know what the Factor I–Factor II correlation was in the English sample, however, since it was not reported.

The British A-R Scale correlated .81 with Wilson and Patterson's C Scale, .56 with Warr, Faust and Harrison's (1967) British Ethnocentrism Scale, .67 with an Intolerance of Ambiguity Scale and .48 with a 20-item version of the D Scale. Overall "Communists," Labour, Liberal and Conservative students scored differently on the test, but only the Conservatives' score was significantly different from any other. Clearer differences were found among active members of student political groups, but even then, Labour and Liberal supporters were not different. There were also relationships with atheism and with church attendance, as there had been in Canada.

The procedures used in collecting the data were reported only sketchily, as were the methods used to draw the samples, the instructions and rationale given the subjects, and the organization of the test materials. Also, no item analyses for the predictive relationships were reported. Finally, although Kohn had the data at hand, he did not explain whether or not the A-R Scale had greater empirical validity with the criteria used than did the C Scale.

Evaluation

It is difficult to assess scales which have small literatures. It is even more difficult to assess the A-R Scale because it is not clear whether it should be considered one scale or two. Kohn himself is plainly uncertain on this very fundamental point. His 1971 paper (with Mercer) on drug use analyzed "authoritarianism-rebellion" scores in terms of one dimension, namely the summed score over the entire test. The 1972 factor analysis led to the two-independent-factors interpretation, as we have seen. The 1974 British data seem inhospitable to this interpretation, however, and Kohn handles the ambiguity by reporting empirical relationships in terms of both overall scores on the scale and scores on the two "subscales." Compounding his problems with the two-factor interpretation is the fact that the two supposedly independent factors have very similar relationships with most of the criteria reported upon in the 1972 and 1974 papers. The closest he comes to setting matters straight is at the end of the 1974 paper (p. 253) when he speculates about the one "thing" the A-R Scale measures.

It is not too difficult to untangle all of this, however, since the only evidence for the two-factor model (the 1972 factor analysis) is open to the more straightforward interpretation given above. In fact, then, the A-R Scale is rather like all the other authoritarianism scales we have studied in this critique: very multidimensional, weak, and possessing an unimposing (and very underreported) pattern of association with other variables.

EVALUATION OF THE EXISTING SOCIAL PSYCHOLOGICAL LITERATURE ON RIGHT-WING AUTHORITARIANISM

This review of the research on right-wing authoritarianism is probably one of the most exhaustive and exhausting critiques to be found in experimental psychology. It may also be one of the most depressing: after 35 years of research involving hundreds of studies,[33] using many thousands of subjects, and costing quite a large amount of money, we may rightly ask ourselves what we really know about right-wing authoritarianism. I submit that we still know practically nothing. (I hope the reader does not believe, after completing this review, that this opinion is being offered recklessly and without a detailed examination of the facts.)

I stated in the Introduction that one of the major goals of this critique would be to illustrate how pointless it is in the long run to do the kind of research we have just examined. Right-wing authoritarianism has been one of the most heavily investigated topics in social psychology, so the failure to make progress seems to indicate that something is terribly wrong with the way this research has proceeded. It is not hard to identify several major failings, nor is it difficult to find other literatures suffering from the same fatal problems. We might summarize them as follows:

1 Conceptualizations have been very casually constructed: From the mushiness of the Berkeley model to Kohn's confusion over the relationship between authoritarianism and rebelliousness, the theoretical models advanced have been loosely concocted and sometimes downright superficial. Defining elements have been stuck together, added and deleted and added again, and have hardly ever been given the sort of detailed

exposition which convinces one that the investigator himself has a clear idea of what he is talking about. One can hardly imagine a greater handicap for scientific investigation than such muddled thinking at the gate. But such has been the rule, not the exception, in this literature.

2 Scales have usually been developed very quickly and published long before they were ready for useful scientific investigation: A question which never seems to have been asked is, "Why should test development have been halted when it was?" The Berkeley investigators did three item-analysis studies, developing their scales, and then stopped; Eysenck did one; Rokeach, five; Wilson, three; Lee and War, one; and Kohn, two. Each of these scales is quite deficient psychometrically, as we have seen, and would certainly have profited from more work. Why then were they published when they were?

The most general answer is that scale development ended when the test had an "acceptable" level of reliability. But "acceptable reliability" varies from investigator to investigator, and is typically between .75 and .82 where a third or more of the test's variance is still unreliable. Sometimes even these levels were achieved only by making the test longer — by adding more and more loosely related items, at terrible cost to the scale's unidimensionality.

It may be that the tests' inventors, and the hundreds of investigators who used the scales in their research programs, did not appreciate how unreliable and invalid the tests were. Or, they may have known it but thought that "poor measures are better than no measures at all." But are they? Where have they got us in over three decades?

3 The research which has been done with these scales has been quite deficient methodologically: We sometimes find the most elementary errors in the research. More often, however, we find disturbing omissions: It is important to describe sampling procedures and sample compositions, instructions used, procedures followed, the reasons why some subjects were discarded, mean scores, which statistical tests were used, and so on. Similarly, it is important to mention data on reliability, variance accounted for, correlations between factors and tests of significance. "Simple oversight" cannot justify inappropriate and irrelevant comparisons, ignoring disconfirmations for the few findings that "came through," and so on. It is not disturbing that we seldom encounter item analyses in this literature? And that investigators have been so amiss in testing their scales against others when claiming superior validity?

Another way in which researchers have seemed unwilling to acknowledge difficulties in their findings is in their tendency to "snowball" partial confirmations from previous studies into an impressive array of citations which supposedly demonstrate a model's wide-ranging validity. Outright failures and qualified successes often become unqualified successes soon after they were first reported. Bibliographic citations are sometimes highly selective and self-serving. Contradictory interpretations from different studies live independent lives. Glowing appraisals of one's own "highly successful" and "remarkable" findings can be found, as we have seen, in research programs which have been anything but highly successful.

None of this ultimately does the scientific community any good. Mushy concepts and poor scales and crummy experiments do not lead to anything lasting and worthwhile. All the cosmeticizing and disguising and slanting and crowing in the world is still going to leave us, plop, in square one as far as understanding human behavior is concerned.

4 The vast majority of papers in this literature report the results of one-shot, unreplicated studies: In this literature we seldom find a series of investigations which obtained an initial finding, tested its generalizability, explored its nuances, and then reported the results to the scientific community. Instead, we find, again and again, instances in which a one-shot finding (a) could not be replicated at all, or (b) proved far more restricted than was initially supposed, or (c) was far more complicated than had been imagined. Typically, the literature then ties itself into an unfathomable knot, as one-shot study piles on top of one-shot study. Then the area is abandoned. That, in microcosm, is what has happened to research on authoritarianism. Right-wing authoritarianism has not gone away by 1981, but researchers have, bewildered and disgusted.

"First rights" to replication belong to the initial investigator, and he ought to exercise that right before he publishes his findings. Why does research have to be reported one drip at a time? Whatever happened to the norm that scientists ought to be careful about what they say and believe?

The papers in this literature are so replete with conceptual, methodological, analytical, and reportorial errors that one should wonder how they were ever accepted for publication. Perhaps editors thought that such papers might stimulate thinking about a problem, lead to more research, and hence contribute to progress. If so, they were playing their role in a cycle which began when a test was offered, even though it was quite poor, and used, because it was better than nothing, or because it seemed "to work," or because everybody else was using it, or because editors were accepting papers based upon it. But where is the progress?

Are the recently proposed models of authoritarianism any better than the first ones? Are the latest research papers any better than those of 30 years ago? Are we closer to understanding right-wing authoritarianism today than we were in 1950? Do we even know how to sensibly and usefully define the term yet?

The question arises as to whether the failures in this field also occur in other areas of investigation. The failures may not be universal, but it is hard to believe from a perusal of the journals that they are not common.

It has been observed lately that social psychology is undergoing a crisis in confidence (Elms, 1975, Moscovici, 1972, Smith 1972, 1973, Greenwald, 1976). There is a distinct lack of optimism among some scholars that this discipline will ever produce the sound explanations of behavior which were once thought to be just a matter of time and money. Research in right-wing authoritarianism is one of our most notable failures, notable because such an enormous effort has been directed at understanding it over the years. But it is easy to see why understanding has not advanced. Scientific research does not necessarily and automatically lead to progress. The fact that research grants are awarded and facilities are made available and studies are plentiful and publications abound does not mean we are getting anywhere as a science, all appearances notwithstanding. All this feverish activity can be largely for naught, ultimately an exercise in futility, if the research industry mainly reinforces behaviors which compromise the scientific endeavor. And to what extent does it not?

The response set issue

2

Many of the conclusions reached in chapter 1 were shaped by the possibility that response sets affect the answers given to authoritarianism scales. Certainly it seemed that such sets had greatly increased the F Scale's correlations with other unidirectionally worded tests. Nevertheless, it has proven exceedingly difficult to find direct proof of this effect, although the search for such evidence is nearly as old as the F Scale itself. This chapter attempts to provide that proof.

HISTORY OF THE DEBATE

By "response sets" here is meant what Cronbach meant in 1946: "any tendency causing a person consistently to make different responses to test items than he would have had the same content been presented in different form" (Cronbach, 1946, p. 476).[1] This is a broad definition, conceivably including such behaviors as (a) marking responses on a certain part of a page (which Likert, 1932 called "space error"); (b) preferring certain categories on a response scale, like "yes" or "agree" when one really has no opinion (Lorge, 1937); and (c) personality-based tendencies to be agreeable and conciliatory.

Although one can imagine many response sets which might affect a unidirectionally worded scale, most speculation about authoritarianism tests has involved "response acquiescence." This label has been attached both to the tendency to use "yes" categories (example #2 above) and to personality-based dispositions to be agreeable (example #3). Concern for the effects of such "yea-saying" dates back at least to Lentz (1938), who suggested that such a set might affect the measurement of "a trait such as conservatism-radicalism."

Controversy over the F Scale

The dates of the papers cited above show that concern about unbalanced attitude measures had been expressed several times before the Berkeley researchers began constructing their scales in the 1940s. The Berkeley team was aware of the potential criticisms and at one point Levinson and Sanford (1944) offered a defense of their first instrument, the unidirectionally worded Anti-Semitism (A-S) Scale, that was allowed to stand for later scales as well (*TAP*, p. 59): (a) individuals showed variability in their responses to the scales; (b) extreme positions were in fact avoided by the subjects; (c) similar results were obtained when a unidirectional protrait scale was placed in a larger questionnaire containing some contrait items; and (d) the Anti-Semitism Scale validly discriminated anti-Semitic people from others.

These arguments do not really address the issue, however. The fact of individual variability does not preclude response sets; the strength of the sets themselves could vary from person to person. Response sets could still be important factors on a test even if they do not carry subjects to extreme responses; in fact, a neutral response could result from a strong "yea-saying" tendency counterbalancing strong disagreement with an item's content. Placing contrait items around a protrait test will not stop response sets from affecting the summed score on the test; the contrait items have to contribute to (half of) the test score. And a test can still have some validity if response sets determine part (or even most) of the scale's variance.

Levinson and Sanford's defense of unidirectionally worded scales notwithstanding, the Berkeley researchers themselves tried to develop some contrait items for their tests. The Political-Economic Conservatism Scale contained a mixture of conservative and liberal items throughout its development. Moreover, a few antiauthoritarian items were tried out in the initial stages of the F Scale's development, although none of them survived the item analyses.

It may be easier to conceive of good items to tap a psychological construct than it is to think of items for its opposite(s). But it is also possible that a tide of response sets, produced by the far more numerous proauthoritarian items, was running against the potential F Scale contraits. As noted in chapter 1, response sets will increase the correlations among protrait items, and also among contrait items. If most of the statements in an item pool are worded in one direction (e.g., the protrait), and items are selected for a scale according to the usual Likert criteria, response sets will bias the selection in favor of the more numerous kind of item (i.e., the protraits).

As we saw in chapter 1, the Berkeley investigators' use of unidirectionally worded scales was soon criticized by other social scientists (Hyman and Sheatsley, 1954), and the issue was substantive. The most impressive finding in the 900-plus pages of *The Authoritarian Personality* was the high correlation developed between the E and F Scales. But this relationship, and those subsequently obtained with other unbalanced measures, could have resulted to an appreciable degree from shared response sets. In particular, it was suggested that response acquiescence could be binding the scales together.

Other investigators have pointed out, however, that if the F Scale is affected by response acquiescence, it might be a blessing in disguise, for the tendency to agree with test items might itself be a manifestation of authoritarianism. According to this argument, which is still unresolved, the unidirectional wording of the test would increase the scale's validity rather than hurt it.

Evidence that the F Scale is susceptible to response sets
How did researchers attempt to determine if the F Scale taps acquiescence or some other response set by virtue of its unidirectional items? In the main two approaches were taken. One approach, used a number of times during the mid-fifties and early sixties, was to construct "reversals" of the original F Scale items. These reversals were items which attempted to say the same thing as the original item, but in the opposite way, so that the authoritarian response was disagreement. Best known among these studies are the papers of Bass (1955), Chapman and Campbell (1957), Christie, Havel and Seidenberg (1958), Jackson and Messick (1957), Leavitt, Hax and Roche (1955), and Peabody (1961)—with the paper by Christie et al. being particularly influential. All of these researchers followed the strategy of administering a set of the original F Scale items and a set of reversals to the same subjects, and then determining the correlation between summed scores on the two sets. If subjects were consistently responding to the content of the items, then one would expect a high correlation between the summed scores (a positive correlation if the keying of the reversals had been inverted). In fact, however, no one ever found a very high correlation. Instead, there was a lot of double-agreeing and double-disagreeing with original reversal pairs, and the investigators took this to be an indication that response sets were at work. For a number of reasons the response set of acquiescence acquired the status of chief culprit (although Rokeach [1963] suggested that the double-agreements and double-disagreements may have been

caused by the subjects' lying, or by "double-think.") The response acquiescence interpretation stood firm until 1965.

A second line of inquiry also seemed to connect acquiescence with the F Scale. Beginning with Cohn (1953), a number of investigators reported positive correlations between scores on the original F Scale and a variety of measures of "yes-saying." Cohn's measure consisted of a collection of seemingly unrelated items from the Minnesota Multiphasic Personality Inventory (MMPI). Chapman and Campbell (1957) used a diverse set of 74 questionnaire items; Bass (1956) developed a Social Acquiescence Scale (SAS) consisting of 56 proverbs and "cultural wisdoms"; Gage, Leavitt and Stone (1957) used a true-false information test with impossibly hard items. Couch and Kenniston (1960) developed a 360-item test supposedly balanced against measuring any psychological construct. All of these researchers found significant correlations between their measures of yes-saying and scores on some version of the original F Scale.

Challenges to the evidence
The conclusion based on these studies—that F Scale scores reflect, in part, yes-saying tendencies, and that such tendencies are manifestations of a general personality structure (Jackson and Messick, 1958)—came a little unstuck in 1962. McGee reported that the F Scale correlated only with verbal-content measures of yes-saying, and that in general six different measures of yes-saying had little relationship with one another. Forehand (1962) reported similar findings among several additional measures of yes-saying.

The major attack on both lines of evidence came, however, in 1965 in an astonishing paper by Leonard Rorer. With regard to the many reversal studies, Rorer argued convincingly that there was no need to attribute the double-agreements and double-disagreements in these studies to response sets, since in numerous examples the yes-yeses and the no-noes were sensible and logically consistent responses. Suppose, for example, a person believed that some, but not all, people need to have complete faith in a supernatural power. Such a person could reject, quite reasonably, both the original F Scale item, "Every person should have complete faith in some supernatural power whose decisions he obeys without question," and its Bass (1955) reversal, "No person should have complete faith in some supernatural power." Since all of the reversal studies used such inadequately reversed items, the fact that such reversed scales did not correlate highly with the original scale proves nothing about response sets. Samelson and Yates (1967) later reinforced this argument by pointing out that the reversal studies did not control for the relative extremeness as well as the direction of the responses to the reversals.

As for the second line of evidence, Rorer argued persuasively that the correlations between F Scale scores and various measures of yes-saying (a) were largely limited to measures using meaningful verbal content; (b) indicated that only a small amount of the F Scale's variance was attributable to such a response set; and (c) could be more parsimoniously explained as being due to shared content. For example, the reader will recall that the SAS (Bass, 1956) consists of numerous proverbs and cultural wisdoms. But the F Scale was intended to measure, among other things, conventionalism. Some of the items on the SAS even sound as though they could come from an authoritarianism scale (which later on, in fact, they did; Pflaum, 1964): "Our chief want in life is somebody who will make us do what we can"; "No principle is more noble or holy than that of true obedience"; "Obedience is the mother of success"; "To be happy, always stay within the law." One can hardly be surprised that responses to these items correlated with responses to the F Scale; the correlation proves nothing about response sets.

Rorer's chief goal was to challenge the widely held conclusion that "response styles" are an identifiable aspect of personality which have significant effects upon personality and opinion inventories.[2] But his observations threw the study of authoritarianism into even greater confusion. Things were bad enough when the interpretation of F Scale scores was clouded by the possibility that the scores reflected response sets. Things were worse when researchers argued about whether response sets would help or hurt the test's validity. Now one was not even sure response sets affected tests like the F Scale.

ADDITIONAL EVIDENCE THAT THE F SCALE IS SUSCEPTIBLE TO RESPONSE SETS

Campbell, Seigman and Rees 1967) observed that Rorer's review of the literature neglected two papers which provided a third line of evidence that the F Scale is susceptible to direction-of-wording effects. These two papers (Chapman and Campbell, 1959a, 1959b) were based on a study in which subjects completed, over two testing sessions, both protrait and contrait versions of the F Scale, E Scale, and the Taylor Manifest Anxiety Scale (MAS) (Taylor, 1953). The contrait version of the F Scale,

TABLE 1

Direction-of-wording in correlations among the F Scale of authoritarian
personality trends, the Ethnocentrism Scale, and the
Manifest Anxiety Scale

Scale	F_p	F_c	E_p	E_c	MA_p	MA_c
F_p	(.71)	.53	.76	.56	.41	.27
F_c	.29	(.42)	.36	.58	.12	.10
E_p	.57	.21	(.80)	.94	.13	.06
E_c	.39	.31	.70	(.69)	.05	.10
MA_p	.32	.07	.11	.04	(.87)	.98
MA_c	.21	.06	.05	.08	.84	(.85)

Note: Reliabilities in the diagonal are based upon Kuder-Richardson Formula 20.
Values above the diagonal are corrected for attenuation. From "Direction-of-wording
effects in the relationships between scales" by D.T. Campbell, C.R. Siegman, and
M.B. Rees, *Psychological Bulletin*, 1967, 68, 293-303. Copyright 1967 by the American
Psychological Association. Reprinted by permission.

which was based on reversals developed by Bass (1955) and Chapman and
Campbell (1957), had a very poor reliability (.42) and the usual low
correlation with the original version of the scale (.29). But the E Scale,
and especially the MAS, seem to have been more successfully reversed
(see Table 1). The availability of alternate forms of the same test, differing
totally in the direction of their items' wording, enabled one to test for
direction-of-wording effects on the original F Scale.

Table 1 shows that the original F Scale (F_p) had higher correlations
with the protrait versions of both the E and the MAS than with the contrait versions. The differences were statistically significant, whether
corrected for attenuation or not. While the data are not consistently
convincing (the contrait version of the F Scale [F_c] shows direction-of-
wording effects for the E Scale, but not for the MAS), Campbell et al.
found similar relationships in other studies for both the F and the Dogmatism Scales.

FURTHER RESEARCH ON RESPONSE SETS
AND THE F SCALE

The results of Campbell, Seigman, and Rees (1967) are an extension of
our earlier observation that the F Scale correlates much higher with
protrait-worded tests than it does with other measures. While they

strongly imply that response sets affect answers to the F Scale, they do not directly show this. We do not know how well the content of the contrait version represented the issues presented by the original F Scale. Nor do we know how much of the very large difference in shared variance attributed to direction-of-wording effects is actually due to differences in content. Furthermore the results do not indicate the nature of the effects at work. The higher correlation F_p had with E_p might have been caused by double-agreement or double-disagreement or both. Finally, they do not indicate whether the F Scale's validity is improved or hindered by these direction-of-wording effects. These are the questions I set out to answer in 1968.

The strategy followed
Unlike Campbell et al., my goal was to write a balanced F Scale whose content was nearly identical to the original's. Comparing this test, on which direction-of-wording effects would cancel out when the item scores were summed, with the original F Scale would then directly indicate any effects due to response sets.

The reader who has plowed through the critique of the F Scale in chapter 1 will understand that I was not attempting to develop a viable measure of authoritarianism by balancing the F Scale. A hodge-podge of items balanced against response sets is still a hodge-podge of items. Instead, the research was undertaken solely to answer the questions raised above about response sets, for clarification of the F Scale's literature, and for the insights we might gain about the factors which shape responses to attitude scales.

The research program involved four steps. First, I developed a set of F Scale reversals whose meanings were the opposite to the originals. There was nothing new in this approach; the trick was to do it. Secondly, I substituted these items into the F Scale, along with their opposite keying, thus balancing the summed score on the test against response sets. The variance of this balanced scale and that of the original were each partitioned in a way that isolated direciton-of-wording effects. Thirdly, I identified the response sets at work. And finally, I compared the empirical validities of the two scales to see if the response set effects increased or detracted from the original F Scale's usefulness.

Developing true reversals: criteria for adequate contrait items
The experience of previous investigators indicated that researchers cannot intuitively judge if a contrait item raises the same issues, in all their

nuances, that the original items do. Questionnaire statements have different meanings for different people. I therefore decided to test contrait versions of the F Scale's items until I found a set whose statistical properties matched those of the originals. This proved to be a long but unavoidable process.

It may appear easy to determine if a contrait item is evoking the opposite response from a protrait item. People who strongly agree with the protrait item should strongly disagree with the contrait; those who slightly disagree with the first should slightly agree with the second, and so on.* But there are several reasons why matters do not turn out so neatly. For one thing, there is instability in subjects' responses to surveys, and considerable instability when responses are analyzed item by item. A subject who strongly agrees with an item may only slightly agree with the same item a week later—or even disagree with it. The measurement error attending the original F Scale statements limits the degree to which the contrait items can match the protraits. Beyond this, there is the object of the search: response sets that produce double-agreements and/or double-disagreements. The more response set determine answers to original F Scale items, the harder it will be for any contrait item to evoke opposite responses.

These considerations bear significantly on the criteria for measuring a reversal's adequacy. First of all, the correlation between responses to the protrait and contrait items should be high if the reversal captures the essence of the original item. But it can only approach the protrait's test-retest reliability, and response sets could keep it far short of that. The one-week test-retest reliability of most original F Scale items is between .60 and .70. I tried for protrait-contrait correlations of at least .40, and higher if possible.

Secondly, the mean of responses to the contrait item should, with reversed keying, approximately equal the protrait's mean, if response sets of yea-saying and nay-saying are equally strong. Again, measurement error produces an instability of about ± 0.40 for most items upon retesting. I therefore tried to develop contrait items whose mean would be within 0.40 of the protrait's mean.

Thirdly, the variance of responses to a contrait item should approxi-

---

* The F Scale was developed with a seven-point scoring system, the possible responses ranging from "strongly agree" which was coded a "7" to "strongly disagree" which was coded a "1." "No response" was coded a "4" which represents the neutral point on the response scale.

mately equal the protrait's variance if both items are tapping the same sentiments. The standard deviations of responses to original F Scale items varied about ± 0.20 over a one-week period. I therefore tried to develop contrait items whose variance would match that of the protraits within this limit.

The three criteria above refer to properties of the individual items. I also imposed criteria on the set of original F Scale items which would be replaced to form a balanced scale. It was important that they not be any particular set of items on the scale, especially the items which made the greatest psychometric contribution to the test (e.g., see Table 1 in chapter 1). Reversing a disproportionate number of these statements would give the contrait items on a balanced F Scale greater significance (i.e., higher item-whole correlations) than a more representative set of items would have. It would also be improper to reverse most of the more stable items on the original F Scale, for such contrait items would themselves probably have greater reliability than otherwise warranted. I therefore imposed the following additional set criteria: The replaced items should not have, as a group, unusually high (or low) correlations with the rest of the original F Scale, nor should they have unusually high (or low) test-retest reliabilities. These criteria meant in effect that I could not merely reverse the items on the F Scale which were easiest to reverse, easiest because they were the most meaningful and stable. I also had to reverse a considerable number of the "junk" items.[3]

The item development studies
Beginning in October, 1968, with the contrait items developed by Christie, Havel, and Seidenberg (1958), I conducted ten studies which tested various contrait versions of the items on the F Scale. In all of these studies, introductory psychology students at the University of Manitoba answered the original versions and experimental reversals of F Scale items. I noted the adequacy of each reversal, and this usually led to further item modification and testing. These studies are of little interest in themselves, but the reader can get some idea of the difficulties involved in this process by examining Table 2, which lists 15 unsuccessful attempts I made over a two-year period to reverse item 1 of the F Scale: "Obedience and respect for authority are the most important virtues children should learn." It is instructive to note how many different ways there are to fail to say something.

My tenth and final reversal development study was done in September, 1970, and should be reported in detail, for the data from this investi-

TABLE 2

Fifteen unsuccessful attempts to reverse item #1 of the original F Scale

---

1   Obedience and respect for authority are the least important things children should learn. (Mean off)

2   Obedience and respect for authority are about the least important things children should learn. (Mean off)

3   Obedience and respect for authority are certainly not the most important things children should learn. (Reported in Altemeyer, 1969, but the variance is off)

4   Obedience and respect for authority is one of the least important things children should learn. (Mean off)

5   Obedience and respect for authority are among the less important things children should learn (Mean off)

6   Obedience and respect for authority are among the less important things children need to learn. (Mean off)

7   Obedience and respect for authority are without a doubt not the most important things children should learn. (Correlation off)

8   Obedience and respect for authority are not particularly important things for children to learn. (Correlation, mean and variance all off)

9   There are many things children should learn which are more important than obedience and respect for authority. (Mean off)

10 Obedience and respect for authority are *not* the most important virtues children should learn. (Correlation off)

11 Children should be taught obedience and respect for authority, but there are other much more important things children need to learn. (Mean and variance off)

12 There are many things children should learn which are considerably more important than obedience and respect for authority. (Mean off)

13 Children should be encouraged to doubt and openly question authority rather than learning obedience and respect for it. (Correlation off)

14 Rather than learning obedience and respect for authority, children should be encouraged to doubt and openly question it instead. (Correlation off)

15 There are a great many things children should learn which are more important than obedience and respect for authority. (Mean off)

---

gation determined the reversals which were used to balance the F Scale. Altogether, 516 introductory psychology students at the University of Manitoba,[4] serving in groups of 40–50, completed two versions of the F Scale over a one-week interval. One hundred and two subjects completed the original F Scale at both sessions, thus providing measures of the original items' test-retest reliability. Ninety-six subjects completed "balanced" F Scales at both sessions which used as contrait items the reversals developed by Christie, Havel, and Seidenberg (1958). On Form A of the test the odd-numbered items were contrait, and on Form B, the even-numbered statements were contrait. The sequence of surveys over the two testing sessions was AB for half the subjects, and BA for the rest. Three hundred and eighteen subjects completed one of three other pairs of "balanced" scales in counterbalanced Form A and Form B formats. These scales tested three different reversals which I had developed for each item during the preceding nine studies.[5]

At the first session the subjects were told, in tape recorded instructions, that the questionnaire was a poll of attitudes on social issues. At the second session, the questionnaire was explained as an attempt to measure the "testing reliability" of the poll. The instructions at the second session led subjects to expect the same items they had answered a week ago in either the same or an alternate form. The subjects, however, were asked to respond to the items according to how they felt at the moment, as if they had never seen the statements before. That, it was explained, was crucial in discovering a survey's "testing reliability." Within any given testing session, one-fifth of the subjects provided reliability data on the original scale, one-fifth provided data on the Christie et al. (1958) reversals, and the other three-fifths of the subjects provided data on my three sets of reversals. The survey booklets, which appeared very similar and had the same printed instructions, were distributed in fixed rotating order within the room.

Table 3 presents, for each item on the original F Scale except #13:

1 The test-retest reliability in this study of each original item (column 1).
2 The data from the sample which completed the Christie et al. items in terms of (a) the correlation of each Christie reversal with the corresponding original item (column 2); (b) the mean scores of the original item in this sample and the Christie reversal (columns 3 and 4) — responses to the reversals were scored with inverted keying, thus a good reversal would have approximately the same mean score as the original item; (c) the standard deviation of the responses to each original item in this sample and to each Christie reversal (column 5 and 6).
3 The same indices just described from whatever sample answered what seemed to be the best of my own reversals (columns 7 to 11).

The significance of the data in Table 3 is illustrated in item #1. The original version of this item had a one-week test-retest reliability of .62 in this study. When the Christie et al. sample answered this original item, their mean response was 4.67 (or about half way between the "neutral"

TABLE 3

Results of the September, 1970, reversal development study

Item	Original item's reliability	Christie et al. (1958) Reversals‡					My Best Reversals‡				
		Correlation with the original	X̄ original this sample reversal	X̄ this sample reversal	SD original, this sample reversal	SD reversal	Correlation with the original	X̄ original, this sample reversal	X̄ this sample reversal	SD original, this sample reversal	SD original, SD reversal
	(1)	(2)	(3)	(4)	(5)	(6)	(7)	(8)	(9)	(10)	(11)
1	.62	.08	4.67	4.94	2.07	2.05	.56	3.85	2.82	1.98	1.87
2	.72	.24	5.00	3.87	1.77	1.89	.38	4.98	5.64	1.91	1.47
3	.65	.15	4.72	2.42	1.97	1.66	.42	4.93	4.89	2.00	1.89
4	.74	.51	4.84	3.62	1.88	2.16	.53	5.11	5.11	1.88	1.77
5	.72	-.02	2.58	2.02	2.04	1.52	.46	2.22	2.40	1.77	1.85
6	.74	.08	2.92	2.79	1.79	1.89	.30	3.19	2.72	2.01	1.72
7	.64	.21	3.68	2.73	1.95	1.59	.56	3.72	3.58	2.08	1.98
8	.69	.44	3.66	3.92	1.99	1.98	.49	3.50	4.33	2.01	2.07
9	.69	.26	2.97	3.16	1.97	1.94	.54	2.80	3.20	1.79	2.06
10	.62	.51	3.19	3.66	1.86	2.12	.57	3.12	3.29	1.90	1.95
11	.49	.37	2.42	2.92	1.43	1.65	.40	2.65	2.44	1.58	1.64
12	.66	.23	3.90	3.38	1.92	1.83	.48	3.33	3.40	2.03	2.03
14	.74	.18	4.50	3.71	2.03	2.25	.34	4.50	5.61	1.92	1.66
15	.72	.45	2.86	2.27	2.07	1.67	.47	2.94	3.30	2.09	2.09
16	.63	-.21	2.29	1.64	1.77	1.00	.41	2.30	2.38	1.76	1.79
17	.63	.04	2.93	2.91	1.93	1.97	.50	2.75	2.39	1.95	1.77
18	.74	.63	3.44	4.05	2.05	2.09	.68	3.39	3.70	2.00	1.96
19	.61	-.07	4.46	2.50	1.83	1.58	.21	4.41	4.95	1.94	2.04
20	.72	No reversal was developed by Christie et al.					.49	2.88	2.89	2.07	2.02
21	.61	.23	3.16	2.17	1.94	1.48	.43	2.88	3.29	1.81	1.98
22	.75	-.03	4.34	2.67	1.86	1.53	.20	3.88	4.43	1.94	1.73
23	.55	.11	4.01	3.29	2.08	1.90	.45	3.26	4.51	1.92	2.02
24	.61	-.25	3.64	4.05	1.95	1.69	.47	3.88	3.34	1.84	1.93

25	.67	.32	2.04	2.78	1.62	1.95	.55	2.13	2.33	1.55	1.74
26	.57	.11	2.43	5.04	1.66	1.81	.66	2.22	1.74	1.47	1.34
27	.58	.27	3.90	4.05	2.13	2.03	.30	3.72	3.65	2.17	2.00
28	.66	-.10	3.66	2.32	1.91	1.29	.60	3.41	3.80	1.93	1.90
29	.60	No reversal was developed by Christie et al.					.45	2.82	4.05	1.87	2.06

‡Original items and reversals have been scored with opposite keys. Thus "strong agreement" with an original F Scale item was scored a "7," while "strong agreement" with a reversal was scored a "1."

and "slightly agree" points on the response scale), and these responses had a standard deviation of 2.07. The Christie et al. reversal of item #1 reads: "One of the most important things children should learn is when to disobey authorities." Table 3 reveals that responses to this item were virtually uncorrelated ($r = .08$) with responses to the original item #1. Thus despite the fact that the reversal's mean approximated the original's, and the standard deviations were virtually identical, the reversal could not be accepted. It showed no tendency to evoke the opposite response of that made to the original.

By September, 1970, I was working on my 13th, 14th and 15th attempts to reverse item #1 (see Table 2). The best of these reversals, which happened to be the 15th attempt, had an adequate correlation with the original (.56). But in this sample, where it so happened that subjects expressed a very slight disagreement with the original item, they tended to agree too much with the reversal. Thus the correlation of .56 (–.56 without reversed keying) indicated the original and reversal evoked opposite responses among the subjects. But if the reversal had truly captured the gist of the original, its mean would have been much closer to the original's.

Table 3 shows the following: First of all, while a few of the Christie items approached the criteria for an acceptable reversal, overall these reversals fell far short of the mark. Thus, while the mean test-retest reliability of the original items was .66, the mean of the correlations between each Christie reversal and its original was only .20. (All mean correlations have been calculated following z-transformations.) Furthermore, Table 3 shows numerous instances in which the means and standard deviations of scores were quite discrepant.

The Christie, Havel, and Seidenberg (1958) items are probably the most carefully developed reversals found in the literature, and, as mentioned earlier, I began my reversal development program with them. It would seem, however, that these widely used reversals have very weak relationships with the original F Scale items.

The data in Table 3 also reveal that my own efforts at writing reversals did not meet with universal success. But 18 of the 28 items (viz. numbers 3, 4, 5, 7, 9, 10, 11, 12, 15, 16, 17, 18, 20, 21, 24, 25, 26 and 28) met the criteria for *item* adequacy. I then chose 14 items from these 18 which together would meet the *set* criteria of representative item-whole correlations and reliability. The reversals chosen are presented in Table 4.

The psychometric properties of these 14 items, in terms of the criteria established for reversal adequacy, were as follows:

TABLE 4
The fourteen reversals chosen to balance the F Scale

Original item no.	
3	The human mind is surely capable of discovering all the important things there are to know. It's just a matter of time until all the truths are understood.
4	Human nature does not make war inevitable. Man will undoubtedly establish a peaceful world someday soon.
5	A person should not necessarily put complete faith in some supernatural power whose decisions he obeys without question.
7	A person who has bad manners, habits and breeding is nevertheless still entitled to the respect of "decent" people.
9	Probably no one is born with an urge to jump from high places.
11	We need not react against every single insult to our honor.
12	It is tragic that young people lose their rebellious ideas as they grow older and surrender to the established ways.
15	Sex crimes, such as rape and attacks on children, do not necessarily deserve public whipping, or even imprisonment. Often the people who do these things are mentally ill, and need to be treated with kindness and understanding.
18	Astrology will probably never be able to explain very much.
20	There is no reason to expect that wars and social troubles will be ended someday by an earthquake or flood that will destroy the whole world.
24	Our lives are not controlled to any great degree by plots hatched in secret places.
25	Homosexuals may be sick persons but they are hardly criminals. Others need to understand their feelings and be more accepting of them.
26	The artist and professor are as important to society as the businessman and manufacturer.
28	Familiarity does not breed contempt.

1 The mean test-retest reliability of the replaced items was .67; the mean correlation of the selected reversals with their originals was .53.

2 The mean item score of the replaced originals was 3.26; the mean item score of the selected reversals, with inverted keying, was 3.29.

3 The mean standard deviation of the replaced items was 1.86; the same statistic for the reversals was 1.87.

4 The mean correlation of the replaced originals with summed scores on the original F Scale was .39; the same figure for the nonreplaced items was .41.

5 The mean test-retest reliability of the replaced items, as mentioned above, was .67; the same statistic for the nonreplaced items was .65.

In summary, the data from the September, 1970, study indicated that the 14 reversals listed in Table 4 presented, to a high degree, the same content as the items they replaced, but in a different form. Moreover, the replaced items were an ordinary and representative subset of the statements contained in the original F Scale. A balanced version of the test was apparently at hand.

Comparing the original and Balanced F Scales: winter, 1970, studies
With two forms of the F Scale available, both presenting essentially the same material but differing in the susceptibility of their summed scores to direction-of-wording effects, one could now determine the similarity of scores produced by the two tests. Accordingly, during the last three months of 1970, over 1,000 subjects were run in a series of studies which compared the two scales. The overall design of these investigations is outlined in Figure 1.

Five hundred and forty-two subjects answered an 87-item questionnaire[6] which had the original F Scale at the beginning. One hundred and eight of these subjects, randomly selected, returned for a second testing session a week later and completed the original scale again (Path A). Another 108 subjects also returned a week later, but they then completed the balanced F Scale (Path B).

An additional 531 subjects completed a version of the 87-item questionnaire which began with the balanced F Scale. One hundred and four of these subjects returned a week later and completed the original F Scale (Path C), while another 93 returned to complete the balanced F Scale again (Path D). Subjects in all four paths were drawn from the same introductory psychology classes. They unknowingly assigned themselves to the different paths of the experimental design by the appointment times they chose.

Table 5 summarizes the psychometric properties of the items which composed the original and balanced F Scales. A few of the reversals (especially item #3) did not perform as well as they had in the previous study. But overall the slippage was small, and the "five-point" test of reversal adequacy in this experiment is summarized below:

1 The mean test-retest reliability of the replaced items was .68; the mean correlation of the reversals with the items they replaced was .48.

2 The mean item score of the replaced originals was 3.32; the mean score of the reversals was 3.25.

3 The mean standard deviation of the originals was 1.86; the same statistic for the reversals was 1.83.

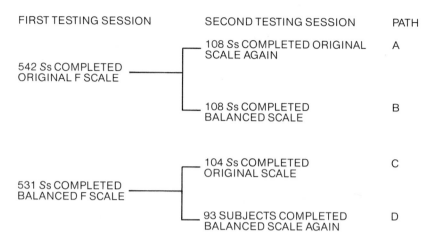

FIRST TESTING SESSION　　　　SECOND TESTING SESSION　　　PATH

108 Ss COMPLETED ORIGINAL　　A
SCALE AGAIN

542 Ss COMPLETED
ORIGINAL F SCALE

108 Ss COMPLETED　　　　　　B
BALANCED SCALE

104 Ss COMPLETED　　　　　　C
ORIGINAL SCALE

531 Ss COMPLETED
BALANCED F SCALE

93 SUBJECTS COMPLETED　　　D
BALANCED SCALE AGAIN

Figure 1
Summary of the design of the winter, 1970, studies

4 The mean correlation of the replaced items with the total scores on the original scale was .36; the same figure for the nonreplaced items was .38.

5 The mean test-retest reliability of the replaced items was, as mentioned above, .68. The same statistic for the nonreplaced items was .67.

These values essentially replicate the findings of the September, 1970, study and confirm the value of the reversals.

One additional feature of the data in Table 5 should be pointed out. The reversals were significantly less reliable as a group (.61) than were the items they replaced on the original scale (.68) ($t = 2.08$; $p < .05$). The lower reliability is due to the nine reversals (numbers 4, 5, 9, 11, 15, 18, 20, 24, and 28)which contained negative qualifiers ("no," "not" or "never"), whose test-retest reliability (.58 on the average) was appreciably lower than that of the items they replaced (.71).[7] The reversals' lower reliability and the likelihood that they were, as a group, somewhat weakened representations of "F Scale sentiment" explains why the sum of scores of the 14 reversals correlated significantly less (.67) with the total score on the balanced scale than did the sum of the 15 remaining items (.80) This fact will leave important implications later in this chapter.

Psychometric properties of the two scales
Table 6 shows the major psychometric properties of the original and

TABLE 5

Comparison of the items on the original and balanced F Scales, winter, 1970, studies

| | Original F Scale | | | | Balanced F Scale | | | | | | |
| | | | | | Original items | | | Reversals | | | |
Item	Mean (N=542)	SD (N=542)	Correl. with summed score (N=542)	Test-retest reliability[a]	Mean (N=531)	SD (N=531)	Test-retest reliability[a]	Mean (N=531)	SD (N=531)	Correl. with original[bc]	Test-retest reliability[d]
1	4.68	1.91	.52	.64	4.70	1.88	.69				
2	4.87	1.85	.27	.69	5.07	1.81	.70				
3	5.10	1.95	.29	.57				4.18	2.05	.10	.74
4	5.27	1.87	.32	.73				4.99	1.83	.36	.58
5	2.65	2.00	.33	.75				2.75	2.05	.47	.62
6	3.00	1.92	.33	.62	3.19	2.00	.68				
7	3.51	1.94	.41	.58				3.31	1.89	.51	.56
8	3.48	1.93	.51	.68	3.50	1.93	.68				
9	3.08	2.03	.16	.74				3.26	2.13	.52	.56
10	3.02	1.85	.33	.70	3.06	1.88	.72				
11	2.62	1.58	.40	.61				2.40	1.57	.45	.38
12	3.56	2.02	.46	.65				3.57	1.94	.44	.67
13	2.60	1.67	.41	.60	2.76	1.76	.62				
14	4.36	2.03	.25	.57	4.53	2.00	.55				
15	3.22	2.18	.48	.69				3.22	2.04	.47	.71
16	2.62	1.88	.36	.77	2.30	1.74	.57				
17	2.84	1.88	.47	.80	2.94	1.91	.79				
18	3.43	1.94	.32	.80				4.26	1.93	.70	.59
19	4.50	1.98	.37	.74	4.62	1.87	.68				
20	3.04	1.98	.35	.63				2.89	1.95	.38	.57
21	3.06	2.02	.39	.55	3.13	1.95	.50				

22	3.77	1.86	.35	.65	3.82	1.85	.68	3.33	1.87	.48	.74
23	3.70	1.96	.40	.59	3.77	1.98	.65	2.22	1.49	.52	.62
24	3.77	1.94	.36	.67				1.58	1.08	.61	.64
25	1.85	1.33	.41	.78							
26	2.09	1.47	.33	.49							
27	3.69	2.03	.40	.58	3.90	2.10	.62	3.47	1.79	.55	.44
28	3.28	1.85	.38	.76							
29	2.74	1.81	.33	.70	2.66	1.86	.71				

aIndicates data are based on responses of subjects in Path A. Figure 1 (N=108)
bcIndicates data are based on responses of subjects in Paths B & C, Figure 1 (N=212)
dIndicates data are based on responses of subjects in Path D, Figure 1 (N=93)

TABLE 6

Psychometric properties of the original and balanced F Scales

	N	Mean	Variance	Test retest reliability	Cronbach "alpha" reliability	Mean interitem correlation
Original Scale	542	99.4	406	.91	.77	.10
Balanced Scale	531	99.4	241	.87	.60	.05

balanced F Scales. The means happen to be identical, while the balanced scale's test-retest reliability is lower, as one would expect from the above discussion. But the biggest difference occurs in the two tests' mean interitem correlations. Responses to the unidirectionally worded original F Scale items correlated twice as well with one another as did those on the balanced scale. This difference in interitem correlations produced a significantly higher alpha value ($w = 1.48$, $p < .001$; see Feldt, 1969) and a significantly higher test variance ($F = 1.68$, $df = 541, 530, p < .0001$) for the original F Scale.

The variance of summed scores on each of the scales can be partitioned into components representing the contributions of 1) the 15 original items common to both scales, and 2) the remaining 14 items which are protrait on the original scale and contrait on the balanced scale. The formula for this partition (see Magnusson, 1967, ch. 4) is

$$S^2_{\Sigma 29} = S^2_{\Sigma 15} + S^2_{\Sigma 14} + 2 \times r_{\Sigma 15, \Sigma 14} \times S_{\Sigma 15} \times S_{\Sigma 14}$$

The values of each of these components for the two scales are given in Table 7.

The figures in Table 7 indicate that a small part of the difference in the two tests' variance is due to a slight difference in the variance of the 15 original items common to both tests. A larger part of the difference may be attributed to the poorer cohesion among the 14 reversals, which was probably caused in the main by their significantly poorer reliability. But, clearly, the major source of the difference in test variance is the huge discrepancy in the correlations between the subsets of 15 and 14 items on each test ($r_{\Sigma 15, \Sigma 14}$). On the original F Scale the subsets correlated .63, but on the balanced scale only .09.

This discrepancy could have been caused by direction-of-wording effects, or they could have been caused by content differences. Any con-

TABLE 7

Components of variance of summed scores on
original and balanced scales, winter, 1970, studies

Scale	N	$S^2_{\Sigma_{29}}$ =	$S^2_{\Sigma_{15}}$ +	$S^2_{\Sigma_{14}}$ +	$2 \times r_{\Sigma_{15}, \Sigma_{14}} \times$	$S_{\Sigma_{15}} \times$	$S_{\Sigma_{14}}$
Original	542	406	142	109	.63	11.9	10.4
Balanced	531	241	135	87	.09	11.6	9.3

tent difference would have to be attributed to the 14 reversals and their protrait counterparts. But we know that on an individual basis the reversals rather faithfully reproduce the content of the originals they replaced — certainly much better than a correlation of .09 would indicate. The major cause of the difference in the two tests' variance, therefore, must be response sets which bound the subsets of 15 and 14 items together on the original scale, but which disassociated the protrait and contrait items on the balanced scale.

A conservative estimate, based upon the figures in Table 7, is that at least 30% of the variance of original F Scale scores in this study was caused by the uncorrected influence of response sets.[8] That is considerably more than can be attributed to any meaningful underlying dimension on the test through factor analysis.

What response sets affect the F Scale?
The difference between scores on the original and balanced F Scales in the winter, 1970, studies might have been caused by yea-saying, nay-saying, or both. Figure 2 displays the distributions of these scores. The original F Scale scores are much more extended than balanced scores on both ends of the distribution, with the extension toward higher scores somewhat more pronounced. The response sets apparently cause some people to get higher scores on the original F Scale than they would have on a balanced test, and cause others to get lower scores.

It is not difficult to find a response set which increases scores on a test like the F Scale. As far back as 1942, Cronbach found that some people tend to say yes or true when they are uncertain of the answers on achievement tests. This yea-saying, or "response acquiescence," has long been hypothesized to affect answers to vague and ambiguous items on attitude scales as well; it has been hitherto impossible to isolate, however, because there are no right and wrong answers to opinion surveys. But the upward extension of scores on the original F Scale, as

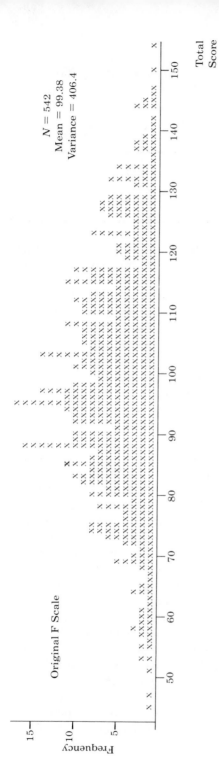

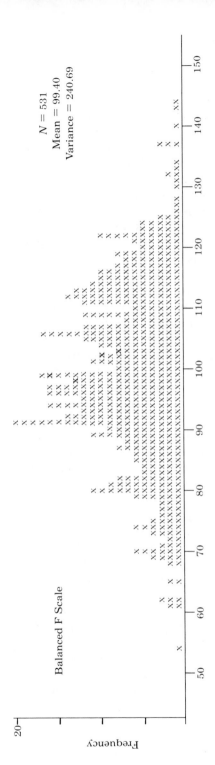

Figure 2
Frequency distribution of scores on original and balanced scales

Figure 2 shows, was caused by some response set to agree with the items, and until evidence of some other phenomenon is obtained, the conclusion that acquiescence affects the F Scale seems reasonable.

What about the extension of scores toward the low end of the scale? Cronbach (1942) also found that some people tended to say no and false when they did not know the answer to objective questions. This nay-saying, which we might call "contrariness," on an attitude scale, has been found to occur about half as often as acquiescence on "objective" tests where the subjects could not possibly know the answers (Fritz, 1927; Berg and Rapaport, 1954; Bass, 1957). It seems to be a little more prevalent on the F Scale, and this may be due to the bizzare nature of many of the original items.[9]

The question arises as to why these response sets of acquiescence and contrariness should determine subjects' answers to such a large extent. Why do not subjects respond more to the content of the items? The answer may be partly that it is not altogether clear what some of the F Scale items mean. But beyond that, the problem may be that the subjects are poorly motivated to consider the items carefully. To them, nothing of consequence is determined by their responses. The same students who will demand twenty minutes to answer ten multiple-choice questions on a quiz will rip through the F Scale in five minutes.[10] They do not deliberate over statements like, "Some people are born with an urge to jump from high places." It is easy to see why tendencies to be agreeable or crabby—be they transient or enduring in the person—could play a strong role in such circumstances.

Do response sets contribute to the original F Scale's validity?
So far, we have found that response sets affect scores on the F Scale, that they control a large part of the test's variance, and that both yea-saying and nay-saying are involved. The remaining question we set out to answer is whether these sets increase or detract from the validity of the original F Scale.

The predictive capabilities of the original and balanced F Scales were compared in the winter of 1970 with a number of variables which have been previously associated with authoritarianism, including both of the variables which we found in chapter 1 to have the most consistent relationships with the original F Scale. The criteria used were (1) sanctioned aggression against an unconventional person, (2) right-wing political sentiment, and (3) continued acceptance of the teachings of one's home religion.

A behavioral measure of sanctioned aggression
Ninety-three of the subjects who had served in the winter, 1970, questionnaire study later participated in an experiment patterned after Epstein's (1965) authoritarian aggression study. The subjects were recruited at the end of the questionnaire study; I told them that one of my colleagues had asked me to sign up subjects for a verbal learning experiment. This route to the subject pool was supposedly being taken to recruit subjects who kept their appointments.

When subjects reported for the verbal learning experiment, each one found a confederate of the same sex also waiting. The experimenter (a male graduate student wearing a lab coat and tie) took both subject and confederate to a laboratory room. The real subject was manipulated, seemingly by chance, into becoming the "teacher" in an experiment on the effects of punishment on learning. The confederate was seated before a memory drum, given a list of nine paired-associate nonsense syllables to learn, and a dummy electrode was attached to his hand.

The subject was then taken next door and seated before a table where he could see, through a one-way mirror, the confederate studying the nonsense syllables. The experimenter explained that the learner was to receive a shock every time he made a mistake, and the strength of shock was up to the teacher. A "shock generator" on the table gave the teacher five options, labelled: 1—slight shock; 2—mild shock; 3—moderate shock; 4—strong shock; and, 5—very strong shock. The shock generator actually delivered no shocks; instead, it recorded the number of times each of the five shock switches was depressed during the experiment, and told the confederate in the adjoining room which "shock" he had supposedly just received. The confederate made 32 programmed errors during eight runs through the list, and gave a standard response to each level of shock, ranging from a brief smile for "slight shock" to a sharp arm jerk and grimace of pain for "very strong shock."

For half of the subjects, the confederate was dressed as an unconventional, deviant member of the student body (a "hippie"); for the other half, the confederate looked like an ordinary student. The dependent variable in the study was the mean level of shock administered for the 32 mistakes.

Scores on the original F Scale were uncorrelated with aggression against "straight" confederates ($r = -.03$; $N = 23$), but were significantly related to aggression against the unconventional students ($r = .37$, $N = 22$, $p < .05$ by a one-tailed test). Scores on the balanced F Scale were not significantly correlated with mean shock delivered to either kind of confederate ($r = .13$ and $.18$ respectively). The original F Scale thus had

TABLE 8

F Scale scores of winter, 1970, respondents
by political party preference

Political party	Original F Scale			Balanced F Scale		
	N	$\overline{X}$	S^2	N	$\overline{X}$	S^2
New Democratic	121	97.7	410.	129	94.7	289.
Liberal	126	101.4	345.	130	100.7	222.
Progressive Conservative	90	106.1	503.	87	105.1	201.
F		4.4			12.1	
p		<.025			<.001	
Number of significant pair-wide contrasts:	1				3	
$\hat{\eta}^2$	3%				7%	

a predictive advantage over its balanced counterpart on this important
behavioral measure.

Political party affiliation

Subjects in the winter, 1970, study were asked to complete a "Demographic Survey" after they had finished the 87-item attitude survey,
ostensibly to gather information about the backgrounds of the student
population enrolled in introductory psychology. After preliminary information on sex, age, year in school, etcetera, had been requested, I asked
those students who were Manitoba residents to indicate which, if any, of
the Manitoba political parties they identified with or preferred.

The major political parties in Manitoba (and in the rest of Anglophone Canada) align from "left" to "right" as follows: The New Democratic Party (NDP), the Liberal Party, and the Progressive Conservative
(Conservative) Party. The mean F Scale scores of those subjects in the
winter, 1970, study who indicated a preference for one of these parties
are given in Table 8. The means on both scales are ranked in the predicted order, and both tests found significant overall differences. The
balanced F Scale's relationship was appreciably stronger than the original's, however, with over twice as much of its variance being related to
party affiliation.

Continued acceptance of the home religion

A short survey of religious beliefs followed the political party poll. Subjects were asked to indicate the religion in which they were raised, and

TABLE 9

Relationships between F Scale scores and
acceptance of home religion

Subjects' home religion	Original F Scale		Balanced F Scale	
	N	r	N	r
Catholics	132	.32‡‡	148	.31‡‡
United Church	91	.03	89	.38‡‡
Anglicans	53	.00	53	.18
Lutherans	19	−.16	20	.41‡
Jews	26	.29	30	.31‡
All subjects	448	.21‡‡	450	.30‡‡

‡ Indicates $p < .05$ by a one-tailed test.
‡‡ Indicates $p < .001$ by a one-tailed test.

also the extent to which they, at the time of the experiment, accepted
the beliefs of that faith. The latter question, answered on a four-point
scale ("not at all," "somewhat," "substantially," and "completely") can
be taken as a measure of authoritarianism insofar as it reflects continued
submission to the authority of the parents who decided what religious
teachings the subjects would receive.[11]

Table 9 presents the correlations each version of the F Scale had with
continued acceptance of the home religion. It shows that the balanced
F Scale had significant relationships with the criterion in the expected
direction in most instances, while the original scale did not. The balanced
scale's relationship over all subjects accounts for twice as much variance
as does the original scale's.

Evaluation

If the reader has been keeping score he knows that there is little to choose
from between the two tests.[12] On one measure the original F Scale had
an important significant relationship which the balanced scale did not.
On the other two criteria, however the balanced scale's relationship was
several times stronger than that of the original. The most defendable
conclusion at this point is that one scale is as good as the other. (This
is confirmed by a more extensive series of experiments conducted in 1973
and reported in chapter 4.)

This conclusion is adequate for our purposes, however, since, on the
face of it, the original scale should be superior because half the items on
the balanced scale have significantly lower reliabilities, overall, than their

counterparts on the original scale. Other things being equal, then, the balanced scale should have less predictive utility because less of its variance is reliable. But "other things" apparently are not equal, since the balanced scale is at least as good as the original. It would seem, then, that the response sets which produce much of the variance of scores on the original scale detract from the scale's predictive usefulness—however much they might improve the internal consistency of the test and inflate correlations with other unidirectionally worded measures.

CONCLUSION

The research program described in this chapter has seemingly answered the pertinent questions which have been raised over the years about the F Scale and response sets.

1 As one would expect from the F Scale's literature and the research of Campbell, Seigman, and Rees (1967), response sets are powerful determinants of F Scale scores. These sets increase the correlations among items worded in the same direction beyond the level waranted by their content per se; and they increase the correlation between tests which are worded in the same direction, beyond the level warranted by their content.

2 Both yea-saying and nay-saying effects have been identified, and have been labelled "response acquiescence" and "contrariness" respectively. It is probable that these sets will particularly affect responses to ambiguous and vague items, and items about which the subject does not have a definite opinion. It has also been proposed that these sets may be common when subjects complete surveys carelessly.

3 While these tendencies to agree or disagree would appear, at least superficially, to be relevant to the construct of authoritarianism, the evidence does not indicate that they improve the F Scale's predictive validity. If anything, in fact, they seem to produce error variance.

The argument over response sets and the F Scale has been "settled" so many times in the past 25 years that it would be foolhardy to suggest that the last word has been spoken on the issue. The matter always seems open to a new twist as researchers produce alternate analyses of old data, or new results to confound our certainties. But if the analysis presented here has merit, the conclusions are significant. Response sets can be powerful forces. Not only can they affect scores on attitude surveys, but they can affect them powerfully. Look again at Figure 2. Perhaps the effects are less dramatic on other tests. But it seems probable that wording all the items on a survey in the same direction—while it may speed up test construction and produce higher levels of internal consistency—can be merely a fast way to ruin the test.

A suggested conceptualization
of right-wing authoritarianism

3

In chapter 2 certain discouraging conclusions were reached about the accomplishments of previous research on right-wing authoritarianism. These conclusions were based in some instances on an assumption that unidirectionally worded authoritarianism scales have their interitem correlations and relationships with other unidirectional tests inflated by response sets. That assumption was supported by the research described in chapter 2. The present literature on right-wing authoritarianism is apparently as uninformative as it was depicted to be in chapter 1.

The rest of this book is concerned with a new conceptualization and measure of this construct which, while limited in many respects, is still believed to be an improvement over the current state of affairs. This chapter offers a detailed definition of what I mean by right-wing authoritarianism, along with a description of the largely inductive way this conceptualization, and an attitude scale to measure it, emerged from a series of eight item-analysis studies. Chapter 4 will present the results of a large-scale "pitting" experiment in which the validity of this approach was compared with that of most of the previous approaches outlined in chapter 1. Chapter 5 will report the results of several studies which have cross-validated the findings of chapter 4 in a variety of populations, and also report some findings on the dynamics of right-wing authoritarianism. We shall then consider evidence bearing on the personal origins of authoritarianism in chapter 6.

DEFINITION OF RIGHT-WING AUTHORITARIANISM

By "right-wing authoritarianism" I mean the covariation of three attitudinal clusters:

1 Authoritarian submission—a high degree of submission to the authorities who are perceived to be established and legitimate in the society in which one lives;
2 Authoritarian aggression—a general aggressiveness, directed against various persons, which is perceived to be sanctioned by established authorities; and
3 Conventionalism—a high degree of adherence to the social conventions which are perceived to be endorsed by society and its established authorities.

Elaboration on terms in the definition
The covariation of the three attitudinal clusters is central to the definition. People who are especially submissive to established authority and who are very conventional, for example, but who are not in general aggressive against sanctioned targets, would not be what I call right-wing authoritarians. Such people might be interesting to study in their own right, and someone else could call such submissive conventionalism "authoritarianism" if he wished. But the right-wing authoritarian, as I mean it, shows all three of the attitudinal clusters listed above. The three are necessary, and together the sufficient defining elements of the psychological construct I am advancing.

By "attitudinal clusters" I mean orientations to respond in the same general way towards certain classes of stimuli (viz., established authorities, targets for sanctioned aggression, and social conventions).

An orientation to respond is not the same thing as a response, and a controversy has developed over whether attitude measurement predicts behavior well enough to be scientifically useful (Brigham, 1971; Fishbein, 1966, 1967; Fishbein and Ajzen, 1975; Kelman, 1974; Wicker, 1969). The case against attitudes parallels Mischel's (1968) argument against personality traits (see Introduction) and comes to the same point: is it worthwhile discussing individual predispositions to act when they can be so easily overpowered by situational influences?

Milgram's 1974 research on obedience provides a dramatic example of the power of situational forces in a setting quite relevant to our interest here. In one of his studies, a naive subject was placed with two confederates on a "teaching team." At a certain point in the experiment, when the learner (who was supposedly receiving powerful electric shocks) was shouting in pain and demanding to be set free, the two confederates refused to continue. So then did 90% of the real subjects who served in this condition. But, in another condition, the two confederates continued to obey the experimenter without protest, and so did 92% of the real subjects. Whether the subjects defied or obeyed the experimenter was thus almost completely controlled by the behavior of the people they were working with. Individual differences in childhood, religious training, education, orientation to authority, and so forth, were almost totally irrelevant.

In the face of such findings, there is no doubt that situational factors can ride roughshod over individual differences of almost any kind. But that does not mean that differences in orientations toward a class of stimuli will never be predictive of behavior. Milgram's subjects were in a very unfamiliar environment among complete strangers who were programmed to act in certain ways no matter what the subjects did. Most of the time, however, people are in familiar situations interacting with others whose behavior is well known to them, and whose behavior they have partly shaped. Moreover, there is a wealth of evidence showing that, to a considerable extent, people choose to interact with those whom they perceive to hold the same attitudes they do (Berscheid and Walster, 1969). There may be a broad range of everyday situations in which attitudes will be predictive of behavior. As Wrightsman (1977, pp. 342–348) has illustrated, whites with anti-black attitudes will sometimes act without prejudice toward blacks, and liberal whites may sometimes behave prejudicially toward blacks, but there are still other times when the attitudes of whites toward blacks have been correlated with behavior toward blacks in the predicted way.

The "bottom line" here is whether assessments of right-wing authoritarian attitudes will be predictive of "authoritarian behavior."

There is a second reason why the study of attitudes is quite germane here. Many of the "authoritarian behaviors" we should be most concerned about are themselves attitudes, that is, specific attitudes toward public officials and courses of action. The "mood of the people" can affect public policy, sometimes dramatically. This can be seen in each of the three episodes from the early 1970s discussed in the Introduction of this book.

During the "October crisis" in Canada, the Leader of the Opposition, Robert Stanfield, initially opposed the government's use of the War Measures Act to deal with the kidnappings in Quebec. But party officials convinced him that the rank and file of his own party strongly favored being tough with the terrorists. This position was supported by his own mail and by radio phone-in shows (see *Toronto Globe and Mail*, Oct. 20,

1970, pp. 8–9). Thus Stanfield set aside his challenge to the War Measures Act—a challenge which events later proved well-founded—and the Conservatives supported the government.

Spiro Agnew's attacks on the press actually began following critical analyses of President Nixon's speech on Viet-Nam on November 3, 1969. Public opinion clearly supported both the president's Viet-Nam policy and the vice-president's criticism of post-speech "instant analyses" (*New York Times*, November 5, 1969, p. 11; Nov. 15, p. 20; Nov. 20, p. 26; Nov. 22, p. 21). For a while, at least, the attacks worked, as the networks, caught in a hailstorm of public criticism, actually dropped their post-speech commentaries of the president's addresses.

Finally, during the Watergate crisis, we now know that a key part of President Nixon's political defense was the belief that the American people would not want their president impeached. During an April 25, 1973, strategy session with H. R. Haldemann, the president noted his deteriorating position in the opinion polls, but said, "I think there's still a hell of a lot of people out there...[who] want to believe. That's the point isn't it?" Haldemann responded, "Why sure. Want to and do" (*New York Times*, Nov. 22, 1974, p. 20). At the time, the Gallup Poll found that 54% of its sample still approved of the way President Nixon was doing his job (*New York Times*, April 23, 1973, p. 24) and as we saw in chapter 1, the American public stood by Nixon for a very long time afterwards. But eventually they wanted him gone, and in June of 1974 the Democratic House Majority Leader, "Tip" O'Neill, used poll results to show reluctant Democrats that not only was it now safe to vote for impeachment, it was politically expedient to do so (Breslin, 1975, pp. 134–136).

I am not saying that public opinion is always a major determinant of public policy. Polls, for example, have shown that the vast majority of Americans favor tighter gun control legislation, but congress does not pass it. Canadians have favored capital punishment by a wide margin for years, but the Trudeau cabinet has commuted all the death sentences imposed by the courts. Representative government takes law-making one large, deliberate step away from the *vox populi*. But at the same time, the attitudes of the electorate are an important shaper of political behavior, the ultimate determinant of who attains power, and an elected official who pays no attention to his constituents' attitudes is apt to become an ex-official.

The central concern underlying this book is that there may be a vast potential for the acceptance of right-wing totalitarian rule in countries such as Canada and the United States. This acceptance is essentially an attitude, a state of mind, a willingness to see democratic institutions destroyed, which in some people may even be a desire. Right-wing authoritarianism has been defined as a state of mind, rather than a set of acts, but it is still dangerous. The mood of the people can create a climate of public opinion which promotes totalitarian movements. It can intimidate politicians, journalists, and religious leaders who might otherwise oppose repression. It can encourage a bold, illegal, grab for power as it did in Italy in 1922. It can elect a Hitler to office as it did in Germany in 1933.

I do not wish to imply, in concentrating on threats to democracy from the political right, that equally grave dangers cannot arise on the radical left. History has shown that totalitarianism threatens democratic institutions on either side. But I doubt that there is an "authoritarian," as I have defined the term, on the left (Shils, 1954). The radical leftists of the late 1960s who were dynamiting buildings (and thereby driving millions of Americans to rally behind Nixon and Agnew) may be called doctrinaire, dogmatic, fanatic, and many other things. But they were not submissive to established authorities, nor were they particularly conventional.

By submission to established authority I mean a general acceptance of its statements and actions, and a general willingness to comply with its instructions without further inducement.

The right-wing authoritarian believes authorities should be trusted to a relatively great extent, and that they are owed obedience and respect. He believes these are important virtues which children should be taught, and that if children stray from these principles it is the parents' duty to get them back in line. Authoritarians would ordinarily place very narrow limits on people's right to criticize authorities. They tend to believe that officials know what is best, and that critics do not know what they are talking about. Criticism of authority is viewed as divisive and destructive, motivated by sinister goals and a desire to cause trouble.

The authoritarian does not ordinarily feel vulnerable to established authorities. On the contrary, he feels safer if authorities are strong. He supports government censorship in order "to control others," never imagining that the government would feel it necessary to censor what he reads, sees, and hears. His reaction to electronic surveillance, unlawful search, and mail-opening by officials is that only wrongdoers would object. To a considerable extent, he believes that established authorities have an inherent right to decide for themselves what they may do, including breaking the laws they make for the rest of us.

By "established and legitimate authorities" I mean those people in our society who are usually considered to have a general legal or moral authority over the behavior of others. One's parents (at least through childhood), religious officials, certain civic officers (policemen, judges, legislators, heads of governments), and superiors in military service are all established authorities. Bus drivers, life guards, employers, psychology experimenters, and countless others also have legitimate authority in certain situations, but their power is much more limited and situation specific.

The right-wing authoritiarian's submission is not absolute, automatic, nor blind. Like anyone else, he can be put into conflict by orders from above; he will not always accept orders, but he will accept them more often than nonauthoritarians will. Similarly, officials do not all command equal degrees of respect and submission: there are judges with "good ideas" and judges with "bad ideas"; there are "good Popes" and "great presidents" and there are "poor Popes" and "mediocre presidents." The evaluation depends, as with most of us, on the fit between the authoritarian's own ideas and those of the judge, pope and president. However, the right-wing authoritarian is more likely than the nonauthoritarian to submit to established authorities he likes, and to those he does not like.

The construct I am advancing is called "right-wing" authoritarianism because the submission is to established authorities. There is no underlying assumption that the government must be right-wing to command this submission. Right-wing authoritarians would, in general, prefer "right-wing" governments, but the "center-oriented" political parties which typically form the governments in Canada and the United States are quite conventional enough to command the respect and submission of authoritarians. Right-wing authoritarians say they will even submit to legally established left-wing governments, at least more so than nonauthoritarians will submit to a government they do not like.

By "aggressiveness" I mean a predisposition to cause harm to someone. The harm can be physical injury, psychological suffering, financial loss, social isolation or some other negative state which people would usually avoid. Aggressiveness is authoritarian when it is accompanied by the belief that established authority approves it, or that it will help preserve established authority. Police who beat up suspects to make them talk, believing such beatings are sanctioned by their superiors, would be authoritarian aggressive. Citizens who are willing to have the police beat up suspects to obtain confessions, or attack nonviolent demonstrators who are challenging a government policy are also being authoritarian aggressive, even though they do nothing themselves beyond saying that they approve. But home-grown terrorists who dynamite a police station are not authoritarian. Their action is every bit as deplorable, but it is not done in the name of established authority.

The predisposition to authoritarian aggression does not mean that the right-wing authoritarian will always act aggressively when opportunities arise. Fear of retaliation may stop him. There are also prominent social prohibitions against aggression in our culture, which the authoritarian, because he is conventional, fully realizes. This is why the perception of authoritative sanction is important. It disinhibits the aggressive impulse.

Right-wing authoritarians are predisposed to control the behavior of others through punishment. They advocate physical punishment in child-rearing and beyond. They deplore leniency in the courts and believe penal reform just encourages criminals to continue being lawless. They are strong advocates of capital punishment. All in all, there is an "Old Testament harshness" in their approach to human conduct. They consider transgressions against the law very serious offenses and believe punishment will help wrongdoers mend their ways. They also consider criminals repulsive and disgusting, and admit that it feels good to punish someone who has done wrong.

The "various people" who are the targets of authoritarian aggressiveness could be anyone, but unconventional people (including "social deviants" such as homosexuals) and people who are conventional targets of aggression (such as certain minority groups) are attacked more readily than are others. Thus right-wing authoritarianism is expected to be correlated, in general, with ethnic and racial prejudice, because such prejudice is a conventional outlet of aggressive impulses. The authoritarian believes that certain authorities approve of this prejudice, and he may believe that groups such as blacks threaten the established social order. Hence, the aggressiveness in prejudice can be authoritarian. But by no means is all prejudice thought to be linked to right-wing authoritarianism, much less be caused by it, as the Berkeley investigators theorized.

If social deviants and certain minority groups are easy targets of authoritarian aggression, others can be victims as well. The authoritarian is more likely to attack a conventional person than is a nonauthoritarian, if an established authority sanctions it. This power of authority figures to direct the hostility of authoritarians against almost any target increases the danger of authoritarian aggression to all in a society.

By "adherence to social conventions" is meant a strong acceptance of and committment to the traditional social norms in our society. Many such norms are based upon the common teachings of the traditional Judaic-Christian religions. The right-wing authoritarian generally believes in "God's Law," and thinks that the biggest reason there is so much conflict among men is that they are ignoring this law. Within each religion, authoritarians tend to be "fundamentalists," wishing to maintain the beliefs, teachings and services in their traditional form, and resisting change and "liberalization." The adult authoritarian tends to stay close to the childhood teachings of his religion. His idea of God (an old man with a beard) and hell (real fire, for eternity), for example, do not change much as he gets older. Authoritarians reject the idea that people should develop their own ideas of what is moral and immoral since these have already been determined by authorities. They also reject atheists and those "who have rebelled against the established religions," and doubt that such people can be as good as those who attend church regularly.

The right-wing authoritarian's attitudes toward sexual behavior are strongly influenced by his religious principles. Sex outside marriage is basically sinful. Nudity is sinful. Thinking about sex is sinful. Homosexuality is sinful and is a perversion. Many sexual acts, even between married partners, are perversions.

These attitudes toward sex have their parallel in conventional attitudes toward male and female behavior. Authoritarians endorse the traditional family structure in which women are subservient to their husbands. They believe women should, by and large, keep to their traditional roles in society. While a "decent, respectable appearance" is important to both sexes, it is especially important for a woman; while sexual transgression is wrong for both sexes, it is especially wrong for a woman.

There are a host of traditional social norms, besides the above, which the authoritarian endorses. The flag and the national anthem should be honored, as of course the national leaders should be. There is a strong belief that "our customs and national heritage are the things that have made us great," and everyone ought to be made to show respect for them. People should strive to be well-behaved and respectable, and in general stick to the "straight and narrow," nondeviating course. Underlying all of this is the notion that these social norms are moral as well as social imperatives. The authoritarian rejects the proposition that social customs are arbitrary, and one nation's customs can be as good as another's. Other ways of doing things are wrong.

The term "norms" is being used here in the normative, not the descriptive, sense. The right-wing authoritarian's conventionalism is a code of how people ought to act, not how they do. The code is conventional because it is based on long-standing tradition and custom, not because it actually describes how most people are behaving. Thus it may be that most adults in our society engage in sexual intercourse before marriage. The authoritarian may have as well. It is nonetheless a transgression, and the fact that most people are sinning only shows the authoritarian that it is a sinful world.

This is not to say that the authoritarian's adherence to traditional social norms is cast in iron and cannot be changed in his lifetime. But it is more resistant to change than the nonauthoritarian's, and it is more likely to be influenced by the pronouncements of authority figures than by the behavior of his peers.

ORIGIN OF THE CONCEPTUALIZATION

Overview
The conceptualization of right-wing authoritarianism just presented has an inductive base. It was inferred from a series of attitude survey studies conducted over a number of years at the University of Manitoba, in which the pattern of covariation among responses to many hundreds of statements was studied. My first discovery was that submissive, aggressive, and conventional sentiments seemed to covary, while others did not. After determining that this covariation was reliable, I undertook to construct an attitude scale, balanced against response sets and possessing adequate internal consistency, to measure this covariation which I have called right-wing authoritarianism. The rest of this chapter describes this process in detail, while the following chapter takes up the question of whether this approach is valid and useful.

Before proceeding, I should acknowledge that inductive models which prove useful do not take us as far scientifically as deductive models which prove valid. If the construct of authoritarianism I have proposed proves useful for analyzing important behaviors and orientations, that will be a worthy accomplishment. But it will not show us grander truths about human nature, the way the Berkeley approach might have—if it had been successful. Unfortunately the attempt to understand authoritarian behavior by proceeding from a grand theoretical position has not taken us very far, and I am willing to try something smaller first, namely to induce a viable conceptualization of authoritarianism from empirical data. Later on, when we have reason to believe we know what we are talking about and can account for relevant behaviors by approaching the subject this way, we will be able to see which theoretical school can best explain the facts. That will be good enough for me. But some scientists, I know, have little interest in inductive models created in a "theoretical vacuum," and they will be unimpressed with this approach.

The winter, 1970, study

The first study in this program was the winter, 1970, investigation described in chapter 2 in which over a thousand subjects responded to 87 "authoritarianism" items. The first 29 items were either the original or balanced F Scale described in the preceding chapter; the remaining items were 18 statements from the D Scale, 22 items from the Lee and Warr (1969) "balanced F Scale," six items from the Traditional Family Ideology Scale (Levinson and Huffman, 1955), and 12 items of my own.[1] (See Appendix I for copies of all surveys used in the item analysis studies.)

The intercorrelations among responses to the items were calculated and analyzed for patterns of covariation. Overall, there was practically none; the mean interitem correlation among the 87 items was .07. The values for the formal scales were scarcely better, being .10 for the F Scale, .11 for the D Scale, and .11 for the Lee and Warr Scale. The reader will recognize that these results approximate the values found in previous research on these scales.

There was only one pattern of covariation within the 87 x 87 correlation matrix worthy of note, and the ten items which most covaried in this cluster (all of which were worded in the same direction) are listed in Table 1. The reader may agree that most common among these items are conventional sentiments that youth ought to submit to familial and social authority, and expressions of hostility toward those who do not do so. The items concerning "sex crimes," "women who want to remove the word "obey," "the divine origin of the family," and "the facts on crime" suggested to me in 1970 that the underlying sentiments of submission, aggression, and conventionalism might extend to matters other than just "the youth."

The average interitem correlation among the ten items listed in Table 1 was .27, which is compromised, however, by the probability that response sets increased the real correlation among the content of these unidirectionally worded items. None of the 18 contrait items in the questionnaire (or 32 such items in surveys which began with the balanced F Scale) was among the most tightly connected members of this cluster.

Five of the items in Table 1 also appear in Table 1 of chapter 1, which contains the items on the original F Scale initially found to have the

TABLE 1

The ten most interconnected items in the winter, 1970, questionnaire

Item No.	Source	Item
1	Original F Scale	Obedience and respect for authority are the most important virtues children should learn.
8	Original F Scale	What the youth needs most is strict discipline, rugged determination, and the will to work and fight for family and country.
12	Original F Scale	Young people sometimes get rebellious ideas, but as they grow up they ought to get over them and settle down.‡
15	Original F Scale	Sex crimes, such as rape and attacks on children, deserve more than mere imprisonment; such criminals ought to be publicly whipped, or worse.‡
17	Original F Scale	There is hardly anything lower than a person who does not feel a great love, gratitude and respect for his parents.
31	Lee & Warr	The minds of today's youth are being hopelessly corrupted by the wrong kind of literature.
32	TFI	Women who want to remove the word "obey" from the marriage service don't understand what it means to be a wife.
40	TFI	The family is a sacred institution, divinely ordained.
50	Lee & Warr	In the final analysis parents generally turn out to be right about things.
67	Lee & Warr	The facts on crime and sex immorality suggest that we will have to crack down harder on some people if we are going to save our moral standards.

‡ Indicates the item was replaced by a reversal in the balanced F Scale which half the subjects completed. Interitem correlations were calculated for original and reversed items separately. The reversals did not correlate nearly as well as the originals with the rest of the items in the table.

greatest covariation with the rest of the test. These same items continued to form the psychometric core of the F Scale in subsequent studies reviewed in chapter 1. Now I found that the only appreciable clustering observed among responses to some 87 "authoritarianism" items tested in the winter of 1970 involved essentially what occurred on the F Scale, supplemented by similar items from other scales. None of the other traits supposedly represented on the F, D, and Lee and Warr Scales (e.g., "anti-intraception," "power and toughness," "superstition and stereotypy") formed a substantive cluster in the correlation matrix.

It should be noted again, as it was in chapter 1, that many of the items in Table 1 can be interpreted to tap several of these sentiments simultaneously. The main idea in "Obedience and respect for authority," for example, is a conventional sentiment about submission to parental authority. The item, "there is hardly anything lower," on the other hand, shows an aggressive attitude toward children who are not submissive. The Lee and Warr item on "crime and immorality" in turn combines aggressive ("crack down harder") and conventional ("save our moral standards") sentiments. The simultaneous tapping of these common themes probably contributed to their covariation. But the covariation was there.

The June, 1971, study
Several months later I administered a very similar 87-item survey to a sample of adult males drawn from the nonstudent population of Winnipeg. The subjects were recruited through newspaper ads which promised a five-dollar payment for two hours of experimental participation. People who phoned for appointments were told that subjects were being recruited from the general public so that studies run during the school year with students could be checked against nonstudent samples.

Fifty-three men were recruited in this way. Their age ranged from 20 to 60 and averaged 31.5. There were a few more blue-collar than white-collar occupations represented in the sample. Thirty-nine of the subjects had completed high school, but only eight had gone further. Conversations with the subjects at the end of the experimental session indicated most of them had volunteered for the study either because they needed the money or because they were interested in psychology. The group was certainly not a random sample of adult males living in the city; it was, however, a different peculiar sample from the traditional student one.

When the subjects reported for their appointments they were paid, taken to a small room which was divided into testing cubicles, and asked to complete an 87-item social opinion poll. The survey consisted of the items used in the winter, 1970, studies, except that they were rearranged to spread the items from the scales systematically throughout the questionnaire (e.g., every third item was from the original F Scale). I also had revised most of the 12 items of my own invention.

The average correlation among the 87 items was a little larger (.10) among the nonstudents than it had been among the students several months earlier. This produced a larger variance in test scores (e.g., 533 on the F Scale among the nonstudents, compared to 406 among the students). The mean interitem correlations on the two unidirectionally worded scales rose a bit (the F Scale to .12, the D Scale to .13); that of the balanced Lee and Warr Scale dropped a bit to .10. But obviously

TABLE 2

The ten most interconnected items in the June, 1971, questionnaire

Item No.	Source	Item
3	Original F Scale	Obedience and respect for authority are the most important virtues children should learn.
13	Lee & Warr	The minds of today's youth are being hopelessly corrupted by the wrong kind of literature.
24	Original F Scale	What the youth needs most is strict discipline, rugged determination, and the will to work and fight for family and country.
25	TFI	A child who is unusual in any way should be encouraged to be more like other children.
31	Dogmatism Scale	In this complicated world of ours the only way we can know what's going on is to rely on leaders or experts who can be trusted.
32	Lee & Warr	The facts on crime and sex immorality suggest that we will have to crack down harder on some people if we are going to save our moral standards.
36	Original F Scale	Young people sometimes get rebellious ideas, but as they grow up they ought to get over them and settle down.
45	Original F Scale	Sex crimes, such as rape and attacks on children, deserve more than mere imprisonment; such criminals ought to be publicly whipped, or worse.
51	Original F Scale	There is hardly anything lower than a person who does not feel a great love, gratitude and respect for his parents.
75	Original F Scale	Homosexuals are hardly better than criminals, and ought to be severely punished.

none of these changes, consistently attributable to greater response set effects among the nonstudents, amounted to much. Responses to each of the pre-existing scales were still quite inconsistent internally.

Examination of the 87 x 87 intercorrelation matrix again revealed one dominant cluster, and its ten most interconnected items are listed in Table 2. It can be seen that seven of these items are carry-overs from Table 1; the three items which did not reappear were still associated with the cluster, but not as tightly as before, relative to other items. The three replacemnts ("a child who is unusual," "in this complicated world," and "homosexuals") strengthened my opinion that the cluster tapped sentiments of submission, aggression and conventionalism, and two of the three implied that the sentiments covaried in matters besides that of "the youth."

Six of the items in Table 2 are from the original F Scale, and all of them may also be found in Table 1 of chapter 1. Also, all of the items in Table 2 are again worded in the protrait direction. Their mean interitem correlation was very high, relative to earlier experience (.39).

I concluded from the winter, 1970, and June, 1971, studies that sentiments of submission, aggression and conventionalism covaried in several areas of social concern.[2] The covariation was by no means dramatic (and it will be seen that it never again approached the value of .39 found among the items in Table 2). Moreover, it occurred almost exclusively among protrait items, and had probably resulted from response sets to a considerable extent. But it was the only substantive pattern of covariation found among the items tested.

The next step was to test the reliability and the generalizability of this clustering. In particular, I considered it essential to see if contrait items could be written which would covary "appreciably" with the cluster found in these studies.

The September, 1971, study
Next, I administered a 54-item questionnaire to 526 introductory psychology students at the beginning of the academic year in 1971. The survey included all of the items in Tables 1 and 2, although a few of them were reworded into contrait form. Other items which had shown weaker tendencies to correlate with the "central cluster" in the preceding studies were again included, in many cases somewhat modified. Quite a number of new contrait items were also included, as well as several ethnocentrism items and some "loser-in-life" statements (Sauer, 1967).

The covariation among responses to the items was examined as before, and a balanced 20-item mock scale was constructed, consisting of the ten protrait and ten contrait items in the questionnaire with the best correlations with one another. This "scale" had a mean interitem correlation of .15, with the protraits intercorrelating .21 on the average, the contraits .15, and the protrait-contrait correlations averaging .12. The Cronbach alpha coefficient of internal reliability was .78.

The twenty items which formed this mock scale are listed in Table 3. The reader will perhaps agree that both protrait and contrait items express sentiments of submission, aggression and conventionalism. It should also be noted that none of the ethnocentrism items and "loser-in-life" items correlated highly enough with the statements in Table 3 to earn a place on the "scale."

TABLE 3

The twenty items which formed the mock scale in the September, 1971, study

Item No.	Source	Item
3	U of Manitoba	Marijuana will probably turn out to be one of man's most beneficial discoveries.‡
7	Reversal of item from original F Scale	Homosexuals may be maladjusted people but they are hardly criminals. Others should try to understand their feelings and be more accepting of them.‡
9	U. of Manitoba	The police and the army have gotten far too much power in this country.‡
10	Dogmatism Scale	Basically there are two kinds of people in the world: those who are for the truth and those who are against it.
11	Lee & Warr Scale	Disobedience to the government is often justified.‡
13	Modification of item from Traditional Families Inventory	If a child starts becoming unconventional, his parents should see to it he returns to the normal ways expected by society.
15	Modification of item from Traditional Families Inventory	Women should always remember the promise they make in the marriage ceremony to obey their husbands.
19	Modification of F Scale item	There is hardly anything lower than a person who is disrespectful toward parents who have made many sacrifices for him.
20	U. of Manitoba	It is all right for a person to use pornography to reduce his sexual tensions.‡
21	U. of Manitoba	Atheists and agnostics are probably just as good and virtuous as those who strongly believe in God.‡
22	Modification of Lee & Warr item	The minds of today's youth are being hopelessly corrupted by the wrong kinds of literature and films.
23	Modification of Lee & Warr item	People who abuse the flag or who refuse to serve in the armed forces should be treated with tolerance and understanding.‡
30	Original F Scale	Obedience and respect for authority are the most important virtues children should learn.
31	U. of Manitoba	There are probably very few "lazy cheaters" on the welfare rolls. Nearly all of the people receiving welfare would probably rather work for a living, but cannot because of disabilities or circumstances beyond their control.‡
32	Modification of Lee & Warr item	The facts on crime and sexual immorality show we will have to crack down harder on deviant groups if we are going to save our moral standards.

TABLE 3 — *Continued*

Item No.	Source	Item
40	Reversal of F Scale item	It will be tragic if today's youth loses its rebellious ideas as they grow older.‡
44	Modification of Lee & Warr item	Life in the military has an unhealthy influence on most men.‡
46	U. of Manitoba	It may be old fashioned nowadays but having a neat, tidy appearance is still the mark of a gentleman and a lady.
48	Original F Scale	Sex crimes, such as rape and attacks on children, deserve more than mere imprisonment. Such criminals ought to be publicly whipped, or worse.
51	Original F Scale	What the youth needs most is strict discipline, rugged determination, and the will to work and fight for family and country.

‡ Indicates the item is worded in the contrait (antiauthoritarian) direction.

The October, 1971, Winnipeg adult study

Just as before, in October, 1971, I administered my latest survey to both student and nonstudent samples; I recruited a similar sample of 49 male nonstudents from Winnipeg through newspaper and radio advertisements to complete the 54-item survey described above. Results very similar to the October, 1970, findings were obtained, but the pattern of covariation among the items again indicated that response sets were a stronger determinant of nonstudent responses. The average correlation among the 10 protrait items in Table 3 was .34 (compared to .21 in the student sample). The average correlation among the 10 contrait items was the same as that for the students: .15. The mean protrait-contrait correlations was .10 (compared to .12 earlier), and the overall mean interitem correlation among the 20 items was .17, yielding a slightly higher alpha coefficient of .80.

To summarize, the student and nonstudent studies conducted in the fall of 1971 confirmed the previous interpretation that sentiments of submission, aggression and conventionalism covaried in such samples. Moreover, by inspecting the items which covaried most, I found that these sentiments appeared in a number of different contexts. Submission was not just owed to parents (items 19, 30, 40, and 51) and husbands (item 15), but also to government (items 11 and 23) and its agencies (items 9 and 44). Aggression was not just directed at rebellious youth (items 19 and 51) but also toward "deviants" (item 32), homosexuals (item 7), sex criminals (item 48) and welfare recipients (item 31). The conventionalism extended to "the normal ways expected by society" (item 13), "a neat, tidy appearance" (item 46), belief in God (item 21) and rejection of marijuana (item 3), pornography (item 20) and "the wrong kinds of literature and films" (item 22). In short, the sentiments seemed broadly based; one could consider them general predispositions to react similarly to different kinds of stimuli. They seemed similarly organized in the rather dissimilar student and nonstudent samples.

By the same token, other attitudes did not covary with this cluster, even at the very modest levels involved in the cluster itself. Virtually all of the ethnocentrism and prejudice items tested (see Appendix I, Questionnaire III, items 1, 4, 14, 26, 35, and 43) were poorly related with the central cluster. So also were several "peer conformity" items (numbers 18, 24, and 41), which suggested to me that the conventionalism was not an orientation to one's contemporaries, but rather that it was directed toward more established social authorities such as the family, the church, and the government. This also seemed obvious from the reactions of students to statements regarding marijuana, "a neat, tidy appearance," "the wrong kinds of literature and films," and so forth.

It was through this process of item creation and testing, of determining what covaried and what did not, that the construct which the reader encountered at the beginning of this chapter began to take shape in my mind.

It was also obvious that direction-of-wording effects affected responses to the items, and that any potential scale would have to be balanced with equal numbers of protrait and contrait statements to control these effects. In this regard, the protrait items were far ahead of the contraits in terms of interitem cohesion.

This was true partly because by 1970 the available pool of protrait "authoritarianism" items was far larger than that of the contraits. But it is also harder to think of the opposite of a construct.

The January, 1972, study

I continued testing new items and additional elements for the "central cluster" early in 1972 when I administered a 50-item questionnaire to a new sample of 500 introductory psychology students. The 10 protrait and 10 contrait items which most covaried in this study are listed in Table 4. Eight of the former but only six of the latter were "repeats"

TABLE 4

The twenty items which formed the mock scale in the January, 1972, study

Item No.	Source	Item
6	U. of Manitoba	It is permissable for one to ignore laws that seem unjust and unfair.‡
7	Original F Scale	Sex crimes, such as rape and attacks on children, deserve more than mere imprisonment. Such criminals ought to be publicly whipped, or worse.
8	U. of Manitoba	Atheists are no doubt as good and virtuous as those who attend church regularly.‡
12	Modification of item from TFI	If a child starts becoming unconventional, his parents should see to it he returns to the normal ways expected by society.
13	U. of Manitoba	Such things as flags and national anthems ought to be deemphasized in order to promote the idea that all men are brothers.‡
14	Modification of F Scale item	It will be tragic if today's rebellious youth lose their revolutionary spirit as they grow older.‡
18	Modification of F Scale item	There is hardly anything lower than someone who is disrespectful toward parents who have made many sacrifices for him.
20	U. of Manitoba	It may be old-fashioned nowadays, but having a neat, tidy appearance is still the mark of a gentleman and a lady.
23	Modification of Lee & Warr item	The facts on crime and sexual immorality show we will have to crack down harder on deviant groups if we are going to save our moral standards.
27	Modification of Lee & Warr item	People who abuse the flag or who refuse to serve in the armed forces should be treated with tolerance and understanding.‡
31	Modification of item from TFI	Women should always remember the promise they make in the marriage ceremony to obey their husbands.
34	F Scale	Obedience and respect for authority are the most important virtues children should learn.
35	Modification of F Scale item	Homosexuals may be maladjusted people but they are hardly criminals. Others should try to understand their feelings and be more accepting of them.‡
36	Modification of Lee & Warr item	The minds of today's youth are being hopelessly corrupted by the wrong kind of literature and films.
38	Lee & Warr Scale	Disobedience to the government is often justified.‡
39	U. of Manitoba	Laws ought to be strictly enforced, no matter what the consequences.
41	Modification of Dogmatism Scale item	In the long run it is best to associate mostly with those background and beliefs are the same as our own.

TABLE 4 — *Continued*

Item No.	Source	Item
42	U. of Manitoba	The police have gotten far too much power for the good of the country.‡
44	U. of Manitoba	Rules about being polite and "well-mannered" are stupid relics of the past and ought to be ignored.‡
45	U. of Manitoba	Youngsters should be encouraged to marry whomever they wish when they grow up, regardless of nationality, race or creed.‡

‡ Indicates the item is worded in the contrait (antiauthoritarian) direction.

from Table 3. The reader may agree that most of the new items ("ignore laws," "flags and anthems," "laws" and "rules") tap further sentiments of submission, aggression, and conventionalism.[3]

The intercorrelations among the items in Table 4 were a little higher than those in Table 3: .29 on the average among protraits; .20 among contraits; .17 among protrait-contrait matchups; and .20 overall. The mock scale presented in Table 4 had an alpha coefficient of .83.

The October, 1972, study

I made an intensive effort to develop the "ethnocentrism cluster" on my surveys when classes resumed in the fall of 1972. Eighty-five items, including 22 designed to tap ethnocentric sentiments, were administered to 559 students over two testing sessions held one week apart. Two sessions were held because in many cases I was testing two versions of the same item, which I thought best answered on separate occasions.

The results of this study provided continued support for the covariation of submission, aggression and conventionalism, but not of ethnocentrism. None of the 22 ethnocentrism items included in the questionnaire (see Appendix I) covaried appreciably with the "central core" in the correlation matrix. Table 5 lists the items from this core which formed a 20-item mock scale. Fifteen of these statements are "repeats" from earlier mock scales, eleven of which (numbers 15, 16, 32, 34, 38, 40, 42, 61, 70, 77, and 82) were part of the central cluster, in one form or another, for at least three studies. The new statements ("easy on drug offenders," "less attention to the Bible," "army and priesthood," "parents are right" and "forces of law and order") all seem to be tapping the same sentiments of submission, aggression, and conventionalism. The items they replaced from the previous mock scale which also seemed to tap these sentiments

TABLE 5

The twenty items which formed the mock scale in the October, 1972, study

Item No.	Source	Item
6	U. of Manitoba	The courts are right in being easy on drug offenders. Punishment would not do any good in cases like these.‡
15	U. of Manitoba	Atheists are no doubt just as good and virtuous as those who attend church regularly.‡
16	Original F Scale	Young people sometimes get rebellious ideas, but as they grow up they ought to get over them and settle down.
22	U. of Manitoba	People should pay less attention to the Bible and the other old traditional forms of religious guidance.‡
26	U. of Manitoba	Rules about being "well-behaved" and respectable are chains from the past that we have to break and throw away.‡
32	Original F Scale	Obedience and respect for authority are the most important virtues children should learn.
34	Modification of item from TFI	Women should always remember the promise they make in the marriage ceremony to obey their husbands.
38	U. of Manitoba	It may be considered old-fashioned by some, but having a decent, respectable appearance is still the mark of a gentleman and, especially, a lady.
40	Modification of Lee & Warr item	The facts on crime and sexual immorality show we will have to crack down harder on deviant groups if we are going to save our moral standards.
42	Modification of Lee & Warr item	Disobedience to the government is very often justified.‡
50	U. of Manitoba	Organizations like the army and the priesthood, which make their members submit to the commands of superiors, have an unhealthy effect upon people.‡
61	U. of Manitoba	Homosexuals are just as good and virtuous as anybody else, and there is nothing really wrong with being one.‡
64	U. of Manitoba	Laws have to be strictly enforced if we are going to preserve our way of life.
66	Lee & Warr Scale	In the final analysis parents generally turn out to be right about things.
70	Modification of F Scale item	There is hardly anything lower than someone who is disrespectful toward his parents. We are duty-bound to honor our father and mother all our lives.
77	Modification of Lee & Warr item	Certain groups are poisoning the minds of today's youth with the wrong kind of music and films.
78	Modification of Lee & Warr item	Groups which abuse the flag should be treated with tolerance and understanding.‡
81	U. of Manitoba	The so-called "forces of law and order" in this country threaten our freedom a lot more than the groups they say are subversive.‡

TABLE 5 — *Continued*

Item No.	Source	Item
82	Modification of item from TFI	If a child starts becoming unconventional, his parents should see to it he returns to the normal ways expected by society.
84	U. of Manitoba	Such things as flags and national anthems should be deemphasized, to promote the idea that all men are brothers.‡

‡ Indicates the item is worded in the contrait (antiauthoritarian) direction.

("ignore laws," "sex crimes," and "police power" in Table 4) did not do much poorer in the present study; their replacements were just better.

The mean correlation among the protrait items in Table 5 was .32, that among the contrait items was .25, that among the protrait-contrait pairs was .23, and that among all twenty items was .26. The alpha coefficient of this mock scale was .87.

The January, 1973, study
Sixty-two items were administered to 457 additional introductory psychology students at the beginning of 1973 in two sessions held one week apart. This time the order of presentation of the items was systematically counterbalanced (see Appendix I). Most of the items tested were those which covaried in earlier studies, which were often administered in two different forms in the two testing sessions. Some other submission, aggression, and conventionalism items were tried as well, as were seven ethnocentrism items.

The results closely mimicked those of the preceding several studies. The usual core of the cluster appeared, with a few new submission, aggression and conventionalism items replacing some earlier statements. None of the ethnocentrism items "made the team."

The intercorrelations among the items were not, as high as those found in the October, 1972, study. The twenty most interconnected items (see Table 6) had the following mean intercorrelations: protrait items — .34; contrait items — .21; protrait-contrait items — .19; overall — .23. The alpha coefficient of this latest mock scale was .85.

The September, 1973, study: the initial version of the RWA Scale
The mock scales extracted from the October, 1972, and January, 1973, studies had mean interitem correlations of .26 and .23 respectively. These

TABLE 6
The twenty items which formed the mock scale in the January, 1973, study

Item No.	Source	Item
2	U. of Manitoba	Capital punishment should be completely abolished.‡
6	U. of Manitoba	Atheists and others who have rebelled against the established religions are no doubt every bit as good and virtuous as those who attend church regularly.‡
8	U. of Manitoba	Our prisons are a shocking disgrace. Criminals are still people, not some kind of animal, and are entitled to much better treatment than they are presently getting.‡
11	U. of Manitoba	It may be considered old-fasioned by some, but having a decent, respectable appearance is still the mark of a gentleman and, especially, a lady.
12	U. of Manitoba	The courts are right in being easy on drug offenders. Punishment would not do any good in cases like these.‡
13	Original F Scale	Young people sometimes get rebellious ideas, but as they grow up they ought to get over them and settle down.
16	U. of Manitoba	Organizations like the army and the priesthood, which make their members submit to the commands of superiors, have an unhealthy effect upon people.‡
19	U. of Mantioba	Homosexuals are just as good and virtuous as anybody else, and there is nothing really wrong with being one.‡
23	U. of Manitoba	Rules about being "well-behaved" and respectable are chains from the past that we have to break and throw away.‡
25	U. of Manitoba	Criminals, loafers and other immoral people usually think leniency and kindness are signs of weakness, so it's best for everyone concerned to use a firm hand when dealing with them.
27	U. of Manitoba	When you get right down to it, there's really no reason to play the national anthem before football games, etc. Such superficial displays of patriotism have little to do with what it really means to be a Canadian.‡
29	U. of Manitoba	A parent, boss or military commander who demands complete obedience from his "subordinates" is just showing how insecure and incompetent he is.‡
45	U. of Manitoba	People should pay less attention to the Bible and the other old traditional forms of religious guidance, and instead develop their own personal standards of what is moral and immoral.‡
46	Modification of Lee & Warr item	The facts on crime, sexual immorality and the recent public disorders all show we will have to crack down harder on deviant groups and troublemakers if we are going to save our religious standards and preserve law and order.

TABLE 6 — *Continued*

Item No.	Source	Item
48	U. of Manitoba	Some people need to be reminded that our customs, moral discipline and national heritage are the things that have made us great.
49	Original F Scale	Obedience and respect for authority are the most important virtues children should learn.
51	Modification of Lee & Warr item	In the final analysis parents, civil authorities and the proper spiritual leaders generally turn out to be right about things.
53	U. of Manitoba	Laws have to be strictly enforced if we are going to preserve our moral standards and way of life.
55	Modification of item from TFI	If a child starts becoming a little too unconventional, his parents should see to it he returns to the normal ways expected by society.
62	U. of Manitoba	It may be all right to criticize someone while he's running for office, but once a man becomes the leader of our country, we owe him our strongest loyalty.

‡ Indicates the item is worded in the contrait (antiauthoritarian) direction.

Note: the order of presentation of the items was counterbalanced. "Item Nos." given above are those of one of the four formats used. (See Appendix I.)

values are about twice as large as those found on earlier "authoritarianism" scales. This level of internal consistency gave the mock scales alpha reliabilities ≥ .85 (or a signal-to-noise ratio greater than 2 to 1), which I believe, most behavioral scientists would agree, is adequate for many research uses. Thus by the fall of 1973 I not only believed that sentiments of authoritarian submission, authoritarian aggression, and conventionalism reliably and broadly covaried, but I also thought that a psychometrically viable scale to measure this covariation was at hand.

I conducted one more item analysis study at the beginning of the 1973-74 academic year, using 253 students who responded to 70 items over the course of two testing sessions held one week apart. Most of the items tested were some variant of items presented in Tables 1–6 of this chapter, and the purpose of the study was to test different versions of these statements for best fit with one another. Seven ethnocentrism items which had shown at least some tendency to covary with the central cluster were also included in the questionnaire, as were five "life-is-a-jungle" (Maslow, 1943) and several "will power" statements. Again, the order of presentation of the 70 items was systematically counterbalanced.

The interitem correlation matrix was analyzed as before, and the most highly intercorrelated twelve protrait and twelve contrait items were selected to form the initial version of a test I have called the "Right-Wing Authoritarianism" (RWA) Scale. These items are listed in Table 7. The reader has encountered nearly all of them, in one form or another, in the preceding item analysis studies. All of them, it seems to me, tap sentiments of authoritarian submission, authoritarian aggression, and conventionalism as defined at the beginning of this chapter.[4]

The mean intercorrelation of the protrait items in the September, 1973, study was .33, that of the contrait items was .22, and that of the protrait-contrait correlations, .18. Overall, the mean interitem correlation among the 24 statements was .23, and the alpha coefficient of the scale was .88.[5]

Summary of the conceptual history of the RWA Scale
The conceptual roots of the RWA Scale trail back to research on the F Scale reported 30 years ago.[6] As was noted in chapter 1, the items on that test are even more loosely connected empirically than they are theoretically, but there is a psychometric core to the test which has appeared rather consistently across samples and years. The items in that core seemed to me to tap hostile, conventional, and submissive attitudes. When I tested an item pool consisting of the F, D, Traditional Family Inventory, and Lee and Warr Scales in 1970 and 1971, the same kinds of items clustered, and nothing else did, in both student and nonstudent samples. All of these items were worded in the protrait direction, but later studies in 1971 found that contrait items expressing unconventional, rebellious or pacifist sentiments also tied into the cluster. Moreover, the cluster now involved a wide range of social contexts (e.g., marijuana, homosexuality, submission to the government, women's rights, pornography, childrearing, respect for the flag, and welfare) whose breadth implied that the dispositions to submission, aggression and conventionalism were not all that situation specific or issue specific.

Four further item development studies strengthened these perceptions. New items written to tap the three sentiments almost always tied into the central cluster as expected, though naturally to varying degrees. Mock scales composed of the most highly intercorrelated items furthered the impression, across successive studies, that sentiments of submission, aggression, and conventionalism were manifest in a wide range of social issues (e.g., submission to established religions, the sanctity of customs, prison reform, the effects of army life, personal modesty,

TABLE 7

The initial version of the Right-Wing Authoritarianism Scale

Item No.	Source	Item
1	U. of Manitoba	A lot of our society's rules regarding modesty and sexual behavior are just customs which are not necessarily any better or holier than those which other people follow.‡
7	U. of Manitoba	Youngsters should be taught to refuse to fight in a war unless they themselves agree the war is just and necessary.‡
9	U. of Manitoba	A "woman's place" should be wherever she wants to be. The days when women are submissive to their husbands and social conventions belong strictly in the past.‡
10	U. of Manitoba	Our prisons are a shocking disgrace. Criminals are unfortunate people who deserve much better care, instead of so much punishment.‡
17	U. of Manitoba	In these troubled times laws have to be enforced without mercy, especially when dealing with the agitators and revolutionaries who are stirring things up.
18	Modification of item from TFI	If a child starts becoming a little too unconventional, his parents should see to it he returns to the normal ways expected by society.
20	Original F Scale	Obedience and respect for authority are the most important virtues children should learn.
21	U. of Manitoba	The courts are right in being easy on drug offenders. Punishment would not do any good in cases like these.‡
23	U. of Manitoba	People should pay less attention to the Bible and the other old traditional forms of religious guidance, and instead develop their own personal standards of what is moral and immoral.‡
24	U. of Mantioba	It's one thing to question and doubt someone during an election campaign, but once a man becomes the leader of our country we owe him our greatest support and loyalty.
25	Modification of Lee & Warr item	The facts on crime, sexual immorality, and the recent public disorders all show we have to crack down harder on deviant groups and troublemakers if we are going to save our moral standards and preserve law and order.
34	U. of Manitoba	One good way to teach certain people right from wrong is to give them a good stiff punishment when they get out of line.
39	Modification of item from TFI	Women should always remember the promise they make in the marriage ceremony to obey their husbands.
44	U. of Manitoba	National anthems, flags, and glorification of one's country should all be deemphasized to promote the brotherhood of all men.‡

TABLE 7 — *Continued*

Item No.	Source	Item
46	U. of Manitoba	Our customs and national heritage are the things that have made us great, and certain people should be made to show greater respect for them.
50	U. of Manitoba	Homosexuals are just as good and virtuous as anybody else, and there is nothing wrong with being one.‡
51	U. of Manitoba	Organizations like the army and the priesthood have a pretty unhealthy effect upon men because they require strict obedience of commands from superiors.‡
52	U. of Manitoba	Laws have to be strictly enforced if we are going to preserve our way of life.
53	U. of Manitoba	It may be considered old-fashioned by some, but having a decent, respectable appearance is still the mark of a gentleman and especially a lady.
55	Original F Scale	Young people sometimes get rebellious ideas, but as they grow up they ought to get over them and settle down.
56	U. of Manitoba	Capital punishment should be completely abolished.‡
62	U. of Manitoba	Rules about being "well mannered" and respectable are chains from the past which we should question very thoroughly before accepting.‡
64	U. of Manitoba	Atheists and others who have rebelled against the established religions are no doubt every bit as good and virtuous as those who attend church regularly.‡
69	U. of Manitoba	Being kind to loafers or criminals will only encourage them to take advantage of your weakness, so it's best to use a firm, tough hand when dealing with them.

‡ Indicates statement is worded in antiauthoritarian direction.
Note: the order of presentation of the items was counterbalanced. "Item Nos." given above are those of one of the four formats used. (See Appendix I).

capital punishment).

Every bit as significant as the discovery of what covaried was the discovery of what did not. Compared to the conceptualizations of authoritarianism which have been advanced in the past, which have typically involved about 10 components, the present model is positively lean. Of course, not every "component of authoritarianism" which has ever been proposed was tested, but many pertinent ones were. None of these ever permanently joined the central core. Authoritarianism apparently need not be as "multifactored" a construct as previous theorists have argued (and scales have required).

TABLE 8

Measures of internal consistency of the scales listed in Tables 1-7

Study	No. Items	Average Correlation among				
		Protrait Items	Contrait Items	Protrait-Contrait Pairs	All Items	"Alpha" Coefficient
Non-students						
June, 1971	10	.39	—	—	—	—
October, 1971	20	.34	.15	.10	.17	.80
Students						
Winter, 1970	10	.27	—	—	—	—
September, 1971	20	.21	.15	.12	.15	.78
January, 1972	20	.29	.20	.17	.20	.83
October, 1972	20	.32	.25	.23	.26	.87
January, 1973	20	.34	.21	.19	.23	.85
September, 1973	24	.33	.22	.18	.23	.88

Summary of the psychometric history of the RWA Scale

The psychometric effect of the eight item analysis studies which produced the initial version of the RWA Scale may be assessed by consulting Table 8, which lists the data on the internal consistency of the mock scales composed at each step of the development. From the start, protrait items covaried better than contrait items, and these covariations improved more or less steadily as items from the F Scale and other tests were modified or altogether replaced with new statements. Contrait items started far behind the protraits, having a much smaller prior literature. But they also improved steadily. As the protrait-protrait, and contrait-contrait correlations improved, the protrait-contrait relationships began to make headway against the strong direction-of-wording effects we first encountered with the F Scale in chapter 2. As both sets of items increasingly tapped the same underlying sentiments, test content controlled more of the variance of responses to the items. The resulting overall intercorrelation of .23, while quite modest in absolute terms, is about twice as large as that of preceding authoritarianism scales.

Conclusions

The conclusions to this chapter were presented, somewhat unconventionally, at its beginning. There, in the definition of the construct I have proposed, I listed my inferences about the nature of right-wing authoritarianism. The reader has now seen the basis for these inferences and the way in which a scale to measure the construct was developed.

It was my belief, in the fall of 1973, that these item analysis studies had taken that first step toward a scientific understanding of authoritarianism on which we had so consistently stumbled in the past. The conceptualization was tighter than previous efforts, more clearly defined, and more carefully delimited. The operational definition of the construct, the RWA Scale, was necessarily faithful to the conceptualization, since they both grew from the same source (the item analysis studies). The RWA Scale appeared stronger, psychometrically, than its numerous predecessors. Finally, I had a sense, arising from the consistency of the findings over three years, that there really was "something there," and I was now able to lay my hands upon it.

A test of the construct validity of the RWA and five other authoritarianism scales

4

As I noted in chapter 1, the sprawling literature on authoritarianism contains numerous attitude scales which have led more or less independent lives. While various researchers have presented their tests as superior measures of authoritarianism, this proposition has rarely been put to the test, even in cases where an investigator had the necessary data in hand (e.g., Kohn, 1974).

The study about to be described, therefore, is remarkably unprecedented for an empirical science. In it, scores were obtained from nearly a thousand university students on six measures of "authoritarianism": the original F Scale (Adorno et al., 1950); the Dogmatism Scale (Rokeach, 1960); the Conservatism Scale (Wilson and Patterson, 1968); Lee and Warr's (1969) "Balanced F Scale"; Kohn's (1972) Authoritarianism-Rebellion Scale; and the Right-Wing Authoritarianism Scale whose development was described in the previous chapter. Data were also collected on a seventh scale, an improved version of the balanced F Scale described in chapter 2. The construct validities of these tests were then assessed, following the pattern used in chapter 1, (a) by examining the unidimensionality of responses to the scales, and (b) by examining their relationships with various measures of authoritarian dispositions and behavior.

The first criterion, unidimensionality, requires little elaboration. The greater the extent to which items on a scale tap a large number of loosely related sentiments, the poorer the validity of the test as a measure of a single construct. The interitem correlations of each test were therefore examined as direct evidence of each scale's unidimensionality. In addition, a factor analysis was performed on the responses to each test as a means of interpreting the major dimensions represented on each scale.

The second criterion, relationships with various authoritarian dispositions and behavior, was assessed by obtaining each scale's correlation with the following six indices: (a) subjects' acceptance of acts by government officials which violate the .undamental principles of a democratic society; (b) subjects' orientation to laws as the basis of morality; (c) subjects' punitiveness toward hypothetical persons who have broken the law; (d) subjects' aggression against a peer in a mock-learning laboratory experiment; (e) subjects' continued acceptance, as adults, of the religious beliefs their parents taught them; and (f) subjects' preference for right-wing political parties.

I believe that the conceptualizations of authoritarianism being pitted here can be held accountable to these criteria;[1] they are not unusual among the criteria which have been used in the past to test the validity of authoritarianism scales. Only the laboratory aggression, it is true, is a direct measure of behavior. The rest are paper-and-pencil assessments of dispositions to act, or else orientations toward ideas and groups. While some researchers will dismiss these assessments as being of little interest, they can still be used to compare the scales. Beyond that, I would again submit that "quiet behaviors" such as accepting government injustices, are among the most potentially dangerous authoritarian acts we could have in our society.

METHOD

Subjects

In October, 1973, students in 24 of the 30 day-sections of introductory psychology at the University of Manitoba were invited to sign up for a three-session "study of the social attitudes of Canadian students."[2] Sixty appointment slips for each of twenty different testing "tracks" were distributed in this subject pool. There were approximately 1,900 students enrolled in these sections, most of them Canadians, and nearly 1,100 appointment slips were filled out.

Slightly over 1,000 of these students kept their first appointment. However, 33 of them failed to return to the second testing session one week later. Fourteen of the subjects who had kept their first two appointments then missed the third session. A few other subjects were dropped because they were not Canadian citizens, or because they did not complete all of the seven "authoritarianism" scales over the three sessions.

In the end I had reasonably complete sets of data from 956 subjects.

Procedure
Subjects reported to a moderate-sized classroom in the psychology building. The classroom contained 24 tables (measuring 76 cm. by 152 cm.)
at which two subjects could be seated with a reasonable space between
them. Individual desk-chairs, scattered about in the back of the room,
accommodated overflow from the tables. There were usually about 50
subjects at each testing session; the lowest turnout ever was 32, and the
highest was 63.

Instructions
At one minute past the appointed time of the first session I introduced
myself and passed out survey booklets and pencils to the subjects, asking
them to keep the booklets face down on the table until I had given them
some preliminary instructions. I then carried a cassette tape recorder to
the middle of the room and said:

I think you know that this experiment is being run at a number of different times
during the week. Whenever a study is done in a number of different sessions it is
important to standardize the instructions. Otherwise there is some danger that I
might explain things differently to you here today than I will on [Friday], and that
could conceivably affect the results of the experiment. For that reason I have tape
recorded my instructions to you, and most of what you hear from me today you will
hear over this tape recorder.

The taped instructions proceeded as follows:

This is the first part of Experiment Survey. As you know, this study takes three hours,
and the second and third parts of this study will be held in this same room at this
same time during the next two weeks. Please be sure to remember your appointments for these times, for as was stated on the sign-up booklet you must attend all
three sessions to earn credit in this experiment. The three hours of credit will be given
out at the last session, two weeks from today, to those people who have served in
the three hours of the study.
   Today's task involves filling out a series of questionnaires which ask your opinion
about a number of different things. We shall get into that in a few minutes, but there
are a few things I want to say first about our general procedures here today.
   First of all, because of its purpose, this experiment is open only to students who
are Canadians. If you are not a Canadian, you should tell me so after these instructions are completed, and I shall find a different experiment for you to serve in instead.
   Secondly, you will soon see that your booklet has a survey number written on
it in red ink. I am going to pass an attendance sheet around during the period, on
which I'd like you to print your survey number, your name, the slot in which you

take introductory psychology, and the name of your 17.120 professor. This information is used for two purposes. One, it provides proof for you, just in case you lose your experimental credit record card between now and April, that you did in fact complete one of my questionnaires in this experiment, and are entitled to credit even though you have lost your card. Secondly, I am required to give the Subject Pool office an account of how many credit hours I have given out to each section of the introductory psychology course. That is why I need the information about your 17.120 slot and professor.

Finally, in the way of general remarks, you do not have to answer any particular item on the questionnaire if you do not wish to. This is always true of any experiment run in the psychology department here. There is absolutely no penalty for leaving an item unanswered — not in this or in any other experiment you will ever serve in at the University of Manitoba.

Okay. Enough for preliminaries. Would you please turn over your booklet now.

You can see that there is an IBM response card attached to the first page of the booklet. You will use this card to give your opinion of the statements on the first questionnaire, and I'd like you to peel it off the front page now. Please leave the sticker on the page.

I'd like you to be very careful in marking your responses on the card, because the machine we use to read these cards is kind of old and fussy, and likes to call the most insignificant stray pencil mark a total response. [Please give only one response to each item, and make a definite dark mark in the bubble you have chosen. If you change an answer, please erase the old answer very thoroughly. Please do not make any stray pencil marks on the card.][3] And of course make sure you keep track of which statement you are responding to on the card.

The first questionnaire is part of [an investigation of general public opinion concerning a variety of social issues. You will probably find that you agree with some of the statements, disagree with others, and to varying extents. Please mark your opinion on the IBM card provided, according to the amount of your agreement or disagreement, by using the following scale: Blacken the bubble labeled −3 if you *strongly disagree* with the statement. Blacken the bubble labeled −2 if you *moderately* disagree with the statement. And blacken the bubble labeled − 1 if you *slightly* disagree with the statement; if on the other hand you feel you *slightly agree* with the statement then blacken the bubble labeled +1. And +2 means you *moderately* agree with the statement. And +3 means you *strongly* agree with the statement; if you feel exactly and precisely *neutral* about an item, then blacken the zero bubble.]

Once you have finished the first questionnaire, then go right on to the next task in the booklet. Some of the tasks are to be answered right in the booklet, while others are to be answered on IBM cards. There are instructions at the beginning of each task.

Keep on working until you finish the booklet. You will not have to rush to finish all the material by the end of the period, but you should try to work at a brisk, steady pace. Don't spend a lot of time on any one item or questionnaire.

When you finish the entire booklet, bring all the materials up to the front of the room, and you may leave.

Are there any questions?

At the second and third sessions of the study subjects were reminded of their survey numbers through the attendance sheets signed at the first session, and after brief instructions which once again reminded them to work with care, completed the booklet with their survey number on it.

Description of the surveys
The booklets distributed to the subjects at the first session began with one of the authoritarianism scales being tested (but never with the C Scale). A "Trials" questionnaire followed, which asked the subject what prison sentence he would impose on persons convicted of four different crimes. Another of the authoritarianism scales followed, and the booklet ended with a "Demographic Survey" which asked for information about the student's sex, age, academic major, year in school, religious and political background, father's occupation and urban-rural background.

At the second session, the subjects again encountered one of the authoritarianism scales being tested, and then they answered the C Scale. A "Government Activities Survey" followed, in which the subject was asked to evaluate the seriousness of four incidents in which Canadian government officials were alleged to have broken the law to accomplish certain objectives. The booklet ended with another of the authoritarianism scales.

The third session began with one of the authoritarianism scales. Then the subject was asked to say what he would do in three "moral dilemmas" in which there would be considerable humanitarian or social pressure to break the law. This last session concluded with another of the authoritarianism scales.

The subjects had ample time to complete each booklet. The few who were dropped because they failed to complete all seven of the authoritarianism scales missed an entire scale, probably through oversight. Often the time remaining at the end of each session was used to collect standardization data for other research projects (e.g., Fullerton, 1974).

Ordering of the authoritarianism scales
The C Scale always appeared in the center of the second-session booklet for every subject. The other six scales were rotated systematically through the six "authoritarianism scale" slots in the booklets described above. The C Scale was treated differently from the others because its format is different. Unlike the others, it does not consist of statements with which the subject can disagree or agree, but rather lists 50 things (e.g., "death penalty") which the subject says he is either in favor of, or not. It thus could not be answered on my IBM response card, which had

"bubbles" for thirty-five -3 to $+3$ responses. Its placement at the beginning of any booklet would have caused confusion when the instructions were given and created curiosity among the subjects about the varying composition of their booklets. The simplest alternative was to put this test in the middle of the series. Subjects responded to the C Scale, incidentally, by circling the response alternative of their choice directly on the booklet page, as in Wilson and Patterson (1968).

In all of the $(20 \times 3 =)$ 60 sessions of the experiment each of the six remaining authoritarianism scales began approximately one-sixth of the booklets distributed in the room, and they also shared equally the second scale-slot in the booklets. The pairing of scales in the booklets was rotated systematically, except that the two unidirectionally worded scales, the original F Scale and the D Scale, were always placed in the same booklet. This was done to keep any response set effects which might be triggered by the unidirectional wording from carrying over onto a balanced scale.[4]

Thus the design of the experiment guaranteed that all of the authoritarianism scales (save one) appeared equally in all of the six scale-slots spread across the three sessions of the study. Simple order of presentation effects, such as reactions to the repetition of similar material over time, were in all probability distributed evenly across the scales.

The seven scales themselves are reproduced in Appendix II as they appeared to the subjects. All of the balanced scales (except the C Scale) had their protrait and contrait items arranged in the same sequence. The C Scale was presented in its published form, which systematically alternates conservative and anticonservative items from beginning to end.

Responses to six of the scales were scored with the usual keying (e.g., 1—strong disagreement, 4—neutral or no response, 7—strong agreement for the protrait items, and the opposite keying for contrait items.) C Scale responses were hand-scored according to the published key (2—yes, 1—uncertain or no response, 0—no for conservative items, and the opposite keying for anticonservative items.)

RESULTS: INTERNAL CONSISTENCY OF THE SCALES

The basic psychometric properties of the seven authoritarianism scales pitted in this study are given in Table 1. The level of interitem correlation varied considerably from test to test; but in general the scales ran true to their past performance. The values obtained for the F and D Scales exactly equal those commonly reported in their vast literature, and that

TABLE 1

Basic psychometric properties of the authoritarianism scales

Scale	Number of items	Balanced?	N	Item mean	Test mean	Test variance	Test range	Alpha relia-bility	Mean inter-item correlation
F	29	No	956	3.49	101.1	430	45-175	.81	.13
F$_{bal.}$	29	Yes	956	3.67	106.6	289	50-164	.73	.09
D	40	No	956	3.72	148.7	609	69-233	.82	.10
C	50	Yes	956	0.73	36.5	114	9-69	.77[a]	.06[a]
L&W	30	Yes	956	3.67	110.1	262	42-163	.72	.08
A-R	30	Yes	956	3.95	118.5	309	53-170	.77	.10
RWA	24	Yes	956	3.81	91.4	466	27-157	.88	.23

[a] Internal consistency estimates for the C Scale are based upon a subsample of 199 of the 956 completed surveys. Because subjects answered the C Scale right in the booklet, item scores were only available if the individual answers were transposed to punched cards, etc. It was impractical to do this for all the booklets, so surveys with I.D. numbers whose last two digits were between 41 and 60 (e.g. 741-760) were used as a subsample. (It so happened that 56% of these subjects were males). A spot check of 50 of these 199 surveys found less than 2% error in transposition from booklet to cards.

for the A-R Scale (.10) approximates the value (.12) estimated from Kohn's split-half reliability data on Canadian students. Lee and Warr's scale was more loosely interconnected here than it was among the Princeton students whose responses created it.[5] The RWA Scale's value of .23 exactly replicates the figure found in the preceding month when the scale was composed.

Only the C Scale's level of interitem correlation is surprisingly different from its published values. While not unprecedented (see Wilson, 1973, p. 56), the figure of .06 is less than half the average value previously found with the test (.13). One might attribute the C Scale's poor showing to its appearing so different to subjects from the three "standard format" scales they had previously encountered in the testing sequence. However, most of the high reliabilities summarized by Wilson were obtained from "heterogeneous" samples, which tend to yield higher alphas.

The level of interitem correlation and the length of each test determine its alpha reliability. Table 1 shows that the RWA Scale had the highest reliability (.88), despite its being the shortest test. The other balanced tests all had reliabilities in the .72–.77 range. The reliabilities of the unidirectionally worded F and D Scales must be interpreted cautiously because of the probability that they have been inflated by response sets.

In this regard, one should note that the variance of the original F Scale (430) was again significantly larger than that of its balanced counterpart (289) (t test for a difference between correlated variances, $t = 9.9$, $p < .0001$). The difference in these variances, paralleling that shown in Table 7 of chapter 2, was basically attributable to a very low correlation between the protrait and contrait statements on the balanced scale. Over 30% of the variance of summed scores on the original F Scale was again attributable to direction-of-wording effects, replicating the result of the winter, 1970, Study.

FACTOR ANALYSES OF THE SCALES

The data on interitem correlations reviewed above provide direct evidence on the extent to which responses to each scale covaried. The low level of intercorrelation found on most of the scales, entirely typical of those reported in the previous literature, raise again our old doubts about the extent to which these tests can be measuring a single construct. We shall now turn to factor analytic techniques to interpret what it is the tests are tapping, and to what extent.

Decisions made regarding the analysis
As we saw in chapter 1, factor analysis is commonly used to assess the construct validity of authoritarianism scales, but its use is often unsatisfying. This is because the many different ways responses to a test can be factored produces interpretations of the data, not something inevitable and unambiguous. Within limits, quite different results can be obtained depending on how the factoring proceeds, and because of this and unresolved issues in the theory of factor analysis, the technique can be bent, to some extent, to the will of the investigator.

The issue at hand is the interpretation of what the items on each test have in common with one another. That is, I considered the task to be the explanation of "common variance," which meant that the data should be analyzed by one of the "classical factor analysis" techniques that place estimates of the items' communalities in the diagnonal of the correlation matrix (Harman, 1967). This class of approaches may be contrasted with the "principal components" technique which inserts 1.0's into the diagonals and thus seeks to explain all of the variance on a test, including "error" variance.

The responses to each survey were accordingly factored by the "principal factor" program of the Biomedical Statistical Package (i.e., Program

P4M in Dixon, 1975), with squared multiple correlations between each item and the remaining items on the test used as the initial estimate of communality.[6] Mutually orthogonal factors were extracted so long as their eigenvalue $\geq$ 1.0,[7] and the estimates of the communalities were revised and the factors re-extracted until the communalities did not change by more than .001 from one iteration to the next.

The resulting solutions were then rotated to orthogonal "simple" structure" according to Kaiser's (1958) Varimax technique. Since the models of authoritarianism under consideration consist of theoretically related, not independent factors, oblique rotations were then performed on the Varimax solution according to Hendrickson and White's (1964) "Promax" technique.[8]

Results of the factor analyses
The many intermediate and final results of the factor analyses are far too numerous to be presented in their entirety. Tables 2a and 2b therefore present the following information about the inferred factorial structure of each scale:

1 The number of factors extracted by the program appears first. This is a very basic measure of the factorial simplicity of a test. As one might expect, the longest test (the C Scale) had the most complex structure (seven factors) while the shortest test, the RWA Scale, and the unidirectionally worded F Scale had the simplest structures (just one factor).

2 Next is reported the total amount of the test's variance which was controlled by the extracted factors. It is only a rough indicator of a test's factorial integrity since the factors may have little relationship to one another.

3 The amount of test variance controlled by the factors in the unrotated matrix is then listed. These figures give an indication of the contribution which each successive factor made toward accounting for the test's common variance, and can be used to decide how many factors are worth retaining in describing the factor structure of a test.[9]

4 Table 2a then lists the number of items on each test which had no "appreciable" loadings (i.e., $\geq$ .40) on any of the Varimax-rotated factors. This is an index of the factorial integrity of a test. It can be seen that there were a large number of such unconnected items on all of the tests except the RWA Scale.

5 Finally Table 2a lists the mean correlation found among the Promax-rotated factors. This too is an index of unidimensionality, as a high degree

TABLE 2a

Summary of the factor analyses of the seven authoritarianism scales

Scale	Number of factors extracted	Percent of test variance accounted for by:									No. items with *no* loadings $> .40$ in varimax rotation	Mean correlation among factors in promax rotation
		All extracted factors	Individual factors in unrotated matrix:									
			I	II	III	IV	V	VI	VII			
F	1	14.0	14.0	—	—	—	—	—	—	19	—
$F_{bal.}$	2	14.0	10.4	3.6	—	—	—	—	—	22	.29
D	2	13.1	10.3	2.8	—	—	—	—	—	30	.54
C	7	27.4	8.9	4.6	4.1	3.0	2.6	2.2	2.0	27	.07
L&W	2	16.1	11.9	4.2	—	—	—	—	—	19	.40
A-R	3	25.4	13.8	7.1	4.5	—	—	—	—	14	.08
RWA	1	23.3	23.3	—	—	—	—	—	—	4	—

TABLE 2b
Highest loading items (i.e. ≥ .40) in the varimax rotation (in order of magnitude)

Scale	I	II	III	IV	V	VI	VII
Factor							
F	17 (.560)a, 1, 12, 8, 15, 16, 11, 23, 25, 21 ([14%]b						
Fbal.	1 (.586), 8, 12, 27, 4 [8.0%]	26 (.464), 25 [6.0%]					
D	13 (.499), 32, 40, 11, 12, 8, 27, 22 [8.5%]	25 (.439), 30 [4.6%]					
C	34 (.645), 37, 4,22,18,27 [5.2%]	49 (.618), 15,35,5 [5.1%]	48 (.594) 17,40,42 [3.9%]	8 (.462), 45,2 [3.8%]	43 (.525), 39,12,38 [3.6%]	32 (.620) [2.9%]	25 (.497) [2.7%]
L&W	6 (.570), 19, 2 5, 1, 8, 7 [9.4%]	3 (.449), 4 15, 10 [6.7%]					
A-R	25 (.697), 14, 1, 24, 15, 4, 20, 28 [11.8%]	22 (.560), 27, 23, 6, 5, 11 [8.8%]	17 (.837), 8 [4.8%]				
RWA	7 (.624), 10, 15, 17, 12, 5, 20, 14, 4, 18, 1, 8, 24, 9, 19, 3, 11, 21, 2, 13 [23.3%]						

a Figure in parentheses indicates the loading of the highest loading item.
b Figure in brackets indicates the amount of variance accounted for by the factor.

of intercorrelation indicates the separatable factors are closely related.
6 Table 2b lists the items which had the highest loadings on the
Varimax-rotated factors. (The listing is by item numbers; the items themselves can be found in Appendix II.) The loading of the highest loading
item on each factor is given in parentheses, while the amount of variance
accounted for by each rotated factor is given in brackets. These latter
values represent a redistribution of the total variance controlled by the
retained factors following rotation to simple structure.

Analyses of the inferred factorial nature
of the authoritarianism scales

The original F Scale
The principal factor analysis of the F Scale indicates there is only one
factor of any importance on the test. Its interpretation will be familiar
to the reader, as its five highest-loading items (see Table 2b) all appear
in Table 1 of chapter 1, and are the same items which have traditionally
dominated factor analyses of the F Scale. I conclude therefore, as before,
that the only factor measured by the F Scale worth noting taps sentiments of authoritarian submission, authoritarian aggression and conventionalism. The vast majority of the items on the test have little
association with this factor (or anything else), however, and make the
scale very diffuse.

The weak factorial strength of the F Scale is particularly noteworthy
because all of its items profit from the strong direction-of-wording effects
found in chapter 2. The disassociating power of these effects on balanced
scales can be seen directly by examining the factor analysis of the
balanced version of the F Scale. Two factors were extracted: all of the
protrait items had their higher loading on Varimax Factor I, and all of
the contrait items had their higher loading on Varimax Factor II. These
factors thus simply represent the protrait and contrait items on the test,
and illustrate again the power of the direction-of-wording effects we
isolated in chapter 2.

The Dogmatism Scale
The factor analysis of the D Scale parallels that of the F Scale in several
respects. The first Varimax factor, which appears to represent sentiments
that the world is divided into two camps, and one must not compromise
with the "other side," is definitely relevant to the construct of dogmatism. The second factor, which might be labelled "excitability in argu-

ments," is also conceptually relevant and correlated .54 with the first. The trouble is, like the F Scale, the vast majority of the items on the test have little relationship with these factors, or with anything else. The two factors only control 13% of the test's variance, and overall, the D Scale is even more diffuse than the F Scale.

The Conservatism Scale
As bad as the D Scale's factor structure is, the C Scale's is even worse. It is clearly the most disjointed test in the battery.[10] The only thing which amounts to a "core" in the C Scale data are Factors I and II, which correlated .52 in the Promax rotation and together accounted for 10% of the test's variance. Factor I might be labelled "Sex-related Propriety" while Factor II is the "Religious Conservatism" factor found in most earlier factor analyses of the C Scale. Factors III and V are identifiable ("Ethnocentrism" and "Harsh Discipline" respectively), but they were uncorrelated with the first two, the highest Promax correlation being .06.

The Lee and Warr "Balanced F Scale"
The factor analysis of Lee and Warr's scale indicates that it is a more cohesive test than either of the balanced scales we have reviewed thus far. The two factors extracted accounted for 16% of the test's variance and correlated .40 in the Promax rotation. The highest-loading items on both factors appear to me to be tapping the same sentiments of authoritarian submission, authoritarian aggression and conventionalism which the RWA Scale was intended to measure. (In fact, as I indicated in chapter 3, some of these items were used in the early stages of the RWA Scale's development.) The two factors themselves represent the usual direction-of-wording effect: all of the contrait items had their higher loading on Factor I, while ten of the fifteen protrait items had their higher loading on Factor II.

The Authoritarianism-Rebellion Scale
Although its factor structure accounts for quite a bit more variance than that of Lee and Warr's scale, the A-R Scale is not as unidimensional, since there was virtually no relationship among its three factors. The interpretation of the factors themselves is straightforward. All but one of the protrait items on the test had their highest loading on Factor I; all but two of the contrait items on the test had their highest loading on Factor II; Factor III is an "astrology" factor with just two items loading (at all) on it.

These results are rather similar to Kohn's (1972) original findings, but their interpretation here is quite different. One could argue, as Kohn did in 1972, that Factors I and II represent independent traits of "authoritarianism" and "rebelliousness." (They would be independent in these data too because the Promax correlation between the two factors was −.05.) I would argue instead that the results reflect the usual tendency for differently keyed items to end up on different factors if they are not very strongly bound by their content. And there is practically no linkage between the protrait and contrait items on the A-R Scale. Even the items in each of the fifteen "matched pairs" (see chapter 1) were poorly correlated with one another, averaging just .18.

The Right-Wing Authoritarian Scale
The factor analysis indicates that the RWA Scale is the most unidimensional of the tests being compared. Only one factor was extracted, and that factor accounted for 23% of the test's variance. Nearly all of the scale's items had loadings $\geq$.40 on this factor.

These results do not mean the test measures just "one thing." Like any attitude scale which covers a variety of subjects, most of its variance is "specific" to individual issues or "error" due to instability in the subjects' responses. What the analysis does indicate however is that, to the extent that the items on the scale are measuring some things in common, they are just measuring one thing in common. I submit that "one thing" is the covariation of authoritarian submission, authoritarian aggression, and conventionalism, which I have called right-wing authoritarianism.

The fact that only one factor was extracted indicates that the shared content on the test in this instance overpowered the usual tendency of items to be split by direction-of-wording effects. If one forces a second factor from the RWA Scale correlation matrix, the usual keying differences appear: all of the protrait items have their higher loading on Varimax Factor I, and all but one of the contrait items have their higher loadings on Factor II. These factors account for 15.8% and 11.3% of the test's variance respectively, and correlated .70 in the Promax rotation.[11]

EMPIRICAL RELATIONSHIPS WITH THEORETICALLY RELATED VARIABLES

We turn now to relationships which the seven scales had with variables that, in most instances, are directly connectable to the concept of "authoritarianism" they represent. The extent to which the tests had the anticipated relationships is another index of their construct validity, and the strength of those relationships is a guide to the usefulness of the construct as an explanation of the behaviors involved.

Orientation to established authority and the law

Acceptance of violations of the law by established authorities
One behavior which I believe nearly everyone would consider relevant to "authoritarianism" is the acceptance and endorsement of illegal acts by government officials. Quite a few such acts by North American police and intelligence agencies have been revealed in the 1970s. Not everyone has agreed, however, that such activities as the FBI's attempts to blackmail Martin Luther King into committing suicide, and systematically conspiring to destroy political protest movements, were outrageous abuses of governmental powers. Newspapers have contained editorials and letters from the public expressing the opinion that these deeds were justified because of the threat posed by such men and groups, because one has to "fight fire with fire," and because government officials who make and enforce the laws have the right to decide which laws apply to them. Thus, there are people in our democracies who agree that governmental authorities are above the law and have nearly dictatorial power.

I initially attempted to measure this attitude by gauging subjects' reactions to four cases in which federal government officials had allegedly violated the law to pursue various ends.[12] The violations involved some of the most basic principles of a democratic society: freedom of speech, right to assemble to protest, freedom from illegal search and seizure, and right to due process of law. The four cases used are reproduced below:

1 It has been reported in the press that the RCMP has maintained illegal wiretaps of the telephones of about 60 persons in Quebec since the FLQ crisis of 1970. The persons are believed to be potentially sympathetic to the aims of the FLQ, and the RCMP is reported to be taking no chances that these persons might become active in their support of the outlawed organization. Members of certain radical right-wing groups, such as the Toronto-based Edmund Burke society that staged the attack on Premier Kosegin in Ottawa a while ago, are also reported to have had their phones tapped.

Under current legislation such wiretaps are legally permissable only if a judge has signed a court order authorizing them. The government reportedly has never sought court approval of the wiretaps because they believed the courts would deny them.

The RCMP has denied that the wiretaps exist, and described the report as a "complete fabrication."

If in fact the story is true, how serious a matter would you say the illegal wire-taps are?

2 It was recently reported that a large group of persons who had travelled to Ottawa to protest the government's economic policies were denied permission to assemble and voice their grievances. The group had been quite scathing in its attacks in recent weeks, and the demonstration promised to be a particularly bitter one.

Officials in Ottawa denied the group a parade and assembly permit, and an injunction was issued prohibiting the group from assembling in the vicinity of Parliament. The disorders which occurred during other recent demonstrations was cited as the reason for denying the group's request.

If the story is true, how serious a matter is the government's denial of the group's petition to assemble to protest?

3 It has been reported in the press that customs officials have, for the past two years, been systematically censoring incoming material for certain extremist political groups. Both the Toronto chapter of the North American Nazi Party and several Maoist/Communist groups have complained that it is practically impossible for them to obtain literature and pamphlets from outside the country. Both groups have also complained that postal officials quite often "lose" their mail, and that the RCMP systematically harasses their rallies by arresting guest speakers on trumped-up charges, closing the meeting hall because of "fire safety violations," etc.

If the story is true, how serious a matter is this governmental activity in your opinion?

4 Last summer, newspapers carried accounts of a series of controversial "drug raids" carried out in British Columbia. These raids were conducted by undercover agents who thought they had identified houses in the Vancouver area from which large amounts of illegal drugs were being distributed. The agents organized and carried out "midnight raids" without first securing search warrants and—it turned out—often ended up raiding the homes of totally innocent persons.

The agents defended these actions by citing the fact that on several of the raids they *had* found drugs hidden in houses, and that if they were going to follow up all their leads it was inevitable that sometimes the homes of persons unconnected with drug trafficking would be raided. The agents said they sometimes did not obtain search warrants before conducting their raids because these proceedings could become quite drawn out before a skeptical judge, and their job was to catch drug pushers, not argue with judges.

If the story is true, how serious an abuse of governmental power would you say these raids were?

The reader will note that the victims of the government injustices in the examples were either ordinary citizens, or else both right- and left-wing radical political organizations.

The subjects indicated their reaction to each of the cases on this response scale: 0—not serious at all (they were clearly justified by the circumstances); 1—mildly serious; 2—somewhat serious; 3—pretty

TABLE 3

Scores on the seven authoritarianism scales and acceptance of Government Injustices ($N = 949$)

	Illegal bugging	Denial of right to assemble	Political harassment	Illegal drug raids	Sum of the four	Coefficient of codetermination
Mean	2.51	2.32	2.15	2.72	9.69	
Standard deviation	1.32	1.22	1.38	1.34	3.79	
Scale						
F	−.22	−.22	−.34	−.26	−.36	13%
$F_{bal.}$	−.22	−.22	−.35	−.25	−.37	14%
D	−.09	−.12	−.24	−.17	−.22	5%
C	−.15	−.24	−.28	−.29	−.34	12%
L&W	−.30	−.30	−.40	−.33	−.47	22%
A-R	−.25	−.29	−.35	−.27	−.40	16%
RWA	−.33	−.36	−.46	−.34	−.52	27%

serious; 4—extremely serious (such acts strike at the foundation of a free society). Previous research has shown that the use of ordering numbers, and the adverbs employed above, each give the scale interval properties (Altemeyer, 1970).

The mean intercorrelation among responses to the four government injustices cases was .357 ($N = 949$), giving the summed score over the four cases an alpha reliability of .690.[13]

The mean and standard deviations of the subjects' reactions to these four government injustices are given in Table 3. Also shown are the correlations which scores on each of the authoritarianism scales had with these reactions, and the amount of variance (of the summed index) which scores on the authoritarianism scales could account for.

Table 3 shows, first of all, that there was a considerable acceptance of the governmental injustices among these Canadian university students. Seldom did the mean evaluation reach 3.0 ("pretty serious"), and only a small number of the subjects thought the cases were "extremely serious."

The various authoritarianism scales correlated significantly and negatively with indignation over these alleged government acts in every instance. Understandably, the correlations with the four-case summed score are almost always higher than those associated with any particular case, as the summed score is a more stable index, poor reliability and all.

The RWA Scale had a significantly higher correlation with the summed score than did any other scale (t test for differences between correlations obtained with the same population), and accounted for 27% of the variance of reactions to government injustices.

Acceptance of law as the basis of morality
The authoritarian's willingness to let officials "be a law unto themselves" does not mean that he considers laws mere formalities. It is almost axiomatic that authoritarians believe the rules issued by authority must be obeyed by the rest of society. The dictates of authority, being the criterion of right and wrong, serve as the basis of morality. It is not simply that moral judgments cannot supercede laws; moral judgments are not made. Authorities have done the judging already. Authoritarians would be people for whom "I was following orders" would be a morally sound justification for almost any act.

Not everyone holds so simple a view of morality, of course. Piaget (1932) and Kohlberg (1963, 1968) have developed models of the stages through which moral thought normally progresses as children grow older. Kohlberg's model is the more differentiated, detailing six types of moral reasoning ranging from the most primitive Type I ("punishment and obedience orientation") to the most advanced Type VI ("morality of individual principles of conscience").[14]

This typology was developed from research in which children responded to a series of moral dilemmas during a two-hour interview. Kohlberg later developed a scoring system for use with survey versions of his dilemmas, but researchers have found very few Type I's (and VI's) among university students with this system (Haan, Smith and Block, 1968; Fishkin, Keniston and McKinnon, 1973). I also discovered that Kohlberg's original problems did not place adults in very strong dilemmas (e.g., almost all said they would steal a drug from a pharmacist to save their spouse's life). For these reasons, in 1972, I began to develop an analog to Kohlberg's measure, which would place university students in greater conflict than the "children's dilemmas" did, be reliably scorable in a survey format, and produce greater numbers of (law = morality) Type I's for research with authoritarianism.

Subjects serving in the pitting experiment were asked to respond to three moral dilemmas during the third session of the study. The stories used are reproduced here:[15]

1 An acquaintance of yours asks you to do him a favor so he can save some money

on his income taxes. During the year he paid people to do odd jobs around his shop. Altogether he paid out about $100 for this sort of thing, but he did not know he had to get receipts from his helpers, and he does not know how to reach them now to get the receipts. It is a legitimate expense and the shopkeeper is entitled to use it as a deduction on his tax form. But the tax rules say he *must* have a receipt signed by the person who received the money. And this the shop owner does not have and cannot get.

The shopkeeper asks you to say *you* received the money, and to sign a fake receipt for it. Would you do so?

(You should assume that saying you received the money will not increase your own taxes.)

2 You read in the paper that a person in your city is near death from a special kind of cancer. There is one drug which the doctors think will save him. It is a form of radium that a scientist in your city has recently discovered. The drug does not cost much to make, but the scientist is making a big profit on it. He pays $100 for the radium but is charging $10,000 for it. The scientist knows a man is dying, but says "I discovered the drug and I'm going to make money from it."

It so happens you work in the same building as the scientist, and you know the drug is stored in a cabinet in the scientist's office. If you can get the drug the doctors will administer it, but the sick person needs the drug in the next 24 hours or it will not do him any good. There is simply no way you can raise $10,000 in such a short time, and the scientist has refused to give anyone any credit. It is apparent that no one else cares about the sick man.

Would you break in and steal the drug?

3 You are an unemployed parent with five children and you live in a slum in a large city. You have not held steady employment for over a year and have been living off unemployment compensation and then welfare. With a great deal of skimping you can just barely make ends meet with your monthly check.

The welfare laws allow you to earn up to $30 per month in odd jobs. Any money you earn over $30, however, is taken off your welfare check. An acquaintance of yours has recently offered you $60 per month to take care of her two children one day a week. You have explained that any payment over $30 does you no good, and offered to take care of the children every other week instead, for $30. Your acquaintance however, says that she needs a steady sitter every week, and suggests that you both say the payment was $30, when in fact it will be $60.

The extra $30 per month which you could keep by this arrangement would certainly come in handy. It would mean your family could have meat for supper two days a week instead of one, and your children could have things like new shoes when they need them. There has been no increase in welfare to compensate for the inflation that has raised prices recently, and in fact a change in the welfare law has been proposed which would allow recipients to earn up to $75 extra per month, instead of just $30. It will be some time before this change can actually be made in the law, however.

Would you make the arrangement with your acquaintance to earn $60 per month while reporting it only as $30?

After subjects indicated whether they would obey the law or not,

TABLE 4

Response alternatives given subjects after Moral Dilemma No. 1

(Type)a	
	Please check the alternative below which comes closest to being *your* main reason for deciding what you did in the situation above.
I	Signing the receipt would be against the law and therefore *wrong*. Laws are laws and were meant to be obeyed.
II	There is a certain amount of risk that one will be caught and punished for breaking the law.
II	No judge or jury would convict one of a crime in a case such as this.
III	Any good person would sign the receipt in that situation.
III	Any good person would obey the law in that situation.
III	Since the shop owner is an acquaintance, one feels some obligation to help him.
IV	One cannot expect others to obey the law if he does not obey it himself.
V	Laws are the basis of society and should be obeyed even if they are misguided, if we are going to have a smoothly running society.
VI	A person should do what is *just*, whether it is legal or not.

a The reader will note I have moved punishment-oriented reasoning from Type I to Type II (without doing too much damage to the "naive instrumental hedonism" of the latter) to isolate in Type I those subjects who believe that laws must be obeyed no matter what.

As will be apparent later, the results of the pitting study would be the same if the punishment-oriented subjects were reclassified as Type I's.

they gave their reasons in two ways. First they wrote down the most important considerations that entered their minds as they thought about the issue. Secondly, they responded to a checklist of possible reasons for reaching their decision. These checklists contained what I thought were the most obvious Type I and Type II, etcetera reasonings which a person might use in each case. The checklist for the first case is presented in Table 4.

The three open-ended responses were scored by the author according to the type of reasoning which seemed most prominent in the protocol. These and the three checklist responses produced six indications of the subject's type of moral reasoning. If four of these were in agreement, the subject was classified as being a particular type of moral thinker.[16]

Table 5 shows the mean and standard deviations of the scores obtained on the seven authoritarianism scales by those subjects who were assigned to a particular type in the scoring system. It can be seen that over half of the subjects (58%) showed too much diversity in their responses to

TABLE 5

Scores on the authoritarianism scales of subjects having identifiable types of moral reasoning

Scale	Stage I (N = 66)		Stage II (N = 109)		Stage III (N = 68)		Stage VI (N = 154)		F	Percent of variance accounted for ($\hat{\eta}^2$)
	$\bar{X}$	S	$\bar{X}$	S	$\bar{X}$	S	$\bar{X}$	S		
F	114.8	18.4	105.3	20.5	106.0	17.3	91.1	20.7	26.7	16.9%
F$_{bal.}$	119.2	13.8	111.1	16.2	106.9	13.1	97.6	18.7	31.2	19.2%
D	159.8	25.8	154.5	22.9	149.8	23.8	140.7	26.6	11.5	8.1%
C	45.7	11.0	37.3	9.6	36.6	9.1	32.4	10.5	26.8	17.0%
L&W	123.6	12.5	115.2	13.6	112.8	12.6	99.5	16.5	51.9	28.4%
A-R	131.3	15.4	125.5	13.7	119.3	14.6	107.2	21.4	39.1	23.0%
RWA	113.5	15.6	100.4	18.5	94.3	14.7	74.2	22.3	79.7	37.8%

be classified. It should also be noted that Types IV and V are not included in the table; there were too few of them (eight and seven respectively) to warrant meaningful comparison with the rest of the stages.[17]

Inspection of the means in Table 5 will also reveal that, with one exception, the scores on the authoritarianism scales decrease regularly from Type I to Type II to Type III to Type VI. A one-way analysis of variance ("fixed effects model," Weiner, 1962) was performed on these scores for each scale, and the resulting values of the F ratios and percentages of variance accounted for ($\hat{\eta}^2$) are also reported in Table 5. All of the F values were statistically significant, but they varied considerably. The RWA Scale differentiated among the types of moral reasoning to a substantially larger degree than did the others. The Type I RWA Scale mean was significantly larger than that of Types II, III and VI (post-hoc t test with individual alpha set at .01) all of which in turn were significantly different from one another.

PUNITIVENESS TOWARDS SANCTIONED TARGETS

Punishment of lawbreakers

Most of the conceptualizations of authoritarianism being considered either state or imply that persons who score high on their scales will manifest "authoritarian aggression" or be "insistent upon strict rules and punishments." While it is not always clear exactly what these phrases were intended to mean, it is a common premise that in some situations, at least, authoritarians are particularly inclined to be aggressive. It is especially common to find expectations that authoritarians are punitive against such targets as minority groups, social deviants and "common lawbreakers." These predictions were tested through the "trials" measure administered at the first testing session.

The four cases used are reproduced here:[18]

1 You are a judge presiding at the trial of "The People vs. Robert Smith." Evidence introduced in court indicates that on the evening of May 23rd, 1973, a Mr. Matthew Burns (a 47-year-old, Caucasian, accountant) was walking to his car in a hotel parking lot when he was stopped by a man who produced a pistol and demanded Mr. Burns' wallet. Mr. Burns complied, but as the robber ran from the scene Mr. Burns ducked into a doorway and began shouting "stop that man."

These cries were heard by a policeman cruising nearby in a partol car who after a short chase apprehended a Mr. Robert Smith (a 28 year-old, Caucasian of no fixed address or occupation). The police officer saw Mr. Smith throw what proved to be Mr. Burns' wallet down a sewer as he was being pursued. Smith matched the general description Mr. Burns gave of his assailant, but Mr. Burns was unable to identify

Smith "with absolute certainty" because it was dark in the parking lot at the time of the robbery.

Smith told the court he saw *another* man running from the parking lot, and then he found the wallet. He began to run after picking up the wallet because he heard the police siren and realized how incriminating the circumstances were. That was also, according to Smith, the reason he threw the wallet down the sewer.

Smith has a record of two previous "mugging" arrests and one prior conviction. He was found guilty of robbing Mr. Burns by the jury, and it is your duty now to declare sentence. A second conviction of armed robbery of this sort is punishable by up to ten years imprisonment, with parole possible after 1/3 of the sentence has been served.

When asked if he had anything to say before being sentenced, Smith said again that he was innocent. What sentence would you give?

2 You are the judge hearing the case of "The People vs. Jerimiah Lockwood. Mr. Lockwood (a 52-year-old, Caucasian, businessman) is the President and principal owner of Lockwood Industries. Following an audit of his tax returns the federal government charged the millionaire Mr. Lockwood with evading over $120,000 in personal income taxes over a five-year period. Mr. Lockwood at first pleaded innocent to the charges, but after records presented in the trial showed conclusively that he had evaded at least that much in tax payment, Mr. Lockwood changed his plea to guilty.

The law carries an automatic fine of 20% on such evasion (which amounts to $24,000 in this case) plus of course, repayment of the back taxes at 9% interest. It is also possible for you to give a jail sentence of up to 10 years, with parole possible after 1/3 of the sentence has been served.

To how many years of imprisonment would you sentence Mr. Lockwood?

3 You are a judge sitting in the case of "The People vs. Gerald Franklin." Mr. Franklin (a 46-year-old, Caucasian, policeman) has been charged with assault with a deadly weapon. The charge arose from events surrounding the arrest of a Mr. Stephen Lewis (a 19-year-old apprentice carpenter of Oujibway Indian ancestry) last September 3rd.

On that day, which was Labor Day, Mr. Lewis was part of a small group of demonstrators who were carrying signs in front of the offices of the Building Trades Union. The signs, and leaflets which the group was distributing, accused the unions of employing "racist discrimination" against Indians by denying them membership in the union, and hence employment on construction sites around the city.

Officer Franklin was in charge of a small detachment of police assigned to keep order in the area of the demonstration. At one point, however, a scuffle broke out between Lewis and a man who had tried to rip down the sign Lewis was carrying. Franklin had both men placed under arrest. Evidence given in court indicated, however, that as Mr. Lewis was being taken to the squad car he began calling the policemen present "pigs" and "fascists." Lewis was then placed in handcuffs and put in the back seat of a patrol car, but he continued to call the policemen these names.

Officer Franklin then got into the backseat of the car with Lewis and as the car was being driven away was seen by several people to strike Lewis repeatedly with his nightstick and fists.

Both the policeman driving the car and Officer Franklin testified that Lewis continued to call them names as the car drove away, and Officer Franklin has admitted striking the prisoner, but said it was necessary to subdue Lewis who was attempting to escape. Lewis, on the other hand, says he stopped calling the policemen names once the car was being driven away, and denies that he was trying to escape at the time he was struck. It took 12 stitches to close the wounds in Lewis' head.

The jury has found Officer Franklin guilty of common assault. Officer Franklin has been accused of "police brutality" by others before, but this is the only time he has been brought to court.

Common assault is punishable by up to ten months in jail, with probation possible after 1/3 of any sentence has been served. What sentence would you give Officer Franklin?

4 You are the judge in the trial "The People vs. Clifford Jones." According to evidence submitted in the case, a Miss Louise McKeet (a 23-year-old, Caucasian secretary) was asleep in her apartment on July 7, 1972 when about 1:30 a.m. a man broke through a rear window. The man threatened Miss McKeet with a knife, took $47 from her purse, and then sexually assaulted her. The intruder then struck Miss McKeet several times about the face, producing lacerations and bruises, before fleeing.

A Mr. Clifford Jones (a 25-year-old Caucasian [or Negro] unskilled laborer) was arrested in the neighborhood by police an hour later. He was positively identified by Miss McKeet in a police lineup, and his fingerprints were found on the window through which the intruder forced his entry.

He was found guilty of theft, assault and rape by a jury, and is now before you for sentencing.

Clifford Jones has been arrested previously for common assault and has one previous conviction for breaking and entering. His attorney has pointed out during the trial that Mr. Jones came from a broken home and that despite his past record has recently been showing signs of rehabilitation. He has held a steady job for six months. Unfortunately, the defense attorney noted, Mr. Jones met some old friends from his criminal past on the night of July 6th, became quite drunk, and reverted to his old habits.

The charges of which Mr. Jones has been found guilty are punishable by from one to twenty years imprisonment in this particular province, with probation possible after one third of the sentence has been served.

To how many years of imprisonment would you sentence Mr. Jones?

The reader will note that two versions of Trial #4 were used in this study. Although the victim (Miss McKeet) was presented as a Caucasian in both cases, half of the subjects were told that the rapist was white, and the other half was told that he was black.

The means and standard deviations of the "sentence" imposed by the subjects are listed in Table 6, along with the correlations found between scores on the authoritarianism scales and the sentences imposed in each case. All of the scales have positive and usually statistically significant relationships with the length of sentence imposed in three of the cases. The one interesting exception involved the policeman convicted of com-

TABLE 6

Relationship between scores on the authoritarianism scales and
sentences imposed for various criminal acts ($N = 954$)

	Mugging	Tax evasion	White rapist	Black rapist	Police brutality	Sum of all but brutality	Coefficient of codeter- mination
Mean	3.64	3.45	10.78	9.57	7.36	24.3	
Standard deviation	2.73	2.93	5.44	5.25	3.19	12.3	
Scale							
F	.18	.10	.26	.24	−.13	.24	6%
$F_{bal.}$	.15	.11	.32	.26	−.14	.25	6%
D	.12	.11	.15	.13	−.07	.17	3%
C	.18	.14	.22	.24	−.11	.25	6%
L&W	.18	.07	.32	.26	−.20	.24	6%
A-R	.17	.08	.32	.22	−.15	.23	5%
RWA	.27	.12	.38	.34	−.17	.33	11%

mon assault, where scores on the scales tended to be negatively, though
very weakly related to punitiveness. In general, the correlations were
strongest with sentences of the rapist and the mugger, perceptibly lower
with the sentencing of the millionaire tax evader, and were lowest (i.e.,
least positive) in the case of the policeman.

The scores obtained in all the cases except the "police brutality" case
were combined into a total score, whose correlations with the authoritarianism scales are reported in Table 6 along with the coefficients of
co-determination.[19] The RWA Scale again had a significantly higher correlation with this criterion than any of the other scales. It only accounted
for 11% of the variation of the three-case summed score, but the very low
reliability of this index must be kept in mind.

The scales' correlations with punitiveness toward the black rapist
were usually quite close to the figures for the white rapist. The fact that
the sentences given the black rapist were significantly lower than those
given the white lawbreaker ($t = 3.48$, $p <.001$) suggests these subjects
may have suspected the case was an indirect measure of prejuduce.

Punishment of peers in a learning situation
The Berkeley theory of the authoritarian personality explicitly predicts
that authoritarians will tend to punish unconventional people and minority groups. But it and other theories are mute about whether or not

authoritarians are also more aggressive against "ordinary people," although, as we saw in chapter 1 (Table 4), there is some evidence that in fact they are.

By point of comparison, the conceptualization of right-wing authoritarianism presented in chapter 3 defined authoritarian aggression as a general aggression directed against various people when sanctioned by authority figures. The "various people" were not just members of minority groups or social deviants but could be anyone, including peers, if the aggression appeared to be sanctioned. This expectation, and the prediction that authoritarians are more likely to aggress against members of a minority gorup, were tested through the bogus "shocking-learning" experiment in the fall of 1973.

Male subjects were recruited for this experiment at the end of the third session of the questionnaire study at the University of Manitoba. I announced to the students that one of my colleagues had asked me to distribute a sign-up booklet for one of his studies to the male subjects present. The subjects believed that my colleague was taking this route to the subject pool because he wanted to recruit subjects who would keep their appointments. I said I did not know what the experiment would be about, but that since my colleague's main area of interest was verbal learning the experiment would probably involve memorizing words or nonsense syllables.

One hundred and fifty-two male students signed up for this study, but 25 (16%) failed to keep their appointments. Of the 127 who did, 12 were from sections of introductory psychology which had already read about Milgram's studies of obedience. An additional 10 subjects were lost because of experimental flubs or chance events. Because of these losses, only 105 subjects were actually run in the experiment.

The procedures used in this study have already been described in chapter 2. In this particular run, half of the subjects served with male confederates who wore yarmulkas and thus appeared to be Jewish; the other half of the sample served with the same confederates, except the latter were bareheaded.

A postexperimental interview was held in an attempt to determine if the subject believed the experiment's cover story. Because of the difficulties in separating naive from aware subjects (Altemeyer, 1971), the interviewer was instructed to disqualify all subjects who seemed to have any suspicions about the experiment. Of the 105 subjects who served in the experiment, 26 were dropped as being non-naive. In all probability there were other undeceived subjects who slipped through this net.[20]

TABLE 7
Aggression against peers in the "Shocking Experiment"

	Victim was "Jewish" and was recognized by S as such.	Victim was "not Jewish" and was recognized by the subject as such.	Combination of all Ss for whom the victim-manipulation worked.	All naive Ss, whether the victim-manipulation worked or not.	Coefficient of codetermination
Sample size	35	30	65	79	
Mean shock	2.52	2.37	2.45	2.41	
Standard deviation	0.68	0.75	0.71	0.74	
Scale					
F	.24	.32	.30‡	.33‡	6-11%
$F_{bal.}$	.18	.36‡	.29‡	.24‡	3-13%
D	.13	.06	.12	.15	0-2%
C	.00	.20	.10	.12	0-4%
L&W	.29	.36‡	.33‡	.32‡	8-13%
A-R	.29	.27	.30‡	.25‡	6-9%
RWA	.41‡	.45‡	.44‡	.43‡	17-20%

‡p < .05

Table 7 lists the mean of the shocks delivered by the naive subjects, and also the correlations between the authoritarianism scales and this index of aggression. The first two columns present these figures for just those subjects who indicated on a postexperimental questionnaire that the manipulation of the confederate's Jewish or non-Jewish identity had been noticed. Since there was no evidence that this identity made any difference, the data from the two conditions were pooled and are presented in the third column of Table 7. The fourth column reports the correlations for all of the naive subjects, including the five serving in the "Jewish condition" who did not notice that the confederate appeared Jewish, and the nine who said the learner was Jewish when he was not wearing a yarmulke.

Most of the scales had at least some significant correlations with aggression in the study. However, the RWA scale again had the highest correlation in each of the comparisons listed in Table 9, and it was usually significantly higher than that of any other scale. RWA Scale scores accounted for 17% to 20% of the variance in punishment.

The fact that the RWA Scale had the strongest relationship with sanctioned aggression against a peer coincides with all of the findings we have considered so far. In addition, the study confirms the prediction that authoritarianism is not just related to aggression against minority groups and social deviants, but will be related to that against "ordinary people" as well if it is sanctioned by authority. On the other hand, the finding that authoritarianism was not more highly correlated with aggression against "Jewish" victims disconfirms all predictions, including my own, that it would be. For the moment, we are confounded and disconfirmed.

RELIGIOUS AND POLITICAL AFFILIATION

Continued acceptance of the home religion
One aspect of people's lives which can be taken as an index of authoritarianism is the extent to which they continue, as adults, to accept the religious beliefs they learned in their youths. This acceptance may represent a continued submission to the authority of the parents (and their designated religious authority, the church). It may also be that the broad agreement in the teachings of most organized religions in our culture constitute, almost by definition, the conventional moral values of our society.

There can be many reasons besides authoritarianism that people continue to accept the home religious beliefs. The teachings could make a great deal of sense to them, following examination, and be accepted for exactly that reason. The continued acceptance could be based on strong social motivations such as a desire to remain part of a valued group of peers. It could be a fixed and necessary part of a romantic relationship. And so on. There is no a priori reason to expect authoritarianism to be the most powerful determinant of "keeping the faith." But it seems plausible that it can be one of the determinants, and the conceptualizations of authoritarianism based upon submission to authority and conventionalism can be expected to show such a relationship.

This expectation was tested by a single item on the "Demographic Survey" administered at the end of the first session, which read, "How completely would you say you now presently accept the beliefs and teachings of the religion in which you were raised?" The response scale that subjects used was:[21] 0 — not at all; 1 — somewhat; 2 — substantially; 3 — completely.

Table 8 presents the correlations which each scale had with continued religious acceptance. Most of the scales had significant relationships with responses to the "how completely" question, but the C Scale had a significantly stronger relationship than any other test. Overall C Scale scores accounted for 28% of the variance in acceptance.

TABLE 8

Scores on the authoritarianism scales and acceptance on beliefs
and teachings of the home religion

	Jews	Anglicans	United	Lutherans	Catholics	All subjects
	N					
	86	120	207	49	305	897
Scale						
F	.35	.21	.22	.31	.31	.29
$F_{bal.}$	.36	.25	.26	.24ns	.27	.30
D	.36	−.12ns	.19	.17ns	.29	.24
C	.28	.32	.46	.54	.58	.53
L&W	.36	.31	.36	.37	.46	.42
A-R	.27	.29	.45	.27ns	.35	.37
RWA	.33	.25	.37	.41	.41	.39

Note: All correlations are statistically significant except those labelled "ns."

Preference for right-wing political parties

Our final criterion of right-wing authoritarianism is the obvious one of identification with right-wing political movements. Presumably, such authoritarians would generally find the policies and goals of such movements more appealing than those of "central" parties, which in turn would be preferable to those of "left-wing" parties.

I do not mean, in making this general prediction, to ignore the complexities of the political process in democratic government. It is often difficult on particular issues to delineate simple left-to-right positions, and sometimes "left-wing" parties support bills which have "right-wing" overtones, and vice versa. Nor do I propose for an instant that persons who claim to be "liberals" are necessarily nonauthoritarian, or that all "conservatives" are authoritarian.

Still in all, there is a broad, general understanding in Canada, which is evident in news reports, editorial analyses, parliamentary debate, and election campaigning that the major federal parties are aligned, from left to right, as follows: the New Democratic Party, the Liberal Party, and the Progressive Conservative Party. If scales purporting to measure right-wing authoritarianism have any meaningful association with right-wing political movements, they ought to show the expected relationship with political party preference.

Subjects were accordingly asked, on the Demographic Survey com-

TABLE 9
Scores on authoritarianism scales and federal political party affiliation

	New Democratic Party ($N = 133$)		Liberals ($N = 411$)		Progressive Conservatives ($N = 147$)			
Scale	$\overline{X}$	S	$\overline{X}$	S	$\overline{X}$	S	F	$\hat{\eta}^2$
F	97.8	21.8	101.0	19.3	109.4	19.4	13.7	4%
F$_{bal.}$	103.4	18.1	106.5	15.8	114.1	15.7	17.2	5%
D	149.0	22.0	149.8	24.4	155.0	25.0	3.1	1%
C	33.6	10.9	36.9	10.4	40.9	10.5	17.0	5%
L&W	105.9	17.2	110.9	14.8	118.3	13.2	25.0	7%
A-R	114.4	19.1	119.1	15.7	127.3	14.7	23.5	6%
RWA	85.0	22.8	92.0	19.9	103.2	17.5	30.2	8%

pleted during the first testing session, to indicate which federal political party they "most identified or associated" themselves with. Table 9 contains the mean and standard deviations of the scale scores obtained by those subjects who indicated such an identification. With one exception, the mean scores of the Canadian subjects rise regularly from the NDPs through the Liberals to the Conservatives. ANOVAs of the scale scores by party affiliation indicated overall statistically significant differences for each scale. The RWA Scale did a marginally better job of differentiating the subjects. Post hoc analysis revealed that the NDP mean on the RWA Scale was significantly lower than the Liberal Party mean, which in turn was significantly lower than the Conservative Party mean.

EVALUATION OF THE RESULTS OF THE PITTING EXPERIMENT

Relative performance of the scales
The evaluation of the pitting experiment poses no great problem. The RWA Scale was superior to the other tests as far as internal consistency and factor structure were concerned. It also was the best predictor of authoritarian dispositions and behavior on five of the six criteria used. In short, the RWA Scale was the best measure of authoritarianism tested in the study.

The other tests fared less well, to varying degrees. Overall, Lee and Warr's Scale did the next best job in terms of both psychometric properties and relationships with the six criteria. The C Scale had a high correlation with continued acceptance of the home religion; this fact reinforces the view that the test measures mainly religious and sexual conservatism, but otherwise has little to offer the study of authoritarianism. Neither, it would seem, do the F, D, or A-R Scales.[22]

Item analysis of the RWA Scale's relationship with the criterion measures

Several research literatures were criticized in chapter 1 because investigators had casually attributed relationships found with the summed score on a test to the content of the test as a whole, when the relationships might easily have occurred mainly because of those items which had obvious connections with the criterion. It is possible, accordingly, that the RWA Scale's correlation with the Government Injustices measure was due to the existence of those items on the test which directly tap sentiments about government power. The other items may have been unrelated. Similarly, the "scale's relationship" with sentencing in the Trials cases may simply have arisen from the items on the test which directly measure attitudes toward criminals and the justice system. And it is quite possible that Conservatives scored higher on the RWA Scale than did Liberals and NDPs simply because of the conventionalism items; they may not have also been more submissive and aggressive. If so, Conservatives can be called "conventional," but not "authoritarian" —and that is a big difference. The same possibilities exist for the other criteria.

To what extent then did the items on the RWA Scale have statistically significant associations with each of the six authoritarianism criteria? Table 10 lists these item relationships (in terms of correlation coefficients or ANOVA F's), and for comparison also presents the same analysis for Lee and Warr's Scale.

These data reveal that all of the items on the RWA Scale had significant relationships in the predicted direction with all of the criteria save one. The one exception was the laboratory shocking experiment, with its relatively small samples, where nine item-correlations were nonsignificant. By way of comparison, 70 of the item-relationships on the Lee and Warr Scale failed to attain significance. Furthermore, a third of the scale (viz., items 8, 9, 11, 12, 13, 16, 18, 23, 26, and 27) had nonsignificant relationships with at least half of the criteria, despite the very large sample sizes usually involved. (Not surprisingly, these items also tended to have the weakest item-whole correlations on the test.)

Thus the RWA Scale's relationship with the Government Injustices measure was not simply due to those items on the test which directly

TABLE 10

Predictive validities of the items on the RWA and Lee & Warr scales

RWA Scale

Item#	Government injustices (r's) (N = 948)	Moral dilemmas (F's) (N = 397)	Sum-trials ment (r's) (N = 954)	Shocking experi-ment (r's) (N = 79)	Accept home religion (r's) (N = 897)	Political affiliation (F's) (N = 691)
1	−.19	18.6	.18	.36	.15	3.3
2	−.21	11.3	.14	.14ns	.49	7.5
3	−.25	8.2	.11	.02ns	.20	5.6
4	−.27	14.5	.18	.15ns	.22	5.9
5	−.31	21.7	.31	.31	.08	12.5
6	−.24	15.6	.09	.33	.13	6.2
7	−.33	27.1	.23	.43	.24	10.5
8	−.33	18.2	.20	.29	.26	10.8
9	−.26	19.0	.27	.20	.12	13.1
10	−.29	27.9	.17	.29	.21	9.8
11	−.28	14.4	.10	.09ns	.21	6.8
12	−.26	26.3	.24	.39	.15	6.0
13	−.26	20.1	.12	.16ns	.10	6.4
14	−.24	12.5	.16	.23	.21	9.8
15	−.33	17.8	.23	.39	.16	11.6
16	−.17	13.6	.09	−.01ns	.40	7.1
17	−.35	29.4	.15	.32	.11	9.0
18	−.29	12.1	.15	−.10ns	.15	11.0
19	−.31	16.8	.25	.31	.20	9.4
20	−.27	26.3	.12	.12ns	.18	3.1
21	−.23	18.2	.10	.31	.17	3.4
22	−.13	7.2	.10	.20	.20	13.5
23	−.23	20.4	.07	−.03ns	.25	7.2

Lee & Warr Scale

Item#	Government injustices (r's) (N = 948)	Moral dilemmas (F's) (N = 397)	Sum-trials ment (r's) (N = 954)	Shocking experi-ment (r's) (N = 79)	Accept home religion (r's) (N = 897)	Political affiliation (F's) (N = 691)
1	−.25	13.9	.13	.17%ns	.26	2.7ns
2	−.19	8.8	.11	.00ns	.48	9.0
3	−.18	5.8	.11	.23	.06ns	6.3
4	−.13	3.6	.09	.23	.08	1.5ns
5	−.20	6.7	.06ns	.20	.17	1.4ns
6	−.25	19.4	.09	.09ns	.30	3.0ns
7	−.24	15.9	.23	.21	.27	7.7
8	−.19	9.4	.05ns	.02ns	.05ns	5.3
9	−.04ns	1.9ns	.01ns	.02ns	−.03ns	5.8
10	−.20	5.5	.13	.14ns	.14	1.2ns
11	.03ns	1.1ns	−.02ns	.06ns	.10	0.0ns
12	−.02ns	0.1ns	.04ns	−.17ns	.07	0.1ns
13	.02ns	0.6ns	−.08‡	.07ns	−.09‡	0.3ns
14	−.13	5.8	.07	.10ns	.19	0.9ns
15	−.24	6.0	.12	.18ns	.13	2.7ns
16	−.03ns	1.2ns	−.04ns	.08ns	.00ns	1.0ns
17	−.19	5.7	.07	.05ns	.13	1.8ns
18	−.03ns	0.9ns	−.03ns	.20	.01ns	5.8
19	−.33	18.1	.09	.11ns	.19	9.7
20	−.19	7.5	.11	.18ns	.20	3.3
21	−.18	12.0	.09	.07ns	.23	3.2
22	−.16	21.3	.10	.25	.13	7.0
23	−.14	7.5	−.01ns	−.28‡	.12	0.3ns

24	-.29	25.8	.23	.30	.08	8.2

24	-.10	4.5	.08	.12^{ns}	.44	2.4^{ns}
25	-.24	12.9	.17	.10^{ns}	.09	6.4
26	.07‡	0.8^{ns}	-.05^{ns}	-.04^{ns}	.02^{ns}	6.5
27	-.13	8.1	.08	.03^{ns}	.06^{ns}	2.3^{ns}
28	-.25	16.1	.08	.05^{ns}	.11	3.3
29	-.22	7.9	.31	.28	.11	12.3
30	-.27	17.8	.16	.35	.02^{ns}	6.7

ns Indicates the relationship is *not* statistically significant.

‡ Indicates a statistically significant relationship in the *wrong* direction.

‡‡ Indicates the items themselves may be found in Appendix II.

concern governmental power. All of the items on the test, including those which have no apparent connection with such matters, were significantly associated with tolerance for highhanded government activity. Similarly, all of the RWA Scale statements, not just the "crime and punishment" items, were significantly associated with punitiveness in the Trials survey. Political party differences were found not only in the conventionalism items, but also in those whose manifest content involves submission and aggression. People who completely accepted the teachings of the home religion scored higher on all of the test's items, not just the few religious ones. And so on.

We should note that the "significant" correlations under discussion ranged as low as .07, and few of them accounted for an appreciable amount of criterion variance. Responses to individual items are quite unstable, and even with perfect reliability, some of the item relationships would still be unimpressive. But nearly every one points in the expected direction, and we can say that the vast majority of the 144 associations do exist in the population sampled. That is quite a large conclusion.

The data in Table 10 are the fruits of the labor invested in developing the RWA Scale. To an appreciable extent, the items on the test, despite their wide-ranging content, measure one underlying dimension. While any particular item will naturally have a higher correlation with criterion behavior that is directly connected to its content, responses to the items on the test are sufficiently intercorrelated so as to give wide-based association with the various authoritarianism criteria. The other scales miss this by a wide margin; they have too many items with no relationship with one another, let alone with the criteria.

CROSS-VALIDATION STUDIES OF THE PITTING EXPERIMENT

Nothwithstanding its scope, large sample, and lack of precedent in the authoritarianism literature, the above pitting experiment shows only that the RWA Scale does relatively well within the population in which it was developed. It is possible that idiosyncracies among the attitudes of University of Manitoba students, captured by the RWA Scale but naturally missed by all the others, contributed appreciably to the test's performance. To check on this possibility, I therefore repeated the pitting experiment with four other samples: (a) 113 introductory psychology students at the University of North Dakota, tested in December, 1973; (b) 148 similar students at the University of Alberta, tested in January,

1974; (c) 172 more introductory psychology students at the University of Western Ontario, tested in February, 1974; and, (d) 56 nonstudent Winnipeg males tested during the summer of 1974.[23]

The University of North Dakota Study

The instructions and procedures used in the University of North Dakota Study and the other cross-validation studies closely approximated those used in the Manitoba experiment. The North Dakota booklet began with either the Lee and Warr or the RWA Scale, followed by the four-case Trials and an Americanized Government Injustices measures. The RWA or the Lee and Warr Scale then appeared, followed by the Demographic Survey.

Overall, the RWA Scale was again the better measure. Its mean interitem correlation (.18; $\alpha = .84$) was much higher than the Lee and Warr Scale's (.04; $\alpha = .56$). Its factor structure (the two-factor direction-of-wording model) was much simpler. Its correlation with the Trials measure was significantly higher (.45 vs. .28), as was its Government Injustices correlation (-.48 vs. -.34). It better distinguished Democrats from Republicans (RWA means = 97.5 and 109.9 respectively, F = 7.2; Lee and Warr Scale means = 112.3 and 120.3, F = 6.7). The only criterion on which the Lee and Warr Scale proved superior was continued acceptance of the home religion (.42 vs. .34).

The University of Alberta Study

The booklet for the University of Alberta Study contained the same surveys used in North Dakota, except the C Scale was added to the middle of the questionnaire, and six Trials cases were used instead of four.

Again the RWA Scale proved to be the superior measure. It had higher interitem correlations (mean = .18; $\alpha = .84$) than either the Lee and Warr Scale (.06; $\alpha = .66$) or the C Scale (.07; $\alpha = .79$). Its factor structure, the two direction-of-wording dimensions, was much simpler. Its correlation with the trials measure (.39) was significantly higher than the Lee and Warr Scale's (.25) or the C Scale's (.10), and its relationship with the Government Injustices cases (-.46) was the highest (Lee and Warr = -.44; C Scale = -.35). NDP students scored lowest and Progressive Conservatives highest on all three scales, but Lee and Warr's test best distinguished among these groupings (F = 15.7); RWA Scale's F = 13.8; C Scale's F = 12.4. The C Scale in turn had the highest correlation with continued religious acceptance (.48) while the other tests both correlated .35 with this measure.

The University of Western Ontario Study
Either Kohn's A-R Scale or the RWA Scale appeared at the beginning
of this booklet, followed by six Trials and four Government Injustices
cases; the RWA Scale or A-R Scale then appeared, followed by the
Demographic Survey. The booklet ended with a role-playing assignment
described below.

Once more the RWA Scale did the best job. Its interitem correlations
averaged .18 (α = .84) compared to .07 (α = .69) for the A-R Scale.
Its factor structure was simpler, being the same two-factor direction-of-
wording model found previously. Its correlations with the Trials measure
(.47) and the Government Injustices cases (.51) were higher than the
A-R Scale's (.38 and -.40 respectively). Both tests distinguished among
political party identification in the usual way, but the RWA Scale's differentiation was stronger (F = 10.0 vs. F = 6.5). The A-R Scale was superior
only on the continued religious acceptance criterion (.36 vs. .33).

The role-playing task at the end of the booklet required subjects to
answer the RWA Scale again, only this time as they thought either the
Canadian Prime Minister, Pierre Trudeau, or Richard Nixon, or Adolf
Hitler would answer it. "Trudeau's" mean score was 107.4, "Nixon's" was
135.2, and "Hitler's" was 145.2 (F = 54.2). All role-played means were
significantly higher than the students' own scores (mean = 93.1) and
significantly different from one another. The difference among the three
sets of scores is the largest found so far with the RWA Scale, in fact,
with ($\hat{\eta}^2$) = 42.6%. "Hitler's" mean score, furthermore, was close to the
maximum possible score on the scale (168), with all but six of the items
having a mean greater than 6.0 on a seven-point scale. If Hitler's can be
considered a highly authoritarian image, this extremely high score can
be taken as further evidence of the validity of the RWA Scale.

The Winnipeg Adult Study
Letters were sent to 380 Winnipeg households randomly selected from the
telephone directory and from the voters lists prepared for the 1974
Canadian federal election. These letters solicited men between 20 and 60
years old who were native Anglophone nonstudent Canadians to serve
in a "public opinion poll" being administered in respondents' homes.
A payment of $2.00 was offered to participants. Follow-up telephone
calls reached 258 of these households, 141 of which reported having
someone in the family who met our criteria. Sixty-five men agreed to
serve in the study, and 56 of these proved available for a testing session.

The mean age of the 56 men in the group was 35.1 years; the average formal education level was 12.4 years. Eighteen were blue collar workers, six were artisans, 22 held white collar jobs, and six were professionals. As a group they were younger, better educated, and more "white collar" than are Winnipeg males in general. They were not therefore a representative sample of the particular population we tried to contact; but it was a different population from the ones used before, and there was no apparent reason why they, like the university students before them, did not constitute a fair sample for the pitting experiment being performed.

The booklet used in this study began with the RWA Scale, followed by the C Scale. Subjects then responded to seven trials and six Government Injustices cases, and finally a brief Demographic Survey.

Once again, the RWA Scale proved to be the superior measure. Its mean interitem correlation was .19 (α = .85), while that of the C Scale was .09 (α = .83). Its factor structure, the same direction-of-wording model found with students, was much more simple. Its correlation with the Trials measure was higher (.43 vs. .40), as it was with the Government Injustices measures (−.54 vs. −.46). Both scales showed the usual ordering of political affiliations, but the RWA Scale drew a sharper distinction (F = 3.24 p < .05, vs. F = 2.86, p < .08; df = 2,40). The only measure on which the C Scale proved superior was, as before, continued religious acceptance (r = .49 vs. .34 for the RWA Scale).

Since both the RWA and C Scales were significantly related to subjects' education (−.36 and −.41 respectively), and education in turn was related to scores on most of the criteria,[24] a partial correlation analysis was employed to control the influence of education on the scales' relationships with the Trials, Government Injustices and religious acceptance measure. The RWA Scale's coefficients dropped to .35, −.49 and .29 re pectively, while the C Scale's figures were reduced to .31, −.39 and .45. All of these correlations remained statistically significant.

Evaluation of the cross-validation studies
While the margin of difference in the cross-validation studies was not as great as it was in the University of Manitoba pitting experiment, the verdict must again go to the RWA Scale. Its internal consistency in all four samples was much greater than any of the other tests, as was its factor structure. It was consistently poorer at predicting religious acceptance, but on the other criteria it was almost always stronger. There was, in short, no evidence that the RWA Scale's relative superiority as a measure of authoritarianism is limited to the Manitoba student population in which it was developed.

*Evaluation of the RWA Scale's absolute level
of performance in the pitting studies*

So far we have been discussing the RWA Scale's performance in relative terms. But there is a more important question: is the scale's performance good enough, in absolute terms, to be scientifically useful in our attempts to understand human behavior?

This question leads us into a very gray area. Any accounting of the variance of some interesting human behavior is a step forward when we are otherwise ignorant, and obviously the greater the variance accounted for, the bigger the step. But experimental psychology has not adopted a convention for an "important relationshp" the way it has for a "statistically significant" one. One researcher's "great leap forward" may seem unimpressive to another.

Perhaps we can gain some definition in this gray area in the realization that human behavior is often shaped by many factors. As validity coefficients loll around in the .20 to .30 range, where they have often fallen in the authoritarianism literature, about 4% to 9% of the criterion variance has been accounted for.[25] One can claim to have explained some of the variation in the criterion, but it is quite possible that there are many other covariates at least as important, if not more so. However, as the validity coefficients rise to the .40 to .50 range, and one is explaining at least one-sixth of the criterion variance (compared to one-twenty-fifth or one-eleventh) the chances that there are many other, more important factors go down dramatically. If one-sixth of the variance is in hand, there can at most be four independent variables with larger relationships; in all likelihood, however, there would be fewer (if any). One can say, therefore, though it is quite arbitrary, that when a test accounts for a sixth or a fifth of a criterion's variance, it is a major covariant of the criterion. At most there can only be a few other variables as important.

With this as a benchmark, RWA Scale scores have, in the pitting studies, proved to be "major covariants" of: (a) subjects' acceptance of government injustices; (b) subjects' use of law as a basis of morality; (c) subject's punitiveness against certain people convicted of crimes; and (d) subjects' aggressiveness in a punishment-learning situation. The test did not account for a major part of the variance of continued acceptance of the home religion, and political party affiliation.

Of these two shortcomings, the latter is the greatest both in magnitude and in theoretical significance for a construct named right-wing authoritarianism.[26] NDPs, Liberals and Conservatives did not differ all that much in RWA Scale scores. But, on the other hand, the subjects who said they preferred one or the other of these parties were not necessarily interested in politics. In the University of Manitoba study, for example, there were no significant differences in the RWA Scale scores of NDPs, Liberals and Conservatives who said (on another question) they had "no interest" in politics ($N = 43$; $F = 0.97$). Among subjects "moderately interested" in politics ($N = 476$) the RWA Scale scores of the three parties were all significantly different, but the relationship ($F = 15.4$) only accounted for 6% of the variance. But among the 169 "quite interested" subjects, not only did the NDP, Liberal, and Conservative party means (76.9, 84.1 and 101.8 respectively) differ significantly, but the relationship accounted for 16% of the variance.

Thus the differences in party authoritarianism were strongly, and sensibly moderated by the interest subjects had in politics. Few variables are going to be related to political party preference among subjects who have no interest in politics. Right-wing authoritarianism becomes a sharper discriminator among party supporters as interest increases.

To summarize, then, RWA Scale scores appear to have scientifically important relationships with most of the authoritarianism criteria under consideration. Where it falls short of such achievement, if fails for understandable reasons. But to put all of this into perspective, we should not lose sight of all the variance still unexplained. Even a "25% accounting" —good for our science at this time and worthwhile in its own right— still leaves a 75% mystery. Some of this would be made up by more reliable measures of both test and criteria, it is true. But beyond that there is a definite limit to how complete an accounting any measure of personal authoritarianism can make of behavior. Authoritarianism is not the only reason people accept government injustices, are hostile toward wrongdoers, continue to accept their home religion, support political parties, and so on. We are far too complicated for that.

WHAT IS "EXPLAINED" BY RWA SCALE COVARIATION?

We should, in ending this chapter, address the issue of what we have really accomplished by "accounting for" whatever criteria variance we now have within our grasp. For developing correlations of .40 or .50 does not necessarily mean we understand the criteria better; we may simply be re-naming the phenomena. For example, we have seen that C Scale scores correlate highly with continued religious acceptance. But when we realize that the test mainly measures sexual and religious conservatism, all we have really found is that people who continue to accept their home religions are religiously more conservative than those who do not. That is not very informative.

Have we done anything different with the RWA Scale? I think so. The item analysis indicates that continued religious acceptance, aside from the expected connection with conventionalism, is associated with the belief that young people should submit to their parents. Furthermore, such people also tend to believe that citizens should submit to government, that authorities should have vast powers, and that people who protest against authorities should be silenced. In short, continued acceptance of the home religion, to a considerable extent, appears to be part of a more general tendency to submit to established authority. Furthermore, many of these "very religious" persons have surprisingly strong aggressive impulses toward certain kinds of targets. All of this is provocatively more than discovering that "religious people tend to be religious."

What we have discovered, in a nutshell, is that sentiments of authoritarian submission, authoritarian aggression and conventionalism covary appreciably, and that this pattern of covariation is related to a number of seemingly unrelated behaviors in theoretically connectable ways. Social scientists (and journalists and barbers) have been "explaining" authoritarian behavior with "authoritarianism" for many years, but as long as we lacked a well-defined, independent and operationally viable concept of authoritarianism we were merely restating the data. Now we can do more.

I do not mean to exaggerate the accomplishment detailed in this chapter. There is an enormous amount we do not know about right-wing authoritarianism, most particularly its origins, and the ways it interacts with situational factors in determining behavior (topics we shall take up in the next chapters). But at least we appear to be underway in the study of "that authoritarianism" which so many have said exists in our society, but which we have not been able to get a satisfactory grip on before.

Explorations of the dynamics and covariates of right-wing authoritarianism

5

By the "dynamics" of right-wing authoritarianism I mean the way RWA Scale scores interact with other variables in accounting for behavior. The "other variables" can be measures of additional aspects of the actor, such as mental health or dogmatism. They can be stimulus properties of other persons, such as characteristics of government leaders or targets of aggression. They can be aspects of situations, such as the behavior of others or the reinforcement contingencies for performing certain acts. All of these factors can interact with personal authoritarianism in shaping behavior.

There are at least two good reasons for studying these dynamics. Experience has shown that trait analyses of behavior will be seriously incomplete if the effects of situational variables, or other traits, are ignored. As well, such studies can isolate the factors which affect the authoritarian's tendencies to act in nondemocratic and aggressive ways. Such information may prove useful for eventually controlling authoritarian behavior in our society.

In this chapter I shall report the results of several studies of the dynamics of right-wing authoritarianism; and I shall also present evidence linking RWA Scale scores with other variables of interest. Some of these variables are additional criteria of authoritarianism, such as Americans' reactions to the "Watergate crisis." Others, such as relationships with gender, education and social desirability influences, are of a more technical interest. I hope that all of these will increase our understanding of where authoritarianism is found in our society and how it operates.

The chapter begins with a description of the samples used in the studies and the procedures followed. The results obtained are then discussed under the following rubrics: (a) RWA Scale relationships with political matters; (b) the dynamics of authoritarian aggression; (c) authoritarianism and religion; (d) demographic covariates of RWA Scale scores; (e) social desirability effects on the RWA Scale; and (f) cross-sectional changes in authoritarianism scores over time.

THE SAMPLES AND PROCEDURES USED IN THE STUDIES

The results described in this chapter are based upon studies of three different populations: (a) introductory psychology students at five American universities, tested in the Fall of 1974; (b) introductory psychology students at the University of Manitoba, tested every fall from 1973 through 1979; and (c) the parents of some of these Manitoba students, tested in the fall of 1976, 1978 and 1979.

American student studies
Students at the Universities of Alabama ($N = 177$), Indiana ($N = 200$), Virginia ($N = 196$), Wyoming ($N = 54$) and at Penn State University ($N = 145$) were tested between September 25 and October 24, 1974. I administered the surveys at all the sites except Wyoming, testing in classrooms but not during class time. The students, who served for experimental credit, were led to believe I was a visiting psychologist conducting a nation-wide public opinion survey for the "North American Survey Research Associates." The instructions and procedures closely followed those used in the pitting experiment (see chapter 4), except that in order to secure the cooperation of the host universities it was necessary to test the students anonymously.[1]

Manitoba student studies
This population was described in chapter 2, and the 1973 study was described in chapter 4. Thereafter, I administered survey booklets in the early fall every year to between 407 and 747 introductory psychology students according to the procedures described in the last chapter. In 1976, 1978, and 1979 I also taught introductory psychology and involved 241, 337, and 463 of my students in this research program, under an altered "cover story." I told my own students that survey booklets were routinely administered at the beginning of the course, and that different professors contributed different research instruments to this "Psychometric Survey." I specifically told my classes that none of the material was my own, having previously announced that my research interest lay

in group dynamics. The remaining instructions and procedures closely approximated those used with students drawn from my colleagues' classes.[2]

Manitoba parents studies

After my introductory psychology students had finished the Psychometric Survey, which usually took two 50-minute class sessions, I announced that the psychology department was interested in obtaining nonstudent samples for a similar survey study. Specifically, if the students addressed an envelope to their parents, the department would mail them surveys with an accompanying letter from me soliciting their participation. (A copy of the letter is reproduced in Appendix IV.) Students were promised an experimental credit for returning one or two completed surveys.

In the three studies involving my own students, 80%, 83%, and 72% of the subjects asked that booklets be sent home, and completed surveys were returned from 80%, 82%, and 81% of these households. In the vast majority of cases, both parents filled out surveys when two booklets were sent out. The final parent sample sizes were 261, 402, and 437 respectively in the three years, of which about 53% were mothers.

As far as I can determine, there has been no authoritarianism-based self-selection bias in the samples obtained. In the most recent study, for example, the mean RWA Scale score (on a 30-item version of the test described below) of the students who tried to involve their parents was 124.9, while the mean score of those who did not was 123.9 ($t = 0.34$, $p < .40$). The RWA Scale scores of parents who declined to participate are unknown, but the students whose parents participated and the students whose parents declined did not differ significantly (means $=$ 126.2 and 119.2 respectively; $t = 1.68$, $p < .10$).

In each of the three samples the parents' mean age was about 48 years and their mean level of formal education was about 12 years. Approximately two-thirds lived in Winnipeg. Their occupations varied widely, but there were fewer blue-collar and more white-collar homes than one would find in an unbiased sample of Manitoba adults. While the parents may be reasonably representative of the mothers and fathers in our society whose children attend large public universities, any extrapolation to the larger population of "Canadian parents" or "Canadian adults" would probably be unwise.[3]

Psychometric properties of the RWA Scale in these samples

The American students responded to the original 24-item version of the RWA Scale (see Table 7 in chapter 3). The mean interitem correlation of responses to this test varied from .19 to .23 at the different sites, with corresponding alpha reliabilities of .85 to .89. Mean scores on the test showed more site-to-site variation than was found among the Canadian students involved in the pitting studies, ranging from 84.4 at the University of Virginia to 106.6 at the University of Alabama. Factor analyses revealed the usual two highly correlated (.69) direction-of-wording factors, accounting for 29.4% of the test's variance in the combined sample.

The Manitoba samples described above did not all answer the same version of the RWA Scale. Over the years the initial 24-item test evolved through further item analysis studies into a 26-, 28-, and 30-item scale.[4] These tests were naturally very similar to one another, but each successive scale represented some improvement over its predecessors. The 30-item RWA Scale used in my 1979 research program, whose results are extensively reported in the following pages, is reproduced in Table 1.

Whatever version of the RWA Scale is under discussion, its mean interitem correlation has always been .18 or greater among the Manitoba students, with corresponding alpha coefficients of .86 or higher. The parents' data have shown similar values. The 30-item test listed in Table 1 had an alpha = .86 among the 1979 students and .89 among the parents. Parents' scores on the test were considerably higher than their children's however, the means being 150.2 versus 126.2 ($t = 10.2, p < .0001$) in 1979, for example. Factor analyses of students' and parents' responses have almost always produced the usual two direction-of-wording factors, correlating about .65–.70 in the Promax rotation and accounting for about 25% to 30% of the test's variance.

The RWA Scale's relatively fine psychometric properties thus have reappeared in each of the populations sampled. It is true that the inter-item correlations decreased somewhat among Manitoba students over the seven years involved. (We shall explore this decrease at the end of this chapter.) But the scale has proven to be relatively unidimensional in every population tested so far, which now includes students at three widely scattered Canadian universities, six similarly scattered American schools, the 1973 sample of Winnipeg males and three samples of middle-aged Manitoba parents. Thus our prime instrument has remained sound across space and time.

RWA SCALE RELATIONSHIPS WITH POLITICAL MATTERS

In this section we investigate further the relationships between authoritarianism and political party preference in American and Canadian

TABLE 1

The thirty-item RWA Scale

Item Number	Item
1	Some of the worst people in our country nowadays are those who do not respect our flag, our leaders, and the normal way things are supposed to be done.
2	It is wonderful that young people today have greater freedom to protest against things they don't like, and to "do their own thing."‡
3	It is always better to trust the judgment of the proper authorities in government and religion, than to listen to the noisy rabble-rousers in our society who are trying to create doubt in people's minds.
4	People should pay less attention to the Bible and the other old traditional forms of religious guidance, and instead develop their own personal standards of what is moral and immoral.‡
5	It would be best for everyone if the proper authorities censored magazines and movies to keep trashy material away from the youth.
6	Our customs and national heritage are the things that have made us great, and certain people should be made to show greater respect for them.
7	The sooner we get rid of the traditional family structure, where the father is the head of the family and the children are taught to obey authority automatically, the better. The old-fashioned way has a lot wrong with it.‡
8	There is nothing wrong with premarital sexual intercourse.‡
9	The facts on crime, sexual immorality, and the recent public disorders all show we have to crack down harder on deviant groups and troublemakers if we are going to save our moral standards and perserve law and order.
10	There is nothing immoral or sick in somebody's being a homosexual.‡
11	Our prisons are a shocking disgrace. Criminals are unfortunate people who deserve much better care, instead of so much punishment.‡
12	Obedience and respect for authority are the most important virtues children should learn.
13	A "woman's place" should be wherever she wants to be. The days when women are submissive to their husbands and social conventions belong strictly in the past.‡
14	People who criticize the police for sometimes using improper procedures are forgetting that the *most* important thing is to get the criminals and troublemakers into jail where they belong.
15	"Free speech" means that people should even be allowed to make speeches and write books urging the overthrow of the government.‡
16	It may be considered old-fashioned by some, but having a decent, respectable appearance is still the mark of a gentleman and, especially, a lady.
17	In these troubled times laws have to be enforced without mercy, especially when dealing with the agitators and revolutionaries who are stirring things up.

TABLE 1 — *Continued*

Item Number	Item
18	Atheists and others who have rebelled against the established religions are no doubt every bit as good and virtuous as those who attend church regularly.‡
19	Young people sometimes get rebellious ideas, but as they grow up they ought to get over them and settle down.
20	Spanking a child only teaches him resentment and fear, and does nothing to teach him right from wrong.‡
21	The courts are right in being easy on drug offenders. Punishment would *not* do any good in cases like these.‡
22	If a child starts becoming unconventional and disrespectful of authority, it is his parents' duty to get him back to the normal way.
23	In the final analysis the established authorities, like parents and our national leaders, generally turn out to be right about things, and all the protestors don't know what they're talking about.
24	Sex criminals should be treated with some sympathy and understanding. Harsh punishments are seldom justified, or do any good, in such cases.‡
25	There is absolutely nothing wrong with nudist camps.‡
26	The *real* keys to the "good life" are obedience, discipline, and sticking to the straight and narrow.
27	It is best to treat dissenters with leniency and an open mind, since new ideas are the lifeblood of progressive change.‡
28	The biggest threat to our freedom comes from the Communists and their kind, who are out to destroy religion, ridicule patriotism, corrupt the youth, and in general undermine our whole way of life.
29	Students in high school and university must be encouraged to challenge their parents' ways, confront established authorities, and in general criticize the customs and traditions of our society.‡
30	One reason we have so many troublemakers in our society nowadays is that parents and other authorities have forgotten that good old-fashioned physical punishment is still one of the best ways to make people behave properly.

‡ Indicates the item is worded in the contrait direction.

Note: As a result of the fall, 1980, experiments, Item 14 above will be replaced by the following, rather chilling statement in future versions of the RWA Scale: "Once our government leaders and the authorities condemn the dangerous elements in our society, it will be the duty of every patriotic citizen to help stomp out the rot that is poisoning our country from within."

samples. Then we shall see how authoritarians reacted to the Watergate crisis in 1974. Finally we shall consider two factors which might affect the way high RWA subjects react to highhanded and illegal acts by government officials.

RWA Scale scores and political party preference
At each of the five American university sites, Republican students scored significantly higher on the RWA Scale than did Democrats, just as they did in the University of North Dakota study reported in chapter 4. The overall means were 103.5 ($N = 162$, $s^2 = 369$) and 89.6 ($N = 226$, $s^2 = 571$) respectively ($t = 6.34$, $p < .0001$) with significant differences appearing on all of the test's 24 items. The relationship accounted for 9% of the variance, comparable to the 8% found in the undifferentiated[5] Manitoba student sample of 1973.

The pattern of RWA Scale association with political party preference found in the 1973 pitting studies continued among Manitoba students through 1976, with NDP supporters always scoring significantly lower than Liberals, and Conservatives scoring significantly higher than both. Beginning in 1977, however, the difference between NDP and Liberal means became nonsignificant. By 1979 the NDP mean (on the 30-item scale) was 120.1 ($N = 130$, $s^2 = 676$), the Liberal mean was 117.7 ($N = 205$, $s^2 = 502$), and the Conservatives' was 128.6 ($N = 271$, $s^2 = 552$). The overall F $= 13.8$ was still highly significant, the Conservatives scoring significantly higher than either the Liberals or the NDP (t's $= 5.18$ and 3.17 respectively). But the latter two were not significantly different ($t = -0.89$). The loss of difference between NDP and Liberal supporters reduced the variance shared with RWA Scale scores to 4%.

If one compares the 1979 data and those obtained in 1973 (Table 9 of chapter 4), two obvious differences appear. The number of Conservative supporters increased greatly, entirely at Liberal expense. Also, NDP scores moved to the right. The flow of support from Liberals to Conservatives among students merely reflects a provincial (and national) trend during the same period (though the trend reversed itself in 1980).[6] The shift in NDP scores appears to have been caused by the gradual disappearance of the party's "left wing" among students. There were always plenty of moderate and high RWA Scale scores among NDP supporters, but they were counterbalanced in the early 1970s to a considerable extent by a sizeable number of very low-scoring party enthusiasts. These "radical leftists" became fewer and fewer as the decade drew to a close, with a consequent rise in the NDP mean to Liberal levels.[7]

The previous finding, that interest in politics moderates the relationship between authoritarianism and party preference, was consistently replicated over the years. In 1979, for example, the association was twice as strong ($\hat{\eta}^2 = 8\%$) among "quite interested" subjects as it was in the overall sample, with party means being: NDP, 107.8 ($N = 26$, $s^2 = 824$);

Liberals, 118.1 ($N = 30$, $s^2 = 480$); and Conservatives, 127.3 ($N = 46$, $s^2 = 894$). Nonetheless, in 1973 the relationship between party preference and authoritarianism among such subjects was twice as stong.

Political party preference was assessed only in the 1978 and 1979 parent studies. In both cases Conservatives scored significantly higher than did Liberals, while Liberals and NDPs did not differ. The results thus parallel those found with concurrent student samples, but in the parents' case the relationship was even weaker, accounting for only 2%–3% of the variance. Among "quite interested" parents, however, it was appreciably stronger ($\hat{\eta}^2 = 8$ and 13% respectively), with the usual overall significant differences and rank ordering of NDPs, Liberals, and Conservatives.

Two facts have thus consistently appeared in the research on RWA Scale scores and party preference among Canadians: (a) Conservatives score significantly higher than Liberals or NDPs; and (b) authoritarianism is more powerfully related to party preference among subjects who take a strong interest in politics than it is in the general sample.

It is harder to say if Liberals tend to be more authoritarian than NDPs. There was a time when they were, among Manitoba (and Universities of Alberta and Western Ontario) students, but lately they have not been.

Whatever changes may have occurred in these relationships over time, authoritarianism has never been found to be an important covariate of party preference in an undifferentiated sample. This will not surprise politicians who know that party choice in the general electorate is determined by an enormous number of factors, of which ideology is hardly first. Among Manitoba students, for example, the strongest determinant of party preference appears to be the parents' orientation. In 1979, for example, 59% of the students who preferred the Conservatives said both their parents were Conservatives; another 21% had one Conservative parent. Only 20% came from Liberal, NDP, or Independent parents. Thus party choice appears to have been "grafted onto" students, and relatively few had a keen interest in politics, party positions, fundamental goals, and so on. Knowledge of such things may be even dimmer in the nonstudent adult population.

RWA Scale scores of role-played members of the
Canadian House of Commons
The finding that RWA Scale scores are only slightly related to political party preference does not necessarily mean that authoritarianism is an

insignificant factor in the political process. As noted several times now, RWA Scale scores consistently differentiate the parties best among the politically interestd. A projection of this relationship suggests that the differences among NDPs, Liberals, and Conservatives would be greatest among those people most actively involved in the political process, that is, politicians. And one can hardly imagine a more crucial place for authoritarianism to be shaping Canada's destiny than among the party caucuses in the House of Commons.

The methodological problems involved in administering the RWA Scale to Members of Parliament in controlled, standardized circumstances appear formidable, and I have never attempted it. I did, however, ask Manitoba students in the 1979 study to answer the RWA Scale (which they had just taken themselves) a second time, with the following instructions: "Suppose this survey were administered to all the current members of the House of Commons who belong to the _____ Party. What do you suppose would be the typical, the most common, response to each item among the _____ caucus in the House of Commons?" NDP, Liberal, and Conservative versions of this task were distributed in fixed, random order among the students in each testing session. Each student role-played just one caucus, and NDP, Liberal, Conservative and Independent students role-played the different caucuses in reasonably equal proportions.

The mean RWA Scale score for "NDP Members of Parliament" (MPs) was 132.3 ($N = 238$, $s^2 = 885$), for "Liberal MPs," 143.9 ($N = 238$, $s^2 = 594$), and for "Conservative MPs," 157.7 ($N = 242$, $s^2 = 396$). All scores were significantly different from one another, with an overall F $= 62.2$, yielding an $\hat{\eta}^2 = 15\%$. There were significant overall differences in role-played responses to all 30 of the items on the test.

Of course, many of these subjects had very little interest in politics, and little idea what the different parties stand for. When we examine the scores role-played by students "quite interested" in politics, the means become, for "NDP MPs," 113.6 ($N = 43$, $s^2 = 1208$), for "Liberal MPs" 132.2 ($N = 30$, $s^2 = 682$), and for "Conservatives" 166.4 ($N = 35$, $s^2 = 475$). Here the overall F was 32.9, with significant differences on all the items again, and an $\hat{\eta}^2 = 39\%$.

We thus see that the images of the party members of the House of Commons were far more differentiated than was the authoritarianism found among their rank-and-file supporters. And that when we examined the opinion of those students we might consider best informed on the matter, the images were strikingly different. Conservative Members of

Parliament appear, to such judges, to be far more authoritarian than Liberal MPs do, while NDP MPs appear significantly less authoritarian than either. The magnitude of the relationship, which is second only to that found with the role-played scores of "Trudeau," "Nixon," and "Hitler" reported in the last chapter, lends credence to the hypothesis that there are sizeable an important differences in authoritarianism among the party caucuses in the Canadian House of Commons.[8]

RWA Scale scores and reactions to Watergate
The Watergate scandal, which eventually forced Richard Nixon from the American presidency, was probably the most dramatic political event in modern American history. Seldom if ever has such a long series of official wrongdoings, emanating from the White House itself, come to light. Seldom if ever have Americans had such cause to wonder if the nation's chief executive should be allowed to finish his elected term of office. Seldom if every have the American people been asked, in the face of mounting evidence to the contrary, simply to believe their President when he said he was innocent of all wrongdoing. In short, the Watergate crisis was a supremely pertinent test of people's tendency to accept the actions and trust the word of an important authority figure. As we saw in chapter 1 Americans were very slow to doubt President Nixon, and even when the indisputable facts of the president's guilt were revealed, 22% of a Gallup sample believed that Richard Nixon did not deserve to be forced from office.

A clear prediction of the model of authoritarianism given in chapter 3 is that authoritarians would have believed President Nixon's account of Watergate longer and thought his crime less serious than would non-authoritarians. This was tested in the American student sample by giving the subjects a chronology of Watergate's major events (Table 2),and asking them to indicate (a) when they first seriously suspected the President was not telling the truth about Watergate, and (b) when they became convinced that he was not telling the truth. Subjects were also asked if they would have wanted their Senators to vote to remove Richard Nixon from office had he stood trial in the Senate; and whether they thought he should have faced criminal trial after his resignation for his Watergate activities.[9]

The median self-reported latency for suspecting that President Nixon was participating in a Watergate coverup was over a year after the break-in: July, 1973. The median latency for becoming convinced of the President's guilt was March, 1974. Eighteen percent of the subjects said, in

TABLE 2

Chronology of "Watergate" events given to American student subjects

1972	
June	Watergate break-in occurs. Nixon says White House not involved.
August	Nixon says a complete investigation shows no White House involvement in Watergate.
September	Grand jury indicts Liddy, Hunt and five others for Watergate break-in.
October	Nixon says he has ordered FBI to make sure there was no White House involvement in Watergate.
November	President Nixon re-elected in landslide over McGovern.

1973	
January	Hunt, others plead guilty to Watergate break-in.
March	Nixon says John Dean will not be allowed to testify in Senate hearings. One of the Watergate burglars says White House officials were involved in Watergate.
April	Nixon announces he has begun new investigations. Haldeman, Erlichman, Kleindienst and Dean resign.
May	The "Ervin" Committee begins televised hearings on the Watergate break-in and coverup. Archibald Cox is named Special Prosecutor by Attorney General Richardson.
June	John Dean testifies that Nixon knew of the coverup. It is learned that tape recordings of White House conversations exist.
July	Nixon refuses to release tapes to Cox. Cox goes to court to get the tapes.
October	Spiro Agnew resigns as Vice-President. Archibald Cox is fired; Attorney General Richardson and his deputy also go.
November	Leon Jaworski is named new Special Prosecutor. Seven tapes are released to him. It is learned one of the tapes has an 18.5-minute gap on it.
December	Nixon reveals his finances, including the fact that he paid very little taxes in 1970 and 1971.

1974	
January	Panel of experts announces the 18-minute gap was caused by deliberate erasure.
March	Haldeman, Erlichman, Mitchell are indicted by a grand jury for Watergate coverup.
April	Nixon refuses to hand over more tapes subpoenaed by Jaworski and the House Judiciary Committee.
May	Nixon releases over 1,200 pages of transcripts of Watergate tapes. Nixon is named as an "unindicted co-conspirator" in the Watergate coverup by the grand jury.
July	Supreme Court rules Nixon must turn over tapes to Jaworski. House Judiciary Committee holds televised hearings, votes to recommend Nixon be impeached.
August	Nixon releases transcripts which show he approved a coverup in June, 1972. President Nixon resigns.

the fall of 1974, that they still were not convinced that Richard Nixon had participated in the coverup.

RWA Scale scores were significantly correlated with the latency of doubt at each testing site, the relationship for the whole sample being .51. The same was true with regard to subjects becoming convinced of Nixon's involvement, the overall correlation being .48.[10] All of the 24 items on the RWA Scale were significantly correlated with these latency measures.

The students' responses to the hypothetical issue of Richard Nixon's trial in the Senate are shown in Table 3 beside the response alternatives employed. A one-way ANOVA of the RWA Scale scores by response categories revealed a significant main effect (F = 40.8; $\hat{\eta}^2$ = 14%). The mean scores of all the categories were significantly different except the first two.

Authoritarian students also tended to support President Ford's pardon of Richard Nixon (Table 4), although the relationship was somewhat weaker (F = 26.1; $\hat{\eta}^2$ = 9%). Post hoc analyses found that those who wanted Nixon brought to trial scored significantly lower on the RWA Scale than did those who endorsed any of the "no trial" alternatives. The other three means did not significantly vary.

The data suggest that authoritarianism was an important determinant of these students' ongoing reaction to the long Watergate saga. The relationships with preferences for Nixon's hypothetical trials are in the expected direction but weaker. The issues are admittedly more complex, and we might also recall the evidence that authoritarians ordinarily tend to be quite punitive toward criminals, a point to which we shall return later.

The most compelling finding in the study, however, is how long it took these subjects to suspect and become convinced of Nixon's wrongdoing. An enormous amount of the Watergate story had been told by July, 1973, and (especially) by March, 1974. The fact that 18% of the students were still not convinced of Richard Nixon's guilt two months (a) after he himself released the "smoking howitzer" transcript which proved he had masterminded the coverup from the beginning, (b) after he had resigned rather than face trial in the Senate, and (c) after he had accepted a full pardon for all the crimes he had committed while serving as president, is truly mindboggling. Were these students more authoritarian than their parents, more authoritarian than their peers who were not in college, and more authoritarian than the rest of the nation? All the evidence suggests otherwise. Were they lying when completing the survey, making it seem as if they were fooled for a longer time than they really were? Not very likely.

TABLE 3
Results of the hypothetical question about forcing Richard Nixon from office

N	Mean RWA	Response alternative
35	111.6	No, because based on the evidence as I understand it, Richard Nixon was *not* guilty of any impeachable offense.
137	104.8	No, because while Nixon may have been guilty of impeachable offenses, the best interests of the country would *not* have been served by removing the President of the United States.
180	97.8	Yes, because while Nixon may or may not have been guilty of impeachable offenses, the best interests of the country required that he be removed from office.
389	85.4	Yes, because based on the evidence as I understand it, Richard Nixon *was* guilty of impeachable offenses and deserved to be removed from office.

TABLE 4
Results of hypothetical question about placing Richard Nixon on trial

N	Mean RWA	Response alternative
16	103.7	No. No president or ex-president should be brought to trial like a common criminal.
173	103.8	No. Mr. Nixon may have been guilty of crimes, but he has suffered enough already.
159	96.4	No. Mr. Nixon may have been guilty of crimes, but the country should be spared the agony of more of "Watergate."
393	86.9	Yes. Justice demands that Mr. Nixon be treated like anybody else who is suspected of wrongdoing.

No, the data confirm what Nixon himself believed and what the opinion polls showed: that the public did not care very much about the president's abuses of power, and gave him all the benefits of doubt. Indeed, he probably would have weathered the storm and finished his term, honored for his accomplishments in foreign relations, had he not been taping every word he said "for history."

THE DYNAMICS OF THE AUTHORITARIAN'S ACCEPTANCE OF GOVERNMENT INJUSTICES

Further RWA Scale relationships with the Government Injustices measure
The abuses of power in the Nixon White House which culminated in the Watergate break-in are examples of the kind of highhanded and often illegal acts committed by authorities which I have termed "government injustices." We saw in the last chapter that RWA Scale scores were

appreciably correlated with tolerance for such acts in all five of the populations sampled in the pitting studies. The same results have consistently been found since.

Among the American students who were tested in 1974, RWA Scale scores correlated −.63 with a six-case Government Injustices (GI) score. All of the 24 items on the scale were significantly correlated with this measure.

RWA Scale scores and GI Scores among Manitoba students and their parents have generally correlated in the .50 to .60 range. A 10-case version of the GI measure used in 1979 had mean intercase correlations of .34 and .46 respectively among 223 of my students and 194 of their parents, with corresponding alpha reliabilities of .84 and .89.[11] RWA Scale scores correlated −.59 and −.54 with the summed GI scores. The parents, incidentally, were significantly less concerned about the alleged acts (mean = 1.50 on a 0-4 scale) than were the students (mean = 2.15) ($t = 7.27$, $p < .0001$). All of the 30 RWA Scale items were significantly correlated with the 10-case summed score, except item 11 (in Table 1) among the parents.

Victim-based factors which might affect reactions to Government Injustices

There are at least two victim-based factors which might affect the authoritarian's reaction to governmental abuses of power: (a) the political leanings of the victims of the abuse; and (b) the conventionality of these victims. According to the first hypothesis, right-wing authoritarians would be more upset by government attacks on right-wing groups than they would by identical attacks on left-wing organizations. According to the second hypothesis, authoritarians would not care about attacks on either right- or left-wing groups, if those groups appeared to be unconventional, deviant, or radical. But they would be relatively concerned about injustices committed against conventional, "respectable" or "normal" people.

The first hypothesis was tested in two Manitoba student studies performed in 1976 and 1978; in each of them, approximately 600 subjects responded to one of two versions of ten government injustices cases. In one version, the victim was a left-wing group (e.g., a Maoist or "socialists" organization:); in the other a right-wing group (e.g., fascist or "ultraconservative" organization).

In only 11 of the (2 x 10 =) 20 cases was authoritarianism more strongly correlated with tolerance of injustices against left-wing groups,

TABLE 5

Effects of varying the conventionality of victims of Government Injustices

Case	Government Injustices	Unconventional victim	rRWA	Conventional victim	rRWA	p
1	Customs Department harassment of	Marxist-Leninist Social Revolutionary Party	−.39	New Democratic Party	−.23	<.05
2	Illegal wiretaps of	"Radical union leader"	−.30	"Moderate union leader"	−.19	<.10
3	Illegal drug raids on	"Slum homes"	−.39	"Wealthy homes"	−.21	<.05
4	Police harassment of	Canadian Fundamentalist Freedom Party	−.36	Progressive Conservative Party	−.16	<.05
5	Denial of assembly to	"An obscure, radical teachers' group"	−.34	"An old, established moderate teachers' group	−.15	<.05

Note: "Form A" booklets, answered by 290 subjects, had unconventional victims for Cases 1 and 3, and conventional victims in Cases 2, 4 and 5. "Form B" booklets, answered by 289 subjects, had conventional victims for Cases 1 and 3, and unconventional victims for Cases 2, 4 and 5. All correlation coefficients are statistically significant.

and in only three of these was the difference statistically significant.[12] There was thus little support for the hypothesis that authoritarians would be more sensitive to government injustices directed at right-wing groups.

The second hypothesis, focusing upon the conventionality of the victims rather than their political leanings, was tested in the 1979 student study. Nearly 600 subjects responded to one of two versions of five cases in which authorities allegedly took identical actions against groups which varied in social respectability. The stories used are summarized in Table 5. Two of the cases varied the apparent conventionality of either a left-wing or a right-wing political organization. The other victims were different kinds of union leaders, teachers' groups, or simply the rich versus the poor.

In each case, RWA Scale scores were more strongly correlated with tolerance of injustices committed against unconventional victims, and in four of these cases the difference was statistically significant. ANOVAs were then performed for each story on the reactions of high and low RWA subjects (upper and lower quartiles) to the different versions of the cases. (These results are summarized in Figure 1). The main effects for Authoritarianism and Versions were usually significant, with high RWA subjects showing less overall concern than lows, and subjects in general being

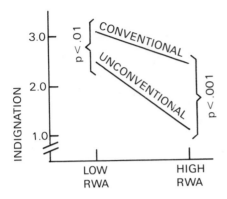

FAUTH. = 48.5 p < .0001
FVER. = 41.7 p < .0001
FINT. = 6.5 p < .02

Figure 1
Case 1   ANOVA of Government
Injustices case varying conven-
tionality of victim

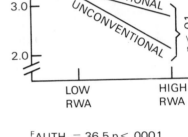

FAUTH. = 36.5 p < .0001
FVER. = 5.5 p < .02
FINT. = 3.2 p < .08

Figure 1
Case 2   ANOVA of Government
Injustices case varying conven-
tionality of victim

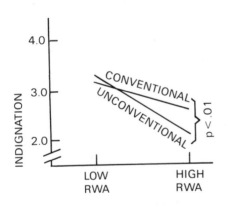

FAUTH. = 62.5 p < .0001
FVER. = 3.05 p < .09
FINT. = 4.00 p < .05

Figure 1
Case 3   ANOVA of Government
Injustices case varying conven-
tionality of victim

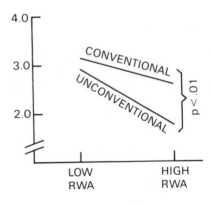

FAUTH. = 50.1 p < .0001
FVER. = 16.2 p < .001
FINT. = 6.6 p < .01

Figure 1
Case 4   ANOVA of Government
Injustices case varying conven-
tionality of victim

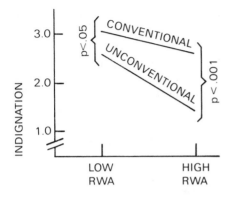

^{F}AUTH. $= 37.1\,p < .0001$
^{F}VER. $= 30.4\,p < .0001$
^{F}INT. $= 6.3\,p < .01$

Figure 1
Case 5   ANOVA of Government
Injustices case varying conven-
tionality of victim

more indignant over injustices committed against conventional groups. The authoritarian x Versions interactions, significant in four of the five cases, are of greater interest. In every case highly authoritarian subjects were less concerned about injustices committed against unconventional groups, while low RWA subjects made a smaller distinction, or none at all.

It is not too surprising that the political orientation of the victims made little difference to the authoritarians. After all, RWA Scale scores are only weakly associated with political party preference. It took an extreme example — the case of a leftist government persecuting the major right-wing party — to get the authoritarian subject to show an even moderate concern about official wrongdoing.

The finding that the victim's social respectability does affect the authoritarian's response is of course congruent with the conventionalism which is one of the defining characteristics of right-wing authoritarianism. High scoring RWA subjects dislike unconventional groups. They have little concern if the government denies dissenters their civil liberties, harasses radical organizations on either the right or the left, or invades the homes of the poor. They seem to think that such groups, by being so different, have forfeited their rights. The logic seems to be: "Good people wouldn't carry on in such a way, so people who do are bad; bad people don't deserve rights, so unconventional groups should be attacked by the government, which is here to protect the good people."

Authoritarians did, in the experimental situation, become relatively concerned about government injustices committed against established, moderate, conventional groups, but they hardly become agitated. The correlations in Table 5 are lower when the victim is conventional, but they are all statistically significant. High RWA subjects still are not as indignant about such abuses of power as low RWA subjects are; they are still more willing to let the government do what it wants against its chosen victims, even respectable ones.

We should note, in closing, that these results suggest that a new political movement will not make much headway with the authoritarians in our society if it is perceived to be radical or extremist. One is inevitably reminded of Hitler in this regard, who dramatically changed his grand strategy for coming to power following the failure of the "beer hall putsch" in 1923. He decided thereafter that he could only gain control of Germany through the constitutional political process, with the help of the established, powerful, institutions in the country. Thus the revolutionary who attempted to overthrow the government by force in 1923 became a strong proponent of "strict law and order" when he emerged from Landsberg Prison in 1924 (Fest, 1973, pp. 194-195).

And it worked, even if Hitler did not believe that "strict law and order" applied to him. And when he came to power through the constitutional process in 1933 and began to impose Nazi control over all the established, powerful, institutions (and everything else) in Germany, the authoritarians may not have minded too much—until they became victims themselves.

THE DYNAMICS OF AUTHORITARIAN AGGRESSION

Further RWA Scale associations with sentencing in the "Trials" measure
Seven Trials cases were administered to the American students. Four involved "unsavory" criminals, namely a juvenile delinquent with a long police record, a political agitator convicted of creating a public disturbance, a drug addict convicted of bank robbery, and an "ex-con" convicted of rape. RWA Scale scores were significantly correlated with the sentences imposed in each of these cases, the relationship across all four being .48. All of the 24 items on the test were significantly correlated with this score.

The other three cases involved "respectable" persons convicted of crimes: the "police brutality" case used in the 1973 pitting experiment, an accountant convicted of assaulting a "hippie" panhandler following an argument, and an American Air Force officer convicted of murder after leading unauthorized bombing raids against Vietnamese villages. RWA Scale scores correlated from −.01 to −.11 with the sentences imposed in these cases, with only the figure for the Air Force officer (−.11) being statistically significant.[13]

RWA Scale correlations with the sentencing of "unsavory" criminals among Manitoba samples have generally been in the .40-.50 range over the years. A 10-case version of the Trials measure was used in the 1979 study. It had mean intercase correlations of .38 and .43 among 233 students and 237 of their parents, with corresponding alpha reliabilities of .86 and .88.[14] RWA Scale scores correlated .52 with the sum of sentences imposed in both samples, with all of the 30 items on the test being significantly correlated with sentencing except items 3, 5, 19, and 28 among the students. There was no difference in the mean sentence imposed by the students and their parents, being 5.4 (on a 0–9 scale) in both cases.

Possible explanations of the authoritarian's punitiveness
What is the motivation behind the authoritarians' punitiveness in the Trials cases? One can imagine many possibilities. Authoritarians may consider the crimes committed more serious offenses than do nonauthoritarians, or they may feel sorrier for the victims. They may have greater faith in the rehabilitative power of long jail terms, in which case their punitiveness is "for the criminal's own good." They may feel the criminal is more blameworthy for his actions. They may derive personal pleasure from punishing wrongdoers. And all of the above may be true; the motivations are not mutually exclusive.

As a test of these possibilities, the 233 students in the 1979 study (who were enrolled in my own classes) were asked to indicate, after proscribing sentence in each of the 10 cases, the following: (a) How serious a crime do you consider the above to be? (b) How sorry do you feel for the victim of the crime? (c) How bad (repulsive, disgusting) do you consider the criminal in this case to be? (d) How much good do you think it will do the criminal, in terms of making him more law-abiding, to send him to jail? (e) How good would it feel personally to administer punishment to this criminal? That is, how satisfying would it be, how glad would it make you feel to be able to punish this man for what he did? All of these questions were answered on a 0–4 scale (e.g., "It wouldn't feel good at all," to, "It would feel extremely good.")

The mean responses to these five questions were 2.33, 2.01, 2.25, 1.42 and 1.12 respectively. RWA Scale scores correlated as follows with the 10-case summed score for each question: "how serious" = .39; "how sorry" = .16; "how bad" = .48; "how much good" = .36; and, "how good would it feel" = .34. All of these coefficients were statistically significant, with the value for "how sorry" being significantly lower than the rest, and that of "how bad" being significantly higher than all the others except "how serious."[15]

These results suggest that authoritarians are particularly likely to feel that "unsavory" criminals such as the ones depicted in these cases are repulsive, disgusting people, and that the crimes they commit are very serious. They also feel that imposing long jail terms will help reform the criminal. They are only marginally more sympathetic toward the victims of the crimes. But the most provocative finding is that punishing such persons, by the authoritarians' own admission, makes them feel "good," "glad," and is "satisfying."

These findings broaden our understanding of the authoritarians' aggression. We could already infer, from their responses to items on the RWA Scale, that they believe in "strict law and order" and the efficacy of punishment. What is striking here is the tendency to see "common lawbreakers" almost as a lower form of life ("repulsive," "disgusting"). "Lower forms of life," one suspects, do not deserve fairness in the authoritarian's mind—no more than dissenters and radicals deserve protection under the law from the government which is supposed to uphold the law.

Victim-based factors which might affect the authoritarian's punitiveness
An obvious hypothesis from the American and Canadian data just reported is that a criminal's conventionality, social respectability, or authority status mediates the relationship between authoritarianism and punitiveness in the Trials cases, though one must note that a "respectable criminal" has still broken the law and hence is unconventional to some extent. This possibility was tested in the 1979 Manitoba student study in which two versions of five Trials cases, varying the status of the criminal, were distributed in fixed, random order among 687 subjects. A summary of the manipulations used is given in Table 6, along with the RWA Scale correlations with punitiveness found in each case.

In each instance, authoritarianism correlated higher with punishment of the low status criminal than it did with punishment of the high status counterpart, but the difference was only significant in three of

TABLE 6

Effects of varying the status of criminals in Trials cases

Case	Crime	Low status criminal	^{r}RWA	High status criminal	^{r}RWA	p
1	Child abuse	Unwed mother	.20‡	Wife of an invest-ment consultant	.10	<.20
2	Common assault	Hippie panhandler (hits accountant)	.31‡	Accountant (hits hippie panhandler)	−.10	<.001
3	Bank robbery	Tramp drug addict	.27‡	Insurance salesman	.13‡	<.06
4	Defrauding government	Welfare recipient (of $3000)	.18‡	Millionaire indus-trialist (of $50,000)	.00	<.01
5	Beating child molester in jail	Another prisoner	.06	Chief of Detectives	−.16‡	<.01

‡ Indicates the correlation is statistically significant.

Note: "Form A" booklets, answered by 347 subjects, had low status criminals in Cases 1 and 3. "Form B" booklets, answered by 340 subjects, had low status criminals in Cases 2, 4 and 5.

the cases. Two-by-two ANOVAs were then used to analyze further the different reactions of high and low scoring RWA subjects to these different criminals. The results, more complex than those obtained in the Government Injustices analyses, are summarized in Figure 2.

The main effects for Authoritarianism and Version were usually significant, with high RWA subjects being more punitive overall and low status victims receiving more punishment. But the interactions between these factors were more varied. In cases 1 and 3 (the two cases for which there was no significant difference in the overall correlations) there was no significant interaction, just the usual pattern of authoritarian subjects being highly punitive. In the "mirror image" case 2, however, high RWA subjects were much more punitive toward a hippie panhandler convicted of assaulting an accountant than they were when the roles were reversed. In case 4, high and low RWA subjects punished equally a tax-evading industrialist, but the high RWA subjects were more punitive toward a "welfare chisler" than were the lows. In case 5, low RWA subjects treated the assailants of an imprisoned child molestor equally, but authoritarians were much less punitive toward a police chief who attacked this prisoner than they were when another prisoner administered the beating.

Except for case 4, where the magnitude of the crimes was so different, low RWA students did not react differently to the status of the criminals. Neither did highs react differently in two of the cases, being just as highly punitive toward the wife of an investment consultant and a

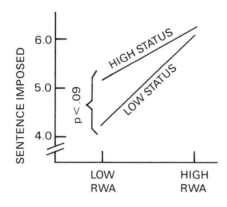

^{F}AUTH. = 14.9 p < .001
^{F}VER. = 2.38 p < .13
^{F}INT. = 0.85 p < .36

Figure 2
Case 1   ANOVA of Trials case
varying status of criminal

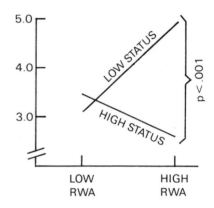

^{F}AUTH. =   3.88 p < .05
^{F}VER. =   9.80 p < .01
^{F}INT. = 19.38 p < .001

Figure 2
Case 2   ANOVA of Trials case
varying status of criminal

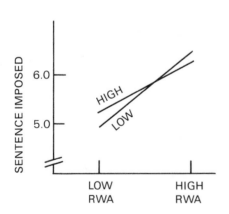

^{F}AUTH. = 22.86 p < .001
^{F}VER. =   0.06 p < .90
^{F}INT. =   0.64 p < .50

Figure 2
Case 3   ANOVA of Trials case
varying status of criminal

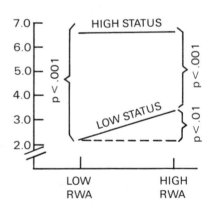

^{F}AUTH. = 5.28 p < .03
^{F}VER. = 202.5 p < .001
^{F}INT. = 4.47 p < .04

Figure 2
Case 4   ANOVA of Trials case
varying status of criminal

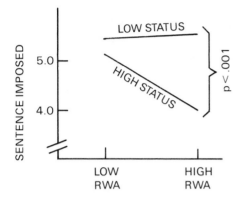

^{F}AUTH. = 3.41 p < .07
^{F}VER. = 8.21 p < .01
^{F}INT. = 4.09 p < .05

Figure 2
Case 5   ANOVA of Trials case
varying status of criminal

businessman as they were toward low status persons who committed the same crimes. However, they were not particularly punitive toward the millionaire industrialist in case 4 (compared to the lows), and they were so positively lenient toward both the accountant in case 2 and the police chief in case 5 that the correlation between authoritarianism and punitiveness in the overall sample was negative.

The implication seems to be that nominal social respectability will not protect a criminal from the authoritarian's punitive impulses. As noted earlier, the supposedly respectable person who commits a crime is disrespectable to some extent because he has broken the law. But why were highs less punitive toward the accountant and the police chief in cases 2 and 5? In both cases, one notes, a "good guy" has aggressed against a social deviant. Similarly in previous studies, RWA Scale scores have been negatively correlated with punishment of a policeman who beat a "troublemaking demonstrator," and the Air Force officer who bombed Vietnamese civilians he suspected were aiding the enemy. As we saw in the last section, the authoritarian may want to attack such targets himself, so he may approve of such aggression and hence be lenient toward high status figures who commit such attacks.

We should also recall the other negative relationship between authoritarianism and punitiveness uncovered in this research program: high RWA American students did not want to punish Richard Nixon for the crimes he committed while president. But this is in keeping with the authoritarian's attitude toward official wrongdoing in general, well documented in the Government Injustices data: authorities, as the source of laws, are also seen as having the power to decide that the laws do not apply to them.

With these notable but understandable exceptions the dominant feature of the data in Figure 2 is the authoritarian's punitiveness. We already knew that high RWA subjects tend to "unload" on low status wrongdoers, whom they see as relatively worthless. Now we find that they are also highly punitive, in some cases, toward higher-status criminals as well. This fact and the finding that high RWA subjects enjoy punishing certain targets supports the hypothesis that authoritarians find such aggression personally reinforcing.

Authoritarianism and prejudice
It was suggested in chapter 3 that, because of their tendencies to aggress against sanctioned targets, authoritarians are likely to be prejudiced against various minority groups who are conventional targets of discrimination. Many ethnocentrism items were tested in the development of the RWA Scale, and a number of them proved weakly correlated with the cluster of submission, aggression, and conventionalism items which ultimately formed the test. But the relationships were not at all strong enough to make ethnocentrism a fourth element in the cluster. The data thus indicated that a weak but positive correlation existed between authoritarianism and prejudice among students, a finding which was later confounded by the failure to obtain higher correlations with aggression against a Jewish victim in the mock laboratory learning experiment.

To further test the relationship between these two constructs I developed a 14-item balanced prejudice scale which was administered to half of my introductory psychology students and to their parents.[16] Mean interitem correlations on this scale were .19 for 245 students and .30 for 237 of their parents, with corresponding (and significantly different) alphas of .77 and .85. The mean scores of the students (47.0, $s^2 = 269$) and parents (49.5, $s^2 = 346$) on this scale were not significantly different, however.

RWA Scale scores correlated .27 with summed prejudice scores among the students, but a significantly higher .43 ($z = 2.00$, $p < .05$) among the parents. All of the RWA Scale items were significantly correlated with the prejudice scores, except items 2, 4, 5, 8, 25, 26, and 29 among the students, and items 4 and 8 among the parents. In both samples though the strongest item correlations tended to be with those statements tapping aggressive impulses (viz. items 9, 10, 11, 14, 17, and 24), none of which mentions any ethnic group and most of which deal with "crime and punishment." This seems to reinforce the explanation of prejudice in high RWA subjects as another form of authoritarian aggression. Just as authoritarians were especially likely to aggress against the "common criminals" whom they saw as disgusting and repulsive, Jews, blacks, Asians and native peoples have historically been treated as "lower forms of life," deserving of discrimination, in North American society. The higher correlation between RWA Scale scores and prejudice among parents suggests, furthermore, that authoritarianism may be an important covariate of prejudice in such populations—though we are still a long way from the .75 coefficient the Berkeley researchers found between the unidirectionally worded E and F Scales.[17]

AUTHORITARIANISM AND RELIGION

Further RWA Scale relationships with continued
acceptance of the home religion
RWA Scale scores correlated .35 to .56 with continued religious acceptance at the five American universities, and was .53 for the sample as a whole. All of the 24 items on the scale were significantly correlated with continued acceptance in the overall sample.

The correlation for Manitoba students has varied from .41 to .52 from 1974 to 1979, being .46 in the 1979 study. All of the test's 30 items had statistically significant correlations with the criterion in this study except items 14, 20, and 24. Data on parents' religion and continued acceptance have not been collected to date.

A more direct way to examine the relationship between religious beliefs and authoritarianism became available with the development of the Christian Orthodoxy (CO) Scale by T. Fullerton and me in the mid 1970s. This balanced 24-item survey measures the extent to which respondents endorse the basic, core teachings of Christianity.[18] Interitem correlations of the test have always been very high; among the 1979 students, for example, they averaged .69, yielding an alpha reliability of .98. Such results reflect the extent to which the Christian faith, probably the most thoroughly taught ideology in our society, is organized in subjects' minds.

The mean score on the CO Scale was 124.3, with a rather hefty variance of 2,314. With considerable strain on the assumption of a normal bivariate distribution (as CO scores tend to be bimodally distributed) the correlation between RWA and CO Scale scores was .47 (23 significant items, religion and sex items most related). This figure, like the correlations with continued religious acceptance, indicates that authoritarianism and religiosity are major covariates among university students.

RWA Scale scores and religious affiliation
Over the years, there have been consistent differences in the RWA Scale scores of students affiliated with different religions. Those with no affiliation (who are mainly agnostics and atheists, about 75% of whom in 1979 stated that they were raised in no religion whatsoever) scored significantly lower than all others, while Jews also tended to score low (see Table 7). Catholics and Protestants in turn scored higher than these groups. In the American sample, Protestant students scored higher than did Catholics. Manitoba student Protestants and Catholics usually did not differ, and therefore authoritarianism has never been as highly related to religious affiliation in these samples as it was among the Americans,[19] as illustrated in Table 7.

Overall, these religious groups gave significantly different answers to all of the items on the RWA Scale used in the American study, and to all of the items used in the 1979 Manitoba student study except item 6. The biggest differences, understandably, occurred on items directly involving religion or sexual morality.

The results described above seem to indicate that authoritarianism and religious variables mutually determine one another. In the first place, it seems clear that different religions produce different levels of authoritarianism in their membership. People raised in no religious system tend to be less authoritarian than those raised in Judaism or Christianity, Jews tend to be less authoritarian than Christians, and there are at least some reliable differences within Protestantism among Manitoba students.

There is no difficulty imagining how these differences, spread across the content of the test, could have arisen. First, there are profound differences among religions in the extent to which members are required to submit to the authority of a governing board, the ministry, and scripture (as interpreted by these authorities). Secondly, religions vary considerably in the extent to which they tolerate, are prejudiced against, and even attack "sinners" and people with different backgrounds or beliefs. Thirdly, organized religions try, to varying degrees, to shape their members' atti-

TABLE 7

RWA Scale scores among students according to present religion

Present religion	1974 American study (24-item RWA Scale)			1979 Canadian study (30-item RWA Scale)		
	N	$\bar{X}$	S^2	N	$\bar{X}$	S^2
"None"	186	76.2	475	93	103.1	676
Judaism	39	83.3	299	47	111.2	506
Catholicism	164	94.9	388	193	127.3	471
Protestantism	349	102.3	441	353	125.3	566
	$F = 67.3$			$F = 29.1$		
	$\hat{\eta}^2 = 21\%$			$\hat{\eta}^2 = 11\%$		

tudes on a host of social issues, such as sexual morality. But together, such attempts promote the three elements of right-wing authoritarianism: authoritarian submission, authoritarian aggression, and conventionalism.

On the other hand, if different religions can produce varying levels of authoritarianism among their faithful, it is also apparent that different levels of personal authoritarianism should produce varying levels of religiousity: authoritarians should be more likely to accept the teachings of the home religion, whatever they were, as a form of continued submission to the authority of the parents, while low RWA subjects should be more likely to develop their own beliefs, and in extreme cases may drop the family religion altogether.[20] And there have been, in every study I have conducted on the matter, significant correlations between RWA Scale scores and continued acceptance of the home religion within every major religious denomination.[21] Within each religion, the authoritarians tend to be the "true believers."

This is not to say that personal authoritarianism is the only source of religiosity, though the size of the correlations certainly indicates that it is a major source. Nor do I want to say that everyone who is an atheist will be less authoritarian than everyone who is a Baptist, though there is not a great deal of overlap in those distributions. But the relationships between RWA Scale scores and religious beliefs have appeared very consistently in the populations studied, and we cannot ignore the apparent connections between the two.

DEMOGRAPHIC CORRELATES OF RWA SCALE SCORES

We shall now briefly consider the relationships between RWA Scale scores and the demographic variables of gender, age, occupational status, and education.

There has been no consistent difference between the RWA Scale scores obtained by males and by females (students or parents) over the years, though the internal consistency of males' responses has tended to be a little higher than females'.

Parents' age, which typically ranged from the upper 30s to the low 60s, has correlated about .15 with RWA Scale scores. No longitudinal research has been undertaken to separate personal history versus cross-sectional interpretations of this small relationship.

Several studies have failed to find a solid relationship between RWA Scale scores and occupational status among parents. Skilled and un-skilled blue-color workers and farmers tended to score about five or 10 points higher on the test than did white-collar workers, managers, and professionals. But there has so far been no difference which makes sense within these clusters of occupations, such as professionals scoring lower than clerks or salesmen, for example.

RWA Scale scores have correlated −.24 to −.30 with the level of formal education among the parent samples. These low coefficients do not support the alternate hypothesis that relationships obtained by the RWA Scale with criterion measures in such samples are appreciably due to mutual correlations with education, which obviously also cannot be the case in student samples where there is no difference in educational level. For example, in the 1979 parents' study, the RWA Scale's correlation with the Government Injustices measure was reduced only from −.54 to −.53 when the effects of education were partialled out, and that with the Trials sentences from .52 to .49.[22] Thus while education may make subjects somewhat less authoritarian, and less likely to accept government injust-ices, and less punitive, it cannot begin to account for the relationships found between these latter variables and scores on the RWA Scale.

Education does have a notable effect on the organization of authori-tarian attitudes among parent samples, however. Parents with a Grade 8 (or less) education typically have alpha levels in the low .70s on the RWA Scale. As subjects' level of education rises, so do the alpha levels rise: from the low .80s for high school, up to the high .80s through university education. Parents who have done postgraduate work of some sort have alphas of about .90.

This relationship between education and alpha levels may well be caused by differences in reading comprehension, which show up in the way subjects use the test's response scale. Poorly educated people are more likely to use the extreme response categories: education correlates

about −.30 with use of the "+3" ("strongly agree") answer, and about
−.15 with use of "−3" ("strongly disagree"). Less educated parents thus
have a net response set for "+3" which on the balanced RWA Scale
reduces the interitem correlations. Better educated parents are more
likely to use the "+1" and "−1" responses, and to approximately equal
extents ($r \approx .25$), more qualified responding that does not result in a
direction-of-wording response set.

Finally, RWA Scale scores have not yet been correlated with scores
on a standardized adult intelligence test. But marks on various objective tests taken in introductory psychology courses are readily available:
in my own classes, authoritarianism has correlated from −.18 to +.06
with grades earned on multiple-choice tests; none of the coefficients has
been statistically significant. Similar results have been found with the
grades earned with other professors, the figures varying so far from −.07
to +.09, all being nonsignificant. Thus if we believe that the grades
students earn in our courses reflect at least to some extent "general
intellectual ability," there is no reason for believing that authoritarianism
is strongly related to intelligence among university students.[23]

SOCIAL DESIRABILITY EFFECTS ON THE RWA SCALE

The response to almost any psychological test can be shaped by respondents' desire to present a positive image of themselves (Crowne and
Marlowe, 1964). There are several reasons, however, why attitude surveys
may be less susceptible to such distortions than are, say, personality
tests: (a) there is no overall social consensus to anchor judgments on
many contentious social issues; and (b) people tend to believe their
opinions are the best ones anyway. It is conceivable therefore, that social
desirability motivations might have little impact on a test like the RWA
Scale.

The issue was tested directly in a 1974 University of Manitoba study
in which students were asked to answer the 24-item RWA Scale either
(a) as subjects usually do, giving their own opinions; (b) under "fake
good" instructions which told them to try to create as socially positive
an image of themselves as possible; or (c) under "fake bad" instructions
which told them to make as socially unattractive an image as possible.[24]
To forestall fears that such answers might be associated with their names,
subjects tested in these three conditions answered their surveys anonymously; that is, they did not follow the usual procedure of putting their
survey number and name on an "attendance sheet." Data for each con-

dition were collected in three different sessions scattered systematically throughout a larger testing program so as to balance time of day, day of week, and classroom time-slots among the three conditions.

The mean RWA Scale score of the 126 subjects who answered RWA Scale in the usual way was 95.3 ($s^2 = 484$). The mean for the "fake good" condition was significantly higher, 109.7 ($N = 131$; $s^2 = 578$); the mean for the "fake bad" condition was 89.8 ($N = 134$; $s^2 = 897$), which was significantly lower than the "normal" mean of 95.3 (but only by a one-tailed test). The significant overall F = 21.2 indicated that 10% of the variance of the scores on the test was determined by these variations in instructional sets.

The direction of these differences is not surprising. Since the RWA Scale taps conventional sentiments, we would expect scores of people trying to make a socially positive impression to be on balance higher than those trying to make a poor impression. What is just as noticeable, however, are the high variances of these faked responses, indicating that there is little consensus about what the "good" and "bad" answers are. This fact, and the small shifts produced by the extremely conflicting instructions, argue that responses to the RWA Scale are not very susceptible to social desirability effects.

A second, if less direct, line of evidence leads to the same conclusion. If social desirability motivations affect the RWA Scale, we would expect higher scores when subjects' responses are linked to their names. In the same 1974 study described above, 140 other subjects answered the survey in the usual way, signing their names and survey numbers on an attendance sheet. Another 123 subjects signed their names directly on the survey booklet. The mean RWA Scale scores of these two groups were 97.3 and 97.2. While in the expected direction, neither mean was significantly different from the 95.3 obtained when subjects were completely anonymous.[25]

CROSS-SECTIONAL CHANGES IN AUTHORITARIANISM SCORES OVER TIME

RWA Scale scores were collected on large samples of introductory psychology students at the University of Manitoba every fall from 1973 through 1979. With only minor exceptions, the sections sampled, the testing site, the booklet format, the instructions used, and (with the loss of some hair) the experimenter were all constant over this period of time. The RWA Scale, it is true, changed, but twelve items (six protrait and six contrait) appeared in every booklet since 1973. These twelve "continuing items" are numbers 9, 10, 17, 20, 21, 23, 25, 46, 53, 55, 62, and 64 in Table 7 of chapter 3.

Figure 3a plots the summed scores of these twelve items over the seven years. A one-way ANOVA reveals an overall significant F (12.2, $p < .0001$), the later scores being in general significantly different from the earlier ones. Moreover, the general tendency appears to be slowly but steadily upwards, though it is too gradual for a significant linear trend. Item analysis reveals that responses to all twelve statements have become significantly more authoritarian, except for the item "A 'woman's place' should be wherever she wants to be...," which has become significantly less authoritarian over the years.

Responses to these same twelve items from the 1976, 1978, and 1979 parents studies also show a significant upward swing in authoritarianism, due entirely to high scores in the last sample; the means were 59.6 ($s^2 = 122$), 59.6 again ($s^2 = 114$), and 63.0 ($s^2 = 170$) respectively (F = 11.0, $p < .0001$). Thus both students and their parents appear to be a little more authoritarian at the end of the 1970s than such people were earlier.

At the same time as RWA Scale scores were slowly increasing among the students, the organization of their responses to the twelve continuing items went down dramatically (Figure 3b). The drop is highly significant ($M = 62.8$, $p < .0001$) (Hakstian and Whalen, 1976). Internal analyses furthermore indicate that the correlations among the protrait items, among the contrait items, and among the protrait-contrait pairs were all sliding down by similar degrees over the years.

The parents data do *not* show a parallel trend, the mean intercorrelation among the twelve items being .18, .16, and .18 in the three successive studies.

The changes in authoritarianism levels among the students and their parents have hardly been large, but they do suggest that at least Manitoba society has become a little more authoritarian lately. It was widely observed that students at the University of Manitoba (and others) in the late 1970s were more "conservative" than were their predecessors ten years earlier. The change may actually have been a little more subtle than that, however. The real difference between 1969 and 1979 on many North American campuses may not have been that the majority of the student body became more conservative, but rather that there were fewer very liberal or "radical" students around at the close of the 70s.

This is borne out by an examination of the distribution of the scores on the twelve continuing items produced by 1973 and 1979 freshmen. In

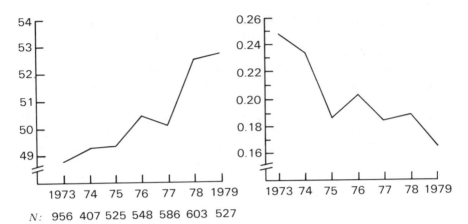

N: 956 407 525 548 586 603 527

Figure 3a   Mean scores
Changes in responses to six RWA scale items over time, University of Manitoba students.

Figure 3b   Mean interitem correlations
Changes in responses to six RWA scale items over time, University of Manitoba students.

Note: The values for the fall, 1980 study ($N = 533$) were essentially those of the 1979 experiment: mean = 52.2, average intercorrelation = .169.

1973, 3.5% of the students had summed scores between the minimum possible, 12, and (2x 12 =) 24; and 11.2% had scores between 25 and 36. In 1979, only 1.3% of the sample had scores between 12 and 24, and 6.5% had scores between 25 and 36. On the other end of the distribution, 1% of the 1973 sample had scores between 73 and the maximum possible (7 x 12 =) 84, and 13.2% had scores between 61 and 72; the figures for 1979 were 1.1% and 16% respectively. Thus the rise in RWA Scale scores over that period of time did not basically occur because the whole distribution shifted to the right. Most of the rise was caused by a thinning of the far left, as noted earlier in the discussion of the shift in NDP student scores over the same interval.

The future shape of the curve in Figure 3a is a matter of speculation. It may continue to rise for all time, but that seems unlikely. Instead, I suspect it will peak at some point and either flatten out or even begin to descend. If significant events in our culture create a student activist left again, the way the civil rights movement and the war in Viet-Nam did in the 1960s, the curve would probably turn downwards. (Events in Canada and the United States in the 1970s and early 1980s suggest that swings in political sentiment toward either the right or the left result in policies which activate the "opposite camp," sometimes producing a counterflow, and other times producing polarization.) On the other hand, perhaps we should not dismiss too casually the possibility that "significant events" couls also have the opposite effect, and drive the curve in Figure 3a to new heights.

The drop in interitem correlations among the twelve continuing items shown in Figure 3b is open to at least three interpretations:

1 It may be that psychological tests, or at least this one, "come apart" over time. Relationships among sentiments may be transient affairs, and the covariation which happens to exist when a test is created may quickly dissolve as items become dated, referrents lose their connotations, and the "semantic map" changes. According to this hypothesis, the curve in Figure 3b will continue to drop until it reaches some minimal level, at which it will stay thereafter.

2 It may be that associations among items can both diminish and grow over time in cycles of regular or irregular periods. Historical events, such as the war in Viet-Nam and the protest against it may have strengthened the associations in people's minds among submitting to the government, maintaining traditional values, controlling the youth, punishing dissenters, and so on. With the resolution of the war and the disappearance of the protest, these issues slowly became more independent. "Unconventional dress" in 1979 did not connote rebellion nearly as much as it did in 1969. But according to this hypothesis it could re-establish tighter connections with defiance of authority, challenging traditional values, and so forth, by 1989, or whenever historical developments start "gluing" attitudes of authoritarian submission, authoritarian aggression and conventionalism closer together again. Therefore this hypothesis predicts that the curve in Figure 3b will eventually bottom out and turn upwards.

3 A third hypothesis is that Figure 3b represents one of the many dismal consequences of the steady decline in reading comprehension skills observed among entering freshmen classes during most of the 1970s. The RWA Scale is not a simple test: most of its items are two or three lines long in the survey booklet, and half of them are worded in the contrait direction, which requires subjects to read the statements carefully if they are going to answer with content consistency. There is plenty of evidence that all this makes the scale more valid, but if the reading skills of students continue to diminish, the interitem correlations should fall even further.

My own guess is that Hypotheses II and III are both right, that is, that students in 1979 are less ideological than they were in 1969, but that future students will be more so, and that almost any self-administered printed survey is going to be hurt by decreased reading skills. But I doubt the slope of Figure 3b can be entirely attributed to whatever loss in reading comprehension has occurred; I suspect that the associations among authoritarian submission, authoritarian aggression, and conventionalism were not as tightly formed among young people in the late 1970s as they were somewhat earlier.

An upward turn in Figure 3b will choose between Hypotheses I and II, but the drop in reading comprehension is more of an "engineering" problem that can perhaps be alleviated by "twisting a few knobs." In the 1979 study I tried two manipulations to correct the situation. The students in 10 of my testing sessions received my standard instructions before answering the RWA Scale at their first testing session. Another 218 students in four other sessions received special instructions which emphasized the importance of the study to me personally and to the scientific investigation of public opinion. These subjects were also urged to read each item carefully: I explained that "carelessness by just a few persons can do great damage to the scientific value of a study." The subjects were also given plenty of time to do a thorough job; I told them to ignore the last quarter of the survey booklet.

The alpha coefficient of the 30-item RWA Scale produced by the 527 "regular instruction" subjects was .86, while, for those who received the special instructions, the figure was .87. While the scores leaned in the hoped-for direction, the difference was not statistically significant ($W = 1.14, p < .15$) (see Feldt, 1969).

When subjects came for a second testing session one week later, they were asked to answer the RWA Scale again, according to how they felt then. Afterwards, they were shown their answers to the same items from the previous week, told to compare the two sets, and then write down their final reaction to each item in light of how they had answered it on the two prior occasions. My hope was that subjects would not make the same misinterpretation mistakes twice, and that discovery of inconsistencies in their answers would produce a more valid final response.

The alpha level of the RWA Scale for the 507 "regular instructions" subjects who kept their second appointments was .88, which was significantly higher than their first session alpha ($W = 1.25, t = 7.88, p < .0001$). (see Feldt, 1980). The alpha coefficient for the 210 returning "special instruction" subjects also increased significantly, to .89 ($W = 1.20, t =$

4.30, $p < .0001$). Item-by-item analysis indicated that most of the changes which took place between the first and third answerings were minor (e.g., from "slightly agree" to "moderately agree"), but on about three items per survey, answers moved across the neutral point of the response scale (i.e., from some level of agreement to some level of disagreement, or vice versa), indicating a more substantial shift of response upon reexamination of the item. Furthermore, the amount of change which took place on an item correlated .47 ($p > .0001$) with the length of the item, meaning that it was the longer, more complicated items which tended to be answered differently the second time.[26]

These results support the hypothesis that drops in reading comprehension will produce error in RWA Scale socres and thus decrease the test's reliability. They also show a way to regain some of what has been lost in Figure 3b, probably more in fact than has been lost since 1973 in diminished reading skills. (The mean intercorrelation among the twelve continuing items in the third set of answers to the survey was .194, compared to .166 for the first session.) Such a gain is not trivial: the change in alpha from .860 obtained overall at the first session to .887 obtained overall at the second session produced a 32% increase in the RWA Scale's signal-to-noise ratio, from 2.8:1 to 3.7:1.

In closing, I might observe that the data in Figure 3 are fairly unique. There has been abundant speculation in historical, political scientific, sociological, and psychological writing about the rise and fall of authoritarianism in societies, and occasionally some fairly ingenious ways to measure such flows indirectly have appeared (Sales, 1972, 1973). But data such as those shown in Figure 3, obtained with an apparently valid and fairly powerful measure of right-wing authoritarianism in highly standardized and well-controlled circumstances are, I think, unprecedented. The pity is that the studies have necessarily been limited to such a narrow population, when for a relatively small amount of money we could by now have had much more representative data on Canadian and American populations.

Summary of the chapter
We have now accumulated a number of findings about right-wing authoritarianism which need to be organized into as neat a synthesis as possible. First of all, we have a considerable amount of evidence supporting the validity and power of the RWA Scale. In every population studied so far, the test has demonstrated adequate if not superior psychometric properties. It remains, even in the face of decreasing interitem correla-

tions and increasing length, an essentially unidimensional measure of the covariance of authoritarian submission, authoritarian aggression, and conventionalism. Improvements in the scale itself and in various criterion measures have brought the validity coefficients from the .40s we frequently saw in chapter 4 into the .50s. Rather large chunks of the variance of certain seemingly diverse attitudes and beliefs (reactions to Watergate, punishment of criminals, religious fervor) can be explained in terms of this construct.

We should note in passing the stability of these findings. The repetitive reporting of factor analyses, validity coefficients, item analyses, and so forth, are tedious, but it is a small price to pay to avoid the chaos characteristic of the literature on the original F Scale, for instance. Furthermore, there is nothing magical about how the research was done: The instruments were reliable, the testing procedures standardized, the samples large, the research program sustained, and the data led the way.

And where have the data led us? I said at the beginning of this chapter that we needed to discover where authoritarianism is found in our society and that we needed to learn how the authoritarian mind operates. Keeping in mind all the limitations imposed by our idiosyncratic samples and particular methodology, I still think we have some very good clues about where to find the authoritarians in our midst. In short, they seem to be all around us. There are authoritarians among the well-educated and the poorly educated, on the political left and the political right, among the rich and the poor, among the atheists and among the ardently faithful, among the young and old, among males and females, and—if anyone doubted it—among Americans as well as Canadians.

Beyond this sound caution against overgeneralizing, there are a few areas in which right-wing authoritarianism seems more concentrated. If our politically interested student judges are correct, it appears to be concentrated among politicians on the right. It can readily be found among fundamentalist Protestants, but also among the "true believers" of any major Christian-Judaic religion. It is a little more concentrated among the poorly educated. Parents are substantially more authoritarian than their university-aged student children.

What have we found about the way the authoritarian mind works? I am struck, most of all, by the way the authoritarian clings to his notion of what is respectable, and how thoroughly he disapproves of those whose behavior falls outside what he considers right and normal. Authoritarians think of themselves as "the good, decent people." Unconventional people, people who are different, are worth less, and sometimes even worthless. "Let the authorities do what they want to the radicals, the deviants, the 'wierdos.'" "Throw the book at them in court." "Send them all back where they came from." And from there it is not too big a step to "Let's get rid of them once and for all."

What is behind this absorption with, and of, the conventional? I was struck by a statement heard in Canada when it was revealed that the RCMP were illegally opening some people's mail: "Only someone with something to hide would object." That's just a little too much a boast of innocence to me; it seems unnecessary. But the authoritarian trots out his respectability at the drop of a hat. It is his badge, his hallmark, his holy medal. Is he trying to convince himself as well as others that he is good in a world crowded with deviants? Does he cling to conventions because he fears his own evil? Does he continually cast stones at "the bad" in hopes that a psychological form of Newton's Third Law will thereby propel him back toward the good?[27] Does he make such a display of his conventionality because he knows, or at least senses, that he has something to hide?

Another thing that impresses me in the findings presented in this chapter is how strong the authoritarians' punitive impulses are. They strike out at a bewildering array of targets if they come across their sights, including a plethora of minority groups, and even some "respectable criminals." This can be taken as the generalized aggressive drive which the Berkeley researchers theorized was integral to the authoritarian personality. Is the hostility there first, looking for a safe place to happen? Or is it a by-product of attitudes that are acquired for other reasons (e.g., imitation of parents), and is the pleasure authoritarians derive from disparaging and hating simply "gravy" from behavior that springs from ordinary roots? How crucial, how necessary is it for the authoritarian not simply to dislike, but to attack others? Or to put the question in its most theoretical clothes: one can readily see why conventional people would also be submissive to established authority, but why do they also tend to be so aggressive as well?

These are psychodynamically intensive questions. We are digging deeper into the authoritarian's personality, but have so far only scratched the surface of the data mass we will need to find the answers. And there are many other questions. Do characteristics of established authorities affect the authoritarian's submission to them?[28] Is the authoritarian particularly likely to aggress if authority figures express hostility toward deviant targets? Does the authoritarian have "perceptual defenses" against violent stimuli, indicating unconscious censoring of his own aggressive impulses? Does his conventionality translate into behavior, or does he "sin" but not accept his impulses and deeds.[29] And so on. There is a very long list of things to find out.

But I do believe we shall find out. One can doubt this of course, but for a long time, many experimental psychologists wondered if *any* study of authoritarianism was either relevant or possible. I hope the reader by now agrees it is both.

Some exploratory findings
on the origins
of right-wing authoritarianism

6

In this chapter we consider the question of how right-wing authoritarianism develops within a person. Two different answers to this question are compared and contrasted: one is based on psychoanalytic theory and the other might generally be called a "social learning" explanation. Some data bearing on these two approaches are also presented.

TWO EXPLANATIONS OF THE PERSONAL ORIGINS OF RIGHT-WING AUTHORITARIANISM

A psychoanalytic explanation
The Berkeley theory of the origins of right-wing authoritarianism was summarized in chapter 1. This account, relying heavily upon Freudian theory and extensively shaped by Frenkel-Brunswik's study of highly prejudiced adults, held that authoritarians were created in a particular family mileau. As one of the Berkeley authors summarized the findings many years later:

> High authoritarians came, for the most part, from homes in which a stern and distant father dominated a submissive and long-suffering but morally restrictive mother, and in which discipline was an attempt to apply conventionally approved rules rather than an effort to further general values in accordance with the perceived needs of the child (Sanford, 1974, p. 147).

A psychoanalytic scenario of how this family background could produce "fascist potential" involves most of the classic ego-defense mechanisms. At some point the child would have reacted aggressively to his stern and distant father, but this would have been met by still more "threatening or traumatic or even overwhelming" punishment, so the hostility toward the father (and authority figures in general) was repressed and replaced through a reaction formation with superficial love and abject submission. The repressed hostility was then projected onto minority groups who were then seen as threatening and offensive, and this perception served as the rationalization for aggression against these groups, which however was really displaced hatred of authority figures.

As we also saw in chapter 1, the evidence which the Berkeley researchers presented in support of this appealing model is singularly unconvincing. Subsequent attempts to test the Berkeley theory have also fallen far short of the mark. The early childhood origins of authoritarianism may be taken for granted in our culture today, and the theory might be valid. But there is little scientific support for it so far.

A "social learning" model
An alternate explanation of authoritarianism's origins can proceed from the definition of right-wing authoritarianism as the covariation of certain attitudes (see chapter 3). The question then becomes, "How did these attitudes arise?" I would suggest that in general people acquire attitudes (a) from other people, through direct tuition and through imitation; and (b) through their own experience with the objects of these attitudes. The determinant of what attitude is learned is the reinforcement the person receives for learning the attitude (which can be vicarious in the case of imitation) and the reinforcement he receives from his interaction with the object of the attitude, according to principles of social learning theory (Bandura, 1964, 1973).

Sources of attitudes
One's parents would naturally be a primary source of attitudes toward authority, aggressive behavior, conventionality, and an enormous number of other topics. Many of these attitudes are intentionally taught, and parents will readily use positive and negative reinforcers to insure that their children's verbal statements and behavior conform to their wishes. Parents can also serve as powerful models (Bandura, Ross & Ross, 1963) for their children, so that even if they do not intentionally teach their children certain attitudes, their offspring can still acquire them by observing the parents' behavior, from conversations around the dinner table, and so forth. And of course children can form attitudes as a result of their own experience with their parents; a college student's

attitudes toward spanking children, which is tapped by the RWA Scale, may mainly reflect his evaluation of how he was disciplined, and that judgment may or may not coincide with his parents' intentions or example.

There are a number of other people whose social roles normally give them the right to directly teach attitudes to children; grandparents, older siblings, ministers, school teachers, and scout leaders may all directly shape a child's opinions, though not usually in contradiction of parental teachings. These "quasi-parents" can also become models whom children imitate, and experiences with them can affect their attitudes in ways the parents may or may not wish.

Even people whom the child has never met, such as TV personalities, advertising executives, or comic book illustrators are allowed to directly shape attitudes on certain topics, and can (themselves or their creations) become models for imitation. The heroes of comic books are later replaced by the characters in novels, movies, and plays which are often written to express and shape social attitudes.

Then there is the peer group, whose influence develops slowly but may eventually rival the parents'. The modes are the same: direct influence attempts, observing peers' behavior and the consequences, and the effects of experience with peers. Again there are adult counterparts to childhood peers: one's spouse, friends, co-workers, and neighbors can all shape our attitudes on social issues.

Beyond this, there are the effects of the environment at large, the world beyond direct experience. People read newspapers, newsmagazines, see the news on television. Whether intentionally "slanted" or not, the news can shape people's attitudes on the issues covered, and can certainly affect sentiments of authoritarian submission, authoritarian aggression, and conventionalism. So can *The Reader's Digest, The Ladies Home Journal,* and *Playboy.*

The development of right-wing authoritarianism
Obviously these sources do not operate evenly over the life cycle. Parental influence is apt to be enormous at first, and for understandable reasons parents do not typically encourage their young children to scrutinize the dictates of authority. Thus in most families children may be taught simply to obey legitimate authority unquestioningly. The other determinants of attitudes most important to the young child (e.g., teachers, extended family) might tend to reinforce this "reflexive" submission. We might thus expect children to have relatively uniform and highly submissive attitudes toward authorities during their early years.

Right-wing authoritarianism probably does not begin to take organized form until adolescence, when our culture increasingly concentrates on preparing the child for the adult status he will soon acquire. Younger children's cognitive abilities are too limited to comprehend the issues involved in the adult world and develop interconnected attitudes on them. But these attitudes can develop and become increasingly organized during adolescence, and with this development comes differentiation in a group of young adults who once might have all agreed that authorities should simply be obeyed.

The parents may still be the most important source of the attitudes which develop then, not just through their teachings and example on an ever-widening range of subjects, but through their relationship with the emerging adult who is apt to be seeking ever-greater autonomy. But peers can also exert powerful influence, not just on clothing and music preferences, but on sexual behavior and attitudes toward authority, hostility toward outgroups, and so forth. Also, through his school work, the movies, and TV, and an occasional news broadcast, the adolescent becomes more aware of the world he is inheriting and the issues which abound in it. But perhaps as important as all these other factors, the teenager now experiences quite a larger slice of life firsthand than ever before. By late adolescence the contemporary teenager will probably have held a succession of jobs, taken trips to distant places, met a wide range of people, and got into situations which a few years earlier he would never have imagined.

Continuation of earlier trends

It is highly probable that the development which occurs at this time will be more a continuation of earlier learnings than a radical departure. The child whose parents have stressed submission to authority, who have emphasized observing the family religion, or have shown hostility toward various groups is apt to form authoritarian attitudes as an adult. His friends, his movies, and his travels have likely been selected by his parents to a considerable extent to reinforce the home influence; and the child who has been reinforced for submission is apt to accept this, indeed to depend on it.

At the other end of the scale, one would find those probably rare children whose parents rewarded independence, had no "enemies list," emphasized no particular religious code, tolerated unconventional ideas and behavior, and in general, nurtured a "question and judge" approach to life rather than "memorize and obey." Adolescents with this sort of past are not likely to become friends with those from firmly authoritarian homes. Their experiences in life are apt to be quite different. Their reaction to common experiences, such as adolescent sexual impulses and high-handed high school teachers, will probably be quite different. The movies they choose to see will often be different. Their interpretation of major news events may well be quite different. And so on. They are headed toward opposite ends of the RWA Scale distribution we find among introductory psychology students.

In between these two extremes lie a thousand less homogeneous patterns. Most parents require submission to their authority, but in moderate amounts overall with perhaps increasing tolerance for independence as the child grows older. Most parents want some conformity to social conventions, but can accept moderate amounts of deviation. Most parents may teach and display hostility toward some groups, but the list may be short and hostility not altogether self-righteous. All of these tendencies would head the child toward moderate levels of adult authoritarianism.

A moderate start toward authoritarianism can occur within a family in other ways. Religious parents are not necessarily highly authoritarian in their dealings with their children, for example. A child may thus receive a thorough schooling in the Ten Commandments and learn to worship a supreme being; but he may also have parents who encourage his independence from them. Atheistic parents, on the other hand, can be highly authoritarian when interacting with their children. The net effect in both cases is an inclination toward a more moderate level of adult authoritarianism than would have been the case had both parent-child relationship and religious influence pointed in the same direction. Other factors in the child's home (the most important probably being different approaches to childrearing by the mother and father) can push in opposite directions and incline the individual away from either high or low authoritarianism as an adult.

When does the development end?
There is no reason to expect that a person's authoritarianism is finally established at the age of 18. Education, and the greater assumption of adult status may further increase the organization of attitudes and the level of RWA Scale scores. Relationships with parents can change (and eventually end), peers can change, roles can change (the shift from childhood into parenthood perhaps being the most significant), the world can change. Modification and change of opinions are possible as long as

new experiences are possible, as long as new models can emerge, as long as reinforcement contingencies can change.

Dramatic changes may be rare, nonetheless, because for the most part life may continue in relatively stable circumstances, and we tend to interpret new experiences in terms of old learnings. But small changes are always possible, and they can accumulate over a period of time. And large sudden changes in the individual and a society can occur—because of economic calamity, domestic upheaval, or war, for example.

The two explanations contrasted

Aside from the fact that the psychoanalytic and social learning theories both hold that authoritarianism is determined by the person's experience, the two explanations have little in common. The model I have advanced, for example, holds that parental behavior is important, but it also lists many other factors that contribute to the development of right-wing authoritarianism. There is no assumption that parental behavior will ultimately be more important than all the rest of these.

As well, the nature of the parental influence is different. I make no case for the stern, distant father and the submissive, long-suffering, morally-restrictive mother as a particularly dangerous combination. It is not necessary that the authoritarian's parents were harsh, cold, and distant. They could have been as close and involved with their child as any other parents, and still could have taught him to obey authority, etcetera. In short the family origins of authoritarianism I am proposing are not nearly as dramatic or as peculiar as those Frenkel-Brunswik proposed.

The explanations also differ on the age at which authoritarianism is created. Like other psychoanalytic explanations, the Berkeley model places great emphasis on early childhood experiences. I have proposed instead that while some authoritarian attitudes are formed during early childhood, the process is hardly completed then. The most dramatic change in the organization of submissive, aggressive and conventional attitudes is expected to occur during adolescence. But I have also argued that neither the organization nor the level of authoritarianism is ever set in concrete.

As important as the above differences are, they are not the most fundamental distinction between the two explanations, which lies in the "mechanisms" theorized to produce authoritarianism. The psychoanalytic theory invokes powerful instinctual forces, a struggle amongst the id, ego and superego, ego defense mechanisms, cathexes, and so forth.

The social learning theory is based more simply upon the concept of reinforcement. It is true that learning theory explanations in 1980 are not nearly as simple, nor simplistic, as they were in 1950. Today we know that reinforcements can be experienced vicariously, can be self-administered as well as encountered from outside, and can be thoughts as well as food pellets (Bandura, 1973, pp. 39–53). Just as important, the individual's role in shaping his own behavior, directly as well as through his effect on how the environment responds to him, is accepted and employed to explain complex social behaviors. But underlying all of this is still the notion of reinforcement and the Law of Effect.

The difference in the theoretical constructs used to explain the development of authoritarianism gives the two approaches different statuses as scientific theories. "Occam's razor" aside, there is little chance of accumulating scientific support of psychoanalytic explanations because so much of the theory is untestable in the sense that it cannot be disconfirmed. Thus if it happened that high RWA subjects tended to speak bitterly of their parents, this would be considered evidence for the stern, distant treatment they received in childhood. But if they turned out to be warm and generous toward their parents, it would be explained as "over-glorification," as a reaction formation against repressed hostility. If there were no tendency to speak in either way, it would be because both reactions occurred and masked one another.

I do not claim, in advancing a learning theory model, that these explanations are always unambiguous, or are subject to general disconfirmation either. But such an explanation does stand upon a enormous accumulation of fact and principle which have proven useful for predicting and controlling behavior. And the model does rely more upon observable, quantifiable events and yields specific hypotheses about the formation of authoritarian attitudes which can be tested. And that is an enormous advantage in this business, as we shall now see as we consider some exploratory evidence on the validity of the two accounts.

FURTHER DATA ON THE BERKELEY THEORY OF THE ORIGINS OF AUTHORITARIANISM

As I noted in chapter 1, the most straightforward test of the psycho-analytic theory of authoritarianism's origins requires veridical measurements of parent-child interactions on a number of dimensions over the childhood years, and then a valid measurement of adult authoritarianism 10 to 15 years later. The methodological problems involved in such a study—such as obtaining a representative sample of parents willing to be studied for years, and observing parental discipline without affecting it—appear formidable, however. Thus even though I believed in the mid 1970s that I had a valid measure of adult authoritarianism, I was not tempted to try for the "straightforward test."

Instead I developed paper-and-pencil measures for collecting retrospective data on the childhoods of the students who served in my Manitoba survey studies.[1] These instruments asked for recollections of certain events which might have occurred 10 to 12 years previously, when the child was seven to nine years old, from both the students and each of their parents.[2] Altogether I developed, between 1976 and 1978, scales for collecting reports on three types of parental behavior highly relevant to the Berkeley theory: parental anger over various childhood offenses, the type of parental punishment used in such cases, and parental interest in the child.

The final version of the Parental Anger Scale (as completed by students)[3] is shown in Table 1. It lists 24 youthful misdeeds which it was thought most children might commit some time or another during the years involved. Student subjects were asked to indicate, on a 0 to +4 scale, how angry their mothers, and their fathers, would have typically become if they had done the things which were listed. Parents in turn were asked to indicate how angry they themselves would typically have become over each misdeed.

The Parental Punishment Scale listed the 24 misdeeds again, and asked the student subjects to indicate how their mothers, and how their fathers, would most typically have punished them for each. Five options were given:

Your mother (father) would typically have *scolded* you, but seldom or never would have given you a spanking.

Your mother (father) would typically have given you a *spanking*, perhaps with a scolding or deprivation of privileges as well.

Your mother (father) would typically have *deprived you of privileges*, (no TV, no candy, 'Go to your room,' etc.), perhaps with a scolding, but seldom or never would have given you a spanking.

Your mother (father) would typically have *expressed sorrow or disappointment* that you had done wrong, asked you to explain yourself, made you apologize to injured parties—perhaps with a bit of a scolding or a deprivation of privilege, but no spanking.

Your mother (father) would not have punished you in any way for the act.

TABLE 1

Items composing the Parental Anger Scale

How angry would your mother (father) have become if she (he) had found out, when you were about 7-9 years old, that you had:

---

 1 ruined a nice or expensive toy (e.g. your major Christmas present) through too rough play or abuse;
 2 stolen a dollar from her purse, the "sugar bowl," etc;
 3 gotten the house dirty by "tracking in" mud, getting dirt on the chesterfield, etc.;
 4 hit a younger brother or sister (or a neighbor's younger child) such that the child began to cry, while having an argument with him/her;
 5 lied to her about something like whether you'd brushed your teeth or fed a pet;
 6 lied to her about something more important, like whether you'd broken a vase, or a window;
 7 used "dirty" or sexual words in your speech;
 8 disobeyed her in a matter like coming straight home from school, or cleaning up your room before going out to play;
 9 disobeyed her in a more important matter, like going somewhere you were forbidden to go, or doing something with other children you were forbidden to do;
10 been caught "playing doctor" (i.e. engaging in childhood sexual play) with some other children;
11 struck her in anger;
12 "sassed" her or showed disrespect in some similar way;
13 failed to clean up a mess you had made that she told you to clean up;
14 started a fight at school;
15 taken (i.e. stolen) another child's toy home with you;
16 "sassed" another adult or showed disrespect toward another adult in some similar way;
17 gotten your "dress up" clothes dirty just before going to Church or some important event;
18 lied to her about whether you had eaten all your supper, or left a book out in the rain;
19 lied to her about something more important, like losing a tool or breaking a nice dish or ornament;
20 been looking at "dirty pictures" in a magazine or book you had found;
21 disobeyed her in a matter like using your spending money to buy things you weren't supposed to have (e.g. a pack of cigarettes);
22 deliberately disobeyed her in front of other children in order to look like a "big shot";
23 been playing with your "private parts" while taking a bath;
24 yelled abusive or angry things at her.

Subjects whose parents used some other form of punishment were asked to leave the item unanswered, and describe on the questionnaire the punishment used. Again, parents also filled out the Parental Punishment Scale, reporting on their own typical reaction to each of the 24 misbehaviors.

The students' version of the Parental Interest Scale is shown in Table 2. It consists of 21 items (18 of which are scored for the mother, and 18 for the father), each answered on a 0 to +4 scale, which tapped the degree to which each parent reportedly had a close, warm relationship with the student when the latter was seven to nine years old. Again, parents reported on their own behavior when they completed this survey.

The 1978 student-parent study

My scale construction program culminated in the 1978 Manitoba student-parent experiment, which was largely devoted to investigating the origins of right-wing authoritarianism. As reported in the last chapter, 322 of my introductory psychology students (166 females, 156 males) and 402 of the parents of 230 of these students served in this study. One hundred and twenty-three of the 230 students were females, and 115 of their mothers and 99 of their fathers completed the survey booklets sent home. The remaining 107 students were males, and completed booklets were received from 96 of their mothers and 92 of their fathers.

Psychometric properties of the "origins" scales

The mean interitem correlation of the students' reports of their mothers' anger was .23, with a corresponding alpha coefficient = .87; the figures for students' reports of fathers' anger were .27 and .90. The mean interitem correlation for the mothers' own reports of their anger was .28, with a corresponding alpha = .90; the figures for the fathers' own reports were .34 and .92. Not surprisingly, the students reported their parents would have become significantly more angry over the misdeeds than the parents said they would have (means of 62.3 vs. 51.9 overall, $p < .001$). Reports of mothers' anger versus fathers' anger were not significantly different in either sample, nor was reported anger at daughters different from reported anger at sons.

The Parental Punishment Scale simply yields the total number of scoldings, the number of spankings, etcetera, received for the 24 offenses, and hence does not lend itself to measures of internal consistency. There were, though, significant differences in the reports obtained from students and parents. Students reported receiving significantly more spankings (mean = 6.0) than parents reported administering (3.9) ($p < .001$). Parents in turn reported using "psychological discipline" (expressing sorrow, etc.) far more often than their children reported they did (6.8 vs. 3.5, $p < .001$). In both sets of data mothers appeared a little more likely to use psychological punishments, while fathers were a little more likely to spank.

TABLE 2

Items composing the Parental Interest Scale

How often did your mother (father) get involved in the following activities with you when you were 7-9 years old?

1   Visiting your school to see how you were doing, or to help with programs at the school.
2   Playing "inside games" with you (e.g., checkers, card games, "board games").
3   Playing with your toys with you (dolls, cars, building toys, etc.)
4   Reading stories or books with you.
5   Having "heart-to-heart" talks with you about your concerns or hers.
6   Going to playgrounds, swimming pools, etc. with you.
7   Going on bike rides or walks with you.
8   Getting your help in projects she was doing.
9   Praising you for your accomplishments.
10 Going to movies, puppet shows, plays, etc. with you.
11 Teaching you some of her skills.
12 Going to watch you perform (e.g., in some sport, music classes, dancing classes, etc.).
13 Making things for you to play with.
14 Giving you a "special time" alone with her.
15 Getting you involved in projects of your own (e.g., growing a garden, collecting something).
16 Having your friends over for lunch, or for play time.
17 Looking after your grooming and appearance.
18 Physically comforting you ("hugs and kisses," holding you).
19 Playing sports with you (ice skating, ball, etc.). (Item 8 on Father's form)
20 Taking you to his job, sporting events, or some other activity he wanted to share with you. (Item 16 on Father's form)
21 Going on recreational drives (Sunday drives) or long walks with you. (Item 17 on Father's form)

There were no significant differences in reported use of scoldings (mean about 9.0 in both samples, for both parents), or deprivations of privileges (mean about 3.0 for all), or "no punishments" (means about 1.6 for all).

The mean interitem correlation on the Mothers' Interest Scale was .34 among the students, yielding an alpha = .90. The corresponding figures for the Fathers' Interest Scale were .39 and .92. Mothers' own reports of their interest had a mean interitem correlation of .30 with an associated alpha of .89; the fathers' own values were .33 and .90. Again students and their parents had different recollections of how much interest had been shown, with the parents' overall mean (38.7) being significantly higher than their children's (32.9) ($p < .001$). Both sources indicated that mothers showed significantly more interest in the children than the fathers did.

Correspondence between the students' and parents' reports
The figures above indicate that both students and parents told, to an appreciable degree, internally consistent stories when they completed the Parental Anger and Parental Interest Scales. But there is also evidence that the stories were not the same. This suspicion is reinforced by the correlations obtained between students' and parents' reports of the same parental behaviors. The coefficient between the two sets of data on mothers' anger was only .17, while that for fathers' anger was .11. The interjudge reliability for mothers' scolding was .02, for mothers' spanking, .37, for mothers' deprivation of privileges, .19, for mothers' psychological punishment, .24, and for mothers' "no punishment," .25. The corresponding figures for fathers' punishments were .12, .32, .24, .22 and .04. The correlation for mothers' interest was .36 and for the fathers, .24.

These meager values cast a long shadow over the validity of the data. Clearly someone is not telling the truth. One might be inclined to suspect the parents more than the children, since it is their behavior being reported upon, and since they consistently paint a better picture of themselves than their children do. But it would be perfectly natural for children to remember spankings better than psychological punishments; and parental anger may well look more intense to the child on the receiving end than it does to the parent. There are no compelling reasons, in short, for trusting either set of reports as an accurate record of what actually took place.

Correlations between parental behavior
and their children's RWA Scale scores
With such serious doubts about the validity of both sets of reports, our examination of the relationships between these reports and the children's authoritarianism must proceed without enthusiasm. The figures obtained, moreover, are hardly encouraging:

1 Students' reports of Mothers' Anger correlated .24 with their own RWA Scale scores; the mothers' own reports of their anger correlated .04 with their children's authoritarianism. The figure for Fathers' Anger was .15 for both reports.

2 Students' reports of mothers' *scoldings* correlated .01 with their authoritarianism; the mothers' own reports, −.06. The figures for fathers' scoldings were .05 and −.03.

3 Students' reports of their mothers' *spankings* correlated .18 with their RWA Scale scores. Their mothers' reports correlated .19. The figures for

fathers' spankings were .15 and .09.

4 Students' reports of their mothers' *deprivations of privileges* correlated −.15 with their authoritarianism, while their mothers' reports correlated −.04. The reports of the fathers' deprivations correlated −.14 and .04

5 Students' reports of their mothers' use of *psychological punishment* correlated −.02 with their RWA Scale scores; the mothers' own reports correlated −.06. The figures for the fathers were −.01 and .02.

6 Students' reports of receiving *no punishment* from their mothers for the misdeeds in Table 1 correlated −.16 with their RWA Scale scores. Mothers' reports of no punishment correlated −.14. The figures for fathers were −.11 and −.10.

7 Finally, students' accounts of their Mothers' Interest in them when they were young correlated −.02 with their authoritarianism, while their mothers' accounts correlated −.01. The values for Fathers' Interest were .07 and .09 respectively.

Research on the childhood origins of authoritarianism has a tortured past, and the study just reported is merely the latest pain in a writhing literature. While it is perhaps a better investigation of the matter than we have had before, insofar as it employed for the first time an apparently valid measure of adult authoritarianism and the other measures had appreciable levels of internal consistency, it still does not provide any answer to the question. If we can trust either the students' or their parents' reports of events which occurred a decade ago, then the uniformly low and often nonsignificant correlations reported above clearly indicate that the Berkeley model is wrong. If, however, we distrust both sets of reports, as well we might, the low correlations prove nothing.

If retrospective reports cannot be trusted, then what we need are actual, but nondisturbing, observations of how a representative sample of children are actually reared, and then we need measures of their authoritarianism when they become adults. Some of the other findings from the 1978 study might tempt one to try such a study. Parents' RWA Scale scores correlated .34 with their reports of their anger, .32 with their reports of how often they spanked the child, and −.35 with their reports of how often they would not have punished the child for the offenses listed. So authoritarian parents may be a bit of the brute that psychoanalytic theory describes the father to be. If we now simply presume that authoritarian parents are likely to produce authoritarian offspring, we can make the connection between parental "harshness" and authoritarianism in the next generation. But surely there are simpler

ways to explain these same facts, including the social learning model
to which we now turn.[4]

Findings relevant to the social learning explanation
of the origins of authoritarianism
I have conducted a number of tests of the social learning explanation
of the origins of right-wing authoritarianism in my student-parent studies
over the years. Data have been collected on the expectation that parents
would want their children to have the same attitudes on the RWA Scale
that they do, and that their children's level of authoritarianism would
be significantly correlated with their own. I have also tested the effect
of parental emphasis of the home religion upon their children's subsequent authoritarianism. And finally I have studied the students' own
attributions of the sources of their attitudes on the RWA Scale.

Do parents want their children to have the same attitudes they have?
A basic assumption of the present model of authoritarianism's development is that parents want their children's attitudes on the issues covered
by the RWA Scale to be like theirs. This was tested in the 1976 study
(see chapter 5) by asking parents, after they had completed the test
themselves, "to answer it again the way you would want your son/
daughter to answer it."

Mothers' wishes for their daughters ($N = 81$) correlated .82 with their
own scores; mothers' wishes for their sons ($N = 56$), .86. Fathers' wishes
for their daughters correlated .93 with their own RWA Scale scores ($N = 69$); Fathers' wishes for their sons, .88 ($N = 46$). None of these correlations was significantly different from any other.

Not only were the correlations quite high, but there was also a close
match in the level of authoritarianism wished. The parents' own mean
score (on the 28-item scale used in 1976) was 130.4; the mean of their
wishes for their children was 129.2 ($p > .50$). There were no significant
sex differences of any kind.

Correlations between students' and parents' RWA Scale scores
Obviously parents want their children to adopt their attitudes on the
kinds of issues raised on the RWA Scale. To what extent do they succeed?
It was possible in each of the 1976, 1978 and 1979 student-parent studies
to determine the correlation between students' RWA Scale scores and
those of their parents. The overall coefficient ranged from .27 to .38,
the latter occurring in the most recent 1979 study. In that investigation,

daughters' authoritarianism correlated .46 with their mothers' ($N = 138$) and .35 with their fathers' ($N = 119$). Sons' RWA Scale scores correlated .37 with their mothers' ($N = 92$) and .36 with their fathers' ($N = 87$). None of these relationships was significantly different from any other; all were statistically significant.

These data demonstrate a modest correspondence between children's and parents' attitudes. An additional issue from a social learning point of view is, however, how well the students' RWA Scale scores correspond to what they think their parents want their attitudes to be. This was tested in the 1976 and 1978 studies when I asked my own introductory psychology students, when they had completed the RWA Scale for themselves, to answer it again as they thought their father, and their mother, would want them to answer it.

The overall correlations between these estimates and the students' own scores were .47 and .50 in the two studies. Again, there were no significant sex differences of any kind in these correlations. The students also rather accurately perceived that their parents would want them to be appreciably more authoritarian than they were: for example, in the 1978 study the students' own mean RWA Scale score was 115.9, the mean of their perceived parents' wishes was 146.8, while the parents' own mean was 138.2.[5]

The size of these correlations, .27 to .38 for real parental scores, .47 to .50 for perceived parental wishes, argue that parents do contribute to their children's authoritarianism.[6] It is also clear that the parents do not produce carbon copies of themselves, their wishes notwithstanding. At best, the correlations only account for 25% of the variance in students' RWA Scale scores, and the students' mean is over a standard deviation lower than their parents.'

Parental influence on their children's authoritarianism
through religious emphasis
As I noted several times earlier, one of the ways in which parents theoretically can shape their children's authoritarianism is by emphasizing the family religion. A 10-item scale was thus developed to collect retrospective reports on this variable and used in the 1978 and 1979 studies.[7]

The mean intercorrelation among students' (and parents') reports of this emphasis was at least .52, with resulting alpha reliabilities of .91 or higher. Moreover there was, in this case, reasonable correspondence between students' reports and their parents', the overall correlation being .70 in the first study and .73 in the second. In both investigations, parents reported emphasizing the family religion significantly more than the children recalled. In both studies all parties agreed the mothers placed significantly more emphasis on the family religion than the fathers did, but that sons and daughters received equal amounts of emphasis. Both parents' and their children's responses indicated that there was a fairly strong correlation (.71 to .80) between the mother's and father's degree of religious emphasis within the family.

There was a reasonably strong relationship (.48 to .53) between the various reports of parental religious emphasis and the extent to which the students still accepted the teachings of the home religion. Students' RWA Scale scores correlated lower, but still significantly, with these reports of parental emphasis, being .28 to .34 for their own accounts, and .23 to .33 for the parents.'

The implication of these results is that parental emphasis increases the chances that their children will retain the family faith, and this in turn increases the chances that their children will score high on the RWA Scale. An item analysis of the religious emphasis–RWA Scale correlations indicates how this effect is obtained. The strongest relationships were with those RWA Scale items which directly involve religion (items 4 and 18 in Table 1 of chapter 5) or sex (items 5, 8, and 25). But they do not end there: 19 of the 30 items were significantly correlated with students' reports of their parents' religious emphasis, and seventeen of these same items correlated significantly with the parents' reports.[8] The extent of these relationships across most of the content of the RWA Scale indicates that strong religious emphasis can affect more than just religious attitudes—though it clearly does not shape answers to all of the items on the RWA Scale.

Students' attributions of the origins of their RWA Scale attitudes
All of the above data suggest that the young adult's level of authoritarianism has been shaped to some extent by his relationship with his parents.[9] They also indicate that there must be other sources of these attitudes. I attempted to identify the other factors which might be involved, in the 1979 study using my introductory psychology students, by asking them where they thought they had acquired their opinions.

At the beginning of the second testing session the subjects were handed a survey which read:

People are not born with opinions about social issues. Instead, they learn to hold certain opinions from their contact with other people and their experiences in life.

The purpose of this survey is to identify the *sources* of the opinions you hold on the 30 issues you answered last week. Why do you have the opinion you do in each case? Where did it come from? Why do you believe what you do, instead of something else? How would *you* explain why you believe what you do?

Many people will say, "I believe what I do because I can see that's the right thing to believe." The trouble with that is that people who believe quite opposite things all think theirs are the naturally right opinions. Our idea about what is "naturally right" has been shaped in us too.

So where *do* our opinions come from? There are a number of possibilities:

1 You may have learned your opinion on an issue from your *parents*. You may hold, with perhaps some modification, the opinion your parents taught you on a subject. Or if they did not directly teach you, you may have picked up their opinion on the matter just from being around them, from knowing how they felt on the subject, from wanting to be like them.

2 You may have basically acquired your opinion on an issue from a *church*, or a church-related experience such as the Bible. Your formal religious training, not by your parents (that's covered above), but in your church, may have been the most basic source of your opinion.

3 You may have basically acquired your opinion on an issue from *school* at some point, from a particular subject or teacher. Your formal education may have been the most direct cause of your opinion.

4 You may have formed your opinion on an issue through your *own direct personal experience*. Something may have directly happened to you, in your contact with the subject matter. You learned your opinion firsthand. You have "been there," you have done it, you have experienced it yourself.

5 You may have formed your opinion on an issue by knowing what happened to *friends or acquaintances*. They have "been there," they have done it, experienced it, and you have learned from their experience.

6 Your opinion on a subject may have been basically shaped by your *friends' opinion* on the subject. You haven't "been there" and neither have they, but you've talked about it or know how they feel, and that has influenced you.

7 You may have formed your opinion from *news reports* on an issue. Newspaper stories, editorials, TV documentaries, magazine articles can shape opinions on an issue.

8 Your opinion may have been basically formed by *fictional accounts* of events. Novels, plays, TV dramas, movies also can shape opinions on an issue.

9 Your opinion may have been formed by some other factor you can identify, not covered in the list above.

10 You may have no idea at all why you believe what you do.

The reader will recognize that the list of options above is based upon the possible sources of attitudes outlined at the beginning of this chapter. The subjects were then asked to think about each of the answers they had given the previous week to the RWA Scale items, and after considering the matter indicate which of the 10 alternatives above best described the basic source of their opinion in each case.

The most frequently cited source was "parents"; this source was named 25% of the time by the students as the most basic source of an opinion. The second most frequently cited source was "own direct personal experience," named 23% of the time. Then came "school" and "news reports," each mentioned in 12% of the responses. "Friend's opinions" was cited 7% of the time, "church" and "friend's experience" each 5%. "Fictional accounts" and category 9, "some other factor," were hardly ever mentioned. (Ten percent of the respondents were in category 10, "I have no idea.")

There were distinct tendencies for the sources to be prominent on certain kinds of issues. "Parents" were mentioned most often as the source of attitudes on child-rearing issues. "Own direct personal experience" had the greatest impact on attitudes toward the role of young people in society, premarital sexual intercourse, and the morality of church-goers versus atheists. "School's" effects were most prominent on civil liberties issues concerning free speech, dissenters and Communists. "News reports" were cited most often on the "crime and punishment" items. The other sources, which were not mentioned very often, had rather diffuse effects, except for "the Church" which had most of its impact on the religion and sex items.

It was possible, by considering the attitudes of the subjects who cited each source, to see if the source apparently promoted authoritarianism or discouraged it. Just as we might surmise from much of the earlier findings, parents appear to be a major source of authoritarian attitudes. On all of the 30 items, students who said they had got their opinions basically from their parents had more authoritarian attitudes than the overall sample did. The individual's "own experiences," on the other hand, seem to lower RWA Scale scores for those who cited such experiences, as did "school." In both cases, subjects who mentioned these sources had lower than average scores on 24 of the 30 items. "News reports" had a mixed effect, depending on the topic involved (e.g., news reports of crime in society appear to have made subjects more authoritarian, but coverage of prison life, less so.) The "church" had a powerful proauthoritarian effect on many issues among the relatively few subjects who cited it as the chief source of an attitude.

Caution is particularly important in interpreting such findings. These results do not tell us how the students actually got their opinions; their attributions could easily be wrong. If they make sense to us, that may only be because the students attributed their attitudes to sensible sources, when the real determinant might have been something else.

The value in the data lay instead in the hints they gave us about where to look for other sources of authoritarianism besides the parents, and the specific areas of life where these determinants might be most important. It is not hard to imagine, for example, which "direct experience" with premarital sex led to the attitude that it is not immoral, nor is it difficult to imagine what was so rewarding about that experience so as to form the opinion. It is a little more challenging to hypothesize which direct experiences in confronting established authorities have been rewarding enough so as to lower the students' level of authoritarianism. But we can try to find out; this may be a useful avenue to explore.

That "school" lowers authoritarianism is corroborated by the cross-sectional negative correlations between education and RWA Scale scores reported in the last chapter. The small size of these relationships indicated however that mere attendance at school does not have much effect; what matters is what is being learned. The students' attributions suggest that "civics" instruction in democratic principles and rights may lower RWA Scale scores among late adolescents. This is certainly a testable hypothesis. So also are the hypotheses that "news reports" affect attitudes in the different ways reported.

The most surprising feature of the attributions data is how little influence is credited to the peer group (categories 5 and 6). It may be that friends are chosen to support pre-existing ideas, but we also expect friends to have a shaping effect afterwards (Newcomb, 1961). We can test this hypothesis by studying the change in RWA Scale scores among students who become friends during their first year at university, compared to changes in a matched gorup of nonfriends.

SUMMARY OF THE CHAPTER

This chapter has presented the results of several years of research on two different theories of the origins of right-wing authoritarianism. The new data presented on the Berkeley theory, like so much that has preceded them, are discouraging and ultimately inconclusive. The evidence on the general social learning theory presented is more encouraging, but is exploratory and seriously incomplete. There are grounds for guarded optimism, however, because the latter approach does seem to generate testable hypotheses. If it is wrong, we should be able to find out and move on from there.

At the moment, however, we can sketch a broad outline of the ontogeny of right-wing authoritarianism which is supported (if not conclusively) by some evidence. Authoritarianism apparently has its beginnings in the child's relationship with his parents, but they are different beginnings from what the Berkeley theorists envisioned. The authoritarian's parents are not necessarily stern, distant, and so forth. What they are apt to be is authoritarian themselves, and they can transmit their attitudes to their children through their teachings, modeling, and other ways of shaping them during the many years of their relationship. Parents are particularly likely to shape authoritarian attitudes on childrearing, but they can also affect their offsprings' opinions on the full range of topics covered by the RWA Scale. Parents do not all have the same attitudes on these issues, but they do want their children to be like them and overall their influence is apparently proauthoritarian.

Various other socializing agencies, frequently chosen by them, reinforce the parents' influence. Organized religion is one of these. The person's authoritarianism as an adult will be partly determined by the religion in which he was raised and the extent to which his parents emphasized observing that religion. Persons who have their opinions basically shaped by their church are likely to be authoritarian.

The major cause of low authoritarianism, apart from those relatively rare parents who intentionally shape their children in that direction, is the child's own direct experience with authorities, and "life" (e.g., sexual activity, modesty, sex roles). It is unlikely that these experiences occur before middle to late adolescence, which is the time when authoritarian attitudes may start becoming organized and low authoritarianism begin to appear within an age-group. Formal education in certain topics during this same period also appears to lower RWA Scale scores.

Though we are discussing the factors which determine the authoritarianism of young adults, it is probably a mistake to think that the process is concluded then, or ever. Major events in the world around us can raise or lower RWA Scale scores.[10] "Peers" may become a powerful force when we get married, or begin a career. Parenthood, the acquisition of social power, and a mortgage, may eventually bring our typical eighteen-year-old's RWA Scale score closer to the level of his 45-year-old parents. And there is no reason to expect the process to end there.

Epilog

It may be that relatively few right-wing authoritarians will make it to the end of this book; but what I have left to say does not apply to them anyway.

First of all, we ought to remind ourselves, lest we become self-righteous, that low and moderate RWA Scale scorers can still do authoritarian deeds. Over the years I have run my bogus punishment-learning experiment four times: in June, 1971, and October, 1971, when the subjects were Winnipeg (nonstudent) males; and in October, 1972 and November, 1973, when introductory psychology students were tested. There was an aspect of this experiment which I have not reported until now. Beside the five-switch "shock box" on the table before the teacher was another device which the research team called Big Red. It was a small metal box with a set of wires running into and out of it, and a large red pushbutton on its face. Above the button was printed: "Danger. Very severe shock. Do not push this button unless you are instructed to do so." Big Red was in plain sight throughout the experiment, but the experimenter made no reference to it after initially pointing it out.

When the confederate had made all the errors he was supposed to, the experimenter said to the teacher: "That concludes the experiment. It's obvious the learner hasn't been trying as hard as he should. Push the red button on your right to administer an extra strong shock as punishment for not trying." Once the experimenter finished this command he started a concealed stopwatch to time how long it took the subject to push Big Red. If the subject declined, the experimenter said quietly but firmly "Go ahead," "Push that big red button," and "Do what I told you to do." However if the subject refused for fifteen seconds, the experimenter stopped pressuring him.

In my four studies, 89%, 86%, 88%, and 91% of the subjects pushed Big Red within fifteen seconds. The mean latencies in fact were 6, 4, 3, and 2 seconds respectively. The vast majority of the subjects did no more than say "You mean this button here," before complying. Most of the delays we had—aside from the very few who steadfastly refused to obey—were with subjects who were afraid that *they* would receive the shock if they touched the second box.[1]

The high percentages of compliance indicate how easily individual differences in attitudes are negated when situational pressures rise. It is true that, in a free-choice situation, high RWA subjects tended to use stronger shocks to teach the confederate his lesson. But it is also true that when commanded to do so, nearly everyone was willing to hurt, possibly severely, another person who really had not done anything wrong. And it did not matter how the subjects' parents had treated them, what religion they were raised in, if they had learned their "civics" lessons well, and so on. These results, of course, are just a small piece of the horror that Milgram has shown us about ourselves.

I have one other previously unreported study to describe. In a way it takes us back to the first page of the Introduction of this book. In the spring of 1977, an officer in the Canadian Armed Forces who was taking a course with me administered a survey to 38 Canadian Armed Forces recruits who had just finished their basic training.[2] These recruits were tested together, with the permission and cooperation of the Canadian Armed Forces, while the officer was in uniform and in the room with them. But they also knew that the officer did not know them personally, and they did not put their names or any other identifying marks on the surveys.

The soldiers were given a set of hypothetical situations and asked if they would obey certain orders in these cases:

Suppose you are stationed near Ottawa. One day the Prime Minister declares that Canada is in a state of emergency. He orders strict censorship of all newspapers, radio and TV stations, suspends the civil liberties of Canadian citizens, and declares Parliament closed until further notice. As there are no laws giving the Prime Minister such powers, he has to rely upon the military to back him up. The military leaders agree to do so, and your unit is ordered to Parliament Hill to keep the House of Commons from meeting. Would you obey this order and move out to take up such positions?

Seventy-six percent of the soldiers said they would.

Suppose a Member of the House of Commons attempted to cross your lines and enter the building. Your commander ordered you to place him under arrest and take him to a military prison. Would you do so?

Ninety-two percent of the soldiers said they would.

Suppose a demonstration was organized to protest the closing of Parliament and a crowd of persons carrying signs and chanting slogans began to march toward your lines. The officer commanding your detachment orders them to stop or they will be fired upon, but they continue to march toward you. The officer orders you to open fire at the crowd. Would you shoot at the demonstrators?

Sixty-three percent of the soldiers said they would.

The situations, as noted, are hypothetical, and one might argue that in the testing circumstances there were powerful "demand characteristics" for the soldiers to say they would obey. But there are also fairly strong demand characteristics when you are in the army and someone gives you a direct order. It may be that the figures above represent the minimum amount of compliance one would find in those circumstances.[3]

In closing, let me give *you* a hypothetical situation. Suppose that tomorrow your prime minister or your president decided to cast aside constitutional government and seize power illegally. Suppose that he had made a deal with a few military leaders, and the armed forces were ordered to back him up. Who would stop this scenario from unfolding? Subordinates in the army? Members of the legislature? The judiciary? An aroused press? University professors? An alarmed, freedom-loving populace?

Now suppose that this dictator, in a move to consolidate his power and forestall counterrevolution, moves to eliminate "dangerous elements" in our country. Someone points at you and me and says, "Better get rid of them fast." The police arrive to arrest us. We are about to disappear into prison forever as thousands upon thousands disappeared into the prisons in Dachau and Moscow, and Santiago and Havana, and Saigon and Phnom Penh, and Tehran and Kampala. Who would try to stop them from taking us away?

Suppose instead that it is only me who is declared dangerous, because I wrote this book. But you are ordered to kill me. Could I count on you to defy that order because it is unjust? Could *you* trust yourself not to do a terrible, unjust act? Before you say "Sure," consider how many of Miligram's subjects could have predicted what they would do in his experiment.

We go to bed at night so secure in our liberties that we do not even notice how free we are and what we have that most people do not. But as long as we do not realize this, as long as a sizeable lot of us have no love for that freedom, and as long as a sizeable lot of us will do what we are told because we have never been trained to do otherwise, that freedom is in grave danger. We sleep soundly at night—but one man could probably take our freedom away from us by the time we awoke the next day. Every year, millions of people around the world awaken to find their rights suddenly "terminated."

Our sleep should be troubled. I wish you a troubled sleep.

APPENDIX I

Questionnaires used in the item analysis studies which led to the initial version of the Right-Wing Authoritarianism Scale

THE WINTER, 1970, STUDIES

1 Obedience and respect for authority are the most important virtues children should learn.

2 No weakness or difficulty can hold us back if we have enough will power.

3 Science has its place, but there are many important things that can never possibly be understood by the human mind.

4 Human nature being what it is, there will always be war and conflict.†

5 Every person should have complete faith in some supernatural power whose decisions he obeys without question.†

6 When a person has a problem or worry, it is best for him not to think about it, but to keep busy with more cheerful things.

7 A person who has bad manners, habits and breeding can hardly expect to get along with decent people.

8 What the youth needs most is strict discipline, rugged determination, and the will to work and fight for family and country.

9 Some people are born with an urge to jump from high places.†

10 Nowadays when so many different kinds of people move around and mix together so much, a person has to protect himself especially carefully against catching a disease from them.

11 An insult to our honor should always be punished.†

12 Young people sometimes get rebellious ideas, but as they grow up they ought to get over them and settle down.†

13 It is best to use some prewar authorities in Germany to keep order and prevent chaos.

14 What this country needs most, more than laws and political programs, is a few courageous, tireless, devoted leaders in whom the people can put their faith.

15 Sex crimes, such as rape and attacks on children, deserve more than mere imprisonment; such criminals ought to be publicly whipped, or worse.†

16 People can be divided into two distinct classes: the weak and the strong.

17 There is hardly anything lower than a person who does not feel a great love, gratitude, and respect for his parents.

18 Some day it will probably be shown that astrology can explain a lot of things.†
19 Nowadays more and more people are prying into matters that should remain personal and private.
20 Wars and social troubles may someday be ended by an earthquake or flood that will destroy the whole world.†
21 Most of our social problems would be solved if we could somehow get rid of the immoral, crooked and feebleminded people.
22 The wild sex life of the old Greeks and Romans was tame compared to some of the goings-on in this country, even in places where people might least expect it.
23 If people would talk less and work more, everybody would be better off.
24 Most people don't realize how much our lives are controlled by plots hatched in secret places.†
25 Homosexuals are hardly better than criminals, and ought to be severely punished.†
26 The businessman and the manufacturer are much more important to society than the artist and the professor.†
27 No sane, decent person could ever think of hurting a close friend or relative.
28 Familiarity breeds contempt.†
29 Nobody ever learned anything really important except through suffering.
30 The legal system in our country is too harsh; courts should show more mercy to people convicted of crimes than they have in the past.
31 The minds of today's youth are being hopelessly corrupted by the wrong kind of literature.
32 Women who want to remove the word "obey" from the marriage service don't understand what it means to be a wife.
33 One way to reduce the expression of prejudice is through more forceful legislation.
34 It is only natural that a person would have a much better acquaintance with ideas he believes in than with ideas he opposes.
35 Fundamentally, the world we live in is a pretty lonesome place.
36 It has gotten to the point that hoodlums get better treatment from lawyers and judges than do the victims of crimes and the police.
37 When it comes to differences of opinion in religion we must be careful not to compromise with those who believe differently from the way we do.
38 If children are told too much about sex, they are likely to go too far in experimenting with it.
39 Honesty, hard work, and trust in God do not guarantee material rewards.
40 The family is a sacred institution, divinely ordained.
41 One of the greatest threats to the true Canadian way of life is for us to resort to the use of force.
42 In the long run the best way to live is to pick friends and associates whose tastes and beliefs are the same as one's own.
43 Most of the people who live on welfare are lazy cheaters who are taking advantage of the rest of us.
44 It is the duty of a citizen to criticize or censure his country whenever he considers it wrong.
45 A child who is unusual in any way should be encouraged to be more like other children.
46 The most important qualities of a real man are determination and driving ambition.

47 There are two kinds of people in this world: those who are for the truth and those who are against the truth.

48 It is only natural and right for each person to think that his family is better than any other.

49 "Mind-expanding drugs" will probably turn out to be enormously valuable to mankind.

50 In the final analysis parents generally turn out to be right about things.

51 Even though freedom of speech for all groups is a worthwhile goal, it is unfortunately necessary to restrict the freedom of certain political groups.

52 A man who does not believe in some great cause has not really lived.

53 A group which tolerates too much difference of opinion among its members cannot exist for long.

54 Most of the problems society is having with its young people nowadays have been caused by the overly permissive way parents have been raising their children lately.

55 The average person hardly has a chance in life anymore.

56 The church has outgrown its usefulness and should be radically reformed or done away with.

57 An unmarried woman who gives birth to two or more children out of wedlock should be forced to have an operation so she can't have any more children.

58 Most honest people admit to themselves that they have sometimes hated their parents.

59 There is a lot more racial prejudice in our society than most people are willing to admit.

60 It is often desirable to reserve judgment about what's going on until one has had a chance to hear the opinions of those one respects.

61 People cannot meaningfully be divided into two distinct classes, the weak and the strong.

62 If pornography helps a person get rid of his sexual tensions, then it is a good thing.

63 It usually helps the child in later years if he is forced to conform to his parents' ideas.

64 Few people deserve the misfortunes they have; for example, the poor people in our society are mostly the victims of hard luck.

65 Most censorship of books and movies is a violation of free speech and should be abolished.

66 Science declines when it confines itself to the solution of immediate practical problems.

67 The facts on crime and sex immorality suggest that we will have to crack down harder on some people if we are going to save our moral standards.

68 There is a divine purpose in the operations of the universe.

69 Some equality in marriage is a good thing, but by and large the husband ought to have the main say-so in family matters.

70 Of all the different philosophies which exist in this world there is probably only one which is correct.

71 A person who thinks primarily of his own happiness is beneath contempt.

72 A world government with effective military strength is one way in which world peace might be achieved.

73 The poor will always be with us.

74 It is only when a person devotes himself to an ideal or cause that life becomes meaningful.

75 Most of the ideas which get printed nowadays aren't worth the paper they are printed on.

76 Disobedience to the government is sometimes justified.

77 Unless something drastic is done, the world is going to be destroyed one of these days by nuclear explosion or fallout.

78 The worst danger to real Canadianism during the last 50 years has come from foreign ideas and agitators.

79 It is better to be a dead hero than to be a live coward.

80 The main thing in life is for a person to want to do something important.

81 Divorce or annulment is practically never justified.

82 We should be grateful for leaders who tell us exactly what to do and how to do it.

83 Members of religious sects who refuse to salute the flag or bear arms should be treated with tolerance and understanding.

84 Most people just don't know what's good for them.

85 Army life is a good influence on most men.

86 Most people just don't give a "damn" for others.

87 In this complicated world of ours the only way we can know what's going on is to rely on leaders or experts who can be trusted.

† Indicates the item was replaced by a reversal (see Table 7 in chapter 2) for half of the subjects.

THE JUNE, 1971, STUDY

1 A world government with effective military strength is one way in which world peace might be achieved.

2 It is only when a person devotes himself to an ideal or cause that life becomes meaningful.

3 Obedience and respect for authority are the most important virtues children should learn.

4 One of the greatest threats to the true Canadian way of life is for us to resort to the use of force.

5 The sooner social conventions like having a neat, tidy appearance are forgotten, the better.

6 No weakness or difficulty can hold us back if we have enough will power.

7 it is only natural that a person would have a much better acquaintance with ideas he believes in than with ideas he opposes.

8 The church has outgrown its usefulness and should be radically reformed or done away with.

9 Science has its place, but there are many important things that can never be understood by the human mind.

10 It is all right for a person to use pornography to reduce his sexual tensions.

11 Some equality in marriage is a good thing, but by and large the husband ought to have the main say-so in family matters.

12 Human nature being what it is, there will always be war and conflict.

13 The minds of today's youth are being hopelessly corrputed by the wrong kind

of literature.

14 Most of the people who come up to you on the street, asking for money, are just poor misfortunates down on their luck.

15 Every person should have complete faith in some supernatural power whose decisions he obeys without question.

16 Fundamentally, the world we live in is a pretty lonesome place.

17 One way to reduce the expression of prejudice is through more forceful legislation.

18 When a person has a problem or worry, it is best for him not to think about it, but to keep busy with more cheerful things.

19 It is only natural and right for each person to think that his family is better than any other.

20 The police and army have far too much power in this country.

21 A person who has bad manners, habits and breeding can hardly expect to get along with decent people.

22 Honesty, hard work, and trust in God do *not* guarantee material rewards.

23 In the long run the best way to live is to pick friends and associates whose tastes and beliefs are the same as one's own.

24 What the youth needs most is strict discipline, rugged determination, and the will to work and fight for family and country.

25 A child who is unusual in any way should be encouraged to be more like other children.

26 It is the duty of a citizen to criticize or censure his county whenever he considers it to be wrong.

27 Some people are born with an urge to jump from high places.

28 A man who does not believe in some great cause has not really lived.

29 Drugs like LSD will probably turn out to be about the best things man has discovered in this century.

30 Nowadays when so many different kinds of people move around and mix together so much, a person has to protect himself especially carefully against catching an infection or disease from them.

31 In this complicated world of ours the only way we can know what's going on is to rely on leaders or experts who can be trusted.

32 The facts on crime and sex immorality suggest that we will have to crack down harder on some people if we are going to save our moral standards.

33 An insult to our honor should always be punished.

34 Any woman should be entitled to as many abortions as she wishes.

35 There are two kinds of people in this world: those who are for the truth and those who are against the truth.

36 Young people sometimes get rebellious ideas, but as they grow up they ought to get over them and settle down.

37 Unless something drastic is done, the world is going to be destroyed one of these days by nuclear explosion or fallout.

38 The most important qualities of a real man are determination and driving ambition.

39 It is best to use some prewar authorities in Germany to keep order and prevent chaos.

40 When it comes to differences of opinion in religion we must be careful *not* to compromise with those who believe differently from the way we do.

41 Science declines when it confines itself to the solution of immediate practical

problems.

42 What this country needs most, more than laws and political programs, is a few courageous, tireless, devoted leaders in whom the people can put their faith.

43 The poor will always be with us.

44 There are probably very few "lazy cheaters" on the welfare rolls. Nearly all of the people receiving welfare would probably rather work for a living, but cannot because of disabilities or circumstances beyond their control.

45 Sex crimes, such as rape and attacks on children, deserve more than mere imprisonment; such criminals ought to be publicly whipped, or worse.

46 Most people just don't give a "damn" for others.

47 Women should always remember the promise they made in the marriage ceremony to obey their husbands.

48 People can be divided into two distinct classes: the weak and the strong.

49 Members of religious sects who refuse to salute the flag or bear arms should be treated with tolerance and understanding.

50 Most of the ideas which get printed nowadays aren't worth the paper they are printed on.

51 There is hardly anything lower than a person who does not feel a great love, gratitude and respect for his parents.

52 The worst danger to real Canadianism during the last 50 years has come from foreign ideas and agitators.

53 The average person still has plenty of opportunity for advancement nowadays.

54 Some day it will probably be shown that astrology can explain a lot of things.

55 In the final analysis parents generally turn out to be right about things.

56 It is better to be a dead hero than to be a live coward.

57 Nowadays more and more people are prying into matters that should remain personal and private.

58 Most of the problems society is having with its young people nowadays come from the older generation's own failures and hypocrisy.

59 There is a divine purpose in the operations of the universe.

60 Wars and social troubles may someday be ended by an earthquake or flood that will destroy the whole world.

61 Disobedience to the government is sometimes justified.

62 Even though freedom of speech for all groups is a worthwhile goal, it is unfortunately necessary to restrict the freedom of certain political groups.

63 Most of our social problems would be solved if we could somehow get rid of the immoral, crooked and feebleminded people.

64 Fundamentally speaking this is a racist society, full of prejudiced people.

65 It usually helps the child in later years if he is forced to conform to his parents' ideas.

66 The wild sex life of the old Greeks and Romans was tame compared to some of the goings-on in this country even in places where people might least expect it.

67 A group which tolerates too much difference of opinion among its members cannot exist for long.

68 Very few people will take advantage of a weakness, or mistake you might make, if you have been nice to them.

69 If people would talk less and work more, everybody would be better off.

70 It is often desirable to reserve judgment about what's going on until one has had

a chance to hear the opinions of those one respects.

71 Most censorship of books or movies is a violation of free speech and should be abolished.

72 Most people don't realize how much our lives are controlled by plots hatched in secret places.

73 A person who thinks primarily of his own happiness is beneath contempt.

74 Army life is a good influence on most men.

75 Homosexuals are hardly better than criminals, and ought to be severely punished.

76 The world would be a much better place if "social graces" like polite conversation disappeared tomorrow and people really said what they felt to one another.

77 If children are told too much about sex, they are likely to go too far in experimenting with it.

78 The businessman and the manufacturer are much more important to society than the artist and the professor.

79 Divorce or annulment is practically never justified.

80 Most people just don't know what's good for them.

81 No sane, decent person could ever think of hurting a close friend or relative.

82 Everyone has both good qualities and bad ones as well. The best of men are still evil in some respects, and the worst of men have good features as well as bad.

83 Of all the different philosophies which exist in this world there is probably only one which is correct.

84 Familiarity breeds contempt.

85 We should be grateful for leaders who tell us exactly what to do and how to do it.

86 The main thing in life is for a person to want to do something important.

87 Nobody ever learned anything really important except through suffering.

THE SEPTEMBER AND OCTOBER, 1971, STUDIES

1 Our country would gain much from a greater exchange of ideas and customs with the other peoples who live on the earth.

2 What this country needs most are some strong, courageous leaders who will not be afraid to take things in their own hands in order to solve our problems.

3 Marijuana will probably turn out to be one of man's most beneficial discoveries.

4 A lot of the arguments you hear against giving minority groups better treatment are just cover-ups for prejudice.

5 Someone who has bad breeding and poor manners is still just as good and worthy a person as anyone else.

6 Aside from a few exceptions, most people just don't give a damn for others.

7 Homosexuals may be maladjusted people but they are hardly criminals. Others should try to understand their feelings and be more accepting of them.

8 Many people who are "outsiders" and lonely as youths become outstanding leaders and make great contributions later on in life.

9 The police and the army have gotten far too much power in this country.

10 Basically there are two kinds of people in this world: those who are for the truth and those who are against it.

11 Disobedience to the government is often justified.

12 The most important thing in life is for a person to devote all his energy to the cause that seems most important to him.

13 If a child starts becoming unconventional, his parents should see to it he returns to the normal ways expected by society.

14 Despite what you may occasionally hear about various ethnic and political groups, our lives are *not* really controlled by plots engineered by semi-secret groups.

15 Women should always remember the promise they make in the marriage ceremony to obey their husbands.

16 In this complicated world of ours the only way we can know what's going on is to rely on leaders or experts who can be trusted.

17 Even though one may try very hard to get ahead in life, he might well fail because things are rigged against him.

18 Differences of opinion in religion and politics should be lessened by everybody giving in a little to the other guy's point of view.

19 There is hardly anything lower than a person who is disrespectful toward parents who have made many sacrifices for him.

20 It is all right for a person to use pornography to reduce his sexual tensions.

21 Atheists and agnostics are probably just as good and virtuous as those who strongly believe in God.

22 The minds of today's youth are being hopelessly corrupted by the wrong kind of literature and films.

23 People who abuse the flag or who refuse to serve in the armed forces should be treated with tolerance and understanding.

24 A young person is foolish if he sticks to habits or customs that make him unpopular and a "square" among his schoolmates.

25 One of the best assurances for peace is for us to have the biggest bomb and not be afraid to use it.

26 In the long run it is best to pick friends and associates whose background and beliefs are the same as your own.

27 One of the *worst* ways to discover the truth about things is to put your trust in just one man or one set of leaders.

28 A proper scientific understanding of sex is one thing, but if children are told too much else about it, it is likely to be bad for them.

29 The older, more standard forms of music and art are a lot better than most of the junk that is turned out nowadays.

30 Obedience and respect for authority are the most important virtues children should learn.

31 There are probably very few "lazy cheaters" on the welfare rolls. Nearly all of the people receiving welfare would probably rather work for a living, but cannot because of disabilities or circumstances beyond their control.

32 The facts on crime and sexual immorality show we will have to crack down harder on deviant groups if we are going to save our moral standards.

33 Human nature being what it is, there will always be war and conflict.

34 Most of the problems a person has nowadays are caused by his own weaknesses and failings, and *not* because others are working against him.

35 There is really *no* way people can be divided into two classes, the weak and the strong.

36 A group which tolerates differences of opinion between its leaders and its members is asking for trouble.

37 The real satisfactions in life come from understanding yourself rather than

becoming famous or championing some great cause.

38 People should probably pay a little less attention to the Bible and other old teachings and instead get involved in the exciting new religions being developed nowadays.

39 Nowadays more and more people are prying into our private lives and trying to control our actions.

40 It will be tragic if today's youth loses its rebellious ideas as they grow older.

41 Anyone can be popular with others if he is shallow enough and willing to be a "yes man."

42 In the final analysis parents generally turn out to be right about things.

43 There may be a few exceptions, but in general members of a racial group are all pretty much alike.

44 Life in the military has an unhealthy influence on most men.

45 The family is a sacred institution, divinely ordained.

46 It may be old fashioned nowadays but having a neat, tidy appearance is still the mark of a gentleman and a lady.

47 Quite a few of the people who come up to you on the street, asking for money, are just poor unfortunates down on their luck.

48 Sex crimes, such as rape and attacks on children, deserve more than mere imprisonment. Such criminals ought to be publicly whipped, or worse.

49 Two of the most important qualities of a real man are gentleness and a relaxed attitude toward life.

50 Christianity may have helped people realize God's loving nature, but people nowadays would be wise to remember what happened to Sodom and Gomorrha.

51 What the youth needs most is strict discipline, rugged determination, and the will to work and fight for family and country.

52 Barnum was probably wrong when he said that there's at least one sucker born every minute.

53 In general full economic security is harmful; most men won't work if they do not need the money for eating and living.

54 Men like J.P. Morgan who advance ruthlessly beating down all competition are examples of mankind at its worst.

THE JANUARY, 1972, STUDY

1 The most important thing in life is for a person to understand himself.

2 Almost anything we do for a good cause is justified if it helps us reach our goal.

3 Nowadays when so many different kinds of people move around and mix together so much, a person has to protect himself especially carefully against catching a disease from them.

4 Most people just don't give a "damn" for others.

5 The self-made man is likely to be more ethical than someone born to wealth and power.

6 It is permissable for one to ignore laws that seem unjust and unfair.

7 Sex crimes, such as rape and attacks on children, deserve more than mere imprisonment. Such cirminals ought to be publicly whipped, or worse.

8 Atheists are no doubt as good and virtuous as those who attend church regularly.

9 There are always the odd exceptions, but in general people of the same race

or ethnic background are pretty much alike.

10   A group which allows its members to disagree publicly with its leaders is almost certain to fail in whatever it does.

11   It is best to enforce laws as leniently as possible, especially when minority groups are involved.

12   If a child starts becoming unconventional, his parents should see to it he returns to the normal ways expected by society.

13   Such things as flags and national anthems ought to be de-emphasized in order to promote the idea that all men are brothers.

14   It will be tragic if today's rebellious youth lose their revolutionary spirit as they grow older.

15   Sooner or later every insult to our honor should be punished—especially those made by our inferiors.

16   It is all right for a person to use pornography to reduce his sexual tensions.

17   When it comes to differences of opinion in religion and morality we must be careful *not* to compromise with those who believe differently from our own kind.

18   There is hardly anything lower than someone who is disrespectful toward parents who have made many sacrifices for him.

19   Marijuana will probably turn out to be one of man's most beneficial discoveries.

20   It may be old-fashioned nowadays, but having a neat, tidy appearance is still the mark of a gentleman and a lady.

21   It is foolish to think that any one class of people is better or more virtuous than all the rest.

22   Life in the military, with its emphasis on discipline and following orders, has a bad effect on most men.

23   The facts on crime and sexual immorality show we will have to crack down harder on deviant groups if we are going to save our moral standards.

24   Most people who dislike modern music and modern art are just showing how narrow-minded and intolerant they are.

25   Future immigrants should only be allowed in if they come from the same places as the people who made this country great in the first place.

26   The best way to discover the truth in this complicated world is to rely on our elected leaders and other officials.

27   People who abuse the flag or who refuse to serve in the armed forces should be treated with tolerance and understanding.

28   If children are told too much about sex, they are likely to go too far in experimenting with it.

29   Clubs and organizations which restrict their membership to a particular kind of person do considerable harm to our society.

30   What the youth needs most is strict discipline, rugged determination, and the will to work and fight for family and country.

31   Women should always remember the promise they make in the marriage ceremony to obey their husbands.

32   People should pay less attention to the Bible and other outdated sources of religious teachings, and instead turn to the modern religions being developed in our own times.

33   Basically there are two kinds of people in the world: those who are for the truth and those who are against it.

34 Obedience and respect for authority are the most important virtues children should learn.
35 Homosexuals may be maladjusted people but they are hardly criminals. Others should try to understand their feelings and be more accepting of them.
36 The minds of today's youth are being hopelessly corrupted by the wrong kind of literature and films.
37 There are probably just as many deviants and perverts among people with our own kind of background as any other.
38 Disobedience to the government is often justified.
39 Laws ought to be strictly enforced, no matter what the consequences.
40 There is nothing wrong with a person doing things his own way and living as he pleases, even if he occasionally irritates others.
41 In the long run it is best to associate mostly with those whose background and beliefs are the same as our own.
42 The police have gotten far too much power for the good of the country.
43 Nearly all of the people receiving welfare would probably rather work for a living, but cannot because of disabilities or circumstances beyond their control.
44 Rules about being polite and "well-mannered" are stupid relics of the past and ought to be ignored.
45 Youngsters should be encouraged to marry whomever they wish when they grow up, regardless of nationality, race or creed.
46 People can be divided into two distinct classes: the weak and the strong.
47 There are too many sporting events on television — especially football games.
48 Students at university should be bound by as few rules and regulations as possible.
49 Only a sick person or a neurotic could be well-adjusted in the kind of society we have now.
50 Most of the great men in history were motivated mostly by self-interest and a thirst for power.

THE OCTOBER, 1972, STUDY

Session I
1 The real patriot will support his government if it is right, but criticize it until it changes when it is wrong.
2 The worst danger to real Canadianism during the past 50 years has come from foreign ideas.
3 There is a divine purpose in the operations of the universe.
4 It usually helps a child in his later years if he is forced to conform to his parents' ideas.
5 In order to get many different kinds of people into each neighbourhood, the government should offer a man a speical bonus if he will sell his house to a member of some minority group.
6 The courts are right in being easy on drug offenders. Punishment would not do any good in cases like these.
7 The minds of today's youth are being purposely corrupted by the literature and movies being distributed by special interest groups.
8 The best way to run almost any group or organization is to have the leaders carry out what most of the members say they want done.

9 Nearly all of the people receiving welfare would rather work for a living, but cannot because of circumstances beyond their control.

10 If the laws against pornography were repealed there would probably be fewer prostitutes and cases of rape in our society.

11 Basically there are two kinds of people in the world: those who are for the truth, and those who are against it.

12 Achieving fairness and equality for all is a lot more important than maintaining "law and order."

13 In the long run it is best to associate mostly with those whose background and interests are the same as our own.

14 Sooner or later every insult to our honor should be punished — especially those made by our inferiors.

15 Atheists are no doubt just as good and virtuous as those who attend church regularly.

16 Young people sometimes get rebellious ideas, but as they grow up they ought to get over them and settle down.

17 The human race will take a giant step forward when all the racial and ethnic barriers are ignored and forgotten.

18 Sex crimes, such as rape and attacks on children, deserve more than mere imprisonment; such criminals ought to be publicly whipped, or worse.

19 Life in the military, with its emphasis on discipline and following orders, brings out the worst in people.

20 Youngsters should be encouraged to marry whomever they wish when they grow up, regardless of race, creed or social standing.

21 Laws must be strictly enforced, no matter what the consequences.

22 People should pay less attention to the Bible and the other old traditional forms of religious guidance.

23 The police and army are getting far too much power in this country.

24 There may be an exception every now and then, but in general people of the same race or ethnic background are pretty much alike.

25 Homosexuals are hardly better than criminals and ought to be severely punished.

26 Rules about being "well-behaved" and respectable are chains from the past that we have to break and throw away.

27 There is hardly anything lower than a person who does not feel a great love, gratitude, and respect for his parents.

28 Some people need to be reminded that our customs and national heritage are the things that have made us great.

29 The minority groups agitating these days for a better deal are entirely justified. They have been held down for years — not by any weakness of their own — but by others who got rich at their expense.

30 People can be divided into two distinct classes: the weak and the strong.

31 It is all right to look at dirty pictures or think about sex if that satisfies some personal need.

32 Obedience and respect for authority are the most important virtues children should learn.

33 No group of people should consider themselves especially important or better than others because of their ancestry or way of life.

34 Women should always remember the promise they make in the marriage ceremony

to obey their husbands.

35 People who abuse the flag, or who refuse to serve in the armed forces should be treated with tolerance and understanding.

36 Nowadays when so many different kinds of people move around and mix together so much, a person has to protect himself especially carefully against catching an infection or disease from them.

37 We should raise our youngsters so that they will refuse to fight in any future wars unless it is absolutely *necessary.*

38 It may be considered old-fashioned by some, but having a decent, respectable appearance is still the mark of a gentleman and, especially, a lady.

39 A good leader is careful not to rely merely on his own judgment of situations; he asks for the advice of his followers and generally does what they want.

40 The facts on crime and sexual immorality show we will have to crack down harder on deviant groups if we are going to save our moral standards.

41 Most children should be guided some in making acquaintances, or else they might mistakenly become friends with the wrong sort of person.

42 Disobedience to the government is very often justified.

43 It is only natural and right for each person to think that his family is better than any other.

Session II

44 Persons who spend a lot of time making unjust criticisms of the government should be thrown into jail.

45 There should only be one anthem and one flag on earth — one that would stand for all of mankind.

46 Individually a person is nothing. The only real identity one can have comes through identifying with a group we naturally belong to, and working with all our might to make it great.

47 Nowadays when all kinds of people can come into contact with us, a sensible person has to worry about catching some sickness or infection from others.

48 Some people on welfare never were taught the responsibility to take care of themselves, so it's not their fault they seem to be "lazy."

49 Rules about being polite and "well-mannered" are stupid relics of the past and ought to be ignored.

50 Organizations like the army and the priesthood, which make their members submit to the commands of superiors, have an unhealthy effect upon people.

51 The more unusual and startling works of art are probably the ones that are saying something new and significant about life.

52 One of the most important truths about life is that nature intended those who have the will power to be strong to dominate the weak.

53 The government should reward in some way people who marry across racial or class differences, for helping destroy these boundaries.

54 Sooner or later every insult and slur against our honor must be punished — especially those made by scum and degenerates.

55 Obedience and respect for proper authority are the most important virtues children should learn.

56 It is best to associate as much as possible with those whose background and interests are the same as our own.

57 Our prisons are a disgrace. Criminals are still people, and are entitled to much better treatment than they are presently getting.

58 Atheists are no doubt just as good and virtuous as those who attend church regularly — if not more so.

59 Young people sometimes get rebellious ideas, but as they grow up they ought to get over them and settle down.

60 The human race will take a giant step forward when all the racial and class barriers are overcome and forgotten

61 Homosexuals are just as good and virtuous as anybody else, and there is nothing really wrong with being one.

62 A leader's job is to lead, and so he must make the decisions for his group according to what *he* thinks is best.

63 Some groups just seem to have a natural weakness for alcohol, and for sitting around doing nothing.

64 Laws have to be strictly enforced if we are going to preserve our way of life.

65 People should pay less attention to the Bible and all the other outdated sources of religious teachings, and instead get involved in the new morality being developed in our own times.

66 In the final analysis parents generally turn out to be right about things.

67 When you get right down to it there are two kinds of people: those like us who are worthwhile, and those who are not.

68 People who commit sex crimes like rape and attacks on children ought to be whipped and beaten to within an inch of their lives.

69 Whoever said, "My country, right or wrong" was a fool, and certainly not a true patriot.

70 There is hardly anything lower than someone who is disrespectful toward his parents. We are duty-bound to honor our father and mother all our lives.

71 Some people need to be reminded that our customs and national heritage are the things that have made us great.

72 It is permissable for one to ignore laws that seem unjust and unfair.

73 Most of the people who are always trying to be different and unconventional in their appearance and mannerisms are just being ignorant and showing they haven't got anything solid to believe in.

74 It is all right for a person to privately reduce his sexual tensions by looking at pornography and other acts.

75 Women were meant to be subservient to man, and should never forget it.

76 No group of people should consider themselves especially important or better than others because of their ancestry or way of life.

77 Certain groups are poisoning the minds of today's youth with the wrong kind of music and films.

78 Groups which abuse the flag should be treated with tolerance and understanding.

79 It may be old-fashioned nowadays, but having a neat, tidy appearance is still the mark of a gentleman and a lady.

80 We should raise our youngsters so that they will refuse to fight in any future wars unless it is absolutely *necessary*.

81 The so-called "forces of law and order" in this country threaten our freedom a lot more than the groups they say are "subversive."

82 If a child starts becoming unconventinal, his parents should see to it he returns

to the normal ways expected by society.

83 The facts on crime and sexual immorality show we will have to crack down harder on deviant groups if we are going to save our moral standards.

84 Such things as flags and national anthems should be de-emphasized, to promote the idea that all men are brothers.

85 You can tell more about a person from knowing who and what his parents were than just about anything else.

THE JANUARY, 1973, STUDY

1 The worst danger to real Canadianism during this century has come from foreign ideas.

2 Capital punishment should be completely abolished.

3 The leader of the country's government is about the last person you can expect to be straightforward and honest with the people.

4 In order to get many different kinds of people into each neighborhood, real estate agents should offer special help to members of minority groups searching for a place to live.

5 There are of course exceptions, but in general people of the same ethnic background tend to act and think alike.

6 Atheists and others who have rebelled against the established religions are no doubt every bit as good and virtuous as those who attend church regularly.

7 Eventually we will have to settle the score with any troublemakers who have insulted our honor.

8 Our prisons are a shocking disgrace. Criminals are still people, not some kind of animal, and are entitled to much better treatment than they are presently getting.

9 Our country's problems would be cleared up in no time if a determined, energetic man were given full powers and turned loose.

10 Disobedience to the government is very often justified.

11 It may be considered old-fashioned by some, but having a decent, respectable appearance is still the mark of a gentleman and, especially, a lady.

12 The courts are right in being easy on drug offenders. Punishment would not do any good in cases like these.

13 Young people sometimes get rebellious ideas, but as they grow up they ought to get over them and settle down.

14 People should pay less attention to the Bible and the other old traditional forms of religious guidance.

15 The facts on crime and sexual immorality show we will have to crack down harder on deviant groups if we are going to save our moral standards.

16 Organizations like the army and the priesthood, which make their members submit to the commands of superiors, have an unhealthy effect upon people.

17 There is hardly anything lower than someone who is disrespectful toward his parents. We are duty-bound to honor our father and mother all our lives.

18 Obedience and respect for proper authority are the most important virtues children should learn.

19 Homosexuals are just as good and virtuous as anybody else, and there is nothing really wrong with being one.

20 In the final analysis, parents generally turn out to be right about things.

21 Such things as flags and national anthems should be de-emphasized, to promote the idea that all men are brothers.

22 Laws have to be strictly enforced if we are going to preserve our way of life.

23 Rules about being "well-behaved" and respectable are chains from the past that we have to break and throw away.

24 If a child starts becoming unconventional, his parents should see to it he returns to the normal ways expected by society.

25 Criminals, loafers and other immoral people usually think leniency and kindness are signs of weakness, so it's best for everyone concerned to use a firm hand when dealing with them.

26 Since a person can only know so much about things in a complicated world like this, the only sensible thing to do is support those in positions of authority, who know what's really going on.

27 When you get right down to it, there's really no reason to play the national anthem before football games, etc. Such superficial displays of patriotism have little to do with what it really means to be a Canadian.

28 Women should always remember the promise they make in the marriage ceremony to obey their husbands.

29 A parent, boss or military commander who demands complete obedience from his "subordinates" is just showing how insecure and incompetent he is.

30 There are an awful lot of lazy bums on welfare nowadays who ought to be cut off without another cent and forced to work like the rest of us.

31 We should raise our youngsters so that they will defy the government and refuse to fight in any future wars unless it is absolutely and clearly necessary for our country.

32 You can tell a lot about a person just by knowing who and what his parents were.

33 We should all identify with the groups we naturally belong to, and work with all our mights to make them great.

34 The real patriot will support his government if it is right, but also criticize it as strongly as anyone else when it is wrong.

35 Some groups appear to have a basic weakness for alcohol, prominscuity, and just sitting around doing nothing.

36 One of the most important truths about life is that those with the greatest will power are meant to rule the rest.

37 Groups which abuse the flag should be treated with tolerance and understanding.

38 There is a divine purpose in the operations of the universe in which we are all destined to play a part.

39 Youngsters should be encouraged to marry whomever they wish when they grow up, regardless of nationality, race, creed or parental objections.

40 The only way to teach some people right from wrong is to give them a good stiff punishment when they get out of line.

41 The so-called "forces of law and order" in this country threaten our freedom a lot more than the groups they say are subversive.

42 It may be considered old-fashioned by those who have been swept up in the "sexual revolution," but having a decent, respectable appearance is still the mark of a gentleman and a lady.

43 The courts are quite right in being easy on drug users. Punishment would do no good at all in cases like these.

44 There is hardly anthing lower than a young person who rebels against his parents' beliefs and guidance.

45 People should pay less attention to the Bible and the other old traditional forms of religious guidance, and instead develop their own personal standards of what is moral and immoral.

46 The facts on crime, sexual immorality and the recent public disorders all show we will have to crack down harder on deviant groups and troublemakers if we are going to save our religious standards and preserve law and order.

47 Organizations like the army and the priesthood, which require their members to obey blindly orders from superiors, have an unhealthy effect upon people.

48 Some people need to be reminded that our customs, moral discipline and national heritage are the things that have made us great.

49 Obedience and respect for authority are the most important virtues children should learn.

50 Homosexuals are just as good and virtuous as anybody else, and in fact someone who openly defies society's standards and says he is a homosexual is in some respects better than most people.

51 In the final analysis parents, civil authorities and the proper spiritual leaders generally turn out to be right about things.

52 There should be only one anthem and one flag on earth—one that would stand for all mankind.

53 Laws have to be strictly enforced if we are going to preserve our moral standards and way of life.

54 Rules about being polite and "well-mannered" are stupid relics of the past and ought to be ignored.

55 If a child starts becoming a little too unconventional, his parents should see to it he returns to the normal ways expected by society.

56 Most of our country's problems could be cleared up in no time if the right man were given full powers and turned loose on the troublemakers and degenerates among us.

57 Certain groups are poisoning the minds of today's youth with the wrong kind of music and films.

58 In the long run it is best to associate mostly with those whose background and beliefs are the same as our own.

59 The chief duty parents have is to raise children who will stand on their own two feet, critically examine the old established order, and make things over the way they see fit.

60 Young people owe it to society to get over their rebellious ideas and settle down as they grow older.

61 Every person has the right to challenge the government when he feels its laws are unjust.

62 It may be all right to criticize someone while he's running for office, but once a man becomes the leader of our country, we owe him our strongest loyalty.

Note: The order of presentation of these items was counterbalanced as follows. Subjects were randomly divided into four approximately equal subgroups. One group answered items 1-31 (above) at the first testing session, and items 32-62 at the second session one week later. Group II answered the items in the sequence 31-1, 62-32. Group III answered the items 32-62, 1-31. Group IV responded to the sequence 62-32, 31-1.

THE SEPTEMBER, 1973, STUDY

1   A lot of our society's rules regarding modesty and sexual behavior are just customs which are not necessarily any better or holier than those which other people follow.

2   The greatest thing a person can have is outstanding will power and determination.

3   A father who demands obedience above all else from his teenage sons and daughters is just showing how insecure and incompetent he is.

4   There is really no need to fill up the halftime of football games with a lot of patriotic mush. Such superficial displays have little to do with genuine patriotism.

5   Just about anyone who commits a violent crime like rape has lost control of himself by then, and ought to be treated with sympathy and mercy in the courts.

6   Most of the people receiving welfare these days are just lazy bums who ought to be cut off without another cent and forced to get jobs like the rest of us.

7   Youngsters should be taught to refuse to fight in a war unless they themselves agree the war is just and necessary.

8   It is a natural and good thing that people like to stick with their own kind and maintain their natural identities.

9   A "woman's place" should be wherever she wants to be. The days when women are submissive to their husbands and social conventions belong strictly in the past.

10   Our prisons are a shocking disgrace. Criminals are unfortunate people who deserve much better care, instead of so much punishment.

11   Our country would be in much better shape if people would just get back to the truths and wisdoms that guided our forefathers.

12   One reason our country is in such a mess nowadays is that our leaders are too gutless to give certain problems the "strong medicine" it will take to get rid of them.

13   The amount of violence shown in films and on television nowadays is every bit as disgusting as the sex shown, if not moreso.

14   It is best always to trust the judgment of the proper authorities, even though it may seem wrong at the time.

15   There is really nothing wrong with being a homosexual, even if it is against the main norms and customs of our society.

16   Organizations like the army and the priesthood, which make their members submit to the commands of their superiors, have a pretty unhealthy effect upon men.

17   In these troubled times laws have to be enforced without mercy, especially when dealing with the agitators and revolutionaries who are stirring things up.

18   If a child starts becoming a little too unconventional, his parents should see to it he returns to the normal ways expected by society.

19   If people could do what they really wanted, most would prefer to live in cooperative harmony with others.

20   Obedience and respect for authority are the most important virtues children should learn.

21   The courts are right in being easy on drug offenders. Punishment would not do any good in cases like these.

22   In a world as tough and dangerous as this one, only the determined and the strong-willed come out on top.

23   People should pay less attention to the Bible and the other old traditional forms of moral guidance, and instead develop their own personal standards of what is

moral and immoral.

24 It's one thing to question and doubt someone during an election campaign, but once a man becomes the leader of our country we owe him our greatest support and loyalty.

25 The facts on crime, sexual immorality, and the recent public disorders all show we have to crack down harder on deviant groups and troublemakers if we are going to save our moral standards and preserve law and order.

26 The main reason certain racial minority groups are not advancing in society is not because they lack drive and determination, but because of systematic discrimination against them.

27 Rules about being "well-mannered" and respectful are merely customs left over from another era, and they probably shouldn't apply to us so much today.

28 The only way to keep some people in line is really to "lower the boom" when they start acting up.

29 Those who have rebelled against their parents' religion are probably just as good and virtuous as their parents.

30 In the long run it is wise to associate mostly with those whose background, ideas and beliefs are the same as your own.

31 In the final analysis parents, civil authorities and the proper spiritual leaders generally turn out to be right about things.

32 The best kind of city to live in is one where lots of different races and cultures coexist and mix together.

33 Political leaders who go around shouting for "law and order" quite often turn out to be the biggest crooks of all.

34 One good way to teach certain people right from wrong is to give them a good stiff punishment when they get out of line.

35 Our kind of society works best when people keep a critical eye on the government and treat its leaders with a certain amount of suspicion.

36 A parent, boss or military commander who demands complete obedience from his "subordinates" is just showing how insecure and incompetent he is.

37 A truly patriotic Canadian is the person who's pushing to get equal opportunities for all, and not the guy who's always saluting the flag and arguing for a big army.

38 Occasionally having strong "will power" helps a person accomplish his goal, but usually it just amounts to foolish stubborness and inflexibility.

39 Women should always remember the promise they make in the marriage ceremony to obey their husbands.

40 One should always give strangers "the benefit of the doubt" when it comes to interpreting their actions.

41 Sex crimes, such as rape and attacks on children, deserve more than mere imprisonment; such criminals ought to be publicly whipped, or worse.

42 There is no weaker defense in a war crime trial than "I was only following orders." No one should follow an order when it is wrong.

43 Some groups appear to have a natural tendency toward alcoholism, promiscuity, and just sitting around doing nothing.

44 National anthems, flags, and glorification of one's country should all be de-emphasized to promote the brotherhood of all men.

45 Our prison system is a scandal. It is society's duty to rehabilitate and help criminals, not to punish them.

46 Our customs and national heritage are the things that have made us great, and certain people should be made to show greater respect for them.

47 The people howling about "injustices" supposedly done by the government are just the same old troublemakers who are always trying to stir things up.

48 The most alarming thing about the movies and television programs being made nowadays is not the amount of sex in them, but the violence.

49 Persons in positions of authority are usually right about things, so it is best to follow their instructions even when one might not agree with them.

50 Homosexuals are just as good and virtuous as anybody else, and there is nothing wrong with being one.

51 Organizations like the army and the priesthood have a pretty unhealthy effect upon men because they require strict obedience of commands from superiors.

52 Laws have to be strictly enforced if we are going to preserve our way of life.

53 It may be considered old-fashioned by some, but having a decent, respectable appearance is still the mark of a gentleman and, especially, a lady.

54 The world is not like a jungle; most people are generous and will not take advantage of you if you look weak and helpless.

55 Young people sometimes get rebellious ideas, but as they grow up they ought to get over them and settle down.

56 Capital punishment should be completely abolished.

57 In this world you either dominate and are on top, or else you get dominated by somebody else and have to crawl on your knees.

58 Virginity in someone 30 years old is probably a sign of fear and conflict, rather than holiness or great will power.

59 It may be all right to criticize someone while he's running for office, but once a person becomes the leader of our country we owe him strong support and loyalty.

60 A lot of our country's problems could be cleared up if the right persons were given full powers and turned loose on the troublemakers and degenerates among us.

61 Our youngsters should be encouraged to marry whomever they wish when they grow up, even if the person chosen comes from a different religious or racial background.

62 Rules about being "well-mannered" and respectable are chains from the past which we should question very thoroughly before accepting.

63 There is hardly anything lower than a person who is disrespectful toward his parents.

64 Atheists and others who have rebelled against the established religions are no doubt every bit as good and virtuous as those who attend church regularly.

65 It is unfortunately true, but in this world you always have to be on your guard against someone attacking or cheating you.

66 A lot of the movies and magazines available nowadays are just disgusting, filthy pornography, and their producers ought to be thrown into jail.

67 Spanking a child is the worst way there is to try to teach him something.

68 Politicians who run for office on a "law and order" platform have a bad habit of taking the law into their own hands when elected and running roughshod over people's civil rights.

69 Being kind to loafers or criminals will only encourage them to take advantage of your weakness, so it's best to use a firm, tough hand when dealing with them.

70 If one thing is clear nowadays, it's that we've got to be suspicious and critical

of the businessmen, military and high government officials who hold the power in our society.

Note: The order of presentation of these items was counterbalanced as follows. Subjects were randomly divided into four approximately equal subgroups. One group answered items 1-35 (above) at the first testing session, and items 36-70 at the second session one week later. Group II answered the items in the sequence 35-1, 70-36. Group III answered the items 36-70, 1-35. Group IV responded to the sequence 70-36, 35-1.

APPENDIX II

The seven authoritarian scales used in the "pitting experiments"

This survey is part of an investigation of general public opinion concerning a variety of social issues. You will probably find that you *agree* with some of the statements, *disagree* with others, and to varying extents. Please mark your opinion on the IBM card provided, according to the amount of your agreement or disagreement, by using the following scale:

Blacken the bubble labeled −3 if you *strongly disagree* with the statement.

−2 if you *moderately disagree* with the statement.

−1 if you *slightly disagree* with the statement.

Blacken the bubble labeled +1 if you *slightly agree* with the statement.

+2 if you *moderately agree* with the statement.

−3 if you *strongly agree* with the statement.

If you feel exactly and precisely *neutral* about an item, blacken the "O" bubble.†

1 Obedience and respect for authority are the most important virtues children should learn.

2 No weakness or difficulty can hold us back if we have enough will power.

3 Science has its place, but there are many important things that can never possibly be understood by the human mind.

4 Human nature being what it is, there will always be war and conflict.

5 Every person should have complete faith in some supernatural power whose decisions he obeys without question. :

6 When a person has a problem or worry, it is best for him not to think about it, but to keep busy with more cheerful things.

7 A person who has bad manners, habits and breeding can hardly expect to get along with decent people.

8 What the youth needs most is strict discipline, rugged determination, and the will to work and fight for family and country.

9 Some people are born with an urge to jump from high places.

10 Nowadays when so many different kinds of people move around and mix together so much, a person has to protect himself especially carefully against catching an infection or disease from them.

11 An insult to our honor should always be punished.

12 Young people sometimes get rebellious ideas, but as they grow up they ought to get over them and settle down.

13 It is best to use some prewar authorities in Germany to keep order and prevent chaos.

14 What this country needs most, more than laws and political programs, is a few courageous, tireless, devoted leaders in whom the people can put their faith.

15 SEE OTHER SIDE.††

15 Sex crimes, such as rape and attacks on children, deserve more than mere imprisonment; such criminals ought to be publicly whipped, or worse.

16 People can be divided into two distinct classes: the weak and the strong.

17 There is hardly anything lower than a person who does not feel a great love, gratitude, and respect for his parents.

18 Some day it will probably be shown that astrology can explain a lot of things.

19 Nowadays more and more people are prying into matters that should remain pesonal and private.

20 Wars and social troubles may someday be ended by an earthquake or flood that will destroy the whole world.

21 Most of our social problems would be solved if we could somehow get rid of the immoral, crooked, and feebleminded people.

22 The wild sex life of the old Greeks and Romans was tame compared to some of the goings-on in this country, even in places where people might least expect it.

23 If people would talk less and work more, everybody would be better off

24 Most people don't realize how much our lives are controlled by plots hatched in secret places.

25 Homosexuals are hardly better than criminals, and ought to be severely punished.

26 The business and the manufacturer are much more important to society than the artist and the professor.

27 No sane, decent person could ever think of hurting a close friend or relative.

28 Familiarity breeds contempt.

29 Nobody ever learned anything really important except through suffering.

 † These instructions began all of the surveys except the Conservatism Scale.

†† Each of the scales (again excepting the Conservatism Scale) was printed on the front and back sides of a single piece of paper.

THE BALANCED VERSION OF THE CALIFORNIA F SCALE

1 Obedience and respect for authority are the most important virtues children should learn.

2 Children do not necessarily owe their parents great love, gratitude and respect. Parents have to deserve such things like everyone else.

3 Science has its place, but there are many important things that can never possibly be understood by the human mind.

4 Human nature being what it is, there will always be war and conflict.

5 A peson should not necessarily put complete faith in some supernatural power

whose decisions he obeys without question.

6 When a person has a problem or worry, it is best for him not to think about it, but to keep busy with more cheerful things.

7 A person who has bad manners, habits and breeding can hardly expect to get along with decent people.

8 What the youth needs most is strict discipline, rugged determination, and the will to work and fight for family and country.

9 Probably no one is born with an urge to jump from high place.

10 Even though all sorts of people mix together nowadays, you don't have to worry very much about catching an infection or disease from them.

11 An insult to our honor should not always be punished.

12 Young people sometimes get rebellious ideas, but as they grow up they ought to get over them and settle down.

13 It is best to use some prewar authorities in Germany to keep order and prevent chaos.

14 What this country needs most, more than laws and political programs, is a few courageous, tireless, devoted leaders in whom the people can put their faith.

15 SEE OTHER SIDE.

15 Sex crimes, such as rape and attacks on children, deserve more than mere imprisonment; such criminals ought to be publicly whipped, or worse.

16 People cannot be divided into two simple classes like "the weak" and "the strong."

17 NO weakness or difficulty can hold us back if we have enough will power.

18 Astrology will probably never be able to explain very much.

19 Nowadays more and more people are prying into matters that should remain pesonal and private.

20 There is no real reason to expect that the world will be destroyed someday by an earthquake or flood.

21 Most of our social problems would be solved if we could somehow get rid of the immoral, crooked, and feebleminded people.

22 The wild sex life of the old Greeks and Romans was tame compared to some of the goings-on in this country, even in places where people might least expect it.

23 "Talking less and working more" wouldn't really help us become better off.

24 Our lives are probably not controlled to any degree by plots hatched in secret places.

25 Homosexuals may be sick persons but they are hardly criminals. Others need to understand their feelings and be more accepting of them.

26 The artist and professor are as important to society as the businessman and the manufacturer.

27 No sane, decent person could ever think of hurting a close friend or relative.

28 Familiarity breeds contempt.

29 Nobody ever learned anything really important except through suffering.

THE DOGMATISM SCALE

1 Canada and Russia have just about nothing in common.

2 The highest form of government is a democracy and the highest form of democracy is a government run by those who are most intelligent.

3 It is only natural that a person would have a much better acquaintance with

ideas he believes in than with ideas he opposes.

4 Man on his own is a helpless and miserable creature.

5 It is only natural for a person to be rather fearful of the future.

6 It is better to be a dead hero than to be a live coward.

7 While I don't like to admit this even to myself, my secret ambition is to become a great man, like Einstein, or Beethoven, or Shakespeare.

8 Most of the ideas which get printed nowadays aren't worth the paper they are printed on.

9 In the history of mankind there have probably been just a handful of really great thinkers.

10 A man who does not believe in some great cause has not really lived.

11 When it comes to differences of opinion in religion we must be careful not to compromise with those who believe differently from the way we do.

12 A group which tolerates too much difference of opinion among its members cannot exist for long.

13 There are two kinds of people in this world: those who are for the truth and those who are against the truth.

14 SEE OTHER SIDE.

14 In this complicated world of ours the only way we can know what's going on is to rely on leaders or experts who can be trusted.

15 The present is all too often full of unhappiness. It is only the future that counts.

16 If a man is to accomplish his mission in life it is sometimes necessary to gamble "all or nothing at all."

17 Even though freedom of speech for all groups is a worthwhile goal, it is unfortunately necessary to restrict the freedom of certain political groups.

18 Fundamentally, the world we live in is a pretty lonesome place.

19 Thre is so much to be done and so little time to do it in.

20 The main thing in life is for a person to want to do something important.

21 There are a number of people I have come to hate because of the things they stand for.

22 It is only when a person devotes himself to an ideal or cause that life becomes meaningful.

23 In times like these, a person must be pretty selfish if he considers primarily his own happiness.

24 The worst crime a person could commit is to attack publicly the people who believe in the same thing he does.

25 My blood boils whenever a person stubbornly refuses to admit he's wrong.

26 It is often desirable to reserve judgment about what's going on until one has had a chance to hear the opinions of those one respects.

27 In the long run the best way to live is to pick friends and associates whose tastes and beliefs are the same as one's own.

28 Unfortunately, a good many people with whom I have discussed important social and moral problems don't really understand what's going on.

29 Most people just don't give a "damn" for others.

30 Once I get wound up in a heated discussion I just can't stop.

31 If given the chance I would do something of great benefit to the world.

32 Of all the different philosophies which exist in this world there is probably only one which is correct.

33 In times like these it is often necessary to be more on guard against ideas put out by people or groups in one's camp than by those in the opposing camp.

34 A person who thinks primarily of his own happiness is beneath contempt.

35 Most people just don't know what's good for them.

36 I'd like it if I could find someone who would tell me how to solve my personal problems.†

37 In a discussion I often find it necessary to repeat myself several times to make sure I am being understood.

38 A peson who gets enthusiastic about too many causes is likely to be a pretty "wishy-washy" sort of person.†

39 In a heated discussion I generally become so absorbed in what I am going to say that I forget to listen to what others are saying.†

40 To compromise with our political opponents is dangerous because it usually leads to the betrayal of our own side.†

　† Items 36-40 of the Dogmatism Scale followed those of the California F Scale, as the IBM card on which subjects marked their responses only had places for 35 items.

THE CONSERVATISM SCALE

Attitude survey: WHICH OF THE FOLLOWING DO YOU FAVOR OR BELIEVE IN? (Circle "Yes" or "No." If absolutely uncertain, circle "?" There are no right or wrong answers; do not discuss; just give your first reaction. Answer all items.)

1 Death penalty	Yes	?	No	26 Computer music	Yes	?	No
2 Evolution theory	Yes	?	No	27 Chastity	Yes	?	No
3 School uniforms	Yes	?	No	28 Fluoridation	Yes	?	No
4 Striptease shows	Yes	?	No	29 Royalty	Yes	?	No
5 Sabbath observance	Yes	?	No	30 Women judges	Yes	?	No
6 Beatniks	Yes	?	No	31 Conventional clothes	Yes	?	No
7 Patriotism	Yes	?	No	32 Teenage drivers	Yes	?	No
8 Modern art	Yes	?	No	33 Apartheid	Yes	?	No
9 Self-denial	Yes	?	No	34 Nudist camps	Yes	?	No
10 Working mothers	Yes	?	No	35 Church authority	Yes	?	No
11 Horoscopes	Yes	?	No	36 Disarmament	Yes	?	No
12 Birth control	Yes	?	No	37 Censorship	Yes	?	No
13 Military drill	Yes	?	No	38 White lies	Yes	?	No
14 Co-education	Yes	?	No	39 Birching (Flogging)	Yes	?	No
15 Divine law	Yes	?	No	40 Mixed marriage	Yes	?	No
16 Socialism	Yes	?	No	41 Strict rules	Yes	?	No
17 White superiority	Yes	?	No	42 Jazz	Yes	?	No
18 Cousin marriage	Yes	?	No	43 Straightjackets	Yes	?	No
19 Moral trianing	Yes	?	No	44 Casual living	Yes	?	No
20 Suicide	Yes	?	No	45 Learning latin	Yes	?	No
21 Chaperones	Yes	?	No	46 Divorce	Yes	?	No
22 Legalized abortion	Yes	?	No	47 Inborn conscience	Yes	?	No
23 Empire-building	Yes	?	No	48 Coloured immigration	Yes	?	No
24 Student pranks	Yes	?	No	49 Bible truth	Yes	?	No
25 Licensing laws	Yes	?	No	50 Pyjama parties	Yes	?	No

LEE & WARR'S "BALANCED F SCALE"

1 The minds of today's youth are being hopelessly corrupted by the wrong kind of literature.
2 The church has outgrown its usefulness and should be radically reformed or done away with.
3 An insult to our honor should always be punished.
4 It is only natural and right for each person to think that his family is better than any other.
5 What a youth needs most is the flexibility to work and fight for what he considers right personally even though it might not be best for his family and country.
6 Most censorship of books or movies is a violation of free speech and should be abolished.
7 The facts on crime and sex immorality suggest that we will have to crack down harder on some people if we are going to save our moral standards.
8 It is the duty of a citizen to criticize or censure his country whenever he considers it to be wrong.
9 The resistance of medical pressure groups may have to be broken by strong governmental action in order for all of the people to get the full medical care to which they are entitled.
10 No person who could ever think of hurting his parents should be permitted in the society of normal decent people.
11 A world government with effective military strength is one way in which world peace might be achieved.
12 SEE OTHER SIDE.
12 Few weaknesses or difficulties can hold us back if we have enough will power.
13 Unless something drastic is done, the world is going to be destroyed one of these days by nuclear explosion or fallout.
14 The poor will always be with us.
15 The worst danger to Canada during the last 50 years has come from foreign ideas and agitators.
16 Science declines when it confines itself to the solution of immediate practical problems.
17 We should be grateful for leaders who tell us exactly what to do and how to do it.
18 One of the troubles with our present economy is that full employment depends on a substantial military budget.
19 As young people grow up, they ought to try to carry out some of their rebellious ideas and not be content to get over them and settle down.
20 In the final analysis parents generally turn out to be right about things.
21 Divorce or annulment is practically never justified.
22 Disobedience to the government is sometimes justified.
23 Honesty, hard work, and trust in God do not guarantee material rewards.
24 There is a divine purpose in the operations of the universe.
25 Army life is a good influence on most men.
26 One way to reduce the expression of prejudice is through more forceful legislation.
27 One of the greatest threats to the Canadian way of life is for us to resort to the use of force.
28 It usually helps the child in later years if he is forced to conform to his parents' ideas.

29 Sex crimes, such as rape and attacks on children, deserve more than mere imprisonment; such criminals ought to be publicly whipped, or worse.

30 Members of religious sects who refuse to salute the flag or bear arms should be treated with tolerance and understanding.

THE AUTHORITARIANISM-REBELLION SCALE

1 Obedience and respect for authority are the most important virtues children should learn.

2 What we need least is an authority to tell us what to do or how to do it.

3 Every person should have complete faith in some supernatural power whose decisions he obeys without question.

4 People can be divided into two distinct classes: the weak and the strong.

5 To be a decent human being follow your conscience regardless of the law.

6 No principle is more immoral than that of obedience.

7 Familiarity breeds contempt.

8 Astrology will never explain anything because it is a fraud.

9 The Canadian way of life is so resistant to progress that revolution is necessary to end its injustices and oppressions.

10 Nowadays, when so many different kinds of people move around and mix together so much, a person has to protect himself against catching an infection or disease from them.

11 Children don't owe their parents a thing.

12 Canada is spiritually predestined to lead the world.

13 Sex crimes like rape and child molesting reflect a sick society, and we must change society rather than punishing individual offenders.

14 Obedience is the mother of success.

15 SEE OTHER SIDE.

15 Strong discipline builds moral character.

16 Canada can't exert moral leadership among nations until it abandons its corrupt material values.

17 Some day it will probably be shown that astrology can explain a lot of things.

18 People of different nationalities, social classes and races should mix together more. Everybody would benefit from it.

19 To know people well is to love them.

20 The true Canadian way of life is dissappearing so fast that force may be necessary to preserve it.

21 Sex crimes, such as rape and attacks on children, deserve more than mere imprisonment; such criminals ought to be publicly whipped, or worse.

22 Obedience is the mother of enslavement.

23 True morality only develops in a fully permissive environment.

24 There is hardly anthing lower than a person who does not feel a great deal of love, gratitude, and respect for his parents.

25 No principle is more noble or holy than that of true obedience.

26 The strong and the weak are not inherently different. They are merely the advantaged and disadvantaged members of an unfair society.

27 Obedience and respect for authority aren't virtues and shouldn't be taught to children.

28 To be a decent person always stay within the law.

29 Our chief want in life is somebody to make us do what we should.

30 Faith in the supernatural is a harmful self-delusion, and submission to religious authority is dangerous.

THE RIGHT-WING AUTHORITARIANISM SCALE

1 Laws have to be strictly enforced if we are going to preserve our way of life.

2 People should pay less attention to the Bible and the other old traditional forms of religious guidance, and instead develop their own personal standards of what is moral and immoral.

3 Women should always remember the promise they make in the marriage ceremony to obey their husbands.

4 Our customs and national heritage are the things that have made us great, and certain people should be made to show greater respect for them.

5 Capital punishment should be completely abolished.

6 National anthems, flags, and glorification of one's country should all be de-emphasized to promote the brotherhood of all men.

7 The facts on crime, sexual immorality, and the recent public disorders all show we have to crack down harder on deviant groups and troublemakers if we are going to save our moral standards and preserve law and order.

8 A lot of our society's rules regarding modesty and sexual behavior are just customs which are not necessarily any better or holier than those which other peoples follow.

9 Our prisons are a shocking disgrace. Criminals are unfortunate people who deserve much better care, instead of so much punishment.

10 Obedience and respect for authority are the most important virtues children should learn.

11 Organizations like the army and the priesthood have a pretty unhealthy effect upon men because they require strict obedience of commands from supervisors.

12 One good way to teach certain people right from wrong is to give them a good stiff punishment when they get out of line.

13 Youngsters should be taught to refuse to fight in a war unless they themselves agree the war is just and necessary.

14 SEE OTHER SIDE.

14 It may be considered old-fashioned by some, but having a decent, respectable appearance is still the mark of a gentleman and, especially, a lady.

15 In these troubled times laws have to be enforced without mercy, especially when dealing with the agitators and revolutionaries who are stirring things up.

16 Atheists and others who have rebelled against the established religions are no doubt every bit as good and virtuous as those who attend church regularly.

17 Young people sometimes get rebellious ideas, but as they grow up they ought to get over them and settle down.

18 Rules about being "well-mannered" and respectable are chains from the past which we should question very thoroughly before accepting.

19 The courts are right in being easy on drug offenders. Punishment would not do any good in cases like these.

20 If a child starts becoming a little too unconventional, his parents should see

to it he returns to the normal ways expected by society.

21 Being kind to loafers or criminals will only encourage them to take advantage of your weakness, so it's best to use a firm, tough hand when dealing with them.

22 A "woman's place" should be wherever she wants to be. The days when women are submissive to their husbands and social conventions belong strictly in the past.

23 Homosexuals are just as good and virtuous as anybody else, and there is nothing wrong with being one.

24 It's one thing to question and doubt someone during an election campaign, but once a man becomes the leader of our country we owe him our greatest support and loyalty.

APPENDIX III

Supplementary rules for scoring the "moral dilemma" protocols

1 Use of phrases such as "It's against the *law*," "It's *illegal*," "It would be *fraud*," "It would be *breaking and entering*" indicate a Stage I response. (Note however, a statement such as "It would be illegal *and I could get sent to jail*" should be scored a Stage II, since the concern with legality seems to be focused on the consequences to the individual.

2 Use of phrases such as "It's *unjust*..." "They have a *right* to..." "It is a *legitimate*..." "It's only *fair*" indicate a Stage VI response.

3 Use of phrases such as "It is wrong" and "It is dishonest" are ambiguous because it is not clear if the act is "wrong" because it is illegal or because it is unjust. If there is no clarification in the rest of the protocol, score it a "?"

4 Fear of conscience can be either a Stage II, in the sense of avoiding the suffering produced by guilt for doing an (externally defined) "bad thing," or it can be a Stage VI, in the sense of avoiding feeling one has not been true to one's (self-adopted) principles. If the rest of the protocol is unclear as to why one's conscience would bother one, score it a "?"

5 Protocols which focus on the subject's relationship with someone else (e.g., acquaintance vs. a friend, stranger vs. acquaintance) should be scored a Stage III. Also, deeds done as a favor to a friend indicate Stage III.

6 Decisions based on some reasonably implied moral principle (e.g., "No scientist's greed should count more than a human life," "A human life is at stake," imply a Stage VI scoring.

7 Use of phrases such as "Because my kids need the food" are ambiguous, because it is not clear if the subject would extend the right to "steal" to every parent with hungry children (Stage VI), just to himself (Stage II) or to himself and his friends (Stage III).

8 It is not unusual for protocols to contain evidence of two (or more) identifiable stages. Unless the subject indicates that one of them is the "basic" or "most important" reason for deciding as he did, give priority to the Stage which is evidenced first. In rare cases, a protocol may be scored as evidencing two stages (e.g., the subject says there were two equally important reasons.)

APPENDIX IV

Letter sent to parents in 1979 study

THE UNIVERSITY OF MANITOBA

DEPARTMENT OF PSYCHOLOGY

WINNIPEG, CANADA
R3T 2N2

October 12, 1979

Dear Parent:

I am the professor of psychology who is teaching Introductory Psychology to your daughter/son this term. As you may know, it is possible for students in this course to earn a small part of their grade by serving as subjects in studies being conducted by members of my department. This enables students to learn about psychological research firsthand, and also helps us do the research on which the science of psychology is based.

One problem with this system, which is widely recognized, is that most of our research is done with university students, instead of with other persons who might be more representative of the population as a whole. A few weeks ago, for example, the students in my classes completed a survey on general social issues, and also another on their childhoods. The researcher involved is interested in collecting data on the same topics from the students' parents.

Your son/daughter indicated, by addressing the mailing envelope, that he/she thought you would not mind completing the parents' version of the survey which is enclosed. If you do so, and have it returned to me within the next week or so, I shall be able to give your daughter or son one "experimental credit" for helping collect the data.

You will note there is <u>no</u> place for you to sign your name on the survey; it is meant to be taken anonymously. The surveys should be returned to me through your child, who will be told to put them into a big box in our classroom. Altogether there will probably be about 400 surveys returned in my classes.

Having said all this, let me also say I want very much to keep you from feeling "pressured" by me or anyone else to complete the survey. The experimental credit involved is only worth a tiny part (1%) of the final grade in the introductory psychology course, and there are many other ways students can easily earn this credit. There is absolutely <u>no</u> penalty to students whose parents decline to participate. So please only complete the questionnaire if you are freely willing to do so.

A general summary of the results of the survey will be given to my students once the results are tabulated -- probably in late March -- and you will be able to find out about these through your daughter or son.

One last thing I would add, if you decide to fill out the survey, is that you do so "on your own." That is, do not consult beforehand with your spouse, child, etc.; please do not fill out the survey all together. It is important for the scientific value of the study that the responses come from <u>individuals</u>.

If you have any questions about this project, please call me at 474-8120.

Yours sincerely,

Robert A. Altemeyer

Robert A. Altemeyer, PhD

Notes

INTRODUCTION

1 Five years later Robert Bourassa, the Liberal Premier of Quebec during the crisis, said he never thought there was any danger of an insurrection (*Toronto Globe and Mail*, October 27, 1975, p. 18).

2 One is inevitably reminded of the reaction of many Germans after the Second World War who refused to believe, or who made excuses for the actions of their previous government. Even after all the brutal facts had been made known, Adolf Hitler was still widely perceived as a "good man who had bad advisors" (McGranahan, 1946).

3 The reader unfamiliar with the controversy which has swirled around this issue is referred to the major papers of Mischel (1968, 1969, 1973, 1979), Alker (1972), Bem (1972), Endler (1973), Bowers (1973), Bem and Allen (1974), Epstein (1979, 1980).

4 There are grounds for other hesitations about Burwen and Campbell's findings, which only pale in significance before the reliability problems. To note the more prominent: the interview subjects were ordered to submit to the one-hour interview, which the authors acknowledged produced a "guarded, deferential attitude that was difficult to overcome"; in the TAT and photo-judging measures attitudes toward "older persons" were considered to be attitudes toward "authority figures"; there was no report on the variability of the scores obtained on the different measures. On a more theoretical note, the comparisons being made were between adults' current statements about their fathers and their current attitudes toward their bosses and symbolic authority, whereas the theories being tested by Burwen and Campbell were of how children's attitudes toward their fathers generalize to other authority figures in childhood. The only theorist the authors quoted (Piaget) explicitly qualified his statements about later generalization with the condition that the child's relationship with his father remain homogeneous throughout youth. Burwen and Campbell reported no attempt to assess this aspect of their subjects' lives.

CHAPTER 1

1 The following scales have knowingly been omitted from the review: Berkowitz and Wolkon (1964), O'Neil and Levinson (1954), Pflaum (1964), Ray (1972), Strick-

land and Janicki (1965), and Webster, Sanford and Freedman (1955). The reason for their exclusion was either a very small literature or very poor evidence for validity (or both).

2 It is not clear how many items there were on the final version of the F Scale. The only definitive listing of items (on pages 255-257 of TAP) contains 29 statements. Elsewhere reference is made to thirty items, and the item analysis results on page 260 of the book refer to thirty items. The varying item appears to be one from an earlier version of the scale: "The true American way of life is disappearing so fast that force may be necessary to preserve it." Obviously the addition or deletion of a thirtieth item will have very little impact upon the characteristics of a scale, and so any study which used either the 29- or 30-item Form 45/40 version of the F Scale will be referred to as having used "the original F Scale."

3 Because so many different versions of the "F Scale" have been used in research, it is difficult to know which studies ought to be included in this review and which ignored. Clearly a study which used 25 of the original F Scale items is relevant; on the other hand, one which used only five original items could very easily be misleading. One could draw a line at 15, requiring that a study use at least half of the F Scale, and that those 15 items constitute at least half of the authoritarianism scale used. However, there are a number of widely-cited studies which used 12, 10 and even nine items from the original scale and there doubtless are some who would think a review which omitted these studies would be seriously incomplete. It is also true that some of these studies used the nine most discriminating items from the F Scale; such a scale would probably correlate more highly with the whole test than one composed of 15 less carefully selected items.

Fortunately there is something of a gap in the literature between five- and six-item "F Scales" and nine-item "F Scales." For that rather inelegant reason, and in the interest of including any research in this review which has a reasonable bearing on the validity of the original F Scale, studies which used as few as nine original F Scale items in their measures of authoritarianism have been included here...provided those items constituted approximately half of the items in the scale. I have also noted studies I have purposely excluded from the review because of their small number of F Scale items.

I have also arbitrarily limited the number of studies to be reviewed by considering only those involving English-speaking samples. That means studies which used Afrikans, German, Indian, Italian, Japanese, Lebanese, Swedish, Yiddish etc. translations of the F Scale have been excluded. The justification for this is apparent I hope. It is hard enough to know what an attitude item means to a sample without the added complications brought about by translations.

I know that I have surveyed the North American literature on authoritarianism much more comprehensively than that of other English-speaking countries, especially those in the Southern Hemisphere. It is possible then that the conclusions drawn at the end of this chapter will apply less to English, Australian, Union of South African, etc. research than they will to that of the United States and Canada.

4 In fact at a later date Christie (1954) stated that the clusters were named before *The Authoritarian Personality* was published, and that a cluster originally named "Inner Control" should have been labelled "Anti-intraception" instead. One can hardly conclude, however, that this designation was achieved independently by

the two research teams. The change in the title could of course confirm the theoretical model anyway, if the cluster involved were loaded with items originally written to measure anti-intraception. But three of the five items in the cluster ("sex crimes," "no sane person," and "a person with bad manners") were written for other traits, and seem to have little to do with "opposition to the subjective..."

It is a little disturbing that a cluster interpretation reportedly agreed to by so many judges can be changed (on such slim evidence) to conform to the Berkeley model. It simply points out again the ambiguous nature of factor interpretation.

5 Purposely omitted from this review is a paper by O'Neil and Levinson (1954) who performed a centroid analysis of a 32-item pool which contained only eight items from the final version of the F Scale... only six of which were considered "authoritarianism" items, incidentally.

6 A clear example of this philosophy has recently been given by a researcher who happens, coincidentally, to be one of the authors of *TAP.* This time the issue is Fromm-Maccoby's (1970) "Love of Life" Scale. Sanford writes: "This instrument has already been called, by a leading psychologist (Smith, 1971), worse than the F Scale in its methodology, and I agree; but it has demonstrated an extraordinary capacity to predict political behavior — for example, in separating McGovern from Nixon supporters in August 1972 (Comstock and Duckles, 1972). Apparently the only thing it has going for it is the fact that it works." (Sanford, 1974, pp. 168-169).

Given that Nixon and McGovern supporters in 1972 probably differed on everything from religious affiliation to tooth paste preference, including a huge number of social attitudes, the fact that a sample of them differed on the Fromm-Maccoby scale is next to useless if one does not know what the scale is measuring. Such scales really do not work at all.

7 Even there it could be argued that Hitler's rise to power was due far more to his nationalistic appeals and the promise of dynamic autocratic leadership following the difficulties of the Wiemar Republic and the Depression than to the anti-Semitism of the NSDAP.

8 Similar relationships have been found in other student samples: Christie and Garcia (1951) found r's of .56 and .63 in their Berkeley and "Southwest City" samples respectively. Kates and Diab (1955) report a similar correlation of .66 among University of Oklahoma students; Kaufman (1957) found an $r = .53$ between scores on a version of the anti-Semitism Scale and 15 unspecified items from the F Scale among St. Louis undergraduates. Gaier and Bass (1959) reported correlations of .60, .62 and .49 among Kansas, Maryland and Louisiana students respectively. The reliability of this finding does not, however, remove the ambiguity of its meaning.

9 There is some evidence that level of education is related to F Scale scores (and prejudice) among nonstudent samples (*TAP*, chap. 8; Christie, 1954; Pettigrew, 1959). This has led some writers in fact to suggest that the scale essentially measures "Social sophistication" (Christie and Cook, 1958) or "breadth of perspective" (Kelman and Barclay, 1963), variables which are strongly shaped by the individual's educational background.

10 Several other studies, using student samples but also the entire F Scale, have contradicted Pettigrew's (1959) results, however. Christie and Garcia (1951) found that students in "a southern state" scored significantly higher on both the E

and F Scales than did their Berkeley counterparts. Gaier and Bass (1959) reported a similar significant difference on both scales between Louisiana and Kansas students, with Maryland students falling in between. And Wrightsman, Radloff, Horton and Mecherikoff (1961), in a study involving over a thousand social science students in California, Connecticut, Minnesota and Tennessee, found that students at one predominantly white school in Tennessee scored highest on "shortened" forms of both the E and F Scale, while those at another were also high on the E Scale and moderate on the F Scale. These and other results which we shall encounter later suggest that, Pettigrew (1959) notwithstanding, the southern United States in both a "high E" and a "high F" area. Of course the relatively high scores on both scales could be due to cultural or personality factors. But Pettigrew's findings probably do not nail down the case for the former, in the United States, as tightly as is often supposed.

11 Excluded from this review are a number of frequently-cited papers which used very short versions of the F Scale: Flowerman, Stewart, and Strauss (1950) used a five-item F Scale to study adults in Baltimore, and Minneapolis. This scale has been used in the "anomie vs. authoritarianism" controversy as well: Srole (1956), Roberts and Rokeach (1956), McDill (1961), and Lutterman and Middleton (1970). Incidentally only one of the five items on this scale was carried over unaltered from the final version of the F Scale. Also excluded is a study by Katz and Benjamin (1960) which used Webster, Sanford and Freedman's (1955) 114-item Social Maturity Scale as the measure of authoritarianism.

12 In a recent paper Sanford (1974) wrote that "acquiescence response set is a factor in the F Scale" and that "correlations of this instrument with other scales made up of positive items . . . are somewhat higher than they would otherwise be. This state of affairs has not, however, washed out any findings of the original study" (pp. 154-155). It is hard to agree with this assessment however. The case in hand indicates that taking response sets into account washes away all but a trace of the major finding of the original study.

13 Calculations of z-values from the data Phares gives in Table 1, p. 390, of his paper yields only nonsignificant effects for the fathers' ratings however, even by a one-tailed test: $z = 1.44$; $p < .07$.

14 A paper by Bieri and Lobeck (1959) which used only six original F Scale items in its authoritarianism scale has been omitted from this review.

15 An interesting feature of French and Ernest's study was an item analysis which showed that most of the items on the F Scale were poorly correlated, if at all, with Military Ideology, even though summed scores on the scale had a substantial relationship. This relationship was found to depend mainly on 11 of the 30 items (including nearly all of those listed in Table 1 of this chapter.)

16 It might be noted that Aumack (1955), in his previously mentioned study of San Quentin inmates, also found that F Scale scores dropped significantly as the length of incarceration increased among his subjects.

17 The main part of Wright and Harvey's study is also somewhat relevant to our concern here. Students attending class together completed rating scales on five topics (e.g., peers, people in general), and five days later they were berated by their instructor for the ratings they had given on one of the topics (the morality of different professions). They then rated the topics again.

The results of this manipulation were evaluated in sometimes obscure ways, but the authors stated that high F subjects were apt to change their ratings on most of the topics more than others (but not, oddly enough, on the topic whose earlier ratings had just been criticized by an authority figure). It was also stated that high F subjects tended to rate the topics high before being criticized, and even higher afterwards. This was interpreted to mean that high F students did not displace aggression to nonauthority figures following the instructor's attack.

18 Few research programs have demonstrated as completely as Milgram's the great power which situational factors, compared to "personality-based" ones, can have on overt behavior. The F Scale relationship reported by Elms and Milgram was apparently detectable only because subjects from very different situations were being compared, and MMPI scores were unrelated to the compliance-defiance variable even then.

Nevertheless the F Scale finding was obtained, as it was in Epstein's studies. Thus when Larsen, Coleman, Forbes, and Johnson (1972) found no relationship between scores on "personality scales" and behavior in the shocking/learning experiment, it is noteworthy that no measure of authoritarianism was included in their test battery.

19 Elms (1972) also reported administering the F Scale to groups of "rightists" and "liberals" in Dallas. He seems to imply (p. 83) that there was not a significant difference in the sets of scores, but did not formally report the results.

20 A number of frequently-cited public opinion polls have addressed themselves to the relationship between authoritarianism and political behavior: Janowitz and Marvick (1953), Campbell, Gruin, and Miller (1954), Lane (1955) and McKinnon and Centers (1956). Unfortunately all of these potentially valuable studies measured authoritarianism with some version of F. Sanford's (1950) A-E Scale, which contains only one unaltered item from the F Scale. Other studies excluded from this review because they used very short versions of the F Scale are Paul (1956), Levinson (1957), Leventhal, Jacobs and Kudirka (1964) and Nudelman (1972).

21 Doubtless there exist published studies on the F Scale which should have been included in this review but which I did not come across in my search. I doubt very much that their absence materially affects the conclusions about to be reached, but of course I may be wrong. As mentioned before I have intentionally limited the review in terms of the (language background of) the subjects sampled and the version of the F Scale used. But I did not omit any study because I did not "like" the results found or the procedures used, as I hope is obvious to the reader. This also applies to the theories considered in the rest of the chapter as well.

22 Besides the topics we have covered, there are quite a few other areas of F Scale research which would test the endurance of the reader. It was initially thought for example that high F subjects tended to project their attitudes onto others, while low F subjects saw others more accurately (Scodel and Mussen, 1953; Scodel and Freedman, 1956). But subsequent research (Crockett and Meidinger, 1956; Schulberg, 1961) has challenged this conclusion rather convincingly. There is some evidence in the field of attitude change that high F subjects are more likely to shift their opinions upon receiving a persuasive communication from an authority (Wagman, 1955). But a considerable amount of other research contradicts this (Wright and Harvey, 1965; Johnson, Torcivia and Poprick, 1968; Johnson and Izzett, 1969; Johnson and Stanicek, 1969, as well as studies we have

reviewed in different contexts: Berkowitz and Lundy, 1957; Lasky, 1962; Johnson and Steiner, 1967). Catholics have been supposed to score higher on the F Scale than Protestants, but even the best known evidence for this (Rokeach, 1960) is itself only partially supportive.

23 There is at least one researcher who has taken Eysenck's side in the debate. Ray (1973, p. 26) wrote that if one realizes that the T Factor is just a projection on to the attitude level of a personality variable which takes different forms in the case of radicals and conservatives, then "most of the attacks by Eysenck's critics... lose their point. Rather than attack the 'purity' of the T Scale or Eysenck's arithmetic, they might do better to investigate his claim that both 'radical-tough' and 'conservative tough' statements correlate with extraversion."

One can make several responses to this. First of all there is no proof that the T Factor is "just a projection..." The evidence which exists on the point is Eysenck's interpretation of the results of his study, and the fact that the T Scale correlates with the Introversion-Extraversion Scale (but not very highly). "Realizing these things" (which the critics did of course) does not change matters one bit. Secondly, even if T cannot be measured independently of R and if the relationship between T and Introversion were high enough to justify calling one essentially a projection of the other, most of the attacks by Eysenck's critics would not lose their point. It is a gross misrepresentation of the facts to say that they would, as the reader can see by reviewing the debate summarised above. Thirdly it is not the critics' responsibility to investigate Eysenck's theory, and it is not hard for me to guess why they and others have not chosen to. Finally the errors in Eysenck's "arithmetic" converted patently nonsignificant and nonsupportive differences into allegedly significant and supportive ones. If it was petty of the critics to point this out, then why should we even bother to conduct studies? Why not simply decide what conclusions we wish to verify, and then say they are true? Why take the chance that the data might subvert our notions?

24 For a much more positive evaluation of the Dogmatism Scale's literature, see Vacchiano, Strauss, and Hochman, 1969.

25 It is not clear what literature is referred to here. The 'labels' cited of course are prominent in the academic journals which are usually considered the scientific literature.

26 There is quite a bit of confusion between Bagley's (1970) and Wilson's (1970, 1973) accounts of the factor analysis of these data. Bagley says only that a Varimax rotation was performed. Wilson, (1973, p. 82) reproduces some of the loadings Bagley gives (1970, pp. 136-137) for the orthogonal Varimax rotation, but says they were from an oblique Promax rotation.

27 Incidentally, Boshier's factors were not all that intuitive; they were merely "cleaner" than those reported in Bagley et al. (1970) for the unrotated matrices. Nias and Wilson also state that Boshier's unrotated results provide "strong support for Wilson's (1970) original finding that virtually all of the 50 items intercorrelate in the predicted manner to give a general factor of conservatism." As slight as that evidence would be, it should also be noted that Boshier's first unrotated factor controlled all of 14% of the total variance on the test.

28 There is another uncertainty about these 496 subjects. As reported above a subsample of them ($N = 244$) was used to determine the split-half reliability of the C Scale, which was found to be .943. But there is no description of who these 244

subjects were nor how they were selected. Another study by Patterson and Wilson (1939) was based on a sample of 412 Christchurch, New Zealand, adults whose occupational breakdowns were extremely similar to those listed for the 496 Christchurch adults who served in Wilson and Patterson (1968). It may be coincidental, or a repeated design. But if both reports were based on largely the same subjects, it should be noted that the subjects were given the option of signing,initialling, or not signing their test forms, (which would be an unusual step in a standardizing study.) This variable was found to control 18% of the variance in C Scale scores, and could obviously confound subanalyses of the data.

29 Wilson and Brazendale (1973) however found no relationship between C Scale scores and the funniness ratings of 42 risqué cartoons given by 358 teachers college students.

30 Curiously Wilson, Ausman and Mathews (1973) did not include a preference for conventional art as one of the hallmarks of the ideal conservative, as Wilson and Patterson (1968) originally had, saying instead merely that he is "conventional" (p. 286). This modification was extremely short-lived, however. Wilson (1973, p. 8) states that the ideal conservative prefers "the conventional in art, clothing, institutions, etc."

Incidentally, in another study, Patterson (1973) reported evidence that high C subjects did prefer representational paintings and disliked abstract ones. The interpretation was made post hoc, however, among stimuli unscaled along this dimension. (The main purpose of the study actually was to see if conservatives would use fewer dimensions to conceptualize a series of paintings, in line with the hypothesis that they are cognitively simple. There was no such tendency, however.

31 Wilson and Lillie agree that the groups do not differ on four "racial prejudice" and four "art" items (although the latter was not mentioned in Wilson, 1973, p. 125). Nor is it likely moreover that the groups differed significantly on "co-education," "women judges," "chaperones," "straight jackets," "fluoridation," "socialism," "cousin marriage," "conventional clothes," and "student pranks"... although again one cannot say for sure.

32 Only three of these 30 items actually appeared on the California F Scale.

33 The reader whose appetite has only been whetted by this review of the published literature on authoritarianism will find in Hanson (1974) a listing of 533 doctoral dissertations on the subjects of authoritarianism and dogmatism.

CHAPTER 2

1 It should be noted that this is approximately the same thing that Rorer (1965, p. 134) called a response style: "a tendency to select some response category a disproportionate amount of time independently of the item content."

2 This issue is broader than our concern here. The interested reader should consult Block, 1965; Bentler, Jackson and Messick, 1971; Block, 1971; Bentler, Jackson, and Messick, 1972; Block, 1972; Samelson, 1972.

3 I cannot claim to have realized all of this when I started out. The criteria actually emerged during the reversal testing program. Thus the balanced scale reported in Altemeyer (1969) was later rejected because it did not meet the "set criteria" described above.

4 Many of the subjects used in the research reported in this book were drawn from the introductory psychology course at the University of Manitoba, so a few words about this subject pool are in order.

    The course itself is a full-year, six credit-hour course and runs from early September to early April. Its normal (day session) enrollment was about 2,500 in September and about 2,100 in April during the years of this research program. It is the largest enrollment of any course at the univesity. Introductory Psychology is a popular option among students majoring in the Faculties of Arts and Science, and it is a required course among most of the "professional" faculties: e.g., Administrative Studies, Nursing, Physical Education, Social Work. At least 80% of the students in the course are freshmen, and are typically about 18 years old. Women tend to outnumber men. Unless otherwise noted, however, all samples used in the studies reported in this book were composed equally of males and females.

    Beginning in 1969, six or seven percent of the grade in the course could be earned through "research activity." Practically all the students choose to earn these marks by serving as subjects in experiments. Since 1970 sign-up booklets for experiments have been passed out to students in class. The booklets used to sign up subjects for my questionnaire studies were entitled "Survey" or "Questionnaire," and described the study as an investigation of public opinion about social issues. Only Canadian citizens were allowed to sign up for the study.

    A general description of the procedures and instructions used in my survey research is given at the beginning of chapter 4.

5 No reversal was attempted for item #13 of the original F Scale. This item refers indirectly to General George Patton's use of Nazis in the administration of post-war Germany and is seriously out of date.

6 The remaining items were drawn from the Dogmatism Scale, the Lee and Warr scale, and some items of my own. This aspect of the Winter, 1970 studies will be taken up in the next chapter.

7 In an earlier unpublished study I found that responses to negative forms of propositions (e.g., "Marijuana should not be legalized") had significantly lower one-week test-retest reliabilities than positive propositions ("Marijuana should be legalized") in 22 out of 30 comparisons.

8 That is, $[406 - 241 - (142 - 135) - (109 - 87)] \div 406$, or $136 \div 406 = 33\%$. This figure corresponds in general to the difference in variance shared by the F Scale with other unidimensionally-worded tests (correlations of .50 to .75 are common), as compared to balanced tests (where correlations in the .20s and .30s are typical). See Table 2 in chapter 1 for examples.

9 About 20% of the students in my samples end up disagreeing with at least three-fourths of the items on the original F Scale. Some of this disagreement may simply be response generalization by those who happen to disagree with most of the content of the test. There are, by comparison, very few students who agree with a high percentage of the statements on the original scale. I believe this is the reason why I found, in almost all my reversal development studies, that original items received higher scores on a balanced scale than they did on the original scale. Subjects did not find themselves disagreeing with a solid majority of the items on a balanced scale. But the effect is very small, and only occasionally statistically significant.

10 I can see the irony in the fact that I have spent far more time trying to write good F Scale reversals than I have spent trying to write good exam questions for the students in my classes.

11 See Altemeyer (1970) for evidence that the adverbs used to define this response scale give the scale interval properties.

12 I also ran two other laboratory studies on "authoritarian" behavior with subjects from the winter, 1970, experiment: the replication of Harvey and Rutherford's autokinetic suggestion study mentioned in chapter 1; and a replication of Deutsch's (1960) study of suspicion and trustworthiness in the Prisoner's Dilemma. Neither version of the F Scale had significant relationships with any of the behavior in these two studies, however.

CHAPTER 3

1 The eighteen items selected from the Dogmatism Scale were those which had the highest item-whole correlations in a previous administration of the test at the University of Manitoba. They were nos. 6, 9, 12, 13, 21, 26, 37 38, 39, 42, 47, 48, 50, 51, 53, 54, 55, and 63 from Forms D and E in Rokeach (1960).

Three other items from the Lee and Warr scale also appeared on the F Scale, so altogether 25 of the 30 Lee and Warr items were included in the questionnaire. The five ommitted items were nos. 5, 17, 20, 24, and 25 from Table 1 in Lee and Warr (1969). Most of these were "quasi-F Scale" items already included in the survey in different form.

The six TFI Scale items were nos. 20, 22, 31, and 57 from Table 1 in Levinson and Huffman (1955), and nos. 39 and 52 from Table 1 in O'Neil and Levinson (1954). Versions of three other TFI items (nos. 21 and 34 in Levinson and Huffman, 1955, and no. 63 in O'Neil and Levinson, 1954) also appeared on the Lee and Warr scale.

2 Subjects who served in my survey studies were usually involved afterwards in additional experiments drawn from the "authoritarianism" literature. Thus subjects from the June, 1971, study served in another run of the bogus verbal learning-aggression study described in chapter 2, a "father-perception" study patterned after Koutrelakis (1968), and they gave person-perception ratings of a hippie confederate. The results of these studies are irrelevant to our purpose here, however, which concerns the pattern of covariation found among responses to survey items.

3 As before, the items in Table 3 which did not "make the cut" to Table 4 did not do all that badly; they just were not in the top 10. But two of the new items ("in the long run" and "youngsters should be encouraged") and part of a third ("such things as flags") definitely seemed to reflect ethnocentrism.

4 The ethnocentrism items tested seemed to be measuring something in common; items 8, 30, 32, and 61 (see Questionnaire VII in Appendix I) for example had a mean interitem correlation of .24. But their mean correlation with the items in Table 7 (i.e., the RWA Scale) was only .12—not nearly good enough to become part of the scale or to justify considering ethnocentrism a component of right-wing authoritarianism.

5 Twenty-four items were used to make up the scale because there were twelve reasonably adequate contrait items available. A scale composed of the best twenty

items, as the mock scales were, would have had a mean interitem correlation of .25 and an alpha coefficient of .87.

6 Someone once called the RWA Scale "the son of the son of the F Scale." It is more accurate to say that the concept of authoritarianism measured by the test originated in observations of what covaried, and what did not, on the F Scale. This observation had to be tested and confirmed many times before it was trusted however. Similarly while the Berkeley theory lists "authoritarian submission," "authoritarian aggression," and "conventionalism" among the traits of the authoritarian personality, there are significant differences in the definitions of these terms in the two models. For example, "authoritarian aggression" in the Berkeley model was only directed at unconventional persons, whereas in my definition the focus is not on the victims, but the reason for the aggression. (I would say that soldiers who obeyed orders to open fire on a Rotary picnic were showing "authoritarian aggression," but the Berkeley model would not.) And of course none of the rest of the Berkeley model ("anti-intraception," "stereotypy," etc.) is included in the present model.

I do not believe that I, at least, would ever have stumbled onto this conceptualization had it not been for the Berkeley research and the F Scale. But the RWA Scale, and the conceptualization it represents, is too different from the F Scale to call them father and son. Nor is the RWA Scale "another F Scale."

CHAPTER 4

1 The specific exception of Rokeach's concept of dogmatism is noted. The D Scale was included in this study because of its occasional use as a measure of right-wing authoritarianism, even though Rokeach advanced it as a measure of "general authoritarianism."

2 Students from the other six sections of the course had served in the September, 1973 study described at the end of chapter 3. See footnote 4 in chapter 2 for a description of the introductory psychology course at the University of Manitoba, and the students who enroll in it.

3 Statements enclosed in brackets were also before the subject on either the questionnaire booklet, or on a custom-made IBM response card which was entitled "North American Survey Research Associates—New York-Toronto." This card contained −3 to +3 "bubbles" for up to 35 items.

4 It was necessary to place items 36-40 of the Dogmatism Scale at the end of the original F Scale to fit responses to all of its items on the IBM response card.

5 As we shall see in chapter 5, interitem correlations on a balanced test rise with education, and about a third of Lee and Warr's standardizing sample were graduate students or Peace Corps volunteers. As well, Princeton undergraduates probably have higher reading aptitudes than Manitoba students.

6 I initially used the SPSS "principal factor" program "PA2" (Nie, Bent, and Hull, 1970), but discovered that this program inserts 1.0s as the communality estimates when it initially extracts the factors. That is, it essentially performs a principal components analysis at this stage of its operation. The intended estimates of the communalities are only used after the number of factors had been determined, and not surprisingly many of the retained factors have eigenvalues less than 1.0.

The SPSS results ascribed more factors to each test than did the Biomedical

Statistical Package program which produced the results in Table 2, as would a straightforward principal components analysis. But the relative performance of the scales was essentially the same.

7 That is, so long as the last-extracted factor could account for at least $1/n$th of the test's variance, where "n" equals the number of items on the test. This will often produce factors of trivial importance, but they can be discarded following inspection of the factor matrix.

8 I wish to thank Professor Marion Aftanas of the University of Manitoba for making this program available.

9 As was noted several times in chapter 1, the fact that the first unrotated factor controls more variance than any of the others is not evidence that the test is unidimensional. This first factor is mathematically defined to maximize variance accounted for, and will always be the largest factor in an unrotated matrix on any test.

10 Again, this analysis produced fewer factors for the C Scale, and the F and D Scales as well, than one usually encounters in their literatures because most of the earlier studies have used principal components analyses.

11 Factor analysis sleuths can deduce that the eigenvalue of Factor II in the unrotated matrix was 0.91: 15.8% + 11.3% − 23.3% = 3.8% additional variance explained by Factor II; .038 x 24 (items in the scale) = 0.91. As will be seen later, it is not unusual to obtain two direction-of-wording factors on the RWA Scale. The small amount of explained variance added by the second factor, and the high correlation between the two factors in Promax rotations does not essentially change the conclusions reached above, however. The RWA Scale is relatively unidimensional, as authoritarianism scales go.

12 The four cases were taken from a set of five which were first tested in the September 1973, study. The fifth case, involving a suspect illegally detained for more than 24 hours by police without charges being laid against him, was not used in the subsequent research because the variance of responses to it was much smaller than that in the other four cases.

13 The one-week test-retest reliability of this measure, established in November, 1973, with another 103 subjects, was .82. The low reliability of the measure, caused mainly by the small number of government injustices cases used, reduced somewhat the experiment's ability to detect differences in the validity of the authoritarianism scales being pitted, to the detriment of the superior scales.

14 For readers unfamiliar with Kohlberg's system, Type I morality is based upon avoidance of punishment and unquestioning deference to authority. Type II reasoning ("Naive instrumental hedonism") is strongly influenced by the personal consequences of acting. Right action is that which satisfies the actor's needs. Type III reasoning is governed by primitive social considerations. Acts which bring approval, that make one "nice" are moral. Type IV reasoning is based upon more abstract social considerations. Persons are envisioned to have social obligations to one another, and moral behavior requires doing one's duty toward others. Type V morality acknowledges individual differences in values, and emphasizes using procedures to reach an acceptable social contract. Laws are not considered written in stone, and should be changed to improve society. Type VI moral reasoning is based upon self-determined, universal ethical principles.

15 These cases were selected from four pretested in the September, 1973, study. The

fourth case, involving a forbidden personal phone call from work, was discarded because nearly everyone said he would make the call, as it was a small matter.

16 The interjudge reliability of these scores was estimated by having two judges (W. Josephson and T. Fullerton, both Ph.D. students the author was supervising) independently score the 103 Session I test-retest protocols according to the descriptions of the stages given above, supplemented by scoring rules given in Appendix III. W.J.'s scorings were 93% in agreement with mine, and T.F.'s 90%. The agreement between the other two judges was 89%. Overall there was unanimous agreement on 89/103 or 86% of the protocols. The "high" level of interjudge reliability was largely attributable to the fact that 3/6ths of the scores (i.e., the checklist responses) on each case were unambiguous. Of the 103 subjects tested in the November, 1973 reliability study, 45 were identified as being a certain definite type. The responses given a week later placed 38 of these 45 (84%) in the same category. Of the 58 subjects who were originally scored as "mixed" types, 48 of them (83%) were again considered mixed upon retesting. Overall 86 of the 103 subjects received the same rating twice.

17 By way of comparison, Kohlberg's scoring system, which also is unable to classify large numbers of subjects, usually finds most college students are Types III, IV or V, with very few Types I, II and VI's (Haan, Smith and Block, 1968). The difference reminds us that the analysis above is not comparable to a "Kohlberg analysis"—but that such an analysis would probably be of little value in an experiment pitting authoritarianism scales.

18 These four cases were pretested in the September, 1973, study to determine if responses to each of them varied enough to use them as criteria in this pitting study. They did in each case.

19 The mean intercorrelation among Trials 1, 2 and 4 was .31, giving the summed score over the three cases an alpha reliability of .57. The one-week test-retest reliability of this summed score was .78. Again, the low reliability of the criterion measure, due mainly to the small number of cases being used, somewhat handicaps the experiment's ability to pit the scales against one another, to the detriment of the more valid scales.

20 I would like to thank Mr. Ted Palys for doing the interviewing in this study.

The difficulties involved in running the "mock learning" aggression study have grown steadily as knowledge of Milgram's research has become more widespread in our culture. Some of the subjects dropped indicated they had never heard of the Milgram research or other related experiments, but most of them said they had learned of the obedience studies in one way or another. Some had read articles in *Psychology Today, Esquire,* or magazine reviews of Milgram (1974). Some of the subjects had seen the Milgram film in introductory sociology or political science courses; one fellow reported seeing the film in high school in rural Manitoba. Also one of the Canadian TV networks carried a "latest psychological research" program the Sunday night before we began our study which carried a segment on Milgram's studies of obedience. Then one of my colleagues volunteered to appear on a Winnipeg open-line radio show to discuss the Milgram research while we were running our experiment.

Kelman (1967) has commented eloquently upon the natural conflict that exists between deception research and the scientist's public responsibility to disseminate his findings. If ever there was a research program that I would have everyone learn about, it is Milgram's. But the increased attention which his studies have received made it rather difficult to study authoritarianism and aggression in the shocking experiment format in the mid 1970s.

21 The one-week test-retest reliability of this item was .89.

22 It should be noted that the balanced F Scale's relationshp with the six criteria were at least as strong as the original F Scale's, despite its items being less reliable as a whole. This confirms the conclusion reached in chapter 2 that the variance contributed to original F Scale scores by response sets is, on balance, "noise."

23 I would like to express my appreciation to Professors Ralphe Kolstoe and Paul Wright at the University of North Dakota, Professors T. Nelson and Alan Dobbs, and Beverly Davidson at the University of Alberta, and Professors W.J. McClelland and Douglas Jackson, and Linda Marland at the University of Western Ontario for their kind assistance in collecting these data. They provided access to their subject pools when a dozen other departments in Canada and the United States had to say no, and they did their very best to give me the best possible testing conditions under the circumstances at each site. I would also like to thank Tim Fullerton for assisting in the collection of the Winnipeg adult data.

24 Level of education correlated .34 with sentencing in the Trials measure. +.28 with tolerance of Government Injustices, and .22 with continued religious acceptance. There was no significant relationship with political party affiliation (and the tendency was for Conservatives to be better educated, contrary to the direction needed for education to control some of the relationship between authoritarianism and political affiliation.)

25 Sarason, Smith and Diener (1975) performed a telling analysis of the variance accounted for in nearly 600 statistical analyses found in the 1972 volumes of the *Journal of Personality and Social Psychology*, the *Journal of Personality*, and the *Journal of Consulting and Clinical Psychology*. The median amount of variance accounted for by "personality" factors in these studies was 3%, by situational factors less than 5%, and by demographic factors 1%. Accounting for even 9% of the variance was a "good show."

26 RWA Scale correlations with religious acceptance, which ranged from .33 to .39 in these pitting studies, have risen to .41 to .55 with later versions of the scale.

CHAPTER 5

1 I would like to express my appreciation to Professor I.J. Salzman. Paula Kaiser and Harriet Rairdon at the University of Indiana, Professors J. Deese and M. Hethrington, and John Miscione at the University of Virginia, Professor D. Runcie and Terry Thomason at the University of Alabama, and Professor M. Noble and Sandra Brook at Penn State, who so kindly arranged my access to their subject pools. Professor Hugh McGinley was kind enough to collect the Wyoming data for me.

2 Over the years I have taken pains to keep knowledge of my research program from the Manitoba populations sampled. For example, feedback to students about the results of my experiments has continued the cover story that the investigations were "broad public opinion polls." Information about a few specific items has been given, and discussions of social desirability and response set effects

have been included, but the concept of authoritarianism has never been mentioned. (Anyone who asked for more complete feedback has always been told whatever he wanted to know; I have never received more than two such requests in a year, however.)

   Similarly there have been no newspaper stories, radio phone-in show appearances, speeches to groups, or any media interviews concerning my research. So far as I have been able to determine, there has been no prior knowledge of this ongoing research program in the populations tested — up to now at least.

3 I have tried several times to obtain funding for nation-wide surveys of authoritarianism and its covariates among representative samples of American and Canadian adults, but without success. A 1975 application to NIMH, reporting the data the reader has already encountered, was denied because assessors doubted that the trait of authoritarianism was a viable scientific concept. A later application to the Canada Council was turned down because there were no pilot data indicating that the surveys could be successfully administered in the context of a Gallup Poll. A subsequent request for pilot testing funds was then rejected because those assessors could see no justification for the large study which might follow.

   The reader who wishes he could see some RWA Scale data from a reasonably representative sample of Canadians or Americans, instead of all these obviously unrepresentative samples, may be assured his frustration is second to mine.

4 In all of my studies the test began with a few "warm-up items" which were usually candidates for future versions of the scale. The contemporaneous version of the test then followed without interruption; e.g., item 1 on the test was usually item 9 in the booklet. Incidentally new items were not incorporated into the scale until they had demonstrated sufficiently high interitem correlations in two successive studies.

5 Because of limited space on the IBM response cards used in the American studies, subjects' interest in politics was not assessed.

6 Comparison with data collected in 1970 (see Table 8 of chapter 2) will reveal the 1973-1979 shift is part of a longer trend. In 1970 the NDP and Liberal parties were the most popular among students, with the Conservatives a distant third. By 1973 the Liberals had pulled way ahead of the other two. By 1979 the Conservatives were by far the most popular. It will be interesting to see if the swing to the right crested in 1979, and now the "wave" will begin rolling back toward the left.

7 The low-scoring students did not become Independents; only 10% of the 1979 students said they were Independents, compared with 26% of the 1973 sample. Rather, as we shall see at the end of this chapter, very low-scoring students were simply a vanishing species by the late 1970s.

8 One also notes the large difference in the sharpness of the images in the minds of these subjects. The variance of the role-played NDP scores is significantly larger than that of the "Liberals," while the Conservative's variance is significantly smaller than either. The sharper image of the Conservatives may be due to their having been in power in the fall of 1979, and consequently having more definitive positions on various issues; or it may be due to the fact that there were more Conservatives in the sample than Liberals or New Democrats.

9 By the time subjects answered these surveys, Richard Nixon had resigned and

accepted a full pardon for all crimes committed while he was President. The conspiracy trial of R. Haldeman, J. Erlichman, J. Mitchell, etc. had not yet begun, however.

10 There was a significant but weak tendency for Republican students to stick with Mr. Nixon longer than Democrats did. The point-biserial correlation between party preference and latency of suspicion for example was .26, which was significantly lower than the .51 RWA Scale correlation. Personal authoritarianism was thus a more powerful covariate of trusting the President than party preference, though the latter may have been a bigger factor among subjects with a keen interest in politics.

11 Approximately half of the students in my own introductory psychology classes, and their parents, were given booklets containing the 10 GI cases. The other students, and their parents, responded to 10 "Trials" cases discussed in the next section.

The ten cases involved: (1) illegal wiretaps of FLQ sympathizers and Edmund Burke Society members; (2) denial of the right of assembly to a radical protest group; (3) customs office harassment of a neo-Nazi gorup; (4) a police burglary of the offices of a left-wing newspaper in Montreal; (5) illegal drug raids; (6) placing "agents provocateurs" in a right-wing group; (7) immigration department discrimination against a radical leftist group; (8) police harassment of a radical right-wing group; (9) illegal opening of mail from Communist and Fascist countries; and (10) deportation of radical activist immigrants.

12 The largest of these differences involved a "mirror image" case of unfair election practices which manipulated the political stance of both the victim and the government. Half of the 1978 sample was told that during a Canadian provincial election an NDP government had discretely threatened corporations with tax investigations if they contributed to the Conservative campaign. The other subjects were told a Progressive Conservative government had similarly threatened labor unions with pension fund investigations if they contributed to the NDP cause. RWA Scale scores correlated $-.05$ with indignation over the former case, and .30 with the latter being significantly larger than the former ($t = 3.05$, $p < .0001$).

An ANOVA of the students' reactions according to story Version and subjects' Authoritarianism (high and low quarters of the RWA Scale distribution) found a significant main effect for the latter ($F = 13.3$, $df = 1$, 301, $p < .001$) and a significant interaction effect ($F = 5.82$, $df = 1$, 301, $p < .02$). The latter was caused by differing reactions of the High Authoritarians to the two cases; they were not very upset about a PC government putting the screws to the NDP ($\bar{X} = 2.35$), but they were significantly more indignant about the NDP doing likewise to the PC's ($\bar{X} = 2.84$, $t = 2.43$, $p < .01$). Low Authoritarians on the other hand were more highly indignant about either party taking unfair advantage of a position of power in an election, and equally so (means $= 3.21$ and 3.02 respectively, $t = 1.01$).

13 This case was written to parallel the pertinent facts in the trial of Lt. William Calley for his part in the massacre at My Lai.

14 The ten cases involved, besides the (1) juvenile delinquent, (2) political agitator and (3) bank robber mentioned above, were (4) a small-time heroin pusher; (5) a "Hell's Angel" convicted of armed robbery; (6) a hippie panhandler convicted of assaulting an accountant; (7) a man who spit at a provincial premier; (8) the owner of several "massage parlors" (9) a child molester; and (10) an "ex-con" who assaulted a police chief.

15 Correlations with the sentences imposed in each case were: "how serious" = .44; "how sorry" = .13; "how bad" = .39; "how much good" = .21; and "how good would it feel" = .42.

16 The items comprising this scale were: (1) There are entirely too many Chinese students being allowed to attend university in Canada; (2) Canadians are not any better than all the rest of the people in the world; (3) The main reason certain groups like our native Indians end up in slums is because of prejudice on the part of the white people; (4) There are far too many Jews in positions of power in our country; (5) Every person we let into our country from overseas means either another Canadian won't be able to find a job, or another foreigner will go on welfare here; (6) Canada should open its doors to more immigration from the West Indies; (7) Certain races of people clearly do not have the natural intelligence and "get up and go" of the white race; (8) The Filipinos and other Asians who have recently moved to Canada have proven themselves to be industrious citizens, and many more should be invited in; (9) It's good to live in a country where there are so many minority groups present, like the Indians, Chinese and Blacks; (10) There are entirely too many people from the wrong sorts of places being admitted into Canada now; (11) Black people as a rule are, by their nature, more violent than white people; (12) The persecution which Jews have endured over the centuries has been the result of prejudice and false stereotypes, and has been totally undeserved; (13) As a group Indians and Metis are naturally lazy, promiscuous and irresponsible; and (14) Canada should open its doors to more immigration from India and Africa.

17 Interpretations of results obtained with "proper name" prejudice scales must be sensitive to the role that social desirability motivations might have played. It will be shown later, however, that the RWA Scale appears to be relatively unaffected by such effects, and thus its correlations with the prejudice scores are unlikely to have arisen to any great extent from a mutually shared social desirability factor.

The difference in RWA-prejudice correlations between students and parents is only partly due to the greater reliability of the scales among the latter. Raising the prejudice scale's alpha to .85 for example would only have raised the RWA Scale's correlation to .29.

18 The 24 items are as follows: (1) God exists as Father, Son, and Holy Spirit; (2) Man is *not* a special creature made in the image of God; he is simply a recent development in the process of animal evolution; (3) Jesus Christ was the divine Son of God; (4) The Bible is the word of God given to guide man to grace and salvation; (5) Those who feel that God answers prayers are just deceiving themselves; (6) It is ridiculous to believe that Jesus Christ could be both human and divine; (7) Jesus was born of a virgin; (8) The Bible may be an important book of moral teachings, but it was no more inspired by God than were many other books in the history of Man; (9) The concept of God is an old superstition that is no longer needed to explain things in the modern era; (10) Christ will return to the earth someday; (11) Most of the religions in the world have miracle stories in their traditions, but there is no reason to believe any of them are true, including those found in the Bible; (12) God hears all of our prayers; (13) Jesus Christ may have been a great ethical teacher, as other men have been in history. But he was not the divine Son of God; (14) God made man of dust in His own image and breathed

life into him; (15) Through the life, death, and resurrection of Jesus. God provided a way for the forgiveness of man's sins; (16) Despite what many people believe, there is no such thing as a God who is aware of Man's actions; (17) Jesus was crucified, died, and was buried but on the third day He arose from the dead; (18) In all likelihood there is no such thing as a God-given immortal soul in Man which lives on after death; (19) If there ever was such a person as Jesus of Nazareth, he is dead now and will never walk the earth again; (20) Jesus miraculously changed real water into real wine; (21) There is a God who is concerned with everyone's actions; (22) Jesus' death on the cross, if it actually occurred, did nothing in and of itself to save Mankind; (23) There is really no reason to hold to the idea that Jesus was born of a virgin. Jesus' life showed better than anything else that he was exceptional, so why rely on old myths that don't make sense; and (24) The Resurrection proves beyond a doubt that Jesus was the Christ or Messiah of God.

19 There have been consistent differences in RWA Scale scores among Protestant denominations in the Manitoba samples over the years. Anglicans and United Church members tend to score lowest, then Lutherans, then Mennonites and finally "Fundamentalists" (e.g., Baptists, Jehovah's Witnesses, Pentecostals). The range of scores in the 1979 student study was 119.2 for the Anglicans, to 146.7 for the Fundamentalists, with the overall $F = 12.9 \, (\hat{\eta}^2 = 14\%)$. Mennonites and Fundamentalists were significantly more authoritarian than Anglicans, United Church members or Lutherans.

There was no such difference among Protestant sects in the American student sample however, with scores (on the 24-item test) ranging from 99.7 for Episcopalians to 107.7 among the Fundamentalists. Presbyterians, Methodists and Lutherans scored in between. ($F = 1.7$, ns.)

20 There have usually been no significant differences between the RWA Scale scores of persons raised in no religion, and persons raised in a religion they later abandoned. Both groups score low on the test.

21 Thus for example in the 1974 American study the correlations were: Jews = .56; Catholics = .46; Episcopalians = .39; Presbyterians = .58; Methodists = .49; Lutherans = .61; and Fundamentalists = .67. In the 1979 Manitoba study the figures were: Jews = .33; Catholics = .52; Anglicans = .51; United Church = .28; Lutherans = .36; Mennonites = .40; and Fundamentalists = .61.

22 Level of education correlated as follows in this sample: with RWA Scale scores, −.24; with the Government Injustices measure, .12; with Trials sentences, −.22. As noted earlier the differences in educational attainment among supporters of the political parties (NDP being less educated) is in the wrong direction to explain any of the relationship between authoritarianism and party preference. Also, the reader will recall, there was no measure of parents' religiosity.

23 In a study conducted in the fall of 1980, as this book was going to press, the Wonderlic Intelligence Test was administered to 185 University of Manitoba introductory psychology students immediately after they had completed the RWA Scale. The raw scores on the 50-item test ranged from 11 to 40, with a mean of 28.4, and a standard deviation of 5.4. The correlation with RWA Scale scores was −.08 ($p < .20$; the correlation was .10 when corrected for attenuation). Thus the possibility that RWA Scale findings in this population have been appreciably mediated by mutual relationships with "general intelligence" appears to be remote.

24 The exact instructions were, "Make as socially pleasing a picture of yourself

as possible. Make yourself look good. Give what you think are, in general, socially desirable answers," or, "Make as socially *un*attractive a picture of yourself as possible. Make yourself look bad. Give what you think are, in general, socially *un*desirable answers."

25   This result was replicated in another Manitoba student study conducted in 1975. In both the 1974 and 1975 experiments, the internal consistency of responses to the RWA Scale increased as subjects' anonymity decreased: from .82 to .87 to .88 in 1974, and from .85 to .88 to .90 in 1975. In both studies the overall differences in alpha levels were statistically significant beyond the .02 level, with M = 8.4 and 7.9 respectively (Hakstian and Whalen, 1976). My interpretation of these results is that students are more careful answering surveys when their names are associated with their responses.

Finally in the same 1974 study the effects of booklet position on responses to the RWA Scale was investigated. For 124 subjects the scale appeared in its customary place at the beginning of the booklet; another 140 subjects encountered the test in the middle of the booklet, following some irrelevant "filler" material. For another 144 subjects the scale appeared at the end of a "filler booklet." The mean scale scores of 95.7, 97.3 and 95.3 were not significantly different, but the test's respective alpha coefficients of .83, .87 and .88 were (M = 7.4; $p < .025$). I suspect this result arises from a "warm up" factor involving familiarity with the survey format and response scale.

26   These results were replicated in the fall, 1980 study, where the alpha coefficient of the RWA Scale rose from .86 at the first testing session to .89 at the second ($N = 505$; W = 1.31, $p < .001$). (There was no "special instructions" condition in this study.) The correlation between the length of the item and the amount of change in responses to it was .46.

27   Thus the following item, borne of this analysis, was tested in the fall, 1980, study: "One of the best ways to keep your own self pure and good is to rebuke, condemn and help punish those who do wrong." Its correlation of .44 with the rest of the RWA Scale was nearly high enough to make it part of the test.

28   In the fall, 1980, experiments 480 Manitoba students were asked to react to policies enacted by a hypothetical future Canadian government. For half of these subjects the policies were radical right-wing (e.g. reversing efforts to redistribute personal wealth, getting the government out of the oil industry, increasing defense spending, reintroducing capital punishment, "getting tough" with Quebec, cracking down on homosexuals, marijuana, and the prison system.) The other subjects responded to an hypothetical left-wing government which introduced quite opposite legislation.

Most subjects disliked whichever of these radical governments they evaluated. When asked how they would react to such a program, only 14 endorsed whatever policies were involved. The other subjects said (on a checklist) they either would reluctantly obey such laws (because "laws are laws," for fear of being punished, or with hatred for the government) or would challenge the laws (through passive resistance, civil disobedience, or by fighting the government's continuation in power.)

High RWA subjects were significantly more likely to accept either kind of radical government than were low RWA subjects, who in fact were usually inclined to challenge either government. The most interesting comparison involves High

RWA students' reactions to a left-wing government (36 of 54 said they would obey its laws, however grudgingly), while 32 of 50 Low RWA subjects said they would challenge a right-wing government ($X^2 = 9.8$, $p < .005$, $\emptyset = .31$).

29 One line of evidence suggests that authoritarians are no more nor less honest than nonauthoritarians. In January of 1978 I gave my introductory psychology students each a "feedback sheet" listing the marks recorded in my grade book for their tests in the first term. I asked the students to check my figures while in class, especially the sum of their scores, since that was the number which would determine their grade. I had, however, purposely given every sixth peson an extra two points (i.e. 2%) through an "adding error." This mistake could conceivably change a C to a C+, a C+ to a B, etc.

Only four of the 58 students who received this bonus reported the mistake to me. Believing that 2% might be too big a gift to turn down, I repeated the experiment the following year, but only made 1% errors. The results however were the same. There was not even a hint of an RWA Scale relationship in either study.

The fact that authoritarians were as likely as everyone else to take their points and run is not necessarily a nonfinding. Since High RWA subjects tend to think they are more moral than others, their immorality may have intrapsychic consequences which less self-righteous persons do not have to wrestle with.

Similarly in the fall, 1980 study students who had completed the RWA Scale were also asked to complete an anonymous sexual activity scale. Responses were received from 80% of 225 females and 84% of 255 males. Nonresponding females scored significantly higher on the RWA Scale than did respondents (means of 137 versus 113, $p < .001$); the figures for males were also significant by a one-tailed test (126 versus 118, $p < .04$). Among respondents, there were weak but statistically significant relationships between reported sexual behavior and RWA Scale scores. For example, the point biserial correlations with virginity among unmarried students were .34 for females and .15 for males. It is entirely possible that data from the nonresponding subjects would have raised these correlations somewhat, but as a group authoritarians are by no means "without sin" (in their own eyes), though they do tend to cast the first stones.

CHAPTER 6

1 The samples and procedures used in these studies are reported in chapters 4 and 5.

2 This age range was a compromise between desires to have accurate childhood memories, and still collect data on such childhood experiences as receiving spankings. A study in 1978 (using students from other sections of introductory psychology than my own) found that the internal consistency and RWA Scale correlations of recollections of the seven to nine age range were a little (but not significantly) higher than those for the ages four to six or 10–12.

3 The surveys were unnamed in the questionnaire booklet.

4 Parental RWA Scale scores were significantly correlated with their reports of their anger over sexual misadventures by their children (items 7, 10, 20, and 23 in Table 1), disobedience (items 8, 9, 21, and 22), and disrespect (items 12, 16, and 24). But authoritarian parents were not particularly likely to become angered by the ruining of a toy, stealing from the parent, hitting a younger child, being lied to, leaving a mess, starting a fight at school, or stealing from another child.

Authoritarian parents thus do not appear to be, in general, angry parents nor do they seem, in general, morally restrictive. They just get relatively angry about the same things that, on the RWA Scale, make them relatively authoritarian: sexual "immorality" and disobedience of authority. If their children later on turn out also to disapprove of sexual "immorality" and disobeying established authorities, the simplest explanation is that they acquired these attitudes from their parents' techings, including punishments. There's no need for the parents to have been cold, distant, generally brutal, and so on.

5 It is entirely possible that students' RWA Scale scores correlate as highly as they do with reports of their perceived partents' wishes because the latter are projections of their own attitudes. To test this possibility I asked a sample of 586 students (none of whom, so far as I knew, had ever seen me before) in 1977 to complete the RWA Scale for themselves, and then as they perceived their fathers, their mothers, and I (the experimenter) would want them to answer the test. "My" mean score (111.2) was nearly identical to the students' own mean (110.2), and far below the mean of the perceived fathers' wishes (147.0) and mothers' (142.2). Perceptions of my wishes correlated .36 with the students' own RWA Scale scores, but only .12 with perceptions of both fathers' and mothers' wishes (t = 5.98, $p < .0001$).

Since I was a complete stranger to the subjects, analagous to the semi-structured stimulus of a TAT card, perceptions of my wishes would appear to be far more susceptible to projection. If the students were also projecting their own attitudes onto their parents' wishes, the correlation between the two sets of perceptions should be much higher than .12.

6 Theoretically we would expect high RWA students to be somewhat closer to their perceived parents' wishes than low RWA students.. This has consistently proven true. Students' RWA Scale scores have correlated about −.50 with the difference between their perceived parents' wishes and their own scores. One should note however that the coefficient has been inflated by using the same data (students' RWA Scale scores) in both parts of the calculation.

7 The scale asked respondents to indicate, on a 0 to +4 scale, the extent to which each parent had emphasized the following while the child was growing up: (1) going to church: attending religious services at church, synagogue or temple; (2) attending "Sunday school": getting systematic religious instruction regularly; (3) reviewing the teachings of the religion at home; (4) praying before meals; (5) reading scripture or other religious material; (6) praying before bedtime; (7) discussing moral "do's" and "don'ts" in religious terms; (8) observing religious holidays; celebrating events like Christmas in a religious way; (9) being a good representative of the faith: acting the way a devout member of your religion would be expected to act; and (10) taking part in religious youth groups.

8 The items which were not significantly related to reports of parental emphasis were nos. 1, 6, 9, 11, 12, 14, 15, 17, 19, 24, and 29 in Table 1 of chapter Five.

9 As the results are correlational, my statements of causality may be challenged. While not wishing to deny that children shape their parents' attitudes to some extent, I do believe that parents have much greater effects on their offspring. Similarly, while the correlation may be due to some "third factor," most of the third factors I can think of (e.g., being raised in the same religion) would operate through the parents.

10 In the fall, 1980, study 494 Manitoba students role-played their responses to the RWA Scale in the year 2000 under one of three conditions: (a) (control) Canada's internal and external situation was essentially the same as today's; (b) Canada faced a grave threat from the Soviet Union over arctic oil resources; (c) Canada was experiencing internal "leftist" strife because of economic hard times. RWA Scale scores in the control group ($\bar{X} = 136.0$) were significantly higher than the subjects' own "1980" scores (121.8). Scores among the "external threat" subjects were not significantly higher than the Controls' ($\bar{X} = 141.8$, $t = 1.87$, $p < .06$). But the mean RWA Scale score in the "internal crisis" condition (151.3) was significantly higher than either of the others.

The last result was due to a rise in scores on 25 of the 30 items on the test, only 15 of which were significantly higher than the Controls' (viz. Items 1, 2, 3, 6, 9, 11, 14, 15, 17, 21, 24, 26, 27, 28, and 30 in Table 1 of chapter 5). Most of these items deal with supporting established authorities and suppressing dissent, as one might expect.

Like all role-played data, these are open to various interpretations. The subjects may well not know how they would react in such situations. But the direction of their error may be to underestimate how authoritarian they would become. The control subjects, for example, "predict" that they will be more authoritarian when they are approximately their parents' contemporaneous age; but they only predict about 60% of the difference actually found between students and their parents in previous studies.

In any event, the data do suggest that authoritarianism levels in a society can be appreciably increased by certain events. Internal strife attributed to leftist movements may drive a population to the right. Foreign threats may have a similar, but weaker effect.

EPILOG

1 When subjects pushed Big Red nothing happened; i.e., the confederate in the next room did not leap out of his chair. The experimenter inspected the shocking mechanism and announced that a high voltage connection had broken. The subject was dehoaxed in a matter of minutes afterwards.

2 These recruits were not selected in any way, except they were the survivors of a group originally twice as large who entered basic training some months earlier.

3 In a similar vein, Kelman and Lawrence (1972) found that 51% of a representative sample of American adults said that, if they had been in the My Lai situation, they too would have shot old men, women, and children. Only 33% of the sample said that they would not have done so.

References

Adorno, T.W. Democratic leadership and mass manipulation, In A.W. Gouldner (Ed.), *Studies in leadership*. New York: Harper, 1950.

Adorno, T.W., Frenkel-Brunswik, E., Levinson, D.J., & Sanford, R.N. *The authoritarian personality*. New York: Harper, 1950.

Alker, H.A. Is personality situationally specific or intrapsychically consistent? *Journal of Personality*, 1972, *40*, 1-16.

Altemeyer, R.A. Balancing the F Scale. *Proceedings of the 77th Annual Convention of the American Psychological Association*, 1969, *4*, 417-418.

Altemeyer, R.A. Adverbs and intervals: A study of "Likert scales." *Proceedings of the 78th Annual Convention of the American Psychological Association*, 1970, *5*, 397-398.

Altemeyer, R.A. Subject Pool pollution and the postexperimental interview. *Journal of Experimental Research in Personality*, 1971, *5*, 79-84.

Asch, S.E. Studies of independence and conformity: A minority of one against a unanimous majority. *Psychological Monographs*, 1956, *70*, No. 9 (Whole No. 416).

Aumack, L. The effects of imprisonment upon authoritarian attitudes. *American Psychologist*, 1955, *10*, 342.

Bagley, C. Racial prejudice and the "conservative" personality: A British sample. *Political Studies*, 1970, *18*, 134-141.

Bagley, C., Wilson, G.D., & Boshier, R. The conservatism scale: A factor-structure comparison of English, Dutch, and New Zealand samples. *Journal of Social Psychology*, 1970, *81*, 267-268.

Bandura, A. Vicarious processes: A case of no-trial learning. In L. Berkowitz (Ed.), *Advances in experimental social psychology*. Vol. II New York: Academic Press, 1965, pp. 1-55.

Bandura, A. *Aggression: A social learning analysis*. Englewood Cliffs, New Jersey: Prentice-Hall, 1973.

Bandura, A. Ross, D. and Ross, S.A. A comparative test of the status envy, social power, and secondary reinforcement theories of indentificatory learning. *Journal of abnormal and social psychology*, 1963, 67, 527-534.

Barker, E.N. Authoritarianism of the political right, center, and left. *Journal of Social*

Issues, 1963, *19*, 63-74.

Barron, F. Some personality correlates of independence of judgment. *Journal of Personality,* 1953, *21*, 287-297.

Bass, B.M., McGhee, C.R., Hawkins, W.C., Young, P.C., & Gebel, A.S. Personality variables related to leaderless group discussion behavior *Journal of Abnormal and Social Psychology,* 1953, *48*, 120-128.

Bass, B.M. Authoritarianism or acquiescence? *Journal of Abnormal and Social Psychology,* 1955, *51*, 616-623.

Bass, B.M. Development and evaluation of a scale for measuring social acquiescence. *Journal of Abnormal and Social Psychology,* 1956, *53*, 296-299.

Bass, B.M. Undiscriminate operant acquiescence. *Journal of Educational Psychological Measurement,* 1957, *17*, 83-85.

Beloff, H. Two forms of social conformity: Acquiescence and conventionality. *Journal of Abnormal and Social Psychology,* 1958, *56*, 99-104.

Bem, D.J. Constructing cross-situational consistencies in behavior: Some thoughts on Alker's critique of Mischel. *Journal of Personality,* 1972, *40*, 17-26.

Bem, D.J., & Allen, A. On predicting some of the people some of the time: The search for cross-situational consistencies in behavior. *Psychological Review,* 1974, *82*, 506-520.

Bentler, P.M., Jackson, D.N., & Messick, S. Identification of content and style: A two-dimensional interpretation of acquiescence. *Psychological Bulletin,* 1971, *76*, 186-204.

Bentler, P.M., Jackson, D.N., & Messick, S. A rose by any other name. *Psychological Bulletin,* 1972, *77*, 109-113.

Berg, I.A., & Rapaport, G.M. Response bias in an unstructured questionnaire. *Journal of Psychology,* 1954, *38*, 475-481.

Berkowitz, L., & Lundy, R.M. Personality characteristics related to susceptibility to influence by peers or authority figures. *Journal of Personality,* 1957, *25*, 306-316.

Berkowitz, N., & Wolkon, G. A forced-choice form of the F Scale—Free of acquiescent response set. *Sociometry,* 1964, *27*, 54-65.

Berscheid, E., & Walster, E.H. *Interpersonal attraction.* Reading, Mass.: Addison-Wesley, 1969.

Bieri, J., & Lobeck, R. Acceptance of authority and parental identification. *Journal of Personality,* 1959, *27*, 74-86.

Block, J. Personality characteristics associated with fathers' attitudes toward child-rearing. *Child Development,* 1955, *26*, 41-48.

Block, J. *The challenge of response sets.* New York: Appleton-Century-Crofts, 1965.

Block, J. On further conjectures regading acquiescence. *Psychological Bulletin,* 1971, *76*, 205-210.

Block, J. The shifting definitions of acquiescence. *Psychological Bulletin,* 1972, *78*, 10-12.

Boshier, R. A study of the relationship between self-concept and conservatism. *Journal of Social Psychology,* 1969, *77*, 139-140.

Boshier, R. To rotate or not to rotate: The question of the Conservatism Scale. *British Journal of Social and Clinical Psychology,* 1972, *11*, 313-323.

Boshier, R. Conservatism within families: A study of the generation gap. In Wilson, G.D. (Ed.), *The psychology of conservatism.* New York: Academic Press, 1973.

Bowers, K.S. Situationism in psychology: An analysis and a critique. *Psychological*

Review, 1973, *80*, 307-336.

Breslin, J. *How the good guys finally won: Notes from an impeachment summer.* New York: Viking Press, 1975.

Brigham, J.C. Ethnic stereotypes. *Psychological Bulletin,* 1971, *76*, 15-38.

Brown, R.W. A determinant of the relationship between rigidity and authoritarianism. *Journal of Abnormal and Social Psychology,* 1953, *48*, 469-476.

Brown, R.W. *Social Psychology.* New York: Free Press, 1965.

Burwen, L. S., & Campbell, D.T. The generality of attitudes toward authority and nonauthority figures. *Journal of Abnormal and Social Psychology,* 1957, *54*, 24-31.

Buss, A.H., & Durkee, A. An inventory for assessing different kinds of hostility. *Journal of Consulting Psychology,* 1957, *21*, 343-349.

Byrne, D. Parental antecedents of authoritarianism. *Journal of Personality and Social Psychology,* 1965, *1*, 369-373.

Caine, T.M., & Leigh, R. Conservatism in relation to psychiatric treatment. *British Journal of Social and Clinical Psychology,* 1972, *11*, 52-56.

Camilleri, S.F. A factor analysis of the F Scale. *Social Forces,* 1959, *37*, 316-323.

Campbell, A., Gurin, G., & Miller, W.E. *The voter decides.* New York: Harper, 1954.

Campbell, D.T., & Fiske, D.W. Convergent and discriminant validation by the multitrait-multimethod matrix. *Psychological Bulletin,* 1959, *56*, 81-105.

Campbell, D.T., & McCandless, B.R. Ethnocentrism, xenophobia, and personality. *Human Relations,* 1951, *4*, 186-192.

Campbell, D.T., & McCormack, T.H. Military experience and attitudes toward authority. *American Journal of Sociology,* 1957, *62*, 482-490.

Campbell, D.T., Siegman, C.R., & Rees, M.B. Direction-of-wording effects in the relationships between scales. *Psychological Bulletin,* 1967, *68*, 293-303.

Chapman, L.J., & Campbell, D.T. Response sets in the F-Scale. *Journal of Abnormal and Social Psychology,* 1957, *54*, 129-132.

Chapman, L.J., & Campbell, D.T. Absence of acquiescence response set in the Taylor Manifest Anxiety Scale. *Journal of Consulting Psychology,* 1959, *23*, 465-466 (a).

Chapman, L.J., & Campbell, D.T. The effect of acquiescence response-set upon relationships among F-Scale, ethnocentrism, and intelligence. *Sociometry,* 1959, *22*, 153-161 (b).

Chown, S.M. Rigidity—a flexible concept. *Psychological Bulletin,* 1959, *56*, 195-223.

Christie, R. Changes in authoritarianism as related to situational factors. *American Psychologist,* 1952, *7*, 307-308.

Christie, R. Authoritarianism re-examined. In R. Christie, & M. Jahoda (Eds.), *Studies in the scope and method of "The authoritarian personality."* Glencoe, Ill: Free Press, 1954.

Christie, R. Eysenck's treatment of the personality of communists. *Psychological Bulletin,* 1956(a), *53*, 411-430.

Christie, R. Some abuses of psychology. *Psychological Bulletin,* 1956(b), 439-451.

Christie, R., & Cook, P. A guide to published literature relating to the authoritarian personality through 1956. *Journal of Psychology,* 1958, *45*, 171-199.

Christie, R., & Garcia, J. Subcultural variation of the authoritarian personality. *Journal of Abnormal and Social Psychology,* 1951, *46*, 457-469.

Christie, R., & Geis, F.L. *Studies in Machiavellianism.* New York: Academic Press, 1970.

Christie, R., Havel, J., & Seidenberg, B. Is the F Scale irreversible? *Journal of*

Abnormal and Social Psychology, 1958, *56*, 143-159.

Christie, R., & Jahoda, M. (Eds.). *Studies in the scope and method of "The authoritarian personality."* New York: Free Press, 1954.

Cohn, T.S. The relation of the F Scale to a response set to answer positively. *American Psychologist*, 1953, *8*, 335 (Abstract).

Coleman, A.M., & Lambley, P. Authoritarianism and race attitudes in South Africa. *Journal of Social Psychology*, 1970, *82*, 161-164.

Comrey, A.L. *A first course in factor analysis.* New York: Academic Press, 1973.

Comstock, C., & Duckles, R. *The assessment of destructiveness in personality: Working papers.* Berkeley, California: Wright Institute, 1972.

Cook, M., & Smith, J.M.C. Group ranking techniques in the study of the accuracy of interpersoanl perception. *British Journal of Psychology*, 1974, *65*, 427-435.

Couch, A., & Keniston, K. Yeasayers and naysayers: Agreeing response set as a personality variable. *Journal of Abnormal and Social Psychology*, 1960, *60*, 151-174.

Coulter, T. An experimental and statistical study of the relationship of prejudice and certain personality variables. Unpublished doctoral dissertation. University of London, 1953.

Crockett, W.H., & Meidinger, T. Authoritarianism and interpersonal perception. *Journal of Abnormal and Social Psychology*, 1956, *53*, 378-380.

Cronbach, L.J. Studies of acquiescence as a factor in the true-false test. *Journal of Educational Psychology*, 1942, *33*, 401-415.

Cronbach, L.J. Response sets and test validity. *Educational and Psychological Measurement*, 1946, *6*, 475-494.

Cronbach, L.J. *Essentials of psychological testing.* (Third Edition). New York: Harper & Row, 1970.

Crowne, D.P., & Marlowe, D. *The approval motive.* New York: Wiley, 1964.

Crutchfield, R.S. Conformity and character. *American Psychologist*, 1955, *10*, 191-198.

Davids, A. Some personality and intellectual correlates of intolerance of ambiguity. *Journal of Abnormal and Social Psychology*, 1955, *51*, 415-420.

Davids, A. The influence of ego-involvement on relations between authoritarianism and intolerance of ambiguity. *Journal of Consulting Psychology*, 1956, *20*, 179-184.

Davidson, H.H., & Kruglov, L.P. Some background correlates of personality and social attitudes. *Journal of Social Psychology*, 1953, *38*, 233-240.

Deutsch, M. Trust, trustworthiness and the F Scale *Journal of Abnormal and Social Psychology*, 1960, *61*, 138-140.

Direnzo, G.J. Dogmatism and presidential preferences in the 1964 elections. *Psychological Reports*, 1968, *22*, 1197-1202.

Dixon, W.J. (Ed.). *BMDP Biomedical Computer Programs.* Los Angles: University of California Press, 1975.

Dustin, D.S., & Davis, H.P. Authoritarianism and sanctioning behavior. *Journal of Personality and Social Psychology*, 1967, *6*, 222-224.

Elms, A.C. *Social psychology and social relevance.* Boston: Little, Brown & Co., 1972.

Elms, A.C. The crisis of confidence in social psychology. *American Psychologist*, 1975, *30*, 967-976.

Elms, A.C., & Milgram, S. Personality characteristics associated with obedience and defiance toward authoritative command. *Journal of Experimental Research in Personality*, 1966, *1*, 282-289.

Endler, N.S. The person versus the situation—a pseudo issue? A response to Alker.

Journal of Personality, 1973, *41,* 287-303.

Epstein, R. Authoritarianism, displaced aggression, and social status of the target. *Journal of Personality and Social Psychology,* 1965, *2,* 585-589.

Eptstein, R. Aggression toward outgroups as a function of authoritarianism and imitation of aggressive models. *Journal of Personality and Social Psychology,* 1966, *3,* 574-579.

Epstein, S. The stability of behavior: I. On predicting most of the people much of the time. *Journal of Personality and Social Psychology,* 1979, *37,* 1097-1126.

Epstein, S. The stability of behavior: II. Implications for Psychological research. *American Psychologist,* 1980, *35,* 790-806.

Eysenck, H.J. Primary social attitudes: I. The organization and measurement of social attitudes. *International Journal of Opinion and Attitude Research,* 1947, *1,* 49-84.

Eysenck, H.J. Primary social attitudes as related to social class and political party. *British Journal of Sociology,* 1951, *2,* 198-209.

Eysenck, H.J. *The structure of human personality.* London: Methuen, 1953.

Eysenck, H.J. *The psychology of politics.* London: Routledge and Keagan Paul, 1954.

Eysenck, H.J. The psychology of politics: A reply. *Psychological Bulletin,* 1956(a), *53,* 177-182.

Eysenck, H.J. The psychology of politics and the personality similarities between fascists and communists. *Psychological Bulletin,* 1956(b), *53,* 431-438.

Eysenck, H.J. Social attitudes and social class. *British Journal of Social and Clinical Psychology,* 1971, *10,* 201-212.

Eysenck, H.J. (and Coulter, T.T.) The pesonality and attitudes of working-class British communists and fascists. *Journal of Social Psychology,* 1972, *87,* 59-73.

Feldman, K., & Newcomb, T. *The impact of college on students.* San Francisco: Jossey-Bass, 1969.

Feldt, L.S. A test of the hypothesis that Cronbach's alpha or Kuder-Richardson coefficient twenty is the same for two tests. *Psychometrika,* 1969, *34,* 363-373.

Feldt, L.S. A test of the hypothesis that Cronbach's Alpha Reliability coefficient is the same for two tests administered to the same sample. *Psychometrika,* 1980, in press.

Ferguson, L.W. The stability of the primary social attitudes. I. Religionism and humanitarianism. *Journal of Psychology,* 1941, *12,* 283-288.

Fest, J.C. *Hitler.* New York: Harcourt Brace Jovanovich, 1973.

Fischer, E. H. Authoritarianism and agreement response style in predicting altruistic attitudes: tests of newly balanced F Scale. *Proceedings of the 78th Annual Convention of the American Psychological Association,* 1970, *5,* 327-328.

Fishbein, M. The relationship between beliefs, attitudes, and behavior. In Feldman, S. (Ed.), *Cognitive consistency.* New York: Academic Press, 1966.

Fishbein, M. A consideration of beliefs and their role in attitude measurement. In Fishbein, M. (Ed.), *Readings in attitude theory and measurement.* New York: Wiley, 1967.

Fishbein, M., & Ajzen, I. *Belief, attitude, intention and behavior.* Reading, Mass.: Addison-Wesley, 1975.

Fishkin, J., Keniston, K., & MacKennon, C. Moral reasoning and political ideology. *Journal of Personality and Social Psychology,* 1973, *27,* 109-119.

Flowerman, S.H., Stewart,N., & Strauss, M. Further investigation of the validity of "authoritarianism" as predictive of ethnic prejudice. *American Psychologist,* 1950, *5,* 307-308.

Forehand, G.A. Relationships among response sets and cognitive behaviors. *Educational and Psychological Measurement,* 1962, *22,* 287-302.

French, E.G. Interrelation among some measures of rigidity under stress and non-stress conditions. *Journal of Abnormal and Social Psychology,* 1955, *51,* 114-118.

French, E.G., & Ernest, R.R. The relation between authoritarianism and acceptance of military ideology. *Journal of Personality* 1955, *24,* 181-191.

Fritz, M.F. Guessing on true-false tests. *Journal of Educational Psychology,* 1927, *18,* 558-561.

Fromm, E. *Escape from freedom.* New York: Holt, Rinehart & Winston, 1941.

Fromm, E., & Maccoby, M. *Social character in a Mexican village: a sociopsychoanalytic study.* Englewood, N.J.: Prentice-Hall, 1970.

Fullerton, J. T. Evaluation of the competence of authors as a function of the author's gender, the sex-relatedness of the article, and the sex of the evaluator. Unpublished MA Thesis, University of Manitoba, 1974.

Gage, N.L., Leavitt, G.S., & Stone, G.C. The psychological meaning of acquiescence set for authoritarianism. *Journal of Abnormal and Social Psychology,* 1957, *55,* 98-103.

Gaier, E.L., & Bass, B.M. Regional differences in interrelations among authoritarianism, acquiescence, and ethnoceentrism. *Journal of Social Psychology,* 1958, *49,* 47-51.

Gallagher, J.J. Authoritarianism and attitudes toward children. *Journal of Social Psychology,* 1957, *45,* 107-110.

Gladstone, R. Authoritarianism, social status, transgression and punitiveness. *Proceedings of the 77th Annual Convention of the American Psychological Association,* 1969, 287-288.

Goldberg, P.A., & Stark, M.J. Johnson or Goldwater?: Some personality and attitude correlates of political choice. *Psychological Reports,* 1965, *17,* 627-631.

Gorfein, D. Conformity behavior and the "authoritarian personality." *Journal of Social Psychology,* 1961, *53,* 121-125.

Gough, H.G. Studies of social intolerance: I. *Journal of Social Psychology,* 1951, *33,* 237-246.

Gough, H.G., Harris, D.B., Martin, W.E., & Edwards, M. Children's ethnic attitudes: I. Relationship to certain personality factors. *Child Development,* 1950, *21,* 83-91.

Granberg, D., & Corrigan, G. Authoritarianism, dogmatism and orientation toward the Vietnam War. *Sociometry,* 1972, *35,* 468-476.

Greenwald, A.G. An editorial. *Journal of Personality and Social Psychology,* 1976, *33,* 1-7.

Gump, P.V. Anti-democratic trends and student reaction to President Truman's dismissal of General MacArthur. *Journal of Social Psychology,* 1953, *38,* 131-135.

Haan, N., Smith, M.B., & Block, J. Moral reasoning of young adults: Political-social behavior, family background, and personality correlates. *Journal of Personality and Social Psychology,* 1968, *10,* 183-201.

Hakstian, A.R., & Whalen, T.E. A k-sample significance test for independent alpha coefficients. *Psychometrika,* 1976, *41,* 219-231.

Handlon, B.J., & Squier, L.H. Attitudes toward special loyalty oaths at the University of California. *American Psychologist,* 1955, *10,* 121-127.

Hanley, C., & Rokeach, M. Care and carelessness in psychology. *Psychological Bulletin*, 1956, *53*, 183-186.

Hanson, D. Dogmatism and authoritarianism: A bibliography of doctoral dissertations. (JSAS MS 1100). American Psychological Association, Washington, D.C., 1974.

Hanson, D.J., & White, B.J. Authoritarianism and candidate preference in the 1972 presidential election. *Psychological Reports*, 1973, *32*, 1158.

Hardy, K.R. Determinants of conformity and attitude change. *Journal of Abnormal and Social Psychology*, 1957, *54*, 289-294.

Harman, H.H. *Modern factor analysis* (2nd Ed.). Chicago: Univeristy of Chicago Press, 1967.

Harris, D.B., Gough, H.G., & Martin, W.E. Children's ethnic attitudes: II. Relationship to parental beliefs concerning child training. *Child Development*, 1950, *21*, 169-181.

Hart, I. Maternal child-rearing practices and authoritarian ideology. *Journal of Abnormal and Social Psychology*, 1957, *55*, 232-237.

Hartley, J., & Holt, J. A note on the validity of the Wilson-Patterson measure of conservatism. *British Journal of Social and Clinical Psychology*, 1971, *10*, 81-83.

Harvey, O.J., & Caldwell, D.F. Assimilation and contrast phenomena in response to environmental variation. *Journal of Personality*, 1959, *27*, 123-135.

Harvey, O.J., & Campbell, D.R. Effect upon judgments of extremity of unlabeled anchors, adaptation range, adaptation duration, and judgmental language. *Journal of Experimental Psychology*, 1963, *65*, 12-21.

Harvey, O.J. & Rutherford, J. Gradual and absolute approaches to attitude change. *Sociometry*, 1958, *21*, 61-68.

Hawthorn, W., Couch, A., Haefner, D., Langham, P., & Carter, L.F. The behavior of authoritarian and equalitarian personalities in groups. *Human Relations*, 1956, *9*, 57-74.

Hendrickson, A.E., & White, P.O. Promax: A quick method for rotation to oblique simple structure. *British Journal of Statistical Psychology*, 1964, *17*, 65-70.

Higgins, J. Authoritarianism and candidate preference. *Psychological Reports*, 1965, *16*, 603-604.

Hites, R.W., & Kellog, E.P. The F and Social Maturity Scales in relation to racial attitudes in a deep south sample. *Journal of Social Psychology* 1964, *62*, 189-195.

Hoffman, M.L. Conformity as a defense mechanism and a form of resistance to genuine group influence. *Journal of Personality*, 1957, *25*, 412-424.

Hollander, E.P. Authoritarianism and leadership choice in a military setting. *Journal of Abnormal and Social Psychology*, 1954, *49*, 365-370.

Hovland, C.I., Janis, I.L., & Kelley, H.H. *Persuasion and communication.* New Haven: Yale University Press, 1953.

Hunsberger, B.E. Religious denomination, education, and university students' reported agreement with parents' religious beliefs. Unpublished doctoral dissertation, University of Manitoba, 1973.

Hyman, H.H., & Sheatsley, P.B. "The authoritarian personality": A methodological critique. In R. Christie & M. Jahoda (Eds.), *Studies in the scope and method of "The authoritarian personality."* New York: Free Press, 1954.

Insel, P., & Wilson, G.D. Measuring social attitudes in children. *British Journal of Social and Clinical Psychology*, 1971, *10*, 84-86.

Izzett, R.R. Authoritarianism and attitudes toward the Vietnam War as reflected in behavioral and self-report measures. *Journal of Personality and Social Psychology,* 1971, *17,* 145-148.

Jackson, D.N., Messick, S.J., & Solley, C.M. How "rigid" is the "authoritarian"? *Journal of Abnormal and Social Psychology,* 1957, *54,* 137-140.

Jackson, D.N., & Messick, S. J. A note on ethnocentrism and acquiescent response sets. *Journal of Abnormal and Social Psychology,* 1957, *54,* 132-134.

Jackson, D.N., & Messick, S. Content and style in personality assessment. *Psychological Bulletin,* 1958, *55,* 243-252.

James, W. *Pragmatism.* New York: Longmans, Green, 1907.

Janowitz, M., & Marvick, D. Authoritarianism and political behavior. *Public Opinion Quarterly,* 1953, *17,* 185-201.

Johnson, H.H., & Izzett, R.R. Relationship between authoritarianism and attitude change as a function of source credibility and type of communication. *Journal of Personality and Social Psychology,* 1969, *13,* 317-321.

Johnson, H.H., & Stanicek, F.F. Relationship between authoritarianism and attitude change as a function of implicit and explicit communications. *Proceedings of the 77th Annual Convention of the American Psychological Association,* 1969, *4,* 415-416.

Johnson, H.H., & Steiner, I.D. Some effects of discrepancy level on relationships between authoritarianism and conformity. *Journal of Social Psychology,* 1967, *73,* 199-204.

Johnson, H.H., Torcivia, J.M., & Poprick, M. Effects of source credibility on the relationship between authoritarianism and attitude change. *Journal of Personality and Social Psychology,* 1968, *9,* 179-183.

Johnson, R.C., Johnson, C., & Martin, L. Authoritarianism, occupation, and sex role differentiation of children. *Child Development,* 1961, *32,* 271-276.

Jones, M.B. Authoritarianism and intolerance of fluctuation. *Journal of Abnormal and Social Psychology,* 1955, *50,* 125-126.

Jourard, S.M. Moral Indignation: A correlate of denied dislike of parents' traits. *Journal of Consulting Psychology,* 1954, *18,* 59-60.

Kaiser, H.F. The varimax criterion for analytic rotation in factor analysis. *Psychometrika,* 1958, *22,* 187-200.

Kates, S.L., & Diab, L.N. Authoritarian ideology and attitudes on parent-child relationships. *Journal of Abnormal and Social Psychology,* 1955, *51,* 13-16.

Katz, I., & Benjamin, L. Effects of white authoritarianism in biracial work groups. *Journal of Abnormal and Social Psychology,* 1960, *61,* 448-456.

Kaufman, W.C. Status, authoritarianism, and anti-Semitism. *American Journal of Sociology,* 1957, *62,* 379-382.

Kelman, H.C. Attitudes are alive and well and gainfully employed in the sphere of action. *American Psychologist,* 1974, *29,* 310-335.

Kelman, H.C. The human use of human subjects. *Psychological Bulletin,* 1967, *67,* 1-11.

Kelman, H.C., & Barclay, J. The F Scale as a measure of breadth of perspective. *Journal of Abnormal and Social Psychology,* 1963, *67,* 608-615.

Kelman, H.C., & Lawrence, L.H. Assignment of responsibility in the case of Lt. Calley: preliminary report on a national sample. *Journal of Social Issues,* 1972, *28,* 177-212.

Kerlinger, F., & Rokeach, M. The factorial nature of the F and D Scales. *Journal of Personality and Social Psychology,* 1966, *4,* 391-399.

Kerpelman, L.C. Personality and attitude correlates of political candidate preference. *Journal of Social Psychology,* 1968, *76,* 219-226.

Kirkpatrick, C. Religion and humanitarianism: A study of institutional implications. *Psychological Monographs,* 1949, *63,* No. 9 (Whole No. 304).

Kirscht, J.P., & Dillehay, R.C. *Dimensions of authoritarianism.* Lexington, Ky.: University of Kentucky Press, 1967.

Kirtley, D., & Harkness, R. Some personality and attitude correlates of dogmatism. *Psychological Reports,* 1969, *24,* 851-854.

Kish, G.B., Netterberg, E.E., & Leahy, L. Stimulus-seeking and conservatism. *Journal of Clinical Psychology,* 1973, *29,* 17-20.

Kogan, N. Authoritarianism and repression. *Journal of Abnormal and Social Psychology,* 1956, *53,* 34-37.

Kohlberg, L. The child as a moral philosopher. *Psychology Today,* 1968, *2,* 24-30.

Kohlberg, L. The development of children's orientations toward a moral order: I Sequence in the development of moral thought. *Vita Humana,* 1963, *6,* 11-33.

Kohn, P.M. The Authoritarianism-Rebellion Scale: A balanced F Scale with left-wing reversals. *Sociometry,* 1972, *35,* 176-189.

Kohn, P.M. Authoritarianism, rebelliousness, and their correlates among British undergraduates. *British Journal of Social and Clinical Psychology,* 1974, *13,* 245-255.

Kohn, P.M., & Mercer, G.W. Drug use, drug use attitudes, and the authoritarianism-rebellion dimension. *Journal of Health and Social Behavior,* 1971, *12,* 125-131.

Koutrelakos, J. Authoritarian person's perception of his relationship with his father. *Perceptual and Motor Skills,* 1968, *26,* 967-973.

Krug, R.E. An analysis of the F Scale: I. Item Factor Analysis. *Journal of Social Psychology,* 1961, *53,* 285-291.

Lambley, P. Authoritarianism and prejudice in South African student samples. *Journal of Social Psychology,* 1973, *91,* 341-342.

Lambley, P., & Gilbert, L.H. Forced-choice and counterbalanced versions of the F Scale: Prediction of prejudiced attitudes. *Psychological Reports,* 1970, *27,* 547-550.

Lane, R.E. Political personality and electoral choice. *American Political Science Review,* 1955, *49,* 173-190.

Larsen, K.S., Coleman, D., Forbes, J., & Johnson, R. Is the subjects' personality or the experimental situation a better predictor of a subject's willingness to administer shock to a victim? *Journal of Personality and Social Psychology,* 1972, *22,* 287-295.

Lasky, J.J. Effects of prestige suggestion and peer standards on California F Scale scores. *Psychological Reports,* 1962, *11,* 187-191.

Lawley, D.N., & Maxwell, A.E. *Factor analysis as a statistical method.* London: Butterworth, 1963.

Leavitt, H.J., Hax, H., & Roche, J.H. "Authoritarianism" and agreement with things authoritative. *Journal of Psychology,* 1955, *40,* 215-221.

Lee, R.E., & Warr, P.B. The development and standardization of a balanced F Scale. *Journal of General Psychology,* 1969, *81,* 109-129.

Lentz, T.F. Acquiescence as a factor in the measurement of personality. *Psychological Bulletin,* 1938, *35,* 659.

Leventhal, H., Jacobs, R.L., & Kudirka, N.Z. Authoritarianism ideology, and political candidate choice. *Journal of Abnormal and Social Psychology*, 1964, *69*, 539-549.

Levinson, D.J. Authoritarian personality and foreign policy. *Journal of Conflict Resolution*, 1957, *1*, 37-47.

Levinson, D.J., & Huffman, P.E. Traditional family ideology and its relation to personality. *Journal of Personality*, 1955, *23*, 251-273.

Levinson, D.J., & Sanford, N. A scale for the measurement of anti-Semitism. *Journal of Psychology*, 1944, *17*, 339-370.

Levitt, E.E. The water-jar Einstelung test as a measure of rigidity. *Psychological Bulletin*, 1956, *53*, 347-370.

Levitt, E.E., & Zelen, S.L. The validity of the Einstellung test as a measure of rigidity. *Journal of Abnormal and Social Psychology*, 1953, *48*, 573-580.

Levitt, E.E., & Zuckerman, M. The water-jar test revisted: The replication of a review. *Psychological Reports, 1959, 5*, 365-380.

Levy, S.G. Citizen responsiveness to governmental injustice. *Proceedings of the 80th Annual Convention of the American Psychological Association*, 1972.

Likert, R. A technique for the measurement of attitudes. *Archives of Psychology*, 1932, No. 140.

Lipetz, M.E., & Ossorio, P.G. Authoritarianism, aggression and status. *Journal of Personality and Social Psychology*, 1967, *5*, 468-472.

Lipset, S.M. Democracy and working-class authoritarianism. *American Sociological Review*, 1959, *24*, 482-501.

Lorge, I. Gen-like: Halo or reality? *Psychological Bulletin*, 1937, *34*, 545-546.

Lück, J., & Gruner, C. Another note on political candidate preference and authoritarianism. *Psychological Reports*, 1970, *26*, 594.

Lipsitz, L. Working class authoritarianism: a re-evaluation. *American Sociological Review*, 1965, *30*, 103-109.

Lutterman, K.G., & Middleton, R. Authoritarianism, anomie and prejudice. *Social Forces*, 1970, *48*, 485-492.

Lyle, W.H., & Levitt, E.E. Punitiveness, authoritarianism, and parental discipline of grade school children. *Journal of Abnormal and Social Psychology*, 1955, *51*, 42-46.

McCurdy, H.G., & Eber, H.W. Democratic versus authoritarian: A further investigation of group problem-solving. *Journal of Personality*, 1953, *22*, 258-269.

McDill, E.L. Anomie, authoritarianism, prejudice, and socio-economic status: An attempt at clarification. *Social Forces*, 1961, *39*, 239-245.

McGee, R.K. The relationship between response style and personality variables: I. The measurement of response acquiescence. *Journal of Abnormal and Social Psychology*, 1962, *64*, 229-233.

McGranahan, D.V. A comparison of social attitudes among American and German youth. *Journal of Abnormal and Social Psychology*, 1946, *41*, 245-258.

McGuire, W. Inducing resistance to persuasion. In L. Berkowitz (Ed.), *Advances in experimental social psychology*, Vol. 1. New York: Academic Press, 1964.

McKinnon, W.J., & Centers, R. Authoritarianism and internationalism. *Pubic Opinion Quarterly*, 1956, *20*, 621-630.

Magnusson, D. *Test theory.* Reading, Mass.: Addison-Wesley, 1967.

Martin, J.G., & Westie, F.R. The tolerant personality. *American Sociological Review*, 1959, *24*, 521-528.

Maslow, A.H. The authoritarian character structure. *Journal of Social Psychology, S.PS.S.I. Bulletin*, 1943, *18*, 401-411.

Medalia, N.Z. Authoritarianism, leader acceptance, and group cohesion. *Journal of Abnormal and Social Psychology*, 1955, *51*, 207-213.

Meer, S.J. Authoritarian attitudes and dreams. *Journal of Abnormal and Social Psychology*, 1955, *51*, 74-78.

Melikian, L.H. Some correlates of authoritarianism in two cultural groups. *Journal of Psychology*, 1956, *42*, 237-248.

Melvin, D. An experimental and statistical study of two primary social attitudes. Unpublished doctoral dissertation, University of London, 1955, (approximately).

Mikesell, R.H., & Persensky, J.J. *British Journal of Social and Clinical Psychology*, 1971, *10*, 383-384.

Milgram, S. Behavioral study of obedience. *Journal of Abnormal and Social Psychology*, 1963, *67*, 371-378.

Milgram, S. Group pressure and action against a person. *Journal of Abnormal and Social Psychology*, 1964, *69*, 137-143.

Milgram, S. Some conditions of obedience and disobedience to authority. *Human Relations*, 1965, *18*, 57-76.

Milgram, S. *Obedience to authority*. New York: Harper & Row, 1974.

Miller, S.M., & Riessman, F. "Working-class authoritarianism": A critique of Lipset. *British Journal of Sociology*, 1961, *12*, 263-275.

Millon, T. Authoritarianism, intolerance of ambiguity, and rigidity under ego- and task-involving conditions. *Journal of Abnormal and Social Psychology*, 1957, *55*, 29-34.

Milton, O. Presidential choice and performance on a scale of authoritarianism. *American Psychologist*, 1952, *7*, 597-598.

Mischel, W. *Personality and assessment*. New York: Wiley and Sons, 1968.

Mischel, W. Continuity and change in personality. *American Psychologist*, 1969, *24*, 1012-1018.

Mischel, W. Toward a cognitive social learning reconceptualization of personality. *Psychological Review*, 1973, *80*, 252-283.

Mischel, W. On the interface of cognition and personality: Beyond the person-situation debate. *American Psychologist*, 1979, *34*, 740-754.

Mischel, W., & Schopler, J. Authoritarianism and reactions to "Sputniks." *Journal of Abnormal and Social Psychology*, 1959, *59*, 142-145.

Mogar, R.E. Three versions of the F-Scale and performance on the semantic differential. *Journal of Abnormal and Social Psychology*, 1960, *60*, 262-265.

Mitchell, H.E., & Byrne, D. Effects of jurors' attitudes and authoritarianism on judicial decisions. *Journal of Personality and Social Psychology*, 1973, *25*, 123-129.

Moscovici, S. Society and theory in social psychology. In J. Israel and H. Tajfel (Eds.), *The context of social psychology*. New York: Academic Press, 1972.

Nadler, E.B. Yielding, authoritarianism, and authoritarian ideology regarding groups. *Journal of Abnormal and Social Psychology*, 1959, *58*, 408-410.

Neuringer, C. The relationship between authoritarianism, rigidity, and anxiety. *Journal of General Psychology*, 1964, *71*, 169-175.

Newcomb, T.M. *The acquaintance process*. New York: Holt, Rinehart & Winston, 1961.

Nias, D.K.B. Attitudes to the common market. A case study in conservatism. In

G.D. Wilson (Ed.), *The psychology of conservatism*. New York: Academic Press, 1973.

Nias, D.K.B, Wilson, G.D., & Woodbridge, J.M. Test-retest results of the conservatism scale completed under conditions of anonymity and identification. *British Journal of Social and Clinical Psychology*, 1971, *10*, 282-283.

Nias, D.K.B., & Wilson, G.D. Interpretation of the factor structure of the C Scale: A reply to Boshier. *British Journal of Social and Clinical Psychology*, 1972, *11*, 324-325.

Nie, N.H., Bent, D.H., & Hull, C.H. *SPSS: A statistical package for the social sciences*. New York: McGraw-Hill, 1970.

Nigniewitzky, R.W. A statistical and experimental investigation of rigidity in relation to personality and social attitudes. Unpublished doctoral dissertation, University of London, 1956.

Nudelman, Arthur E. Authoritarianism, economic liberalism, and political preference. *Psychological Reports*, 1972, *30*, 27-33.

O'Neil, W.M., & Levinson, D.J. A factorial exploration of authoritarianism and some of its ideological concomitants. *Journal of Personality* 1954, *22*, 449-463.

Orne, M.T. Demand characteristics and the concept of quasi-controls. In R. Rosenthal & R.L. Rosnow (Eds.) *Artifact in behavioral reseach*. New York: Academic Press, 1969.

Orpen, C. Authoritarianism and racial attitudes among English-speaking South Africans. *Journal of Social Psychology*, 1971, *84*, 301-302.

Orpen, C., & Rodenwoldt, E. *British Journal of Social and Clinical Psychology*, 1973, *12*, 94-95.

Osgood, C.E., Succi, G.J., & Tannenbaum, P.H. *The measurement of meaning*. Urbana, Ill.: University of Illinois Press, 1957.

Patterson, J.R. Conservatism and aesthetic judgments. In G.D. Wilson (Ed.), *The psychology of conservatism*. New York: Academic Press, 1973.

Patterson, J. R., & Wilson, G.D. Anonymity, occupation and conservatism. *Journal of Social Psychology*, 1969, *78*, 263-266.

Paul, I.H. Impressions of personality, authoritarianism, and the *fait-accompli* effect. *Journal of Abnormal and Social Psychology*, 1956, *53*, 338-344.

Peabody, D. Attitude content and agreement set in scales of authoritarianism, dogmatism, antisemitism and economic conservatism. *Journal of Abnormal and Social Psychology*, 1961, *63*, 1-11.

Pettigrew, T.F. Regional differences in anti-Negro prejudice. *Journal of Abnormal and Social Psychology*, 1959, *59*, 28-36.

Pettigrew, T.F. Personality and sociocultural factors in intergroup attitudes: A cross-national comparison. *Journal of Conflict Resolution*, 1958, *2*, 29-42.

Pflaum, J. Development and evaluation of equivalent forms of the F Scale. *Psychological Reports*, 1964, *15*, 663-669.

Phares, E.J. A note on authoritarianism and attitudes toward parents. *Journal of Clinical Psychology*, 1960, *16*, 389-390.

Piaget, J. *The moral judgment of the child*. New York: Free Press, 1932.

Prentice, N.M. The influence of ethnic attitudes on reasoning about ethnic groups. *Journal of Social Psychology*, 1957, *55*, 270-272.

Ray, J.J. 'A new measure of conservatism': Its limitations. *British Journal of Social and Clinical Psychology*, 1971, *10*, 79-80.

Ray, J.J. Non-ethnocentric authoritarianism. *Australian and New Zealand Journal of Sociology*, 1972, *8*, 96-102.

Ray, J.J. Are conservatism scales irreversible? *British Journal of Social and Clinical Psychology*, 1972, *11*, 346-352.

Ray. J.J. Conservatism, authoritarianism, and related variables: A review and empirical study. In G.D. Wilson (Ed.), *The psychology of conservatism*. New York: Academic Press, 1973.

Richert, K.C. Explorations into the specific behavioral determinants of authoritarianism. *Psychological Reports*, 1963, *13*, 950.

Roberts, A.H., & Jessor, R. Authoritarianism, punitiveness and perceived social status. *Journal of Abnormal and Social Psychology*, 1958, *56*, 311-314.

Roberts, A.H., & Rokeach, M. Anomie, authoritarianism, and prejudice: A replication. *American Journal of Sociology*, 1956, *61*, 355-358.

Robertson, A., & Cochrane, R. The Wilson-Patterson Conservatism Scale: A reappraisal. *British Journal of Social and Clinical Psychology*, 1973, *12*, 428-430.

Rohde, K.J. The relation of authoritarianism of the aircrew member to his acceptance by the airplane commander. *American Psychologist*, 1955, *8*, 323.

Rokeach, M. Generalized mental rigidity as a factor in ethnocentrism. *Journal of Abnormal and Social Psychology*, 1948, *43*, 259-278.

Rokeach, M. Political and religious dogmatism: An alternative to the authoritarian personality. *Psychological Monographs*, 1956, *70*, 1-43.

Rokeach, M. *The open and closed mind*. New York: Basic Books, 1960.

Rokeach, M. The double agreement phenomenon: Three hypotheses. *Psychological Review*, 1963, *70*, 304-309.

Rokeach, M., & Hanley, C. Eysenck's tender-minded dimension: A critique. *Psychological Bulletin*, 1956, *53*, 169-176.

Rorer, L.G. The great response style myth. *Psychological Bulletin*, 1965, *63*, 129-156.

Rorer, L.G., & Goldberg, L.R. Acquiescence in the MMPI? *Educational and Psychological Measurement*, 1965, *25*, 801-817.

Rosenthal, R. *Experimenter effects in behavioral research*. New York: Appleton-Century-Crofts, 1966.

Rosenzweig, S. The picture association method and its application in a study of reactions to frustration. *Journal of Pesonality*, 1945, *14*, 3-23.

Runquist, E.A. Item and response characteristics in attitude and personality measurement: A reaction to L.G. Rorer's "The great response-style myth." *Psychological Bulletin*, 1966, *66*, 166-177.

Sales, S.M. Economic threat as a determinant of conversion rates in authoritarian and nonauthoritarian churches. *Journal of Personality and Social Psychology*, 1972, *23*, 420-428.

Sales, S. Threat as a factor in authoritarianism: An analysis of archival data. *Journal of Personality and Social Psychology*, 1973, *28*, 44-57.

Samelson, F. Response style: A psychologist's fallacy? *Psychological Bulletin*, 1972, *78*, 13-16.

Samelson, F., & Yates, J.F. Acquiescence and the F Scale: Old assumptions and new data. *Psychological Bulletin*, 1967, *68*, 91-103.

Sampson, D.L., & Smith H.P. A scale to measure world-minded attitudes. *Journal of Social Psychology*, 1957, *45*, 99-106.

Sanford, F.H. *Authoritarianism and leadership*. Philadelphia: Institute for Research in Human Relations, 1950.

Sanford, N. Authoritarian personality in contemporary perspective. In J. Knudsen (Ed.), *Handbook of political psychology*. San Francisco: Jossey-Bass, 1974.

Sarason, I.G., Smith, R.E., & Diener, E. Personality research: components of variance attributable to the person and the situation. *Journal of Personality and Social Psychology*, 1975, *32*, 199-204.

Sauer, W. National Socialism: totalitarianism or facism *American Historical Review*, 1967, *73*, 408-422.

Schaefer, E.S., & Bell, R.Q. Development of a parental attitude research instrument. *Child Development*, 1958, *29*, 339-361.

Schneider, J.F. The Conservatism Scale: Independent of SD? *British Journal of Social and Clinical Psychology*, 1973, *12*, 90-91.

Schulberg, H.C. Authoritarianism, tendency to agree, and interpersonal perception. *Journal of Abnormal and Social Psychology*, 1961, *63*, 101-108.

Schwendiman, G., Larsen, K.S., & Cope, S.C. Authoritarian traits as predictors of candidate preference in 1968 United States presidential election. *Psychological Reports*, 1970,*27*, 629-630.

Scodel, A., & Freedman, M.L. Additional observations on the social perceptions of authoritarians and non-authoritarians. *Journal of Abnormal and Social Psychology*, 1956, *52*, 92-95.

Scodel, A., & Mussen, P. Social perceptions of authoritarians and nonauthoritarians. *Journal of Abnormal and Social Psychology*, 1953, *48*, 181-184.

Selznick, G.J., & Steinberg, S. *The tenacity of prejudice: Anti-Semitism in Contemporary America*. New York: Harper, 1969.

Sherif, M. A study of some social factors in perception. *Archives of Psychology*, No. 187, 1935, *34*, *35*, *63*.

Sherwood, J.J. Authoritarianism and moral realism. *Journal of Clinical Psychology*, 1966, *22*, 17-21.

Shils, E.A. Authoritarianism: Right and left. In R. Christie, & M. Jahoda (Eds.), *Studies in the scope and method of "The Authoritarian Personality."* Glencoe, Ill.: Free Press, 1954.

Shoben, E. J. The assessment of parental attitudes in relation to child adjustment. *Genetic Psychology Monographs*, 1949, *39*, 101-148.

Siegel, A.E.,& Siegel, S. Reference groups, membership groups, and attitude change. *Journal of Abnormal and Social Psychology*, 1957, *55*, 360-364.

Siegel, S.M. The realtionship of hostility to authoritarianism. *Journal of Abnormal and Social Psychology*, 1956, *52*, 368-372.

Singer, R.D., & Feshbach, S. Some relationships between manifest anxiety, authoritarian tendencies, and modes of reaction to frustration. *Journal of Abnormal and Social Psychology*, 1959, *59*, 404-408.

Smith, H.P., & Rosen, E.W. Some psychological correlates of worldmindedness and authoritarianism. *Journal of Personality*, 1958, *26*, 170-183.

Smith, M.B. An analysis of two measures of "authoritarianism" among Peace Corps teachers. *Journal of Personality*, 1965, *33*, 513-535.

Smith, M.B. Review of Fromm and Maccoby's "Social Character in a Mexican Village." *Contemporary Psychology*, 1971, *16*, 635.

Smith, M.B. Is experimental social psychology advancing? *Journal of Experimental Social Psychology*, 1972, *8*, 86-96.

Smith, M.B. Is psychology relevant to new priorities? *American Psychologist*, 1973, *28*, 463-471.

Smith, M.B., Bruner, J.S., & White, R.W. *Opinions and personality*. New York: Wiley, 1956.

Srole, L. Social integration and certain corollaries: An exploratory study. *American Sociological Review*, 1956, *21*, 709-716.

Stagner, R. Attitude toward authority: An exploratory study. *Journal of Social Psychology*, 1954, *40*, 197-210.

Stagner, R., & Drought, N. Measuring children's attitudes toward their parents. *Journal of Educational Psychology*, 1935, *26*, 169-176.

Steiner, I.D., & Johnson, H.H. Authoritarianism and conformity. *Sociometry*, 1963, *26*, 21-34.

Steiner, I.D., & Vannoy, J.S. Personality correlates of two types of conformity behavior. *Journal of Personality and Social Psychology*, 1966, *4*, 307-315.

Stewart, G.R. *Year of the oath*. New York: Doubleday, 1950.

Stotsky, B.A., & Lachman, S.J. Differences in political and social attitudes of pro-Stevenson students. *Journal of Social Psychology*, 1956, *44*, 143-144.

Strickland, L.H., & Janicki, W.P. An alternative form of a forced-choice F Scale. *Psychological Reports*, 1965, *16*, 933-940.

Taylor, J.A. A personality scale of manifest anxiety. *Journal of Abnormal and Social Psychology*, 1953, *48*, 285-290.

Thayer, R.E. Attitude and personality differences between potential jurors who could return a death verdict and those who could not. *Proceedings of the 78th Annual Convention of the American Psychological Association*, 1970, 445-446.

Thibaut, J.W., & Riecken, H.W. Authoritarianism, status, and the communication of aggression. *Human Relations*, 1955, *8*, 95-120.

Thomas, D.R. The relationship between ethnocentrism and conservatism in an "authoritarian" culture. *Journal of Social Psychology*, 1974, *94*, 179-186.

Thomas, D.R. Conservatism, authoritarianism and child-rearing practices. *British Journal of Social and Clinical Psychology*, 1975, *14*, 97-98.

Thomas, D.R., Shea, J.D., & Rigby, R.G. Conservatism and response to sexual humour. *British Journal of Social and Clinical Psychology*, 1971, *10*, 185-186.

Thompson, R.C., & Michel, J.B. Measuring authoritarianism: A comparison of the F and D Scales. *Journal of Personality*, 1972, *40*, 180-190.

Titus, H.E., & Hollander, E.P. The California F Scale in psychological research: 1950-1955. *Psychological Bulletin*, 1957, *54*, 47-64.

Tomkins, S. *Polarity Test*. New York: Springer, 1964.

Triandis, H.C., Davis, E., & Takezawa, S. Some determinants of social distance among American, German, and Japanese Students. *Journal of Personality and Social Psychology*, 1965, *2*, 540-551.

Triandis, H.C., & Triandis, L.M. Race, social class, religion and nationality as determinants of social distance. *Journal of Abnormal and Social Psychology*, 1960, *61*, 110-118.

Tryon, R.C. *Cluster analysis*. Berkeley, Calif.: University of California Press, 1939.

Vacchiano, R.B., Scheffman, D.C., & Crowell, A.V. Attitude change as a function of intensive training, dogmatism, and authoritarianism. *Psychological Reports*, 1966, *19*, 359-362.

Vacchiano, R.B., Strauss, P.S., & Hochman, L. The open and closed mind: A review of dogmatism. *Psychological Bulletin*, 1969, *71*, 261-273.

Vaughan, G.M. Authoritarian scales as criteria of conformity. *Perceptual and Motor Skills*, 1969, *28*, 776-778.

Vaughan, G.M., & White, K.D. Conformity and authoritarianism re-examined. *Journal of Personality and Social Psychology*, 1966, *3*, 263-366.

Wagman, M. Attitude change and authoritarian personality. *Journal of Psychology*, 1955, *40*, 3-24.

Warr, P.B., & Coffman, T.L. Personality involvement and extremity of judgment. *British Journal of Social and Clinical Psychology*, 1970, *9*, 108-121.

Warr, P.B., Faust, J., & Harrison, G.J. A British ethnocentrism scale. *British Journal of Social and Clinical Psychology*, 1967, *6*, 267-277.

Warr, P., & Rogers, C. Some personality effects on extreme responding and on the realtive weighing of items in combination. *British Journal of Social and Clinical Psychology*, 1974, *13*, 347-357.

Warr, P.B., & Sims, A. A study of cojudgment processes. *Journal of Personality*, 1965, *33*, 598-604.

Waterhouse, I.K., & Child, I.L. Frustration and the quality of performance. III. An experimental study. *Journal of Personality*, 1953, *21*, 298-311.

Webster, H., Sanford, N., & Freedman, M. A new instrument for studying authoritarianism in personality. *Journal of Psychology*, 1955, *40*, 73-84.

Webster, A.C., & Stewart, R.A.C. Theological conservatism. In G.D. Wilson (Ed.), *The psychology of conservatism:* New York: Academic Press, 1973.

Weiner, H., & McGinnies, E. Authoritarianism, conformity, and confidence in a perceptual judgment situation. *Journal of Social Psychology*, 1961, *55*, 77-84.

Wells, W.D., Weinert, G., & Rubel, M. Conformity pressure and authoritarian personality. *Journal of Psychology*, 1956, *42*, 133-136.

Westie, F.R. A technique for the measurement of race attitudes. *American Sociological Review*, 1953, *18*, 73-78.

Whiting, W.M., & Child, I.L. *Child training and personality: A cross-cultural study.* New Haven: Yale University Press, 1953.

Wicker, A.W. Attitudes vs. actions: The relationship of verbal and overt behavioral responses to attitude objects. *Journal of Social Issues*, 1969, *25*, 41-78.

Williams, E.I., & Williams, C.D. Relationships between authoritarian attitudes of college students, estimation of parents' attitudes, and actual parental attitudes. *Journal of Social Psychology*, 1963, *61*, 43-48.

Wilson, G.D. Personality, GSR conditioning and response to instructional set. *Psychological Reports*, 1968, *22*, 618.

Wilson, G.D. Is there a general factor in social attitudes? Evidence from a factor analysis of the Conservatism Scale. *British Journal of Social and Clinical Psychology*, 1970, *9*, 101-107.

Wilson, G.D. (Ed.) *The psychology of conservatism.* New York: Academic Press, 1973.

Wilson, G.D., Ausman, J., and Mathews, T.R. Conservatism and art preferences. *Journal of Personality and Social Psychology*, 1973, *25*, 286-288.

Wilson, G.D., & Brazendale, A.H. Sexual attractiveness as a predictor of social attitudes and response to risqué humour. *European Journal of Social Psychology*, 1973, *3*, 95-96.

Wilson, G.D., & Lillie, F.J. Social attitudes of salvationists and humanists. *British Journal of Social and Clincial Psychology*, 1972, *11*, 220-224.

Wilson, G.D., & Patterson, J.R. A new measure of conservatism. *British Journal of Social and Clinical Psychology*, 1968, 7, 264-269.

Wilson, G.D., & Patterson, J.R. Conservatism as a predictor of humor preferences. *Journal of Consulting and Clinical Psychology*, 1969, 33, 271-274.

Winer, B.J. *Statistical principles in experimental design.* New York: McGraw-Hill, 1962.

Wright, J.M., & Harvey, O.J. Attitude change as a function of authoritarianism and punitiveness. *Journal of Personality and Social Psychology*, 1965, 1, 177-181.

Wrightsman, L.S. Personality and attitudinal correlates of trusting and trustworthy behaviors in a two-person game. *Journal of Personality and Social Psychology*, 1966, 4, 328-332.

Wrightsman, L.S. *Social psychology* (Second Edition). Monterey, Calif.: Brooks/Cole, 1977.

Wrightsman, L.S., Radloff, R.W, Horton, D.L., & Mecherikoff, M. Authoritarian attitudes and presidential voting preferences. *Psychological Reports*, 1961, 8, 43-46.

Zippel, B., & Norman, R.D. Party switching, authoritarianism, and dogmatism in the 1964 election. *Psychological Reports*, 1966, 19, 667-670.

Zuckerman, M., Barrett-Ribback, B., Monashkin, I., & Norton, J.A. Normative data and factor analysis on the Parental Attitude Research Instrument. *Journal of Consulting Psychology*, 1958, 22, 165-171.

Zuckerman, M., & Oltean, M. Some relationships between maternal attitude factors and authoritarianism, personality needs, psychopathology, and self-acceptance. *Child Development*, 1959, 30, 27-36.

Index